Houghton Mifflin Math

HOUGHTON MIFFLIN BOSTON

Printed in the U.S.A.
ISBN-13: 978-0-618-59092-6
ISBN-10: 0-618-59092-7

3456789-WC-14 13 12 10 09 08 07 06

Program Authors & Consultants

Authors

Dr. Carole Greenes
Professor of Mathematics Education
Boston University
Boston, MA

Dr. Matt Larson
Curriculum Specialist for Mathematics
Lincoln Public Schools
Lincoln, NE

Dr. Miriam A. Leiva
Distinguished Professor of Mathematics Emerita
University of North Carolina
Charlotte, NC

Dr. Jean M. Shaw
Professor Emerita of Curriculum and Instruction
University of Mississippi
Oxford, MS

Dr. Lee Stiff
Professor of Mathematics Education
North Carolina State University
Raleigh, NC

Dr. Bruce R. Vogeli
Clifford Brewster Upton Professor of Mathematics
Teachers College, Columbia University
New York, NY

Dr. Karol Yeatts
Associate Professor
Barry University
Miami, FL

Consultants

Strategic Consultant
Dr. Liping Ma
Senior Scholar
Carnegie Foundation for the Advancement of Teaching
Palo Alto, CA

Language and Vocabulary Consultant
Dr. David Chard
Professor of Reading
University of Oregon
Eugene, OR

Blended Usage Advisor

Houghton Mifflin Math and Math Expressions
Dr. Matt Larson
Curriculum Specialist for Mathematics
Lincoln Public Schools
Lincoln, NE

Reviewers

Grade K

Hilda Kendrick
W E Wilson
Elementary School
Jefferson, IN

Debby Nagel
Assumption
Elementary School
Cincinnati, OH

Jen Payet
Lake Ave. Elementary School
Saratoga Springs, NY

Karen Sue Hinton
Washington Elementary School
Ponca City, OK

Grade 1

Karen Wood
Clay Elementary School
Clay, AL

Paula Rowland
Bixby North Elementary School
Bixby, OK

Stephanie McDaniel
B. Everett Jordan
Elementary School
Graham, NC

Juan Melgar
Lowrie Elementary School
Elgin, IL

Sharon O'Brien
Echo Mountain School
Phoenix, AZ

Grade 2

Sally Bales
Akron Elementary School
Akron, IN

Rose Marie Bruno
Mawbey Street Elementary
School
Woodbridge, NJ

Kiesha Doster
Berry Elementary School
Detroit, MI

Marci Galazkiewicz
North Elementary School
Waukegan, IL

Ana Gaspar
Lowrie Elementary School
Elgin, IL

Elana Heinoren
Beechfield Elementary School
Baltimore, MD

Kim Terry
Woodland Elementary School
West
Gages Lake, IL

Megan Burton
Valley Elementary School
Pelham, AL

Kristy Ford
Eisenhower Elementary School
Norman, OK

Grade 3

Jenny Chang
North Elementary School
Waukegan, IL

Patricia Heintz
Harry T. Stewart
Elementary School
Corona, NY

Shannon Hopper
White Lick Elementary School
Brownsburg, IN

Allison White
Kingsley Elementary School
Naperville, IL

Amy Simpson
Broadmoore Elementary School
Moore, OK

Reviewers

Grade 4

Barbara O'Hanlon
Maurice & Everett Haines Elementary School
Medford, NJ

Connie Rapp
Oakland Elementary School
Bloomington, IL

Pam Rettig
Solheim Elementary School
Bismarck, ND

Tracy Smith
Blanche Kelso Bruce Academy
Detroit, MI

Brenda Hancock
Clay Elementary School
Clay, AL

Karen Scroggins
Rock Quarry Elementary School
Tuscaloosa, AL

Lynn Fox
Kendall-Whittier Elementary School
Tulsa, OK

Grade 5

Jim Archer
Maplewood Elementary School
Indianapolis, IN

Maggie Dunning
Horizon Elementary School
Hanover Park, IL

Mike Intoccia
McNichols Plaza
Scranton, PA

Jennifer LaBelle
Washington Elementary School
Waukegan, IL

Anne McDonald
St. Luke The Evangelist School
Glenside, PA

Ellen O'Rourke
Bower Elementary School
Warrenville, IL

Gary Smith
Thomas H. Ford Elementary School
Reading, PA

Linda Carlson
Van Buren Elementary School
Oklahoma City, OK

Grade 6

Robin Akers
Sonoran Sky Elementary School
Scottsdale, AZ

Ellen Greenman
Daniel Webster Middle School
Waukegan, IL

Angela McCray
Abbott Middle School
West Bloomfield, MI

Mary Popovich
Horizon Elementary School
Hanover Park, IL

Debbie Taylor
Sonoran Sky Elementary School
Scottsdale, AZ

Across Grades

Jacqueline Lampley
Hewitt Elementary School
Trussville, AL

Rose Smith
Five Points Elementary School
Orrville, AL

Winnie Tepper
Morgan County Schools
Decatur, AL

Number Concepts, Addition, Subtraction, and Graphing

Algebra Indicates lessons that include algebra instruction.

3 Subtraction Facts

4 Data, Graphing, and Probability

FINISHING THE UNIT

(WR) Indicates WEEKLY WR READER eduplace.com/map

Numbers Through 100

5 Place Value

Algebra Indicates lessons that include algebra instruction.

6 Number Concepts and Patterns

FINISHING THE UNIT

WR Indicates WEEKLY WR READER eduplace.com/map

Geometry and Fractions

Algebra Indicates lessons that include algebra instruction.

9 Fractions

FINISHING THE UNIT

WR Indicates WEEKLY WR READER eduplace.com/map

Adding Two-Digit Numbers

UNIT 4 Adding Two-Digit Numbers

Algebra Indicates lessons that include algebra instruction.

11 Using Two-Digit Addition

FINISHING THE UNIT

(WR) Indicates WEEKLY WR READER eduplace.com/map

Subtracting Two-Digit Numbers

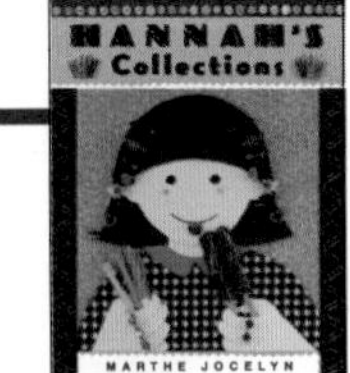

12 Regrouping With Subtraction

Algebra Indicates lessons that include algebra instruction.

13 Using Two-Digit Subtraction

FINISHING THE UNIT

(WR) Indicates WEEKLY WR READER eduplace.com/map

Money and Time

Algebra Indicates lessons that include algebra instruction.

16 Time and Calendar

FINISHING THE UNIT

WR Indicates WEEKLY WR READER eduplace.com/map

Measurement

17 Length

Algebra Indicates lessons that include algebra instruction.

18 Weight, Capacity, and Temperature

FINISHING THE UNIT

(WR) Indicates WEEKLY WR READER eduplace.com/map

UNIT 8 Greater Numbers and Operations, Multiplication, and Division

Greater Numbers and Operations, Multiplication, and Division

Algebra Indicates lessons that include algebra instruction.

21 Adding Three-Digit Numbers

22 Subtracting Three-Digit Numbers

FINISHING THE UNIT

STUDENT RESOURCES

Welcome!

Name ______________________________

What I Know About Math

1. I can write the number that comes after 459.

____

2. I can add two numbers

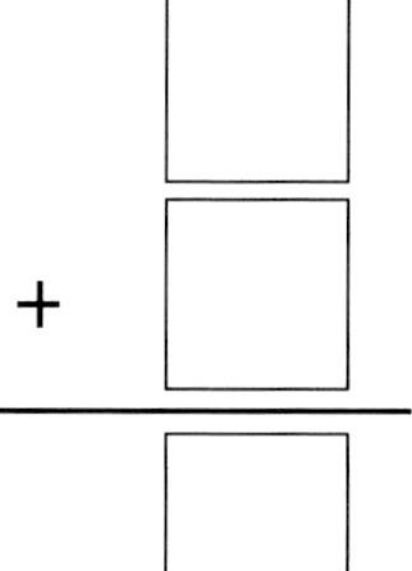

3. I can draw a line 3 inches long.

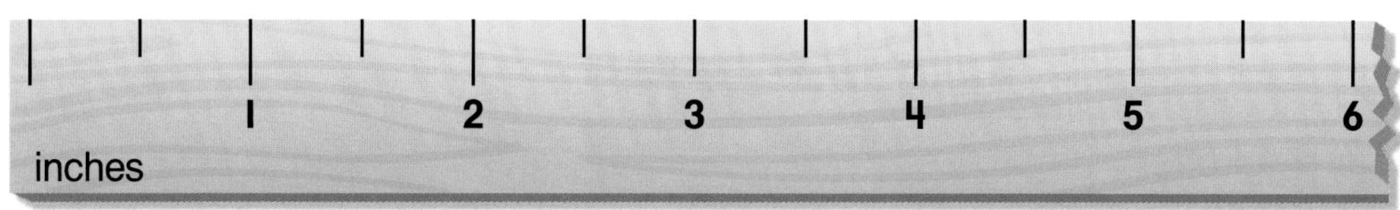

4. I can name these solid shapes. Match each figure with the correct name.

Rectangular Prism

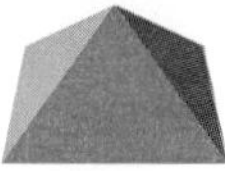

Sphere

Square Pyramid

Cube

5. I can find the value.

$ ___.______

6. I can color to show $\frac{1}{2}$.

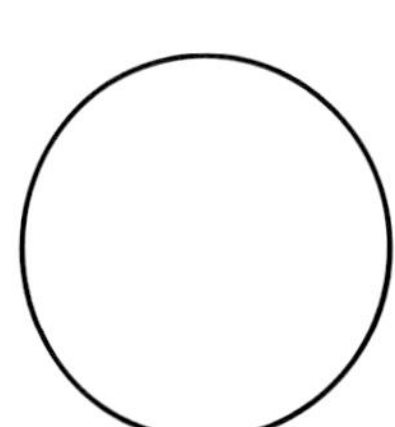

Take a Survey: Graphing

1. Ask 10 friends which of these animals from Africa is their favorite. Make a tally chart.

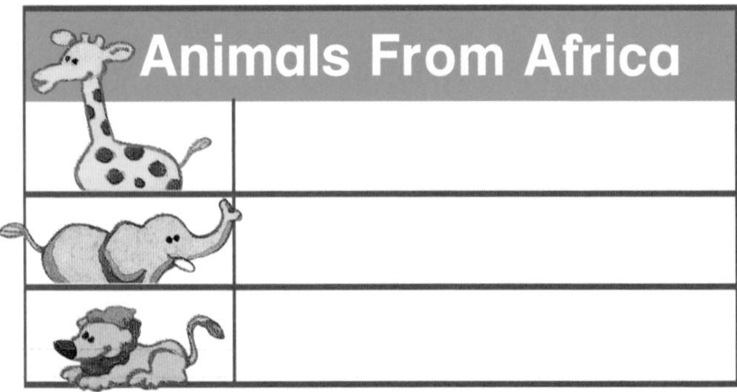

2. Use the tally chart to make a pictograph.

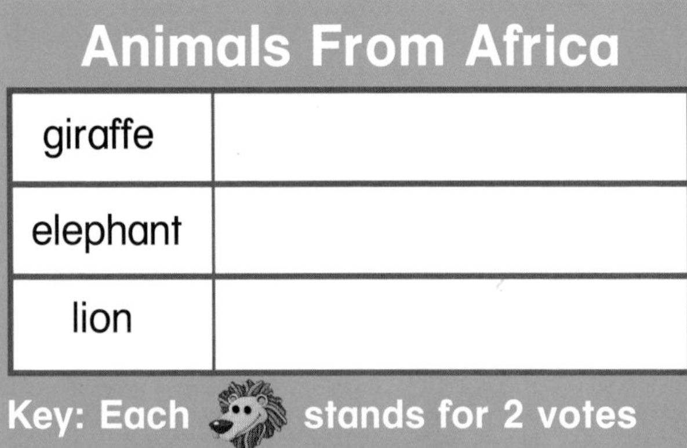

3. Now make a bar graph from the pictograph.

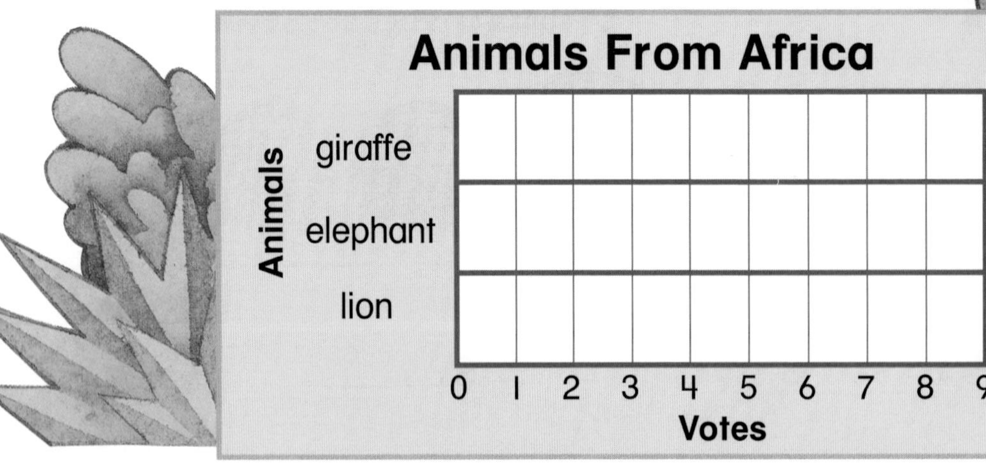

Talk About It

4. Which is your favorite animal from Africa? How would the graph change if your vote were shown?

Name ______________________

Number Patterns

You can make pairs with even numbers.

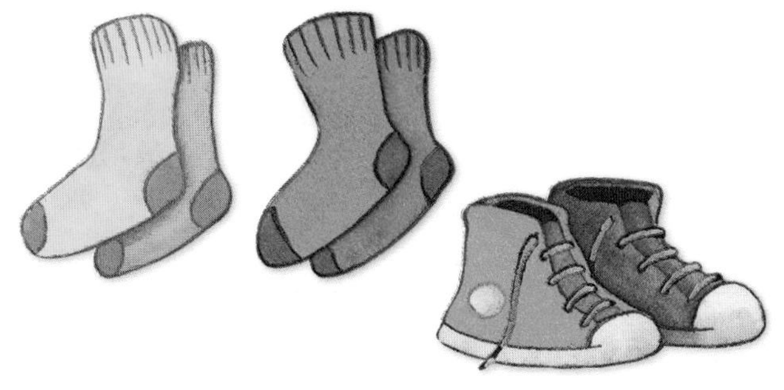

You can not make pairs with odd numbers.

Write the odd numbers between 2 and 10.

1. ______ ______ ______ ______

Write the even numbers between 1 and 9.

2. ______ ______ ______ ______

Skip count by 2s from 2 to 16.

3. 

Skip count by 5s from 5 to 40.

4. ______ ______ ______ ______ ______ ______ ______ ______

Skip count by 10s from 10 to 80.

5. ______ ______ ______ ______ ______ ______ ______ ______

Talk About It

6. Is the number 15 an odd or an even number?
   How did you decide?

Rounding and Estimation

Use this number line to round numbers to the nearest 10.

1. 21 ____ 2. 13 ____ 3. 8 ____ 4. 17 ____ 5. 26 ____

Use this number line to round numbers to the nearest 10.

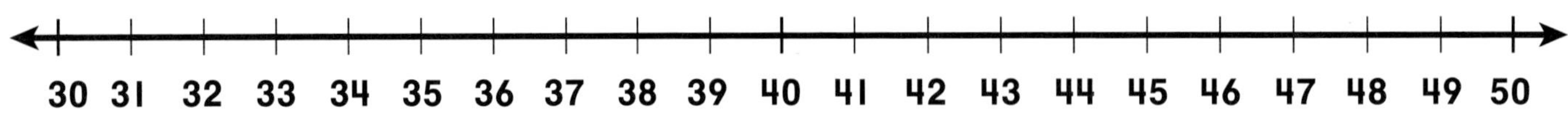

6. 42 ____ 7. 36 ____ 8. 44 ____ 9. 35 ____ 10. 31 ____

Round each number and estimate the sum.

11. 22 + 18 ____ 12. 79 + 11 ____

13. 82 + 16 ____ 14. 38 + 15 ____

Talk About It

15. How might rounding and estimation help you in a store?

Name ___________________________

Count Coins and Bills

Draw a line between the same amounts of money.

1. 

2. 

3. 

4. 

Talk About It

5. What coins can you use to make 65¢?

Trading Bills

1. Cross out the bills that are **not** a fair trade for a $20 bill.

2. Match the money with the price.

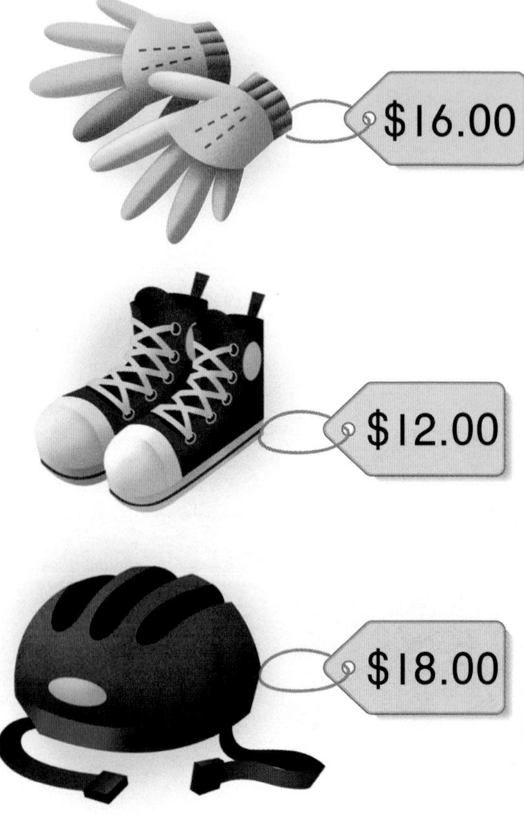

3. **Talk About It** What bills can you use to make $45?

Name ____________________

Basic Facts

You know the strategies that can help you with addition and subtraction facts.

Use counting on to solve.

1. $8 + 2$
2. $6 + 3$
3. $2 + 9$
4. $3 + 7$
5. $9 + 3$

Use doubles to solve.

6. $3 + 3$
7. $7 + 7$
8. $6 + 6$
9. $5 + 5$
10. $4 + 4$

Use counting back to solve.

11. $9 - 2$
12. $11 - 2$
13. $10 - 3$
14. $12 - 2$
15. $10 - 2$

Use related facts to subtract.

16. $12 - 9$
17. $14 - 6$
18. $15 - 7$
19. $11 - 5$
20. $12 - 4$

Talk About It

21. What strategy would you use to solve $12 - 3$? Why?

Fact Families

Complete the fact family.

1.

17	
8	9

$$\begin{array}{r} 8 \\ +\ 9 \\ \hline \square \end{array} \qquad \begin{array}{r} \square \\ +\ \square \\ \hline \square \end{array} \qquad \begin{array}{r} 17 \\ -\ 8 \\ \hline \square \end{array} \qquad \begin{array}{r} \square \\ -\ \square \\ \hline \square \end{array}$$

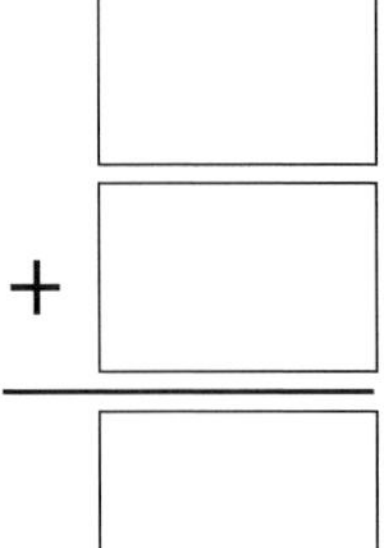

2.

18	
9	9

$$\begin{array}{r} 9 \\ +\ \square \\ \hline \square \end{array} \qquad \begin{array}{r} 18 \\ -\ \square \\ \hline \square \end{array}$$

3.

16	
9	7

$$\begin{array}{r} 9 \\ +\ \square \\ \hline \square \end{array} \qquad \begin{array}{r} 7 \\ +\ \square \\ \hline \square \end{array} \qquad \begin{array}{r} 16 \\ -\ 9 \\ \hline \square \end{array} \qquad \begin{array}{r} 16 \\ -\ \square \\ \hline \square \end{array}$$

Talk About It

4. Look at Exercise 2. Why are there only two facts?

Name ______________________________

Geometry and Fractions

1. Color the spheres blue.
   Color the cubes green.
   Color the square pyramids red.
   Color the cones yellow.

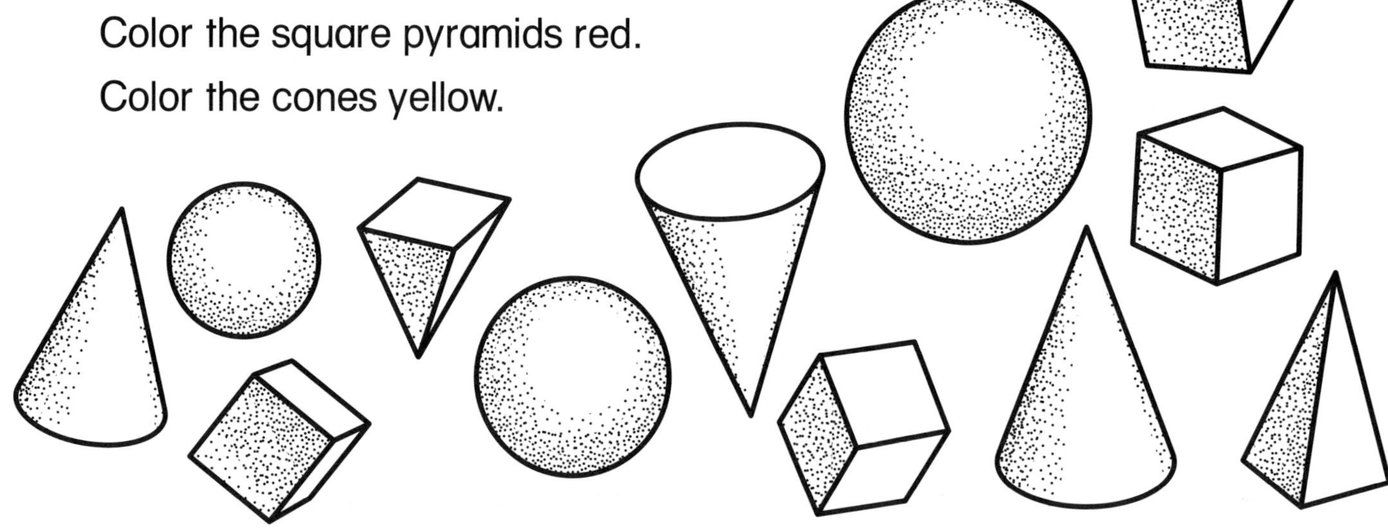

Draw lines to show the fractions.

2. $\frac{1}{2}$

 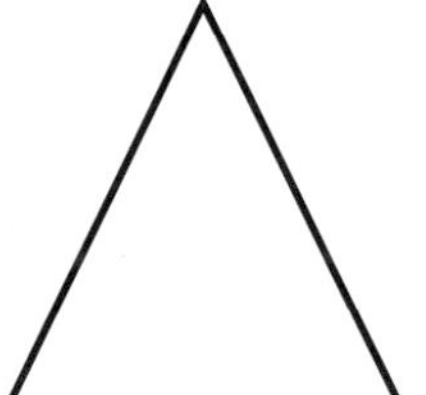  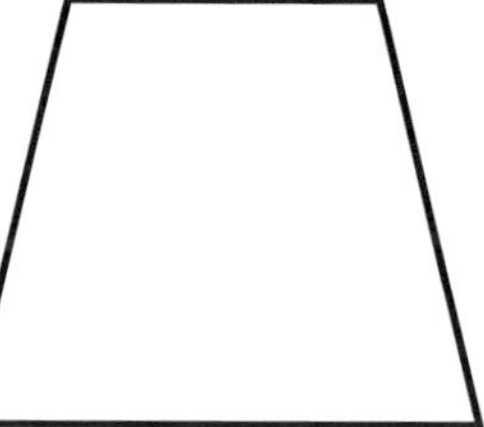

3. $\frac{1}{4}$

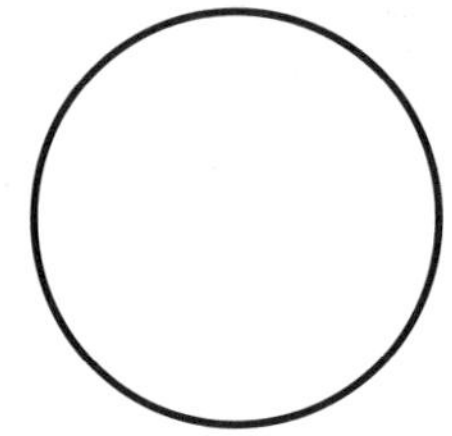   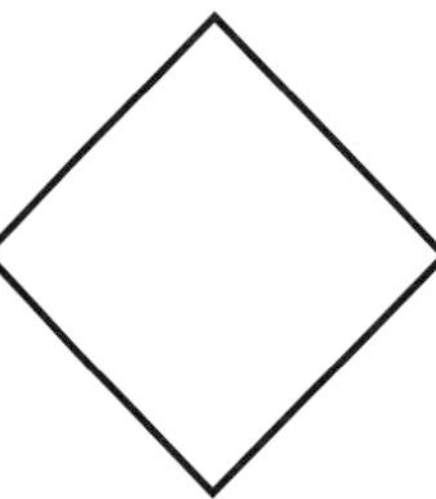

Talk About It

Look at the line you drew to show $\frac{1}{2}$ of the trapezoid.
Is it also a line of symmetry? Why or why not?

Duration and Sequence of Events

1. Circle the activity that usually lasts the longest.

2. Circle the activity that is over the quickest.

Circle the unit you would use to tell

3. the age of your classmate.

hours   days   weeks   years

4. how long it takes to get to school.

minutes   hours   days   weeks

5. Draw the time 1 hour later.

6. Draw the time 3 hours later.

7. Write 1, 2, 3 to show the correct order.

Talk About It

8. Name some reasons you need to be able to tell time.

Counting Kittens

Look back at the story to answer these questions.

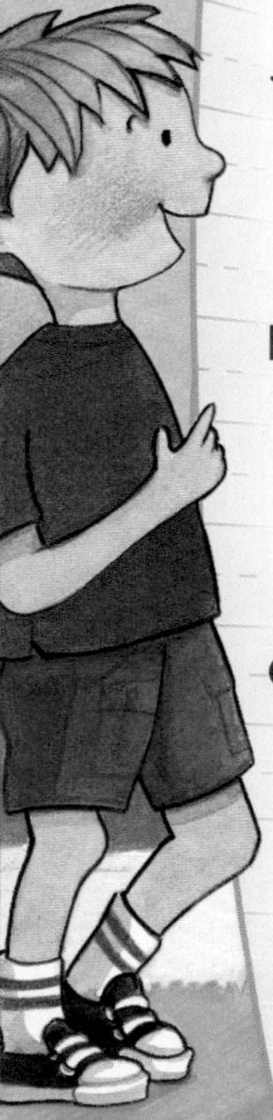

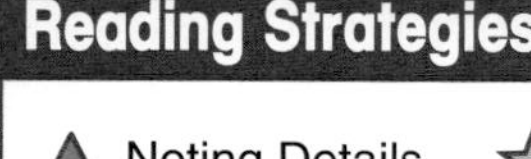

▲ **1.** Look at page 5. How many more kittens did the Johnson cousins take than Layla?

☆ **2.** Do you think Jim is counting on throughout the story or counting back? How do you know?

■ **3.** What if Jim had 3 kittens left to take home at the end of the day? How many kittens would he have had at the beginning of the day?

● **4.** What if you had ten little kittens? How many would you give away? How many would you keep?

Answers

1. 2 **2.** counting back; Possible answer: The value of the numbers decrease. **3.** 12 **4.** Check children's answers to make sure that the sum of the number of kittens given away and the number kept equals 10.

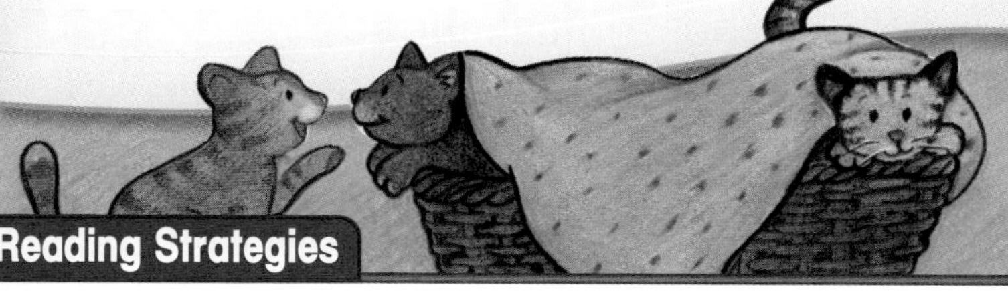

Reading Strategies

▲ Noting Details ☆ Summarize ■ Infer ● Draw Conclusions

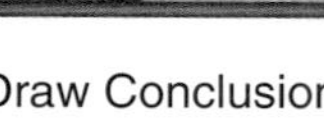

UNIT 1

Good Homes Wanted

written by Rob Arego
illustrated by Deborah Melmon

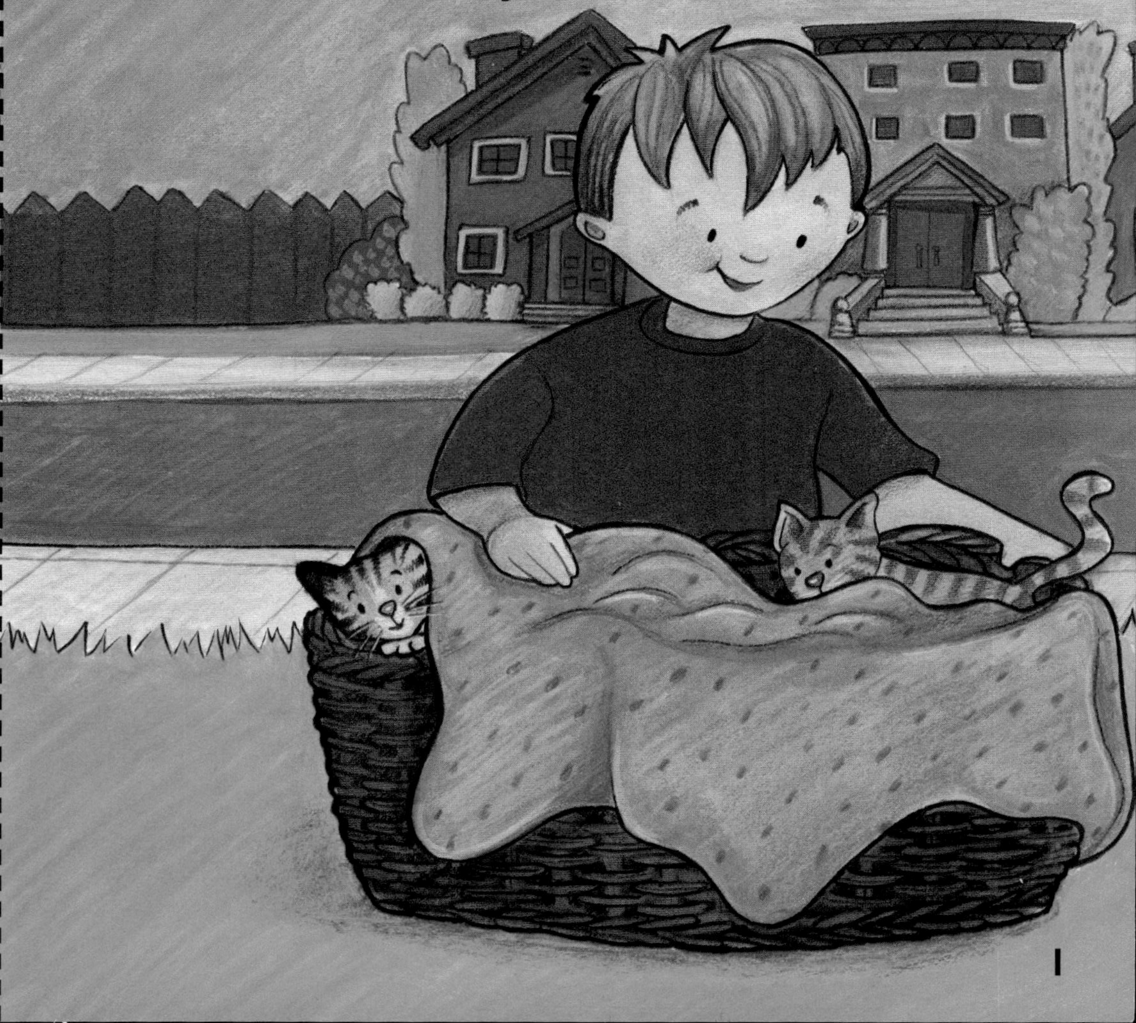

GOOD HOMES WANTED

Jim has 10 little kittens
that need a nice family.
Kate takes 1 with a black-and-white coat,
and so does Mr. Lee.
How many kittens are left?

Now Jim has 1 little kitten
that sits upon his knee.
And whenever anyone asks him, he says,
"This one is coming home with me!"

Now Jim has 2 little kittens
that need a nice family.
The Greens can't choose which kitten to take.
But finally they do agree.
How many kittens are left?

Now Jim has 8 little kittens
that need a nice family.
Mrs. Salas takes 1 with a bushy tail.
It is as cute as cute can be.
How many kittens are left?

Now Jim has 7 little kittens
that need a nice family.
Jamal takes 1 with a spotted coat.
It makes him so happy.
How many kittens are left?

Now Jim has 6 little kittens
that need a nice family.
Layla takes 1 with very long whiskers.
And the Johnson cousins take 3.
How many kittens are left?

UNIT 1

Number Concepts, Addition, Subtraction, and Graphing

From the Read-Aloud Anthology

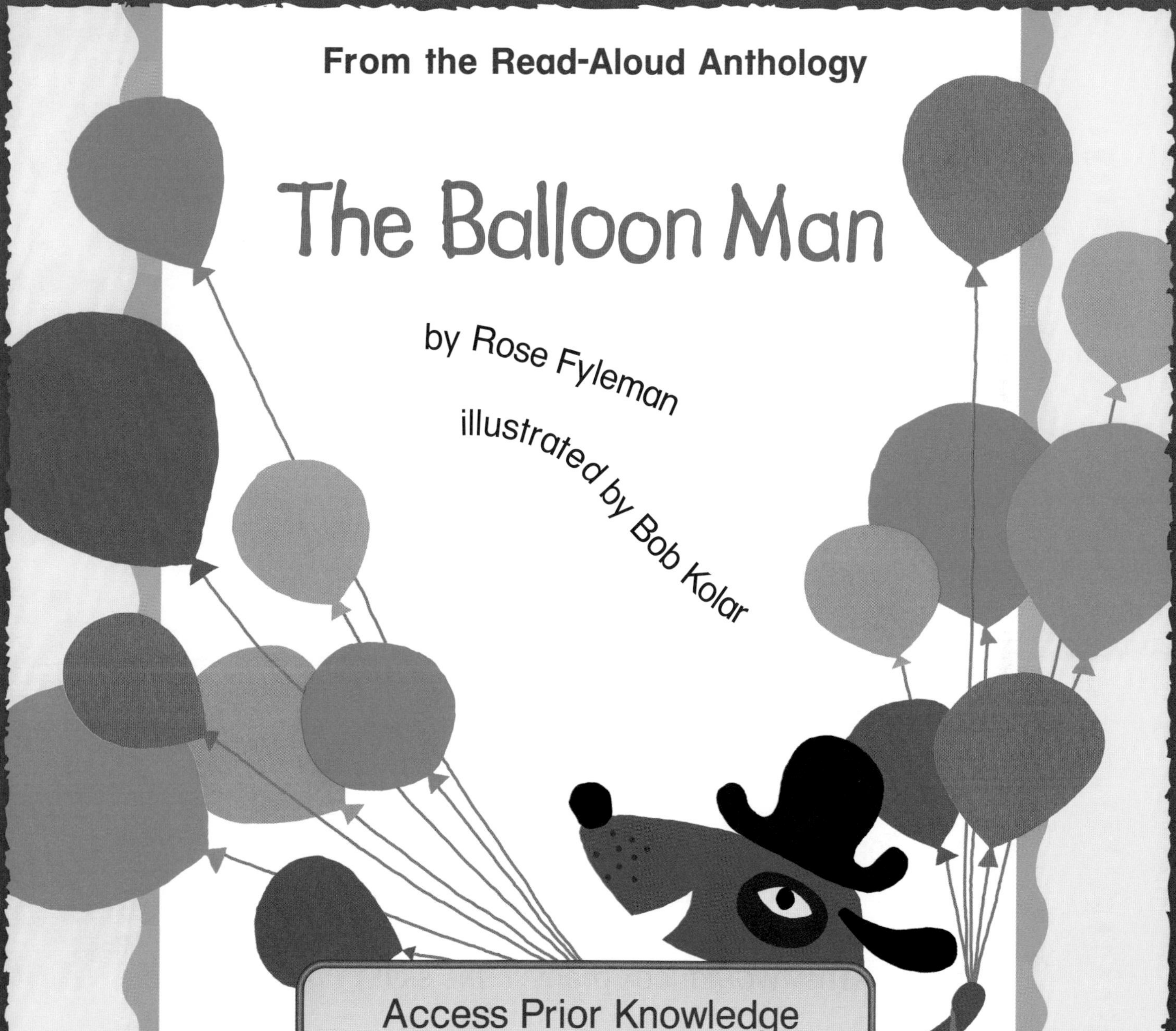

The Balloon Man

by Rose Fyleman

illustrated by Bob Kolar

Access Prior Knowledge

This poem will help you review

- Counting
- Addition and subtraction facts to 10
- Making tally marks

The Balloon Man

He always comes on market days,
    And holds balloons—a lovely bunch—
And in the market square he stays,
    And never seems to think of lunch.

They're red and purple, blue and green,
    And when it is a sunny day
Tho' carts and people get between
    You see them shining far away.

And some are big and some are small,
    All tied together with a string,
And if there is a wind at all
    They tug and tug like anything.

Some day perhaps he'll let them go
    And we shall see them sailing high,
And stand and watch them from below—
    They *would* look pretty in the sky!

Name ______________________

Put an **X** on a balloon. Then make **I** tally mark.

Use the poem and pictures on pages 1b and 1c.
Complete the chart.

1.

	Tally	Total

Use the chart.
Solve.

2. How many more  than  ?

_____ more 

3. How many fewer  than  ?

_____ fewer 

4. How many  and  in all?

_____ in all

5. **Create Your Own** Write a subtraction story about the balloon man holding 10 balloons and then letting some go. Find the answer.

____

____

Dear Family,

My class is starting Unit 1. I will be learning about numbers through 50, addition and subtraction facts, data, graphing, and probability. These pages show some of what I will learn and have activities for us to do together.

From, ______________________

Vocabulary

These are some words and symbols I will use in this unit.

addend Any number being added

addend → $3 + 5 = 8$

sum The result of addition

$4 + 3 = 7$ ← sum

fact family A set of related facts

$6 + 9 = 15$ $15 - 9 = 6$
$9 + 6 = 15$ $15 - 6 = 9$

difference The result of subtraction

$10 - 6 = 4$ ← difference

greater than (>) Used to compare two numbers

$9 > 5$
9 is greater than 5.

less than (<) Used to compare two numbers

$3 < 7$
3 is less than 7.

tally marks Symbols that represent a count

| stands for 1. 𝍸 stands for 5.

estimate To try to determine about how many are in a group

Some other words I will use are **data**, **symbol**, **graph**, **ordered pairs**, **grid**, **survey**, **outcome**, **and predict.**

Vocabulary Activity

Let's work together to complete these sentences.

1. In $13 - 7 = 6$, the number 6 is the ______________.
2. In the statement $8 > 4$, the symbol > means ______________.

How To make 10 to add

In this unit, I will learn strategies to help me remember addition and subtraction facts. This is an example of one strategy I will be learning. Sometimes I will use a ten frame and counters to help.

Making 10 can help you add 7, 8, and 9.

Step 1

Find 8 + 5.

Show 8.

Then show 5.

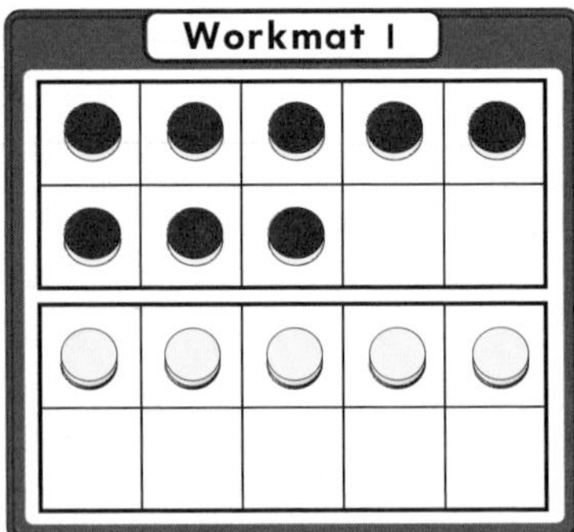

Step 2

Move counters to make 10.

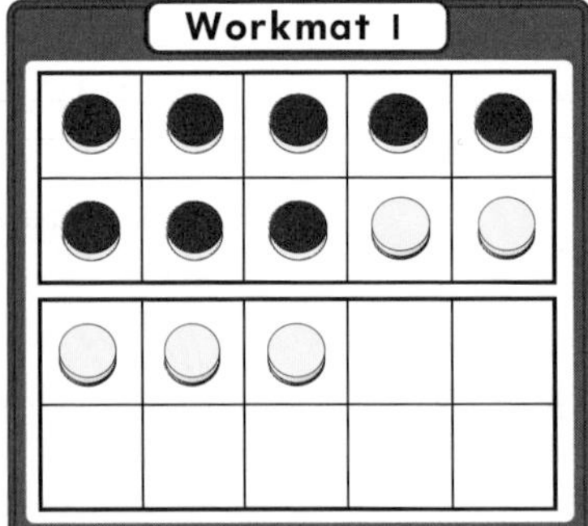

Show 8 + 5 as 10 + 3.

Step 3

Add.

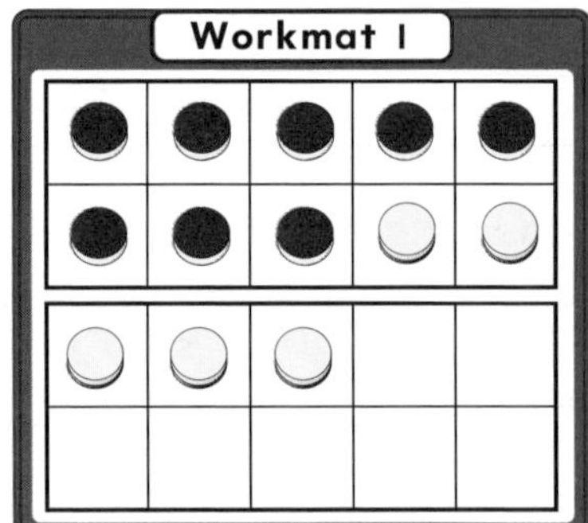

8 + 5 = 13

addend sum

Literature

These books link to the math in this unit. We can look for them at the library.

What's a Pair? What's a Dozen?
Text and illustrations
Stephen R. Swinburne
(Boyds Mill Press, 2000)

More Than One
By Miriam Schlein

Education Place

We can visit *Education Place* at

eduplace.com/maf

for the Math Lingo game, *e*•Glossary, and more games and activities to do together.

Number Concepts Through 50

CHAPTER 1

INVESTIGATION

Find some things in this picture that show 3 or 5. How many ways can you use the picture to show numbers you know?

Storytime

Listen to the street fair story.
Use counters to act out the story.

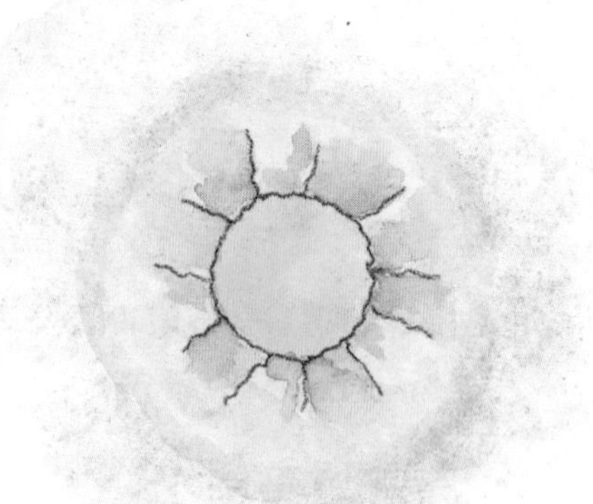

Name ____________________

Reading and Writing Numbers

Objective
Read and write numbers through 50.

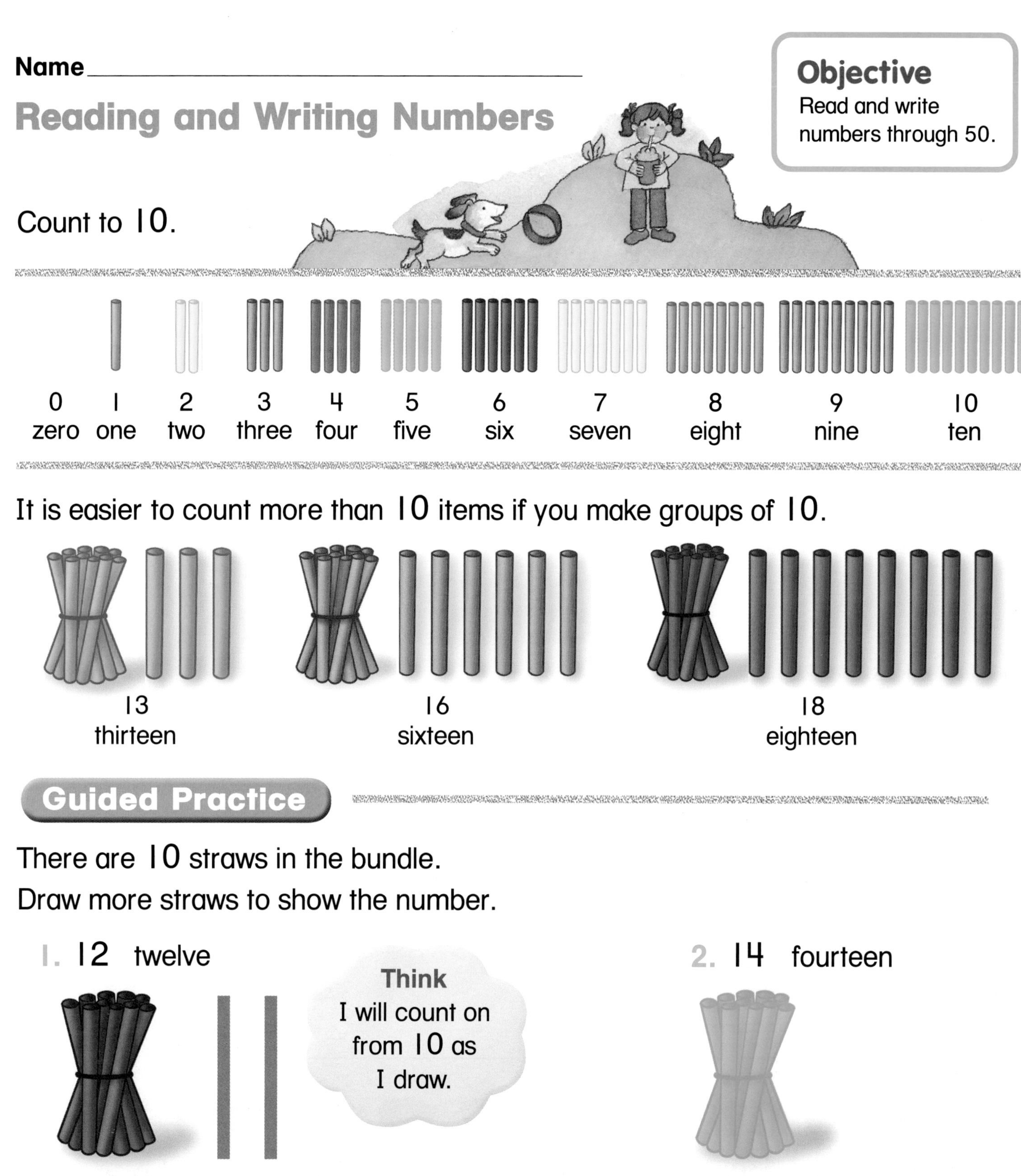

Count to 10.

0	1	2	3	4	5	6	7	8	9	10
zero	one	two	three	four	five	six	seven	eight	nine	ten

It is easier to count more than 10 items if you make groups of 10.

13 thirteen

16 sixteen

18 eighteen

Guided Practice

There are 10 straws in the bundle.
Draw more straws to show the number.

1. 12 twelve

Think
I will count on from 10 as I draw.

2. 14 fourteen

3. 11 eleven

4. 17 seventeen

5. 15 fifteen

Explain Your Thinking Do you think it is quicker to count to 19 using a bundle of 10? Why or why not?

Practice

Remember to count by tens.

Count groups of 10.
Write the number word.

ten
twenty
thirty
forty
fifty
sixty
seventy
eighty
ninety

1. 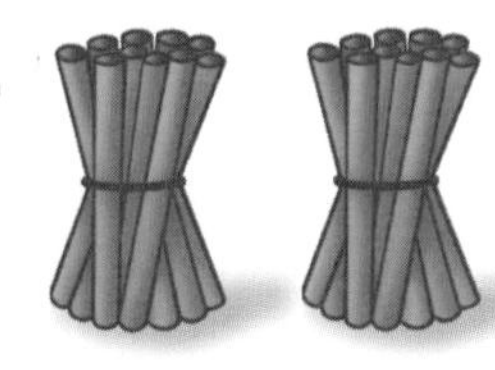

thirty

2.

3. 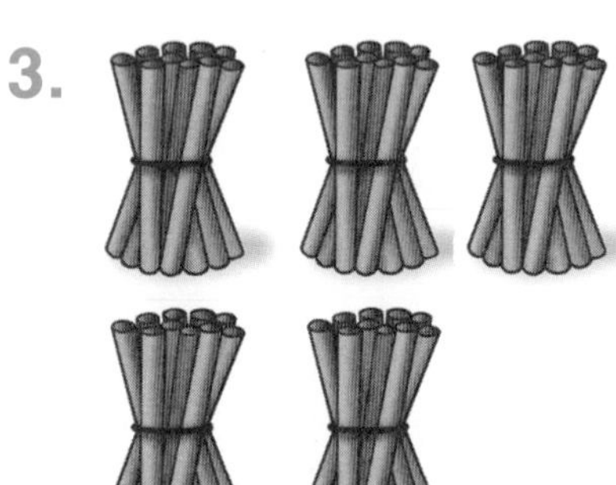

4.

5. 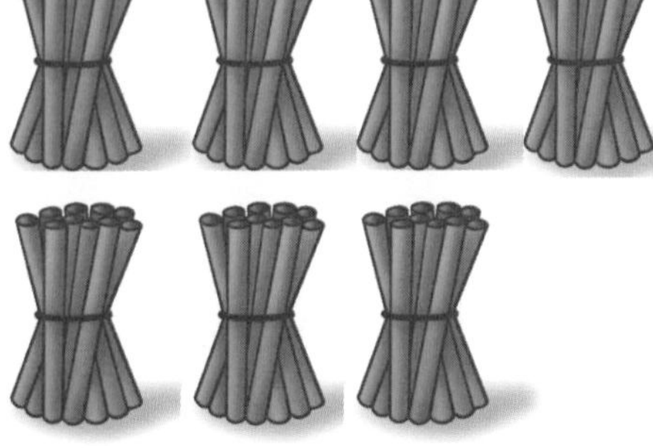

6. 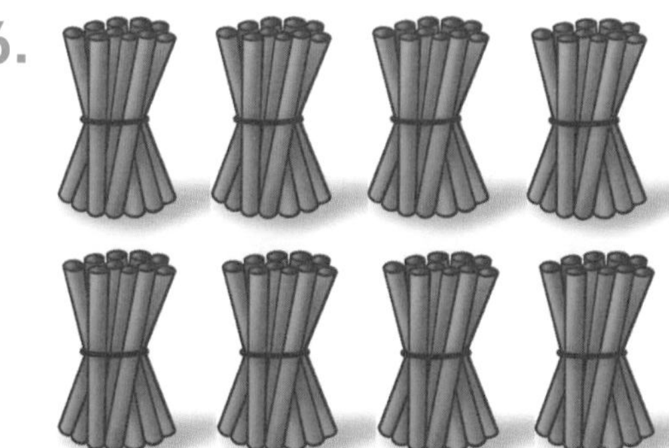

7. 

8. 

9. **Talk About It** Count aloud by ones to fifty. Now count aloud by tens to fifty. Which is faster? Why?

Go on

Name ______________________________

Write how many there are.
Draw a line to the correct number word.

1. 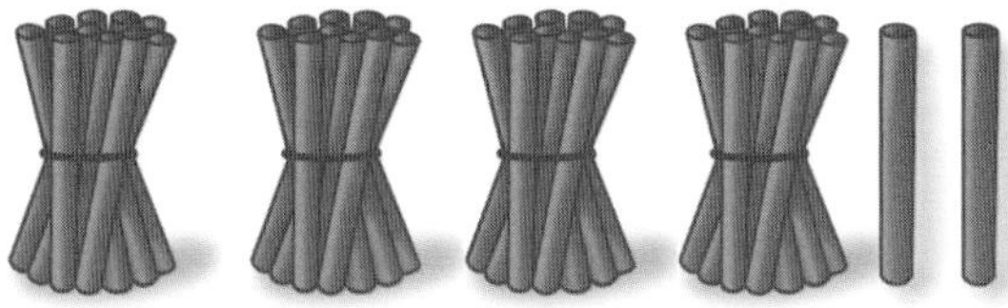 42 — thirty-eight

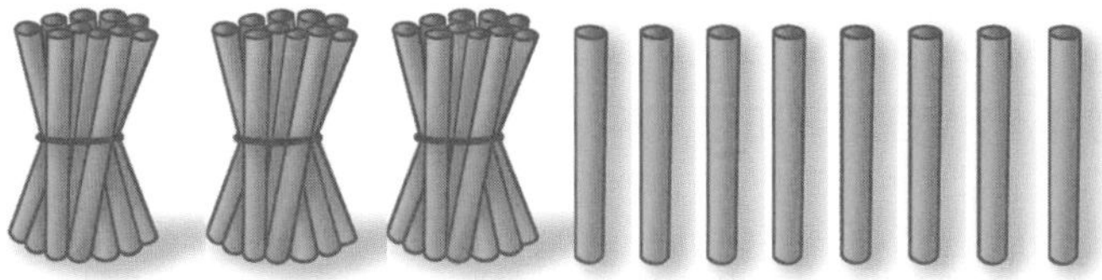

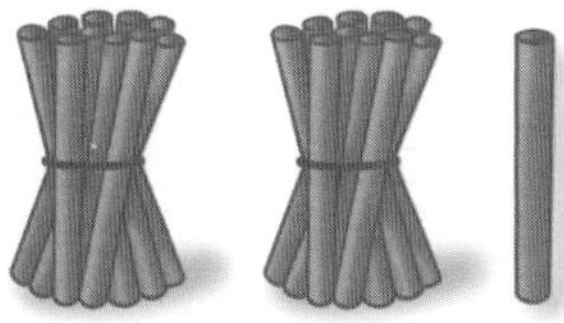

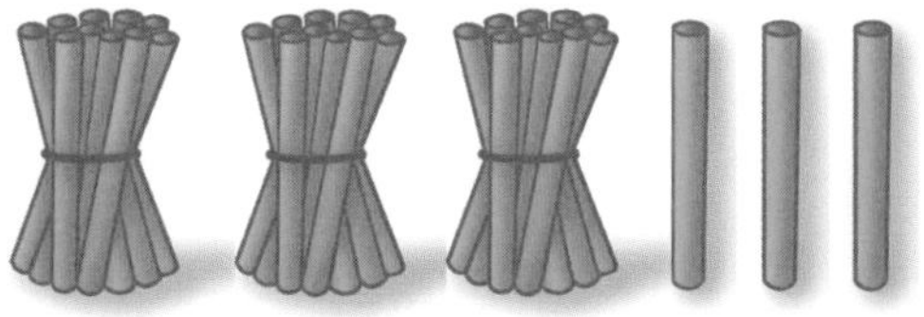

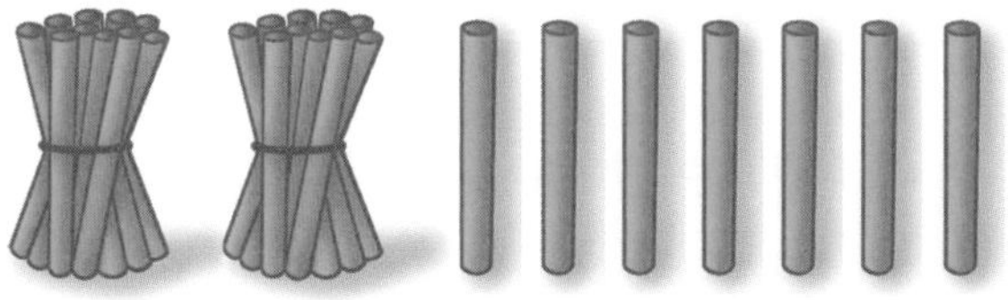

2. ____ — thirty-three

3. ____ — forty-two

4. ____ — twenty-seven

5. ____ — twenty-one

Reading Math ▶ Number Words

Write the number.

6. three ______	7. five ______	8. four ______
thirteen ______	fifteen ______	fourteen ______
thirty ______	fifty ______	forty ______

At Home Write a number word from 11 to 50. Ask your child to read it and write the number.

Activity

Game

Three in a Row

Players: 2

What You Need: Three in a Row picture page, crayons, 2 bags / (LT 8)

How to Play

1. Color the Three in a Row picture page.

2. Cut out the pictures and put them in your bag.

3. Take turns picking a card from each other's bag.

4. Match the cards to the board below.
   Play until someone gets three in a row.

Eight	43	Fifty
Twenty-seven	21	Forty-four
Thirty-two	35	Nineteen

Name ______________________________

Ordering Numbers

Audio Tutor 1/1 Listen and Understand

Objective
Order numbers through 50.

Vocabulary
number line
before
after
less
more

A **number line** can help you count and order numbers.

0 1 2 3 4 5 6 7 8 9 10

These numbers come **before** 5.
4 is just before 5.
4 is one **less** than 5.

These numbers come **after** 5.
6 is just after 5.
6 is one **more** than 5.

Guided Practice

Use the number line below.
Complete the sentence.

10 11 12 13 14 15 16 17 18 19 20

Think
I find 15 on the number line.
I look for the number that comes just before it.

1. _____ is just before 15.
2. 11 is just after _____.
3. _____ is one more than 12.
4. 17 is one less than _____.

Count forward.
Write the missing numbers.

5. 12 13 _____ 15 _____

Count backward.
Write the missing numbers.

6. 18 17 _____ _____ 14

Explain Your Thinking Use the number line. What number is between 12 and 14? How can you use the number line to find the answer?

Practice

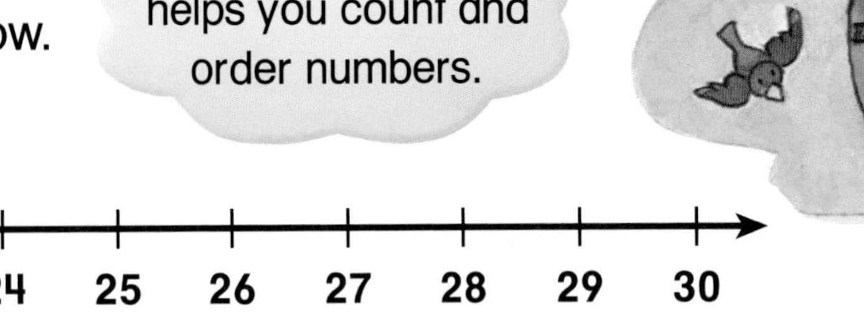

Use the number line below.
Complete the sentence.

20 21 22 23 24 25 26 27 28 29 30

1. 21 is just before 22.
2. 29 is just after ______.
3. ______ is one more than 25.
4. 29 is one less than ______.

Count forward.
Write the missing numbers.

5. 22 ______ ______ 25 26

Count backward.
Write the missing numbers.

6. 28 ______ 26 25 ______

Use the number line below.
Complete the sentence.

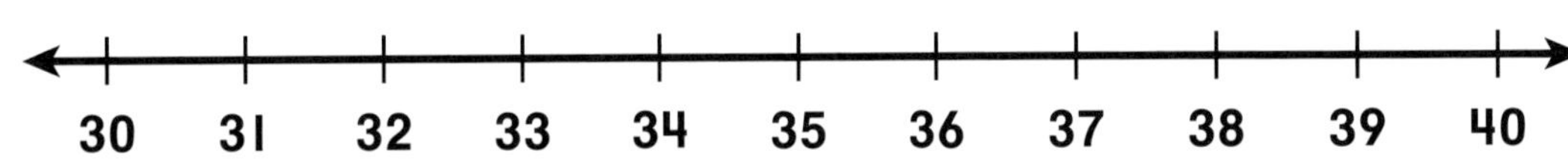

7. ______ is just before 33.
8. 37 is just after ______.
9. ______ is one more than 34.
10. 30 is one less than ______.

Problem Solving ▶ Number Sense

11. Look at these numbers. 45 48 50 49 47 46

Write the numbers in order.

______ ______ ______ ______ ______ ______

At Home Say a number between 10 and 50. Ask your child to tell you the numbers that come just before and just after your number. Repeat with other numbers.

Name ______________________________

Comparing Numbers

Audio Tutor 1/2 Listen and Understand

Objective
Compare numbers through 50.

Vocabulary
more
greater than (>)
fewer
less than (<)

●●●●●
●●●●

▲▲▲
▲▲▲

9 ● 6 ▲

There are **more** ● than ▲.

9 is **greater than** 6.

$9 > 6$

There are **fewer** ▲ than ●.

6 is **less than** 9.

$6 < 9$

Guided Practice

Write how many there are.
Circle the greater number.
Write **more** or **fewer**.

1. ■■■■ ■■■■ ▲▲▲▲▲▲ ▲▲▲▲▲

8 ____ 11 ____ There are ________ ■ than ▲.

2. ●●●●● ●●●●● ■■■■ ■■■

____ ____ There are ________ ● than ■.

Write **>** or **<**.

3. 16 ◯ 24 4. 50 ◯ 27 5. 38 ◯ 42

Explain Your Thinking How can you use **>** or **<** to compare 29 and 42?

Extra Help at **eduplace.com/map**

Practice

Count how many.
Then compare.

Write how many there are.
Circle the greater number.
Write **more** or **fewer**.

1. 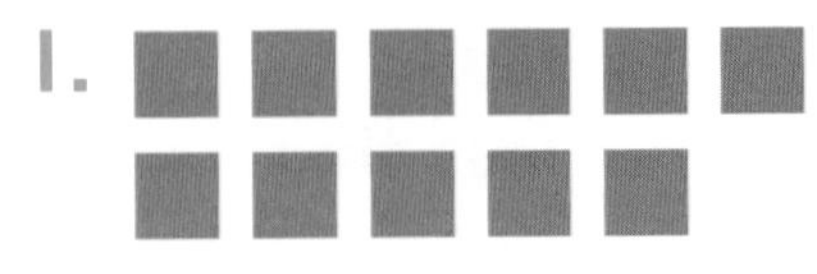 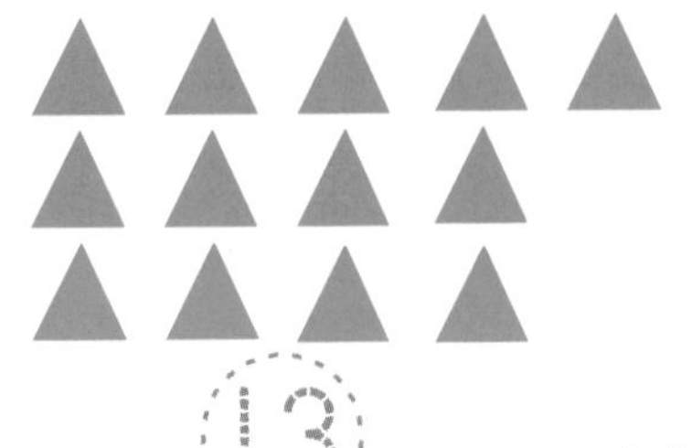

11   13

There are fewer ■ than ▲.

2. ●●●●● ●●●●● 

_____   _____

There are ________ ● than ■.

Write > or <.

3. 25 ◯ 24	4. 33 ◯ 40	5. 38 ◯ 41
6. 19 ◯ 31	7. 30 ◯ 20	8. 50 ◯ 49
9. 0 ◯ 20	10. 11 ◯ 8	11. 44 ◯ 30
12. 29 ◯ 40	13. 17 ◯ 21	14. 25 ◯ 18
15. 35 ◯ 45	16. 41 ◯ 39	17. 49 ◯ 46

Go on

Hands-On

Name ______________________________

Now Try This Estimating More or Fewer

Use cubes.

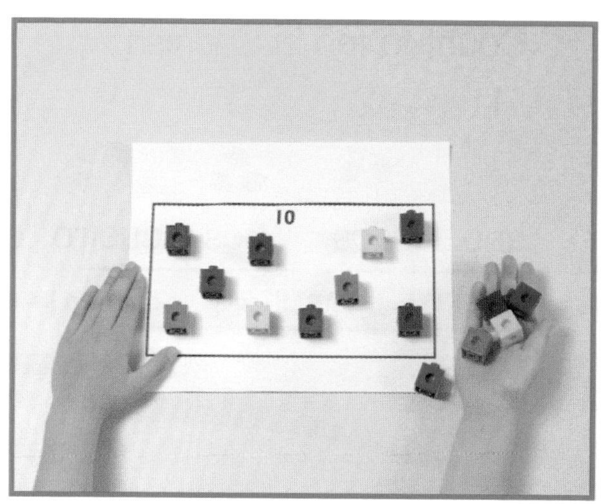

1. Place **10** cubes in the work space below.

2. Take more cubes. Drop them on a separate sheet of paper. Did you drop **more** or **fewer** than **10?** Estimate.

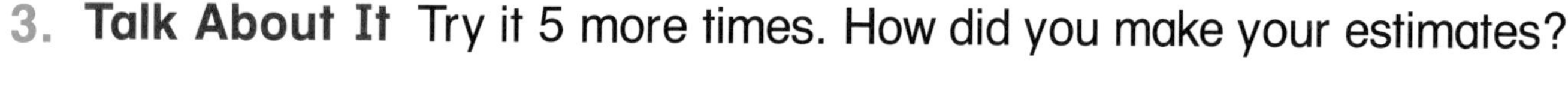

3. **Talk About It** Try it 5 more times. How did you make your estimates?

____

____

10

At Home With your child compare the number of objects in two groups using the terms **more** and **fewer** and the symbols < and >.

Activity

Social Studies Connection

Spanish Numbers

Count to ten in Spanish.

1	2	3	4	5	6	7	8	9	10
uno	dos	tres	cuatro	cinco	seis	siete	ocho	nueve	diez

WEEKLY WR READER eduplace.com/map

Quick Check

Count how many there are.
Write the number and number word.

1. 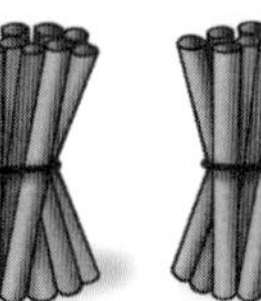 ______ ____________

Use the number line. Complete the sentence.

2. ______ is just before 42.

3. 43 is one more than ______.

4. 49 is just after ______.

5. ______ is between 44 and 46.

Count forward.
Write the missing numbers.

6. 42 43 ______ ______ 46

Count backward.
Write the missing numbers.

7. 50 ______ 48 ______ 46

Write > or <.

8. 27 ◯ 31

9. 43 ◯ 48

10. 34 ◯ 28

Name ____________________

Estimating How Many

 **Audio Tutor 1**/3 Listen and Understand

Objective
Estimate amounts through 50.

Vocabulary
estimate

Use what you know about 10 to **estimate** how many.

Estimate the number of peanuts.

Step 1

Circle a group of ten.

Step 2

Use this group of ten to help you estimate.

Think
About how many tens in all?

Step 3

Write your estimate.

It looks like a little more than 2 tens (20) but much less than 3 tens (30).

about 20

Guided Practice

Estimate how many.

Think
I will circle a group of ten to help me estimate.

1.

Estimate: about ______

2.

Estimate: about ______

Explain Your Thinking Is 20 a good estimate for Exercise 1? Why or why not?

Practice

Think about how many tens in all.

Estimate how many.

1.

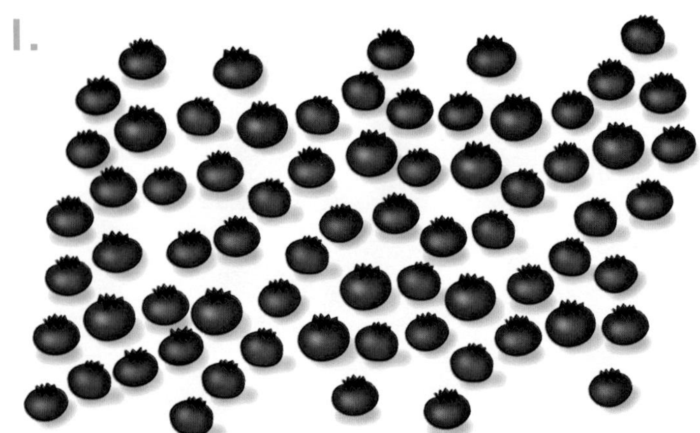

Estimate: about ______

2.

Estimate: about ______

Problem Solving ▶ Reasoning

About how many are there?
Circle the best estimate.

3.

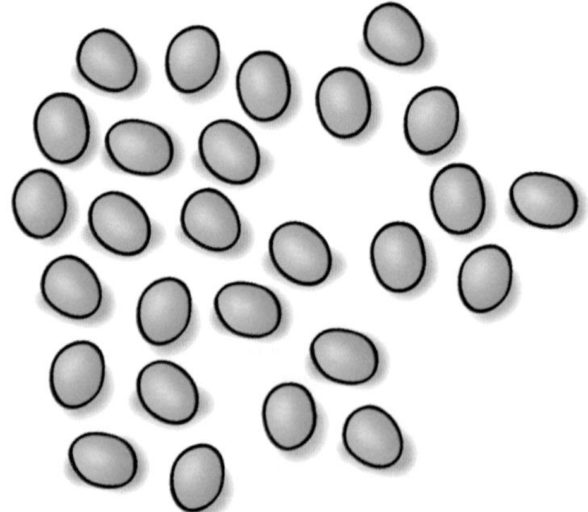

about 30 about 50 about 80

4.

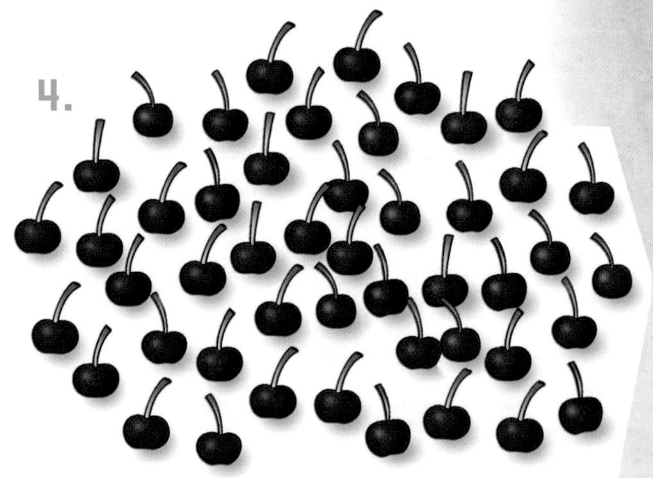

about 20 about 50 about 80

5. **Talk About It** Tell why the estimate you chose was the best. Explain why the other choices don't make sense.

At Home Display a collection of up to 50 small objects. Have your child count out a group of ten of the objects. Then have him or her use this ten to estimate how many there are in all.

Problem Solving

Name ______________________________

Objective
Choose the most reasonable answer.

Reasonable Answers

Each year the town has a street fair.
There are fun things to see and do.

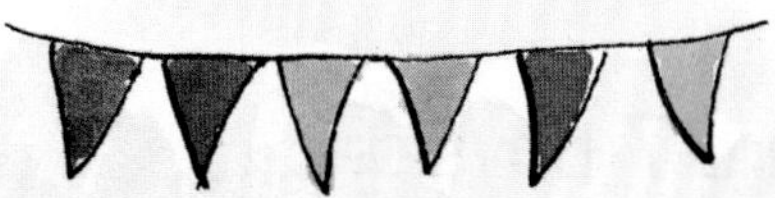

Circle the most reasonable answer.

There are 8 children in line to play a game.
More children come and join the line.
How many children are in the line now?

Choose a reasonable answer.

5 children   8 children   11 children

THINK	DECIDE
What do I need to find?	I need to find how many children are in the line now.
Will my answer be a number, word, or picture?	My answer will be a number.
How do I find the answer?	I will look for clues in the problem.
	Join means to put together. I need to add.
Which number is the most reasonable answer?	The number must be greater than 8.

11 is the most reasonable answer.

There are 11 children in the line now.

Guided Practice

Circle the most reasonable answer.

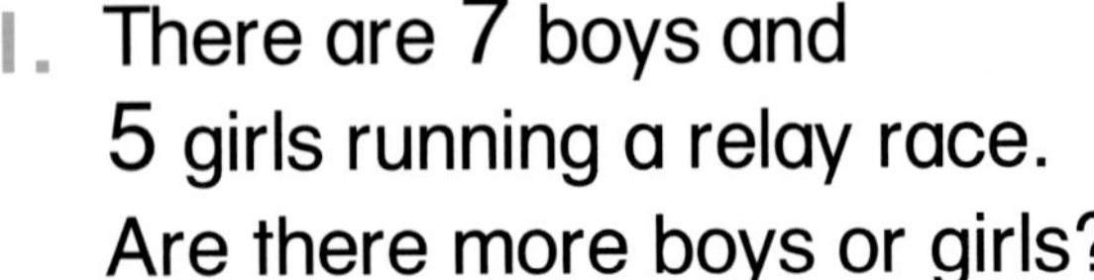

1. There are 7 boys and 5 girls running a relay race. Are there more boys or girls?

Draw or write to explain.

Think
The answer will not be a number or picture.

12 children   more boys   more girls

2. The children are painting a pattern on a banner. What comes next in the pattern?

 ?

Think
There are no numbers or words in the pattern.

square   4   

Practice

3. Tim plays Ring Toss. He has 6 rings to toss into a bucket. He misses on his first 3 tosses. How many tosses does he have left?

3 tosses   none   9 rings

4. There are 6 children making sand art. 4 children join the group. Are there more children or fewer children making sand art now?

10 children   more children   fewer children

At Home Ask your child to explain why the answers he or she chose are reasonable and why the other answer choices do not make sense.

Name ____________________

Now Try This **Number Clues**

Solve.

Draw or write to explain.

1. I am after 18.
   I am before 20.
   What number am I? ________

2. I am between 10 and 15.
   I am greater than 13.
   What number am I? ________

3. I am less than 50.
   I am greater than 48.
   What number am I? ________

4. There are more than 36 dogs.
   There are fewer than 37 cats.
   Are there more dogs or cats? ________

5. Marc has 32 baseball cards.
   Belle has 38 baseball cards.
   Who has more cards? ________

Write About It Choose a number. Write clues to find that number. Give your clues to a friend to solve. ____________________

____

Problem Solving

Math Challenge

Read Between the Lines

Cody is reading a book. He is on a page that is after 30 but before 35. The sum of the two digits equals 6. What page is Cody reading?

______

Key Topic Review

Ordering Numbers

Write the numbers in the boxes on the number line.

1. 26 29 23 22 25 20

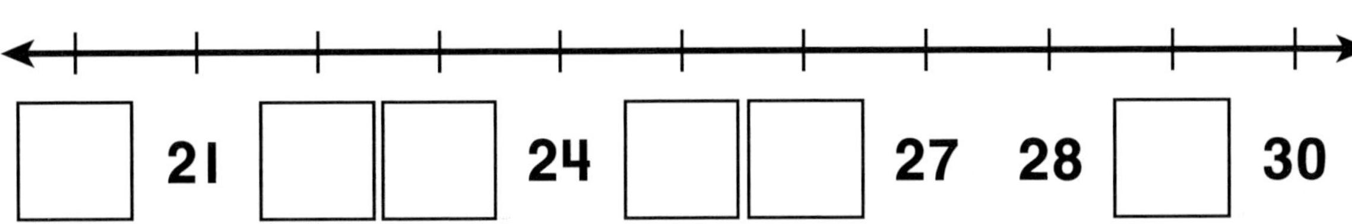

☐ 21 ☐ ☐ 24 ☐ ☐ 27 28 ☐ 30

2. 12 17 11 20 15 18

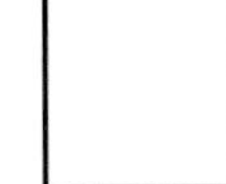

10 ☐ ☐ 13 14 ☐ 16 ☐ ☐ 19 ☐

3. 37 32 33 38 31 35

40 39 ☐ ☐ 36 ☐ 34 ☐ ☐ ☐

Extra Practice at eduplace.com/map

Name ___________________

Vocabulary

Complete the sentence.

fewer
less than
more

1. There are ____________ ● than 5.
2. There are ____________ ▲ than ●.
3. 4 is ____________ 7.

Concepts and Skills

Write how many there are.
Draw a line to the correct number word.

4. 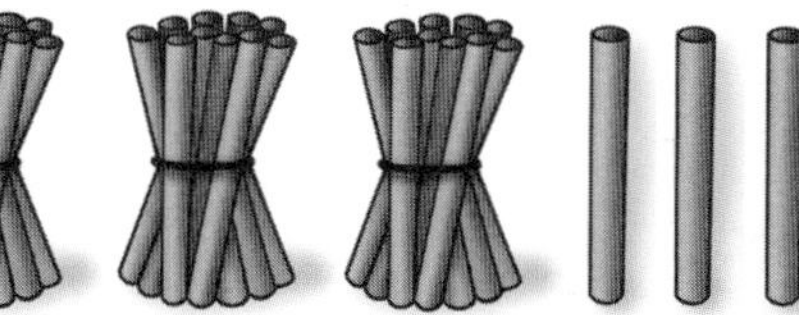 ____

5. 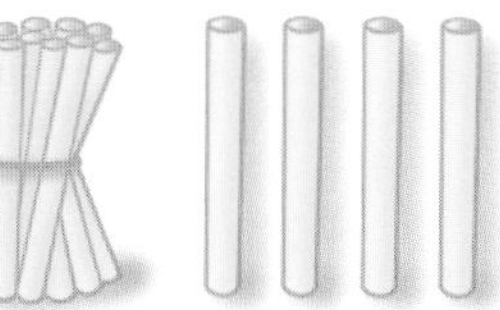 ____

6.  ____

twenty-one

thirty-three

fourteen

Write > or <.

7. 29 ◯ 30
8. 41 ◯ 17
9. 32 ◯ 23
10. 18 ◯ 21
11. 37 ◯ 32
12. 39 ◯ 48

Chapter Review/Test

Use the number line below. Complete the sentence.

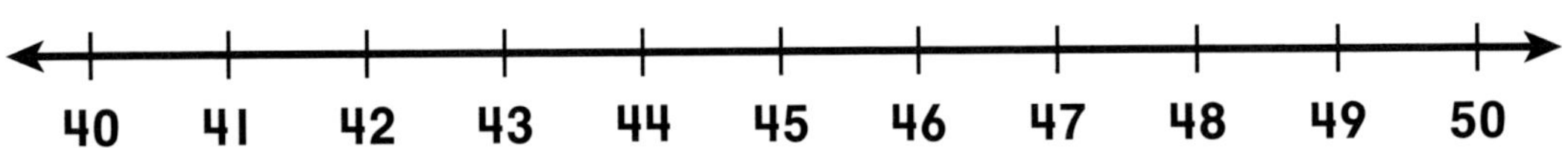

13. 41 is just before _____.

14. 50 is just after _____.

15. 45 is one less than _____.

16. 48 is one more than _____.

Count forward.
Write the missing numbers.

17. 43 44 45 _____ _____

Count backward.
Write the missing numbers.

18. 50 _____ 48 _____ 46

Circle a group of ten. Then estimate how many.

19.

Estimate: about _____

Problem Solving

Circle the most reasonable answer.

20. There are 8 people in line to buy popcorn. 5 more people get in line. How many people are in line to buy popcorn?

Draw or write to explain.

3 people more children 13 people

Addition Facts

CHAPTER 2

INVESTIGATION

How many different addition sentences can you write about this picture?

Apples
5¢

Puppet Path

Start at the bottom.
Follow the sums of 10
to take the puppet back
to the theater.

Name ____________________

Addition Properties

When you **add** numbers, you get a **sum.**

Add numbers in any order.
The sum is the same.

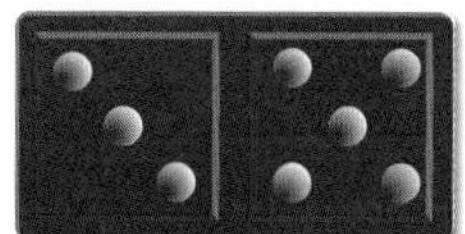

3 + 5 = 8 ← sum

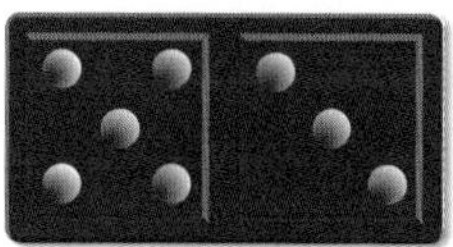

5 + 3 = 8 ← sum

Add zero to any number.
The sum is that number.

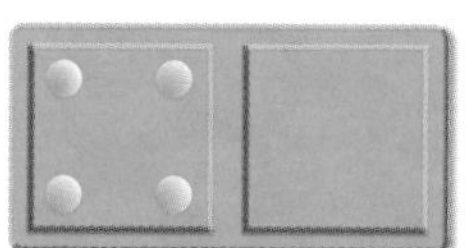

4 + 0 = 4

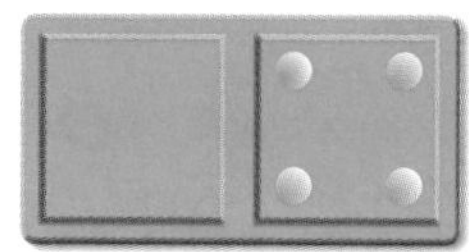

0 + 4 = 4

Objective
Add in any order; add zero.

Vocabulary
add
sum

Guided Practice

Add.

1. 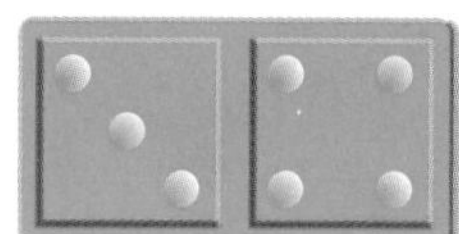

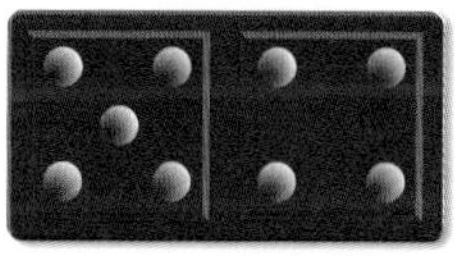

5 + 4 = ____

4 + 5 = ____

Think
I know 5 + 4 and 4 + 5 have the same sum.

2. 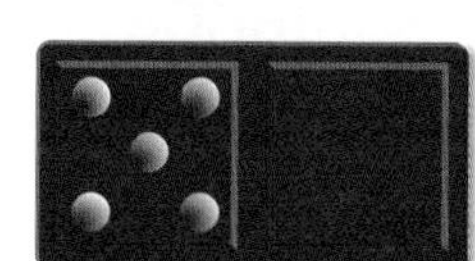

$\begin{array}{r} 3 \\ +4 \\ \hline \end{array}$ $\begin{array}{r} 4 \\ +3 \\ \hline \end{array}$

3. $\begin{array}{r} 5 \\ +0 \\ \hline \end{array}$ $\begin{array}{r} 0 \\ +5 \\ \hline \end{array}$

4. $\begin{array}{r} 2 \\ +1 \\ \hline \end{array}$ $\begin{array}{r} 1 \\ +2 \\ \hline \end{array}$

5. $\begin{array}{r} 7 \\ +0 \\ \hline \end{array}$ $\begin{array}{r} 0 \\ +7 \\ \hline \end{array}$

6. $\begin{array}{r} 2 \\ +6 \\ \hline \end{array}$ $\begin{array}{r} 6 \\ +2 \\ \hline \end{array}$

Explain Your Thinking Why does adding zero to a number not change the number?

Practice

Remember that you can add the numbers in any order.

Add.

1.
$\begin{array}{r} 2 \\ +5 \\ \hline 7 \end{array}$ $\begin{array}{r} 5 \\ +2 \\ \hline 7 \end{array}$

2. 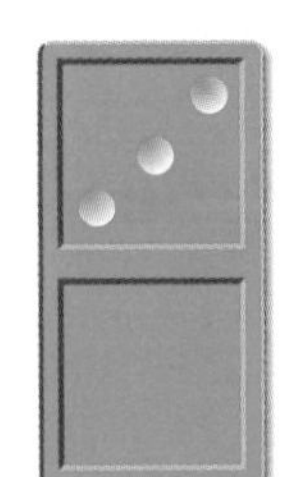
$\begin{array}{r} 3 \\ +0 \\ \hline \end{array}$ $\begin{array}{r} 0 \\ +3 \\ \hline \end{array}$

3. $\begin{array}{r} 4 \\ +1 \\ \hline \end{array}$ $\begin{array}{r} 1 \\ +4 \\ \hline \end{array}$

4. $\begin{array}{r} 8 \\ +2 \\ \hline \end{array}$ $\begin{array}{r} 2 \\ +8 \\ \hline \end{array}$

5. $\begin{array}{r} 0 \\ +7 \\ \hline \end{array}$ $\begin{array}{r} 7 \\ +0 \\ \hline \end{array}$

6. $\begin{array}{r} 6 \\ +1 \\ \hline \end{array}$

7. $\begin{array}{r} 4 \\ +2 \\ \hline \end{array}$

8. $\begin{array}{r} 2 \\ +7 \\ \hline \end{array}$

9. $\begin{array}{r} 2 \\ +0 \\ \hline \end{array}$

10. $\begin{array}{r} 1 \\ +9 \\ \hline \end{array}$

11. $\begin{array}{r} 3 \\ +5 \\ \hline \end{array}$

12. 1 + 5 = ____

13. 8 + 0 = ____

14. 7 + 3 = ____

15. 0 + 10 = ____

16. 1 + 8 = ____

17. 9 + 0 = ____

Algebra Readiness ▶ Number Sentences

Complete the number sentence.

18. 3 + 2 = 2 + ____

19. 6 + 0 = 0 + ____

20. 4 + 1 = ____ + 4

21. 6 + 3 = ____ + 6

22. 5 + ____ = 3 + 5

23. 6 + ____ = 4 + ____

24. **Talk About It** Explain how you found the answer for Exercise 23.

At Home Ask your child to explain why 3 + 5 equals 5 + 3.

Name ______________________

Count On to Add

Objective
Count on using a number line to find a sum.

Vocabulary
number line
equals sign

You can count on using a **number line** to find a sum.

Find 3 + 8.

Start with the greater number.
Start at 8. Count on 3.

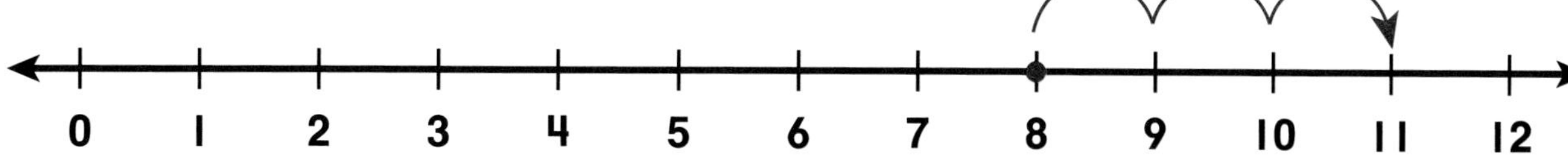

3 + 8 = 11

Remember, the **equals sign** means **is the same as.**

11 = 3 + 8

Guided Practice

Use the number line.
Count on to add.

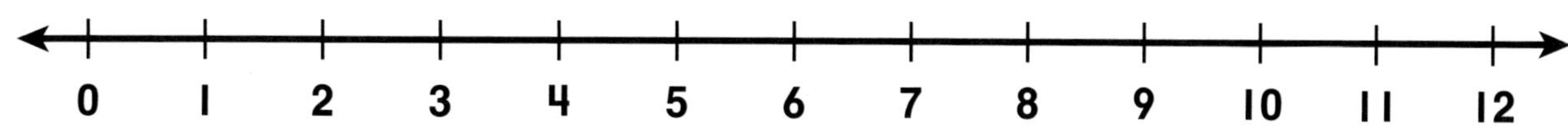

Think
I start with 5 and count on 1.

1. 5 + 1 = ____
2. 3 + 7 = ____
3. 2 + 9 = ____
4. 4 + 1 = ____
5. 8 + 1 = ____
6. ____ = 6 + 3
7. ____ = 5 + 2
8. ____ = 7 + 2

9. $\begin{array}{r} 2 \\ +8 \\ \hline \end{array}$
10. $\begin{array}{r} 3 \\ +5 \\ \hline \end{array}$
11. $\begin{array}{r} 2 \\ +3 \\ \hline \end{array}$
12. $\begin{array}{r} 1 \\ +6 \\ \hline \end{array}$
13. $\begin{array}{r} 4 \\ +3 \\ \hline \end{array}$
14. $\begin{array}{r} 3 \\ +9 \\ \hline \end{array}$

Explain Your Thinking Why is it easier to count on from the greater number?

Practice

Remember to start with the greater number.

Use the number line.
Count on to add.

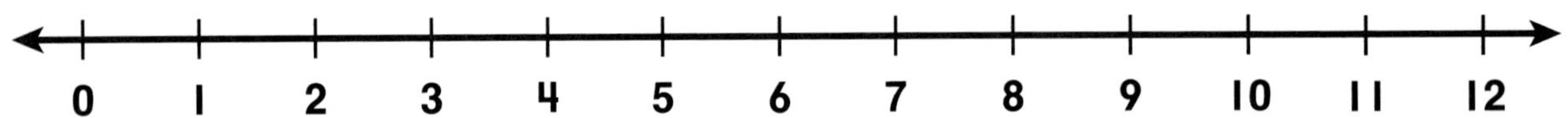

1. $5 + 2 =$ 7
2. $6 + 1 =$ ____
3. $7 + 1 =$ ____
4. $1 + 3 =$ ____
5. $2 + 2 =$ ____
6. $3 + 4 =$ ____
7. $8 + 3 =$ ____
8. ____ $= 8 + 2$
9. $4 + 2 =$ ____
10. ____ $= 3 + 3$
11. $2 + 1 =$ ____
12. ____ $= 9 + 2$

13. $3 + 5$
14. $1 + 7$
15. $2 + 4$
16. $5 + 1$
17. $3 + 1$
18. $6 + 3$
19. $3 + 4$
20. $9 + 3$
21. $8 + 3$
22. $2 + 8$
23. $2 + 7$
24. $6 + 2$

Problem Solving ▶ Reasoning

25. Fred's dad buys 4 children's tickets for the puppet show. He also buys 3 adult tickets. How many tickets does he buy altogether?

Draw or write to explain.

____ tickets

At Home Have your child demonstrate how to use the number line to add.

Name ____________________

Use Doubles Facts

Objective
Use doubles and doubles-plus-one facts to find the sum.

Vocabulary
addends
doubles facts
doubles-plus-one facts

In a **doubles fact** both **addends** are the same.
Doubles-plus-one facts can help you add.

Doubles fact

4 + 4 = 8

addends

Doubles-plus-one facts

  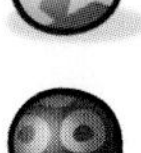  

4 + 5 = 9

5 + 4 = 9

Guided Practice

Find the sum.

1. 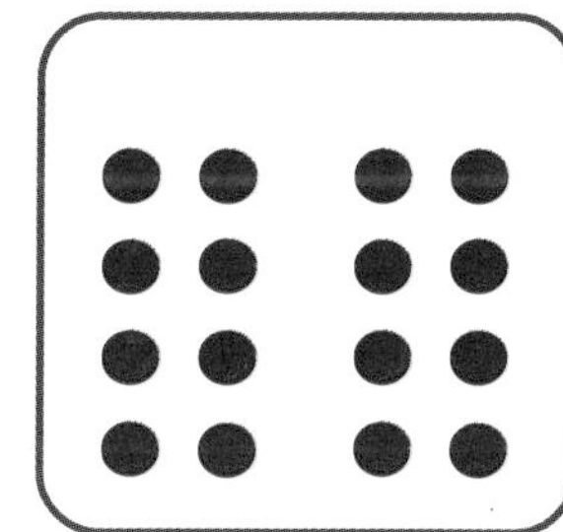

8 + 8 = 16

Think
I can use
8 + 8 = 16
to help me find
8 + 9 and
9 + 8.

8 + 9 = ____

9 + 8 = ____

2. 

7 + 7 = ____

7 + 8 = ____

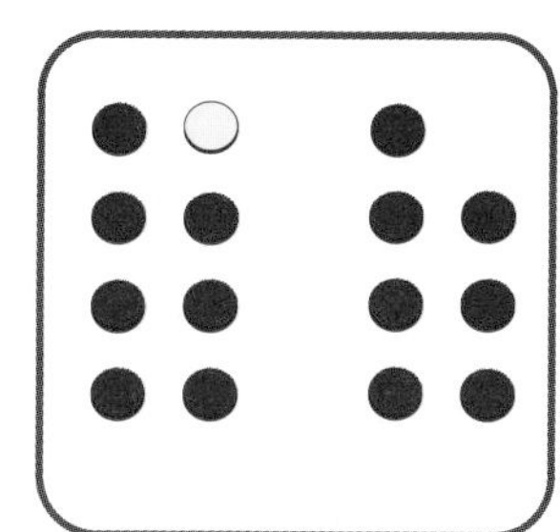

8 + 7 = ____

Explain Your Thinking How does using 4 + 4 = 8 help you solve 4 + 5?

Guided Practice

Find the sum.

3. $5 + 5 =$ _____ $6 + 5 =$ _____ $5 + 6 =$ _____

4. $9 + 9 =$ _____ $9 + 10 =$ _____ _____ $= 10 + 9$

5. $3 + 3$ $4 + 3$ $3 + 4$

6. $7 + 7$ $8 + 7$ $7 + 8$

7. $9 + 9$ $9 + 10$ $10 + 9$

8. $1 + 1$ $2 + 1$ $1 + 2$

Use doubles facts to find the sum of doubles-plus-one facts.

Practice

Find the sum.

1. $8 + 8 = 16$ $9 + 8 = 17$ $8 + 9 = 17$

2. $2 + 2$ $3 + 2$ $2 + 3$

3. $4 + 4$ $5 + 4$ $4 + 5$

4. $6 + 6$ $7 + 6$ $6 + 7$

Go on

Name ____________________

Practice

Find the sum.

5. $9 + 9 =$ ___
6. $5 + 6 =$ ___
7. $8 + 8 =$ ___
8. $4 + 3 =$ ___
9. $1 + 2 =$ ___
10. $5 + 5 =$ ___
11. $3 + 2 =$ ___
12. $5 + 4 =$ ___
13. $7 + 7 =$ ___
14. $6 + 6 =$ ___
15. $7 + 6 =$ ___
16. $9 + 10 =$ ___

17. ____ = 3 + 3
18. ____ = 1 + 2
19. ____ = 4 + 3

Write a doubles fact.
Use the doubles fact to complete the doubles-plus-one fact.

	Doubles	Doubles–plus–one
20.	____ + ____ = 6	____ + ____ = 7
21.	____ + ____ = 12	____ + ____ = 13
22.	____ + ____ = 16	____ + ____ = 17

Problem Solving ▶ Algebra

The sum is given.
Write two addends to make a number sentence.

23. ____ + ____ = 10
24. ____ + ____ = 15
25. ____ + ____ = 11
26. ____ + ____ = 8

At Home Have your child explain what a doubles fact is and what a doubles-plus-one fact is. Work together to make a list of these facts.

Problem Solving

Social Studies Connection

Giant Puppets

The Bread and Puppet Theater and Museum in Glover, Vermont has the largest collection of giant puppets in the world.

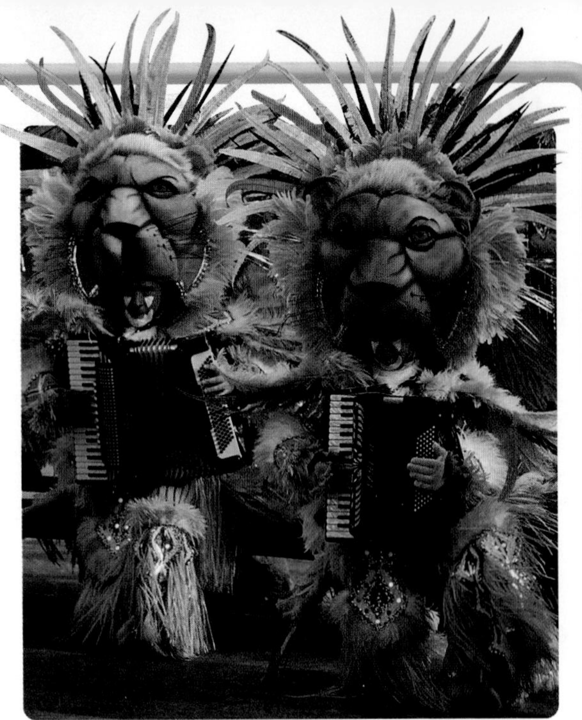

A giant puppet has a mask that is 2 feet tall. The body of the puppet is 4 feet tall.

How tall is the puppet? _____ feet

WEEKLY WR READER eduplace.com/map

Quick Check

Add.

1. $\begin{array}{r} 2 \\ +3 \\ \hline \end{array}$ $\begin{array}{r} 3 \\ +2 \\ \hline \end{array}$

2. $\begin{array}{r} 4 \\ +5 \\ \hline \end{array}$ $\begin{array}{r} 5 \\ +4 \\ \hline \end{array}$

3. $\begin{array}{r} 0 \\ +6 \\ \hline \end{array}$ $\begin{array}{r} 6 \\ +0 \\ \hline \end{array}$

Use the number line. Count on to add.

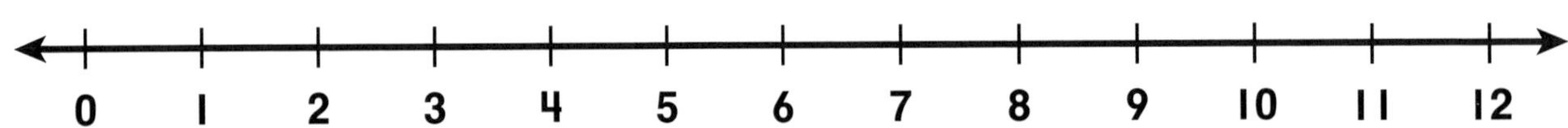

4. $6 + 1 =$ _____

5. $7 + 3 =$ _____

6. $9 + 2 =$ _____

Find the sum.

7. $\begin{array}{r} 6 \\ +6 \\ \hline \end{array}$ $\begin{array}{r} 6 \\ +7 \\ \hline \end{array}$ $\begin{array}{r} 7 \\ +6 \\ \hline \end{array}$

8. $\begin{array}{r} 5 \\ +5 \\ \hline \end{array}$ $\begin{array}{r} 6 \\ +5 \\ \hline \end{array}$ $\begin{array}{r} 5 \\ +6 \\ \hline \end{array}$

9. $\begin{array}{r} 3 \\ +3 \\ \hline \end{array}$ $\begin{array}{r} 3 \\ +4 \\ \hline \end{array}$ $\begin{array}{r} 4 \\ +3 \\ \hline \end{array}$

10. $\begin{array}{r} 8 \\ +8 \\ \hline \end{array}$ $\begin{array}{r} 8 \\ +9 \\ \hline \end{array}$ $\begin{array}{r} 9 \\ +8 \\ \hline \end{array}$

Hands-On

Name ______________________

Add 10

Objective
Find the sum of 10 and a 1-digit number.

Find 10 + 2.

Step 1

Show 10.

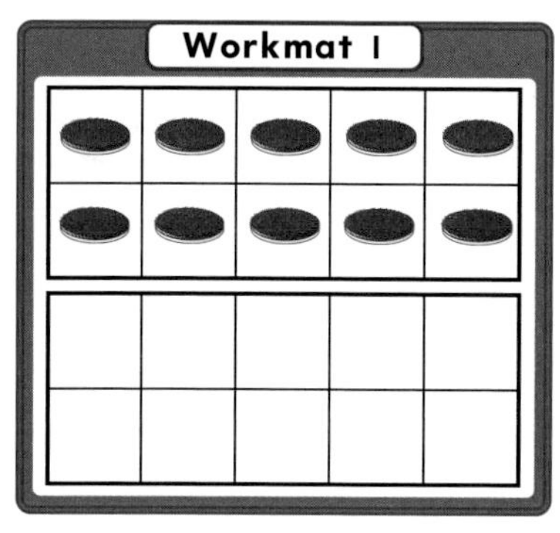

Step 2

Show 2 more.
Write the sum.

10 + 2 = 12

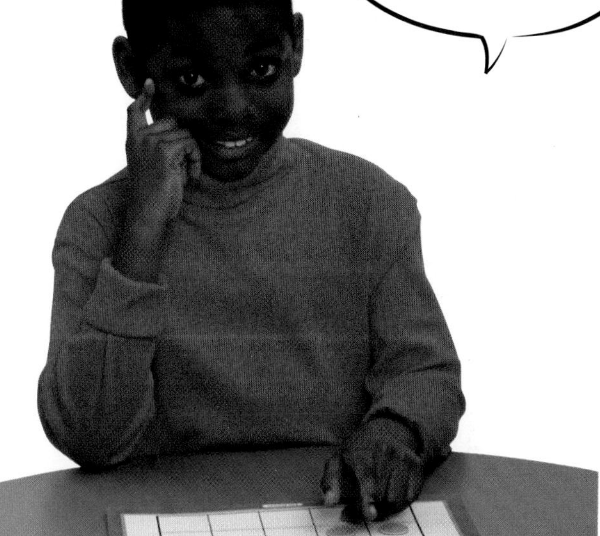

This is 1 ten and some ones.

Guided Practice

Use Workmat 1 with ⬭.
Add.

Think
I show 1 ten and 1 one on the mat.

1. 1 + 10 = ____
2. 6 + 10 = ____
3. 8 + 10 = ____
4. 7 + 10 = ____
5. 10 + 10 = ____
6. ____ = 10 + 4
7. ____ = 10 + 8
8. ____ = 10 + 6
9. ____ = 10 + 3
10. ____ = 10 + 7
11. ____ = 10 + 9
12. 10 + 9
13. 4 + 10
14. 10 + 3
15. 2 + 10
16. 10 + 0
17. 10 + 5

Explain Your Thinking Explain why the sums of 10 + 1, 10 + 2, 10 + 3, 10 + 4, and 10 + 5 form a pattern.

Practice

Think about how adding 10 changes a number.

Use Workmat 1 with [counter].
Add.

1. $10 + 6 =$ 16
2. $9 + 10 =$ ____
3. $10 + 1 =$ ____
4. $7 + 3 =$ ____
5. $9 + 9 =$ ____
6. $10 + 5 =$ ____

7. $\begin{array}{r} 4 \\ +10 \\ \hline \end{array}$
8. $\begin{array}{r} 10 \\ +\ 6 \\ \hline \end{array}$
9. $\begin{array}{r} 7 \\ +10 \\ \hline \end{array}$
10. $\begin{array}{r} 4 \\ +10 \\ \hline \end{array}$
11. $\begin{array}{r} 3 \\ +10 \\ \hline \end{array}$
12. $\begin{array}{r} 10 \\ +\ 5 \\ \hline \end{array}$

13. $\begin{array}{r} 8 \\ +10 \\ \hline \end{array}$
14. $\begin{array}{r} 10 \\ +\ 9 \\ \hline \end{array}$
15. $\begin{array}{r} 1 \\ +10 \\ \hline \end{array}$
16. $\begin{array}{r} 10 \\ +\ 6 \\ \hline \end{array}$
17. $\begin{array}{r} 10 \\ +\ 2 \\ \hline \end{array}$
18. $\begin{array}{r} 9 \\ +3 \\ \hline \end{array}$

19. $\begin{array}{r} 8 \\ +8 \\ \hline \end{array}$
20. $\begin{array}{r} 5 \\ +10 \\ \hline \end{array}$
21. $\begin{array}{r} 6 \\ +10 \\ \hline \end{array}$
22. $\begin{array}{r} 10 \\ +\ 2 \\ \hline \end{array}$
23. $\begin{array}{r} 4 \\ +8 \\ \hline \end{array}$
24. $\begin{array}{r} 9 \\ +10 \\ \hline \end{array}$

Algebra Readiness ▶ Missing Addends

Complete the number sentence to solve.

25. The children make 10 new puppets. Now the class has 17 puppets. How many puppets did the class have before?

Draw or write to explain.

____ $+ 10 = 17$

____ puppets

At Home Ask your child to find the sum of 10 and a 1-digit number such as 10 + 3.

Hands-On

Name ______________________

Make 10 to Add

 **Audio Tutor** 1/4 Listen and Understand

Objective
Make a ten to find sums to 18.

Making a 10 can help you add 7, 8, and 9.

Find 9 + 4.

Step 1

Show 9.
Then show 4.

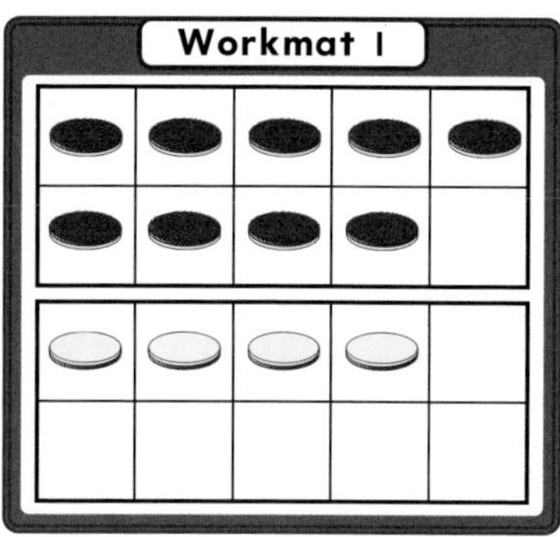

Step 2

Move a counter to make 10.

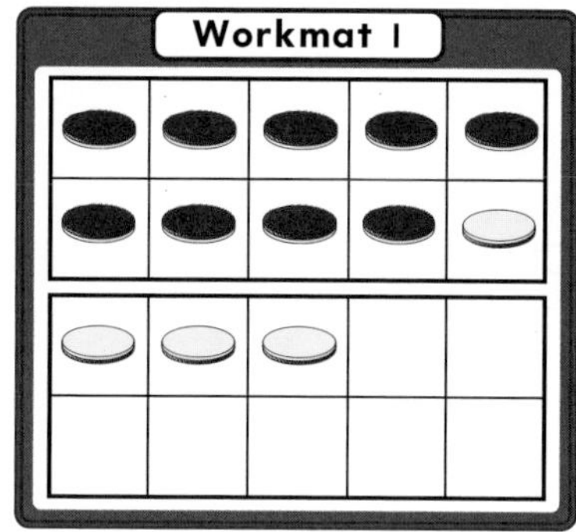

Show 9 + 4 as 10 + 3.

Step 3

Add.

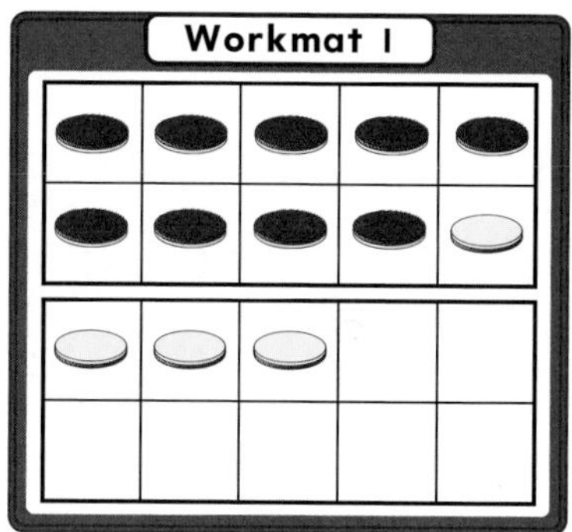

9 + 4 = 13

Guided Practice

Use Workmat 1 with .
Add.

Think
I add 2 to 8 to make 10.

1. 8 + 5 = ______
2. 9 + 7 = ______
3. 9 + 6 = ______
4. 7 + 5 = ______
5. 8 + 4 = ______
6. ______ = 7 + 9
7. 13 = ______ + 7
8. 14 = 8 + ______
9. 9 + 8
10. 5 + 9
11. 7 + 8
12. 7 + 4
13. 8 + 8
14. 6 + 8

Explain Your Thinking How does making 10 help you add 9 + 8?

Extra Help at eduplace.com/map

Practice

Remember to make 10 to help you add.

Use Workmat 1 with counters.
Add.

1. $9 + 6 = 15$
2. $8 + 8 = $ ____
3. $6 + 9 = $ ____
4. $7 + 6 = $ ____
5. $2 + 9 = $ ____
6. $8 + 5 = $ ____
7. $9 + 8 = $ ____
8. $4 + 8 = $ ____
9. $9 + 5 = $ ____
10. $4 + 9 = $ ____
11. $5 + 7 = $ ____
12. $8 + 6 = $ ____

Use Workmat 1 with counters.
Complete each addition sentence.

13.	14.	15.
10 + ____ = 14	10 + 5 = ____	10 + 6 = ____
9 + ____ = 14	____ + 6 = 15	8 + ____ = 16
8 + 6 = ____	8 + ____ = 15	7 + ____ = 16
____ + 7 = 14	7 + 8 = ____	9 + 7 = ____

Problem-Solving ▶ Number Sense

Use the picture to solve the problem.

Draw or write to explain.

16. Lim Sing makes 15 finger puppets. Some of the puppets are in the box. The rest are on the table. How many puppets are in the box?

____ puppets

At Home Ask your child to explain how making a 10 can help you find 8 + 4 and 9 + 2.

Name ____________________

Add Three Numbers

Audio Tutor 1/5 Listen and Understand

Use what you have learned to add three numbers.

Add Zero
Add in any Order
Doubles Fact Plus 1
Count on to Add
Make a Ten
Add Ten

Objective
Add three numbers in any order.

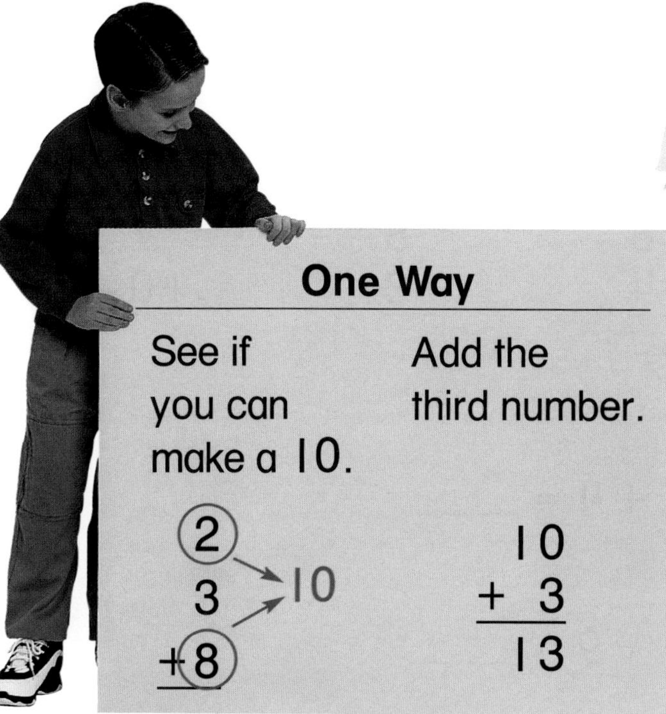

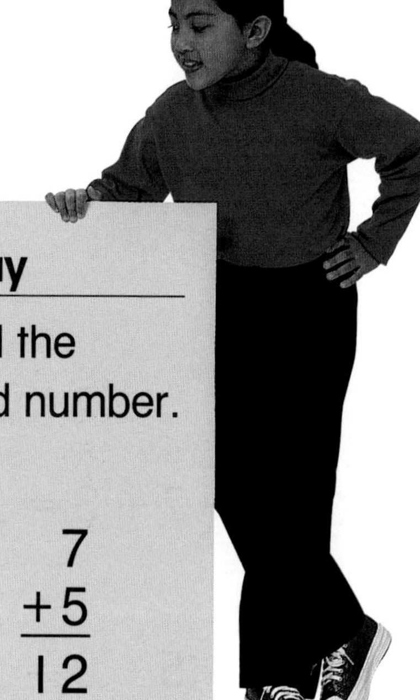

One Way

See if you can make a 10.	Add the third number.
(2) + 8 → 10; 3	10 + 3 = 13

Circled: 2, 8. 2 + 3 + 8

$$\begin{array}{r} 10 \\ +\ 3 \\ \hline 13 \end{array}$$

Another Way

Add two numbers. Add 4 and 3.	Add the third number.
(4) + (3) → 7; +5	7 + 5 = 12

$$\begin{array}{r} 7 \\ +5 \\ \hline 12 \end{array}$$

Guided Practice

Find the sum.
Look for two numbers to add first.

1. $\begin{array}{r} 4 \\ 6 \\ +2 \\ \hline \end{array}$

Think
4 + 6 make 10.
Then I add 2 more.

2. $\begin{array}{r} 2 \\ 7 \\ +8 \\ \hline \end{array}$

3. $\begin{array}{r} 6 \\ 7 \\ +4 \\ \hline \end{array}$

4. $\begin{array}{r} 2 \\ 6 \\ +5 \\ \hline \end{array}$

5. $\begin{array}{r} 2 \\ 6 \\ +8 \\ \hline \end{array}$

6. $\begin{array}{r} 1 \\ 9 \\ +8 \\ \hline \end{array}$

7. $\begin{array}{r} 5 \\ 5 \\ +0 \\ \hline \end{array}$

8. $\begin{array}{r} 4 \\ 2 \\ +5 \\ \hline \end{array}$

9. $\begin{array}{r} 3 \\ 6 \\ +5 \\ \hline \end{array}$

10. $\begin{array}{r} 7 \\ 3 \\ +5 \\ \hline \end{array}$

11. 9 + 1 + 3 = ____

12. 3 + 7 + 4 = ____

Explain Your Thinking Why can you group three numbers in different ways to add?

Practice

Look for two numbers to add first.

Find the sum.

1. 5 + 7 + 5 = 17
2. 4 + 2 + 4
3. 9 + 0 + 1
4. 4 + 2 + 8
5. 3 + 1 + 5
6. 5 + 1 + 9
7. 4 + 4 + 9
8. 5 + 5 + 5
9. 8 + 0 + 3
10. 1 + 6 + 4
11. 2 + 8 + 3
12. 2 + 7 + 0

13. 7 + 7 + 3 = ____
14. 3 + 2 + 4 = ____
15. 5 + 5 + 0 = ____
16. 8 + 1 + 9 = ____
17. 6 + 6 + 4 = ____
18. 2 + 5 + 8 = ____

Reading Math ▶ Vocabulary

Circle the answer.

19. Which number sentence shows a sum of 10?

    4 + 10 = 14   7 + 3 = 10   10 + 1 = 11

20. Which number sentence has three addends?

    2 + 6 + 4 = 12   8 + 5 = 13   9 + 0 = 9

21. Which sign tells you to add?   =   −   +

At Home Ask your child to demonstrate two different ways to add 3 + 7 + 3.

Name ____________________

Draw a Picture

Celia has 6 puppet show tickets. Bernie has 2 more tickets than Celia. How many tickets do they have in all?

Objective
Draw a picture to solve a problem.

UNDERSTAND

What do you know?

- Celia has 6 tickets.
- Bernie has 2 more tickets than Celia.

PLAN

You can draw a picture.

- Draw the part you know: Celia's 6 tickets.
- Draw to find the part you do not know: How many tickets Bernie has.

Think
2 more than 6 is 8.

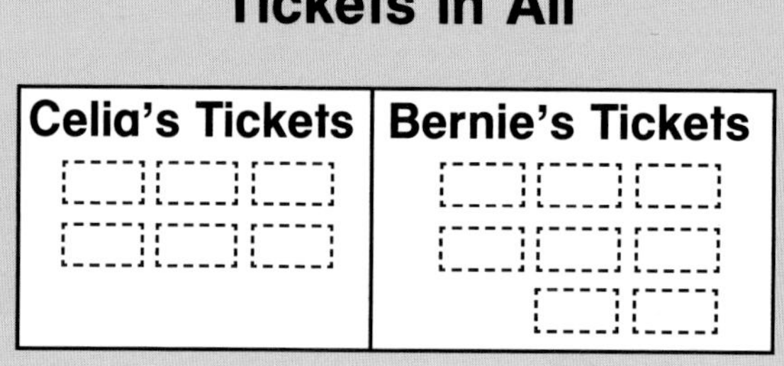

SOLVE

Add to find how many tickets in all.

6 + 8 = 14

Celia and Bernie have 14 tickets in all.

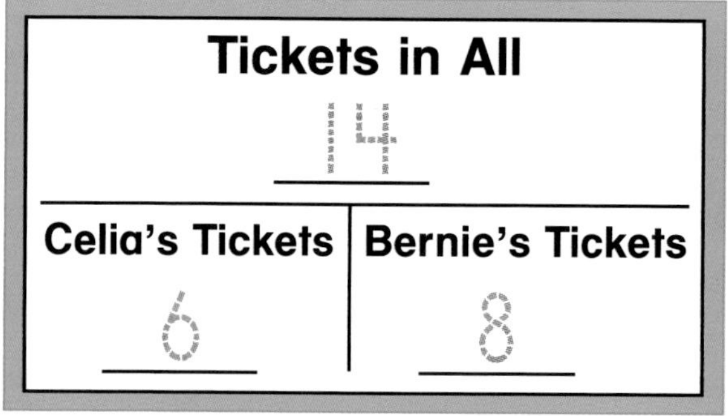

LOOK BACK

Did you answer the question?
How can you check your answer?

Guided Practice

Draw a picture to solve.

Remember:
▶ Understand
▶ Plan
▶ Solve
▶ Look Back

Draw or write to explain.

1. Izzy has 8 hats. Bobo has 3 fewer hats than Izzy. How many hats do they have in all?

Think First I need to find how many hats Bobo has.

_____ hats

2. Maria makes 6 new hats for Izzy. Carl makes the same number of hats for Bobo and 3 new hats for Koko. How many hats do they make in all?

Think I need to find a total for 3 parts.

_____ hats

Practice

3. Mr. Gomez buys 7 tickets. Mrs. Rose buys 2 more tickets than Mr. Gomez. How many tickets do they buy in all?

_____ tickets

4. Izzy has 5 balloons. Bobo has 2 fewer balloons than Izzy. How many balloons do they have in all?

_____ balloons

Go on

Name ______________________

Mixed Problem Solving

Strategies
Draw a picture
Write an addition sentence
Find a pattern

Solve.

Draw or write to explain.

1. Two rows of people watch the marionettes. 5 people are in the first row. 2 more than that are in the second row. How many people are in the second row?

marionette

_____ people

2. A juggler has 2 red blocks, 4 green blocks, and 6 yellow blocks. How many blocks does the juggler have?

juggler

_____ blocks

3. The ventriloquist made this belt for his puppet.

Circle the shape that comes next in the pattern.

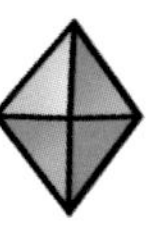

ventriloquist

4. Tina wins 4 prizes at the hand puppet show. Then she wins 2 more. How many prizes does Tina win?

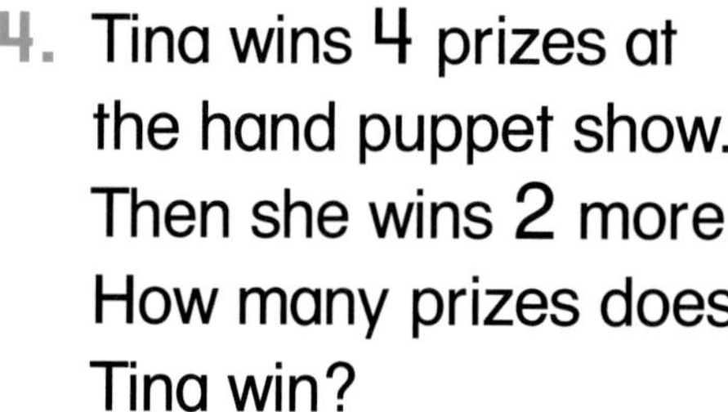

hand puppet

_____ prizes

At Home Make up a problem for your child to solve. Have your child draw a picture to find the answer.

Problem-Solving on Tests • Listening Skills

Open Response

Listen to your teacher read the problem.
Solve.

1. There are 9 people waiting in line to buy tickets. 4 more people join the line. Now how many people are waiting to buy tickets?

Show your work using pictures, numbers, or words.

_____ people

2. Clare makes 8 tacos for her party. Her friend makes 4 more tacos. 10 children come to the party. Are there enough tacos so each child gets one?

____

Multiple Choice

Listen to your teacher read the problem.
Choose the correct answer.

Liam's Score
15

3. 6 ○ 7 ○ 8 ○ 9 ○

4. 6 ○ 10 ○ 12 ○ 14 ○

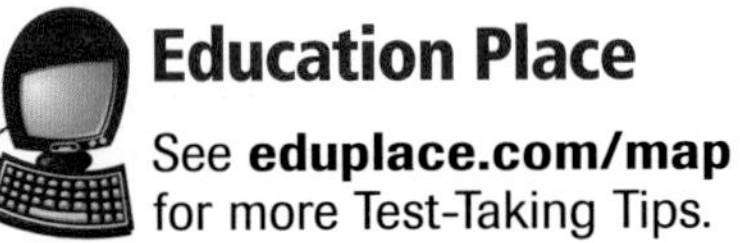

Name____________________________

Now Try This Missing Addends

These shapes are a number code.
Finish the code using the number sentences below.

■ = 5 ● = ____ ▮ = ____

▲ = 3 ⬢ = ____

1. 4 + ■ + ▲ = 12

4 + 5 + 3 = 12

Think
What is the value of the ■?
What is the value of the triangle?

2. ■ + 6 + ● = 11

____ + 6 + ____ = 11

3. ● + ⬢ + ⬢ = 14

____ + ____ + ____ = 14

4. ⬢ + ▲ + ▮ = 18

____ + ____ + ____ = 18

5. ■ + ■ + ■ = ____

____ + ____ + ____ = ____

6. ■ + ⬢ + ▮ = ____

7. ▲ + ▲ + ▮ = ____

Use the code. Write your own number sentence.

8. ____ + ____ + ____ = ____

9. ____ + ____ + ____ = ____

Write About It What is the greatest sum you can make using three of the shapes?

____

Problem Solving

Social Studies Connection

Mayan Counting

In the past, the Mayan people used shells, bars, and dots to show numbers.

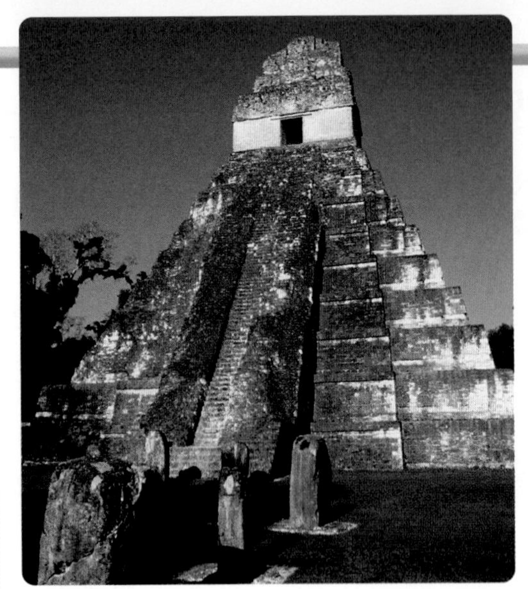

0	1 •	2 ••	3 •••	4 ••••
5 ___	6 •/___	7 ••/___	8 •••/___	9 ••••/___

Use the chart. Show the sum in Mayan writing.

5 + 2 ______ 7 + 3 ______

WEEKLY WR READER eduplace.com/map

Key Topic Review

Ordering Numbers

Write the number.

1. Just Before

	18
	15
	11

2. Just After

12	
18	
16	

3. One More

17	
15	
13	

4. Just Before

	23
	25
	30

5. Just After

28	
29	
23	

6. One Less

25	
27	
20	

Count backwards. Write the missing numbers.

7. 19 ____ 17 16 ____ 14 ____ ____ 11

Extra Practice at eduplace.com/map

Name ____________________  **Chapter Review/Test**

Vocabulary

Complete the sentence.

sum
addend
number line

1. When you add you get a __________.

2. You can use a ______________ to count on to add.

3. The numbers you add are called __________.

Concepts and Skills

Add.

4. $\begin{array}{r} 8 \\ +0 \\ \hline \end{array}$ $\begin{array}{r} 0 \\ +8 \\ \hline \end{array}$

5. $\begin{array}{r} 3 \\ +6 \\ \hline \end{array}$ $\begin{array}{r} 6 \\ +3 \\ \hline \end{array}$

6. $\begin{array}{r} 2 \\ +4 \\ \hline \end{array}$ $\begin{array}{r} 4 \\ +2 \\ \hline \end{array}$

7. 5 + 1 = ____

8. 4 + 3 = ____

9. 2 + 5 = ____

10. 1 + 9 = ____

11. 7 + 2 = ____

12. 3 + 8 = ____

Find the sums.

13. $\begin{array}{r} 4 \\ +4 \\ \hline \end{array}$ $\begin{array}{r} 4 \\ +5 \\ \hline \end{array}$ $\begin{array}{r} 5 \\ +4 \\ \hline \end{array}$

14. $\begin{array}{r} 9 \\ +9 \\ \hline \end{array}$ $\begin{array}{r} 9 \\ +10 \\ \hline \end{array}$ $\begin{array}{r} 10 \\ +9 \\ \hline \end{array}$

15. $\begin{array}{r} 2 \\ +2 \\ \hline \end{array}$ $\begin{array}{r} 2 \\ +3 \\ \hline \end{array}$ $\begin{array}{r} 3 \\ +2 \\ \hline \end{array}$

16. $\begin{array}{r} 7 \\ +7 \\ \hline \end{array}$ $\begin{array}{r} 7 \\ +8 \\ \hline \end{array}$ $\begin{array}{r} 8 \\ +7 \\ \hline \end{array}$

Chapter Review/Test

Add.

17. $\begin{array}{r} 10 \\ +\ 4 \\ \hline \end{array}$

18. $\begin{array}{r} 2 \\ +10 \\ \hline \end{array}$

19. $\begin{array}{r} 8 \\ +10 \\ \hline \end{array}$

20. $\begin{array}{r} 10 \\ +\ 6 \\ \hline \end{array}$

21. $\begin{array}{r} 10 \\ +\ 1 \\ \hline \end{array}$

22. $\begin{array}{r} 9 \\ +3 \\ \hline \end{array}$

23. $\begin{array}{r} 8 \\ +5 \\ \hline \end{array}$

24. $\begin{array}{r} 7 \\ +3 \\ \hline \end{array}$

25. $\begin{array}{r} 9 \\ +8 \\ \hline \end{array}$

26. $\begin{array}{r} 4 \\ +8 \\ \hline \end{array}$

27. $\begin{array}{r} 7 \\ 4 \\ +3 \\ \hline \end{array}$

28. $\begin{array}{r} 5 \\ 7 \\ +5 \\ \hline \end{array}$

29. $\begin{array}{r} 6 \\ 8 \\ +4 \\ \hline \end{array}$

30. $\begin{array}{r} 8 \\ 7 \\ +2 \\ \hline \end{array}$

31. $\begin{array}{r} 1 \\ 9 \\ +6 \\ \hline \end{array}$

Problem Solving

Draw a picture to solve.

Draw or write to explain.

32. There are 12 children in a club. Two children are absent, and 3 children leave early. How many children are left?

_____ children

33. Kevin brings 9 books to the club meeting. Sara brings 2 more books than Kevin. Ernie brings 1 more book than Kevin. How many books are there in all?

_____ books

Subtraction Facts

CHAPTER 3

INVESTIGATION

Compare the number of people in two groups in the picture. How do you find how many more people are in one group than the other?

People Using Math

John Philip Sousa

Do you want to play music in a marching band? John Philip Sousa did.

He began playing music when he was six years old. He learned to play the trombone, the flute, and many other instruments. When John was only 13, he even tried to join the circus band.

After serving in the United States Marine Corps, John wrote many famous songs. He was the leader of several bands, and even got to play for some Presidents. His most famous song was "Stars and Stripes Forever." Can you hum that tune?

John Philip Sousa invented an instrument called the sousaphone.

Use the pictures. Solve.

1. How many more  ? ____ 

2. How many more [drum] than [trombone] ? ____ 

Name ____________________

Subtract All or None

Objective
Subtract all or none.
Vocabulary
subtract
difference

When you **subtract** the answer is called the **difference.**

Find how many balloons are left.

Subtract all.

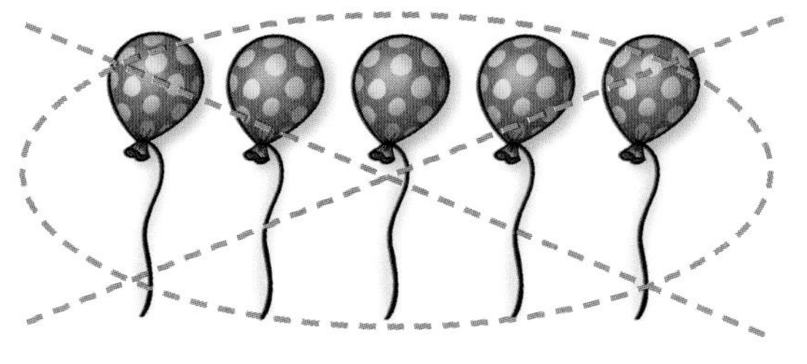

5 − 5 = 0
difference

0 balloons are left.

Subtract none.

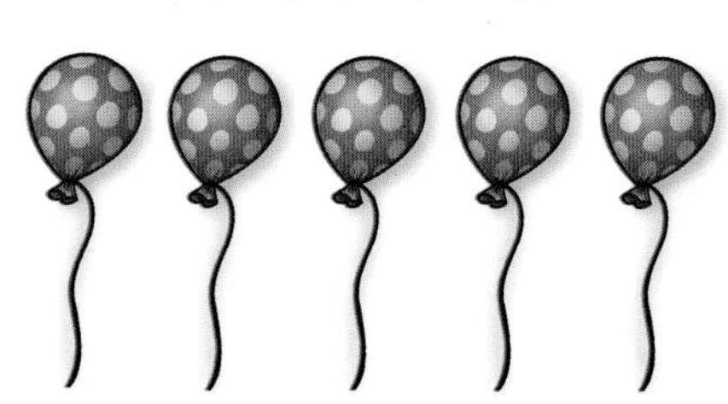

5 − 0 = 5

5 balloons are left.

Guided Practice

Subtract.

1. 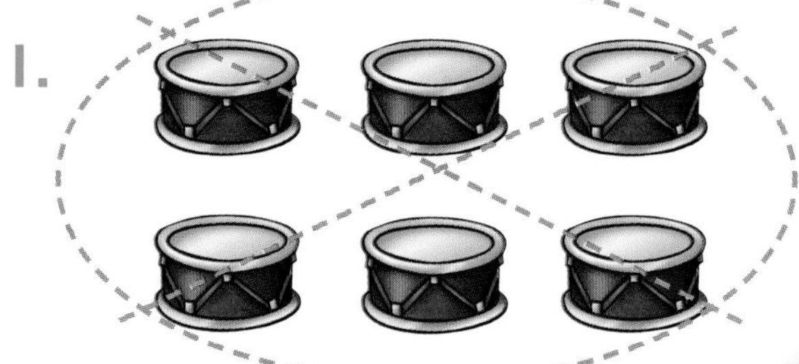

6 − 6 = ____

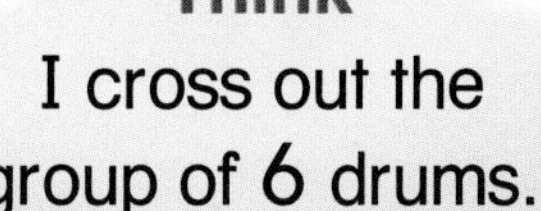

Think
I cross out the group of 6 drums.

2.       

6 − 0 = ____

3. 3 − 3 = ____
4. 8 − 0 = ____
5. 7 − 7 = ____

6. $\begin{array}{r} 2 \\ -0 \\ \hline \end{array}$
7. $\begin{array}{r} 4 \\ -4 \\ \hline \end{array}$
8. $\begin{array}{r} 1 \\ -0 \\ \hline \end{array}$
9. $\begin{array}{r} 9 \\ -9 \\ \hline \end{array}$
10. $\begin{array}{r} 2 \\ -2 \\ \hline \end{array}$
11. $\begin{array}{r} 4 \\ -0 \\ \hline \end{array}$

Explain Your Thinking What happens when you subtract 0 from any number?

Practice

When you subtract 0, the difference is the same as the number you started with.

Subtract.

1. 7 − 0 = ____

2. 

7 − 7 = ____

3. 3 − 0 = ____
4. 9 − 9 = ____
5. 4 − 0 = ____
6. 2 − 2 = ____
7. 9 − 0 = ____
8. 1 − 1 = ____
9. 2 − 0 = ____
10. 3 − 3 = ____
11. 5 − 5 = ____

12. $\begin{array}{r} 8 \\ -0 \\ \hline \end{array}$
13. $\begin{array}{r} 9 \\ -9 \\ \hline \end{array}$
14. $\begin{array}{r} 6 \\ -0 \\ \hline \end{array}$
15. $\begin{array}{r} 5 \\ -0 \\ \hline \end{array}$
16. $\begin{array}{r} 7 \\ -7 \\ \hline \end{array}$
17. $\begin{array}{r} 6 \\ -6 \\ \hline \end{array}$

Algebra Readiness  Number Sentences

Complete.

18. 8 − 8 = ____

8 − 0 = ____

19. 5 − ____ = 0

____ − 0 = 5

20. 3 − ____ = 3

____ − 3 = 0

21. 6 − ____ = 6

____ − 6 = 0

At Home Show your child a group of 9 or fewer objects. Take away all of the objects. Ask your child to say the subtraction sentence.

Name ______________________________

Count Back to Subtract

Objective
Use a number line to count back to find a difference.

Use the number line to help you subtract.

Find 11 − 3.
Start at 11.
Count back 3.

0 1 2 3 4 5 6 7 8 9 10 11 12

11 − 3 = 8

Guided Practice

Use the number line.
Count back to subtract.

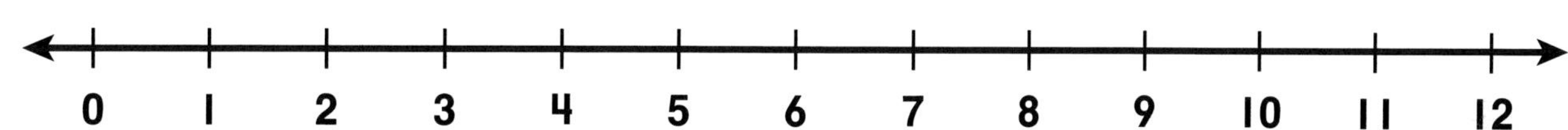

0 1 2 3 4 5 6 7 8 9 10 11 12

Think
I start at 8 and count back 2.

1. 8 − 2 = ____
2. 10 − 1 = ____
3. 9 − 2 = ____
4. 9 − 3 = ____
5. 8 − 1 = ____
6. 9 − 1 = ____
7. 11 − 3 = ____
8. 8 − 3 = ____

9. $\begin{array}{r} 10 \\ -2 \\ \hline \end{array}$
10. $\begin{array}{r} 6 \\ -1 \\ \hline \end{array}$
11. $\begin{array}{r} 7 \\ -2 \\ \hline \end{array}$
12. $\begin{array}{r} 7 \\ -3 \\ \hline \end{array}$
13. $\begin{array}{r} 12 \\ -3 \\ \hline \end{array}$

Explain Your Thinking How does the number line help you subtract?

Practice

Use the number line.
Count back to subtract.

Count back from the greater number.

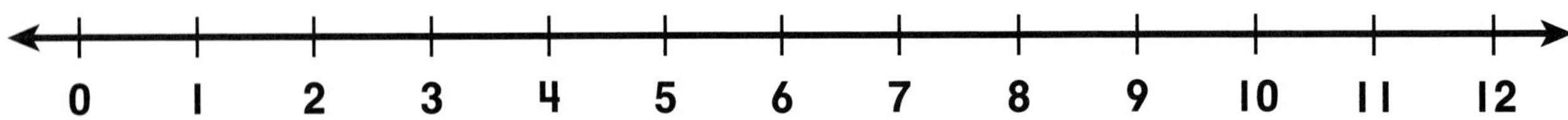

1. 12 − 2 = 10
2. 6 − 3 = ____
3. 5 − 1 = ____
4. 4 − 2 = ____
5. 10 − 3 = ____
6. 8 − 2 = ____

7. $4 - 1$
8. $6 - 2$
9. $10 - 1$
10. $5 - 3$
11. $11 - 2$
12. $3 - 1$

13. $3 - 3$
14. $9 - 1$
15. $8 - 1$
16. $5 - 2$
17. $8 - 0$
18. $7 - 1$

Algebra Readiness ▶ Functions

Follow the rule.
Complete the chart.

19. Subtract 2

9	7
8	
7	
6	

20. Add 3

5	8
6	
7	
8	

21. Subtract 4

12	8
11	
10	
9	

At Home Have your child show you how to find 12 − 3 using a number line.

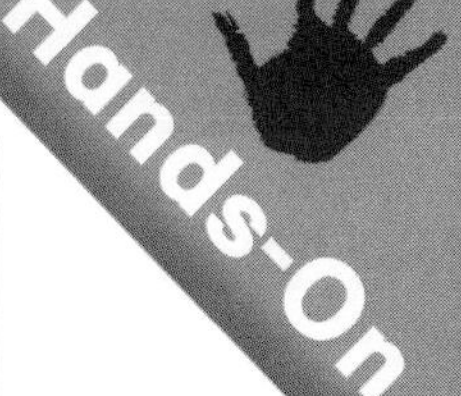

Name ______________________________

Subtract to Compare

Objective
Use subtraction to compare two sets.

 **Audio Tutor 1/6** Listen and Understand

You can subtract to compare two sets.

There are 8 . There are 3 .

How many fewer are there?

8 – 3 = 5

There are 5 fewer than .

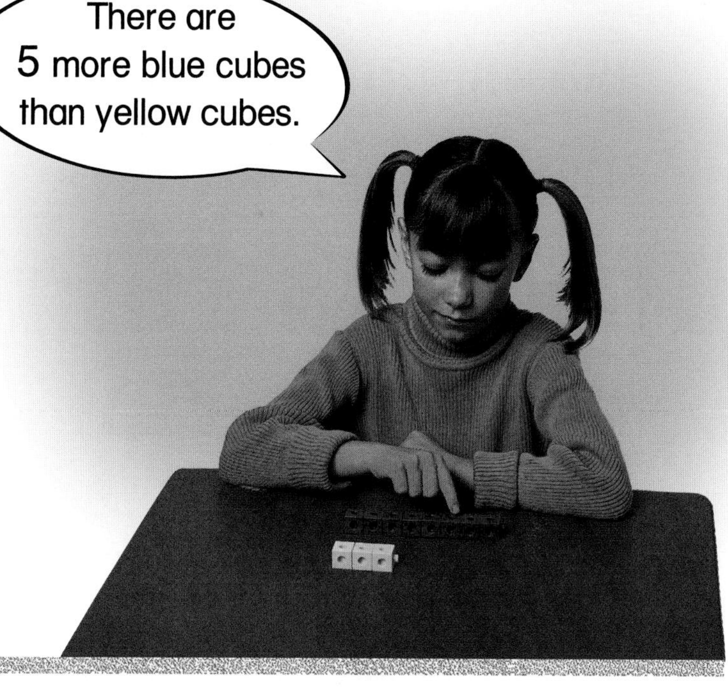

Guided Practice

Use cubes.
Complete the number sentence.

Think
I show 9 yellow and 6 blue.
I need to find how many more yellow cubes than blue cubes there are.

1. 9 6

How many more are there?

9 ____ – ____ = ____

2. 7 4

How many fewer are there?

____ – ____ = ____

3. 9 8

How many more are there?

____ – ____ = ____

Explain Your Thinking How can you find how many more cubes without subtracting?

Practice

You can subtract to find how many more and how many fewer.

Work with a partner.
Share cubes.
Complete the number sentence.

1. 12 5

How many more are there?

12 – 5 = 7

2. 9 4

How many fewer  are there?

_____ – _____ = _____

3. 11 7

How many fewer are there?

_____ – _____ = _____

4. 15 9

How many more 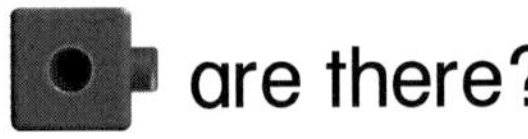

_____ – _____ = _____

5. 10 3

How many more are there?

_____ – _____ = _____

6. 16 7

How many fewer are there?

_____ – _____ = _____

Problem Solving  Data Sense

Use the pictograph to solve the problem.

7. How many more flags than pinwheels are there?

_____ more flags

8. Each child in the parade carries two items. How many children are in the parade?

_____ children

Items in the Parade

flags	► ► ► ► ► ►
banners	► ► ► ► ►
pinwheels	► ► ►

Key: Each ► stands for 2 items.

At Home Have your child tell you how to use subtraction to compare.

Name ______________________________

Use Addition to Subtract

Audio Tutor 1/7 Listen and Understand

Objective
Subtract from numbers through eighteen using addition.

Find 11 − 8.

Use a related addition fact to help you find the difference. What addition fact can you use to find the difference?

8 + __3__ = 11

11 − 8 = __3__

Guided Practice

Use the related addition fact to help you find the difference.

1. Think 5 + 5 = 10.

5 + 5 = ______

10 − 5 = ______

2. 6 + 5 = ______

11 − 5 = ______

3. 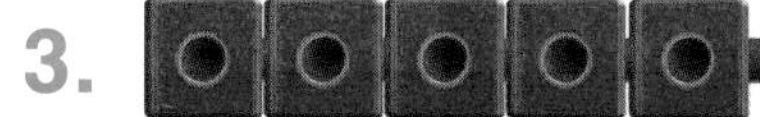

5 + 8 = ______

13 − 8 = ______

4. 

3 + 7 = ______

10 − ______ = 3

5. $\begin{array}{r} 7 \\ +4 \\ \hline \end{array}$ $\begin{array}{r} 11 \\ -\ 7 \\ \hline \end{array}$

6. $\begin{array}{r} 9 \\ +3 \\ \hline \end{array}$ $\begin{array}{r} 12 \\ -\ 3 \\ \hline \end{array}$

7. $\begin{array}{r} 7 \\ +7 \\ \hline \end{array}$ $\begin{array}{r} 14 \\ -\ 7 \\ \hline \end{array}$

Explain Your Thinking How can you use related facts to check subtraction?

Practice

Related facts use the same three numbers.

Add or subtract.

1. $4 + 7 = \underline{11}$

$\underline{11} - 7 = 4$

2. $4 + 6 =$ ______

$10 - 6 =$ ______

3. $8 + 8 =$ ______

$16 - 8 =$ ______

4. $1 + 9 =$ ______

$10 - 9 =$ ______

5. $6 + 8 =$ ______

$14 - 8 =$ ______

6. $8 + 9 =$ ______

______ $- 9 = 8$

7. $2 + 9 =$ ______

$11 -$ ______ $= 2$

8. $9 + 9 =$ ______

$18 -$ ______ $= 9$

Problem Solving ▶ Reasoning

9. Use the numbers to write addition sentences.

3 4 6 9 5

______ + ______ = ______   ______ + ______ = ______

10. Use the addition sentences to write related subtraction sentences.

______ − ______ = ______   ______ − ______ = ______

11. **Talk About It** Explain why the facts in Exercise 9 and 10 are related.

At Home Ask your child to name a related addition fact that could be used to find 13 − 4. Have your child explain why the addition fact can help.

Name ______________________

Now Try This Subtract from Numbers to 20

The same numbers are used in related addition and subtraction sentences.

$\begin{array}{r} 4 \\ +10 \\ \hline 14 \end{array}$ $\begin{array}{r} 14 \\ -10 \\ \hline 4 \end{array}$ $\begin{array}{r} 14 \\ -4 \\ \hline 10 \end{array}$ | $\begin{array}{r} 8 \\ +7 \\ \hline 15 \end{array}$ $\begin{array}{r} 15 \\ -8 \\ \hline 7 \end{array}$ $\begin{array}{r} 15 \\ -7 \\ \hline 8 \end{array}$

1. $\begin{array}{r} 9 \\ +10 \\ \hline 19 \end{array}$ $\begin{array}{r} 19 \\ -10 \\ \hline 9 \end{array}$ $\begin{array}{r} 19 \\ -9 \\ \hline 10 \end{array}$

2. $\begin{array}{r} 10 \\ +6 \\ \hline \end{array}$ $\begin{array}{r} 16 \\ -6 \\ \hline \end{array}$ $\begin{array}{r} 16 \\ -10 \\ \hline \end{array}$

3. $\begin{array}{r} 10 \\ +7 \\ \hline \end{array}$ $\begin{array}{r} 17 \\ -7 \\ \hline \end{array}$ $\begin{array}{r} 17 \\ -10 \\ \hline \end{array}$

4. $\begin{array}{r} 8 \\ +10 \\ \hline \end{array}$ $\begin{array}{r} 18 \\ -10 \\ \hline \end{array}$ $\begin{array}{r} 18 \\ -8 \\ \hline \end{array}$

5. $\begin{array}{r} 9 \\ +9 \\ \hline \end{array}$ $\begin{array}{r} 18 \\ -9 \\ \hline \end{array}$

6. $\begin{array}{r} 8 \\ +8 \\ \hline \end{array}$ $\begin{array}{r} 16 \\ -8 \\ \hline \end{array}$

7. $10 + 7 =$ ______ $17 - 7 =$ ______ $17 - 10 =$ ______

8. $9 + 10 =$ ______ $19 - 10 =$ ______ $19 - 9 =$ ______

9. **Talk About It** If you know the sum $10 + 5$ why do you also know the difference $15 - 5$?

Problem Solving

Music Connection
Singing a Round

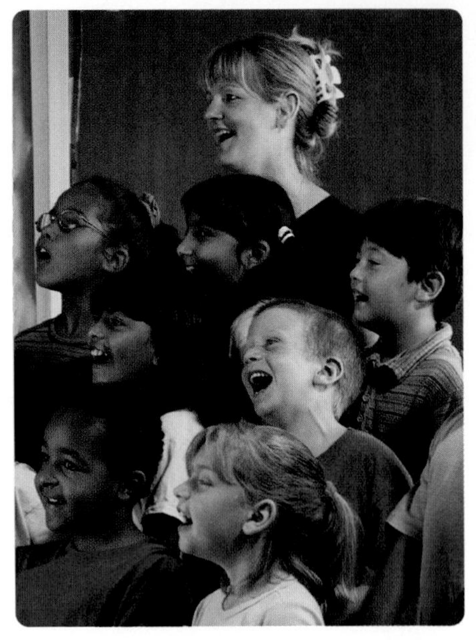

Some songs are sung in rounds. To sing in a round one group starts singing first. After the first line of the song, another group starts singing.

Sing two rounds of "Row, Row, Row Your Boat."

How many more times is the word "merrily" sung than the word "row"? _____

WEEKLY WR READER eduplace.com/map

Quick Check

Subtract.

1. $\begin{array}{r} 9 \\ -0 \\ \hline \end{array}$

2. $\begin{array}{r} 5 \\ -5 \\ \hline \end{array}$

3. $\begin{array}{r} 8 \\ -0 \\ \hline \end{array}$

4. $\begin{array}{r} 10 \\ -10 \\ \hline \end{array}$

5. $\begin{array}{r} 7 \\ -7 \\ \hline \end{array}$

Use the number line. Count back to subtract.

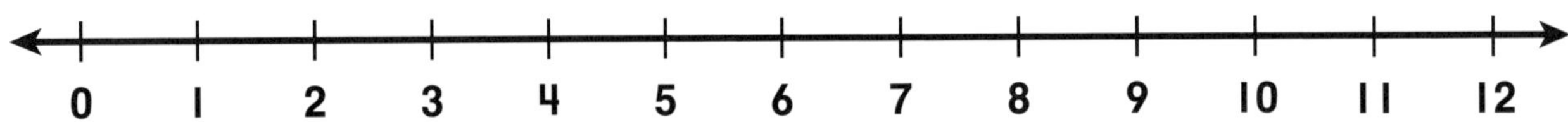

6. $\begin{array}{r} 9 \\ -1 \\ \hline \end{array}$

7. $\begin{array}{r} 10 \\ -3 \\ \hline \end{array}$

8. $\begin{array}{r} 11 \\ -2 \\ \hline \end{array}$

9. $\begin{array}{r} 8 \\ -2 \\ \hline \end{array}$

10. $\begin{array}{r} 12 \\ -3 \\ \hline \end{array}$

Use cubes. Complete the number sentence.

11. 11  3

How many more  are there?

_____ − _____ = _____

Add or subtract.

12. 3 + 9 = _____

12 − _____ = 3

Name ____________________

Number Expressions

Objective
Identify and write different ways to name the same number.

You can use addition and subtraction to name the same number.

These are some names for 7.

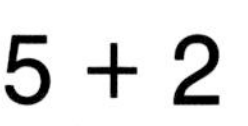

5 + 2   11 − 4   12 − 5   7 − 0

Guided Practice

Circle the names for the number.

Think
I may find more than one way to name 12.

1.  12   8 + 4   12 − 10   7 + 5   12 − 0

2.  4   9 + 6   10 − 6   8 − 4   15 − 9

3.  9   6 + 3   12 − 3   11 − 6   10 − 1

4.  3   10 − 7   3 − 0   12 − 9   3 − 3

Write a name for the number.

5.  14   _____ + _____   6.  8   _____ − _____

Explain Your Thinking Why are 7 + 1 and 14 − 6 both names for 8?

Practice

The sums or differences should equal the number shown.

Write names for the number.

1. (8) 13 − 5   2 + 6   14 − 6
2. (10) 14 − 4   ___ + ___   ___ − ___
3. (5) 5 − 0   ___ − ___   ___ + ___
4. (2) 2 + 0   ___ + ___   ___ − ___
5. (1) 9 − 8   ___ + ___   ___ − ___
6. (11) 5 + 6   ___ − ___   ___ + ___
7. (6) 4 + 2   ___ − ___   ___ + ___

Reading Math ▶ Vocabulary

Which number sentence asks you to find the difference?
Circle it. Find the missing numbers.

8. 8 + 7 = ___   12 − ___ = 5   14 − 6 = ___

9. 14 − ___ = 9   11 − 5 = ___   7 + 6 = ___

10. 9 − 9 = ___   6 + ___ = 13   5 + 5 = ___

At Home Ask your child for two addition facts that name 9 and two subtraction facts that name 9.

Name ______________________

Fact Families

Audio Tutor 1/8 Listen and Understand

Objective
Identify and write fact families.

Vocabulary
fact family

A **fact family** is a set of related facts.

This fact family uses the numbers 17, 8, and 9.
17 is the whole. 8 and 9 are the parts.

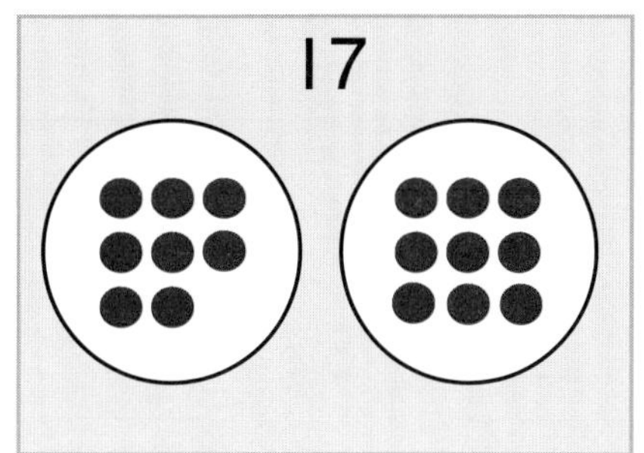

Workmat 2

Whole	
17	
Part	Part
8	9

Fact Family

8 + 9 = 17	17 − 9 = 8
9 + 8 = 17	17 − 8 = 9

Guided Practice

Complete the number sentences for the fact family.

1.

Whole	
14	
Part	Part
7	7

7 + 7 = ____

14 − 7 = ____

Think
Doubles have only two related facts.

2.

Whole	
16	
Part	Part
9	7

9 + 7 = ____

7 + ____ = 16

16 − 7 = ____

16 − ____ = 7

3.

Whole	
15	
Part	Part
9	6

9 + 6 = ____

6 + ____ = 15

15 − 9 = ____

15 − 6 = ____

4. 10 + 10 = ____ 20 − 10 = ____

Explain Your Thinking Why does a double have only 2 related facts?

Practice

A fact family has the same two parts and the same whole.

Complete the number sentences for the fact family.

1.

Whole	
12	
Part	Part
7	5

12 − 5 = 7

5 + 7 = 12

12 − 7 = 5

7 + 5 = 12

2. 7 + 8 = ____

8 + 7 = ____

15 − ____ = 8

15 − 8 = ____

3. 6 + 7 = ____

7 + ____ = 13

13 − 7 = ____

13 − ____ = 7

4. ____ + 5 = 13

____ + 8 = 13

13 − 5 = ____

13 − ____ = 5

5. 6 + ____ = 12

12 − 6 = ____

6. ____ + 9 = 18

18 − ____ = 9

7. 8 + ____ = 16

16 − 8 = ____

Problem Solving ▶ Reasoning

8. Myra's score is 10. She tosses a beanbag and subtracts the number from her score. Now her score is 3.

On which number did the beanbag land?

10 − ____ = 3

9. **Write About It** Explain how you know you are right.

____

____

At Home Ask your child to write the related number sentences with the fact family 9 + 7 = 16.

Name ______________________________

Variables

Objective
Find the missing number in addition and subtraction sentences.

You can use subtraction to find the missing numbers in addition and subtraction sentences.

6 − ▢ = 4

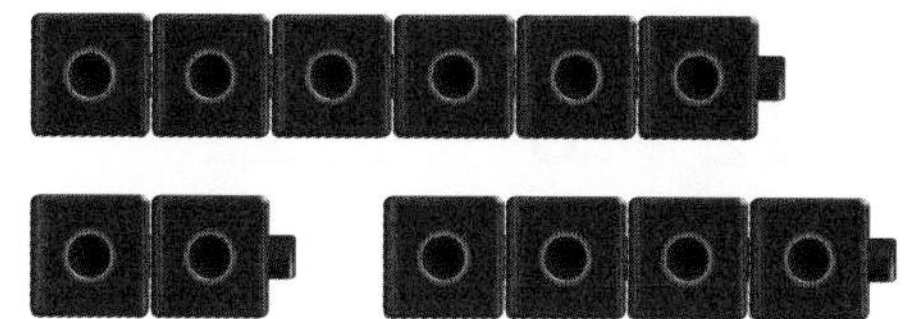

The missing number is 2.

3 + ▢ = 7

Whole	
7	
Part	Part
3	

7 is the whole.
3 is one of the parts.

The missing number is 4.

Guided Practice

Find the missing number.

Think
I subtract 5 from 7 to find the missing number.

1. 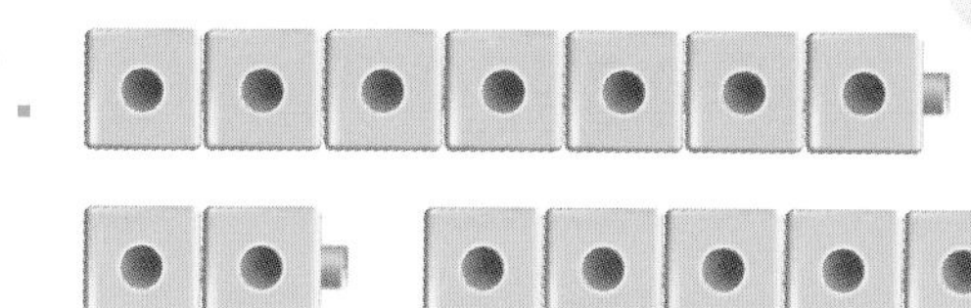

7 − ▢ = 5

Think 7 − 5 = ____

The missing number is ____.

2. 9 + ▢ = 15

Think 15 − 9 = ____

The missing number is ____.

3. 7 + ▢ = 16

Think 16 − 7 = ____

The missing number is ____.

4. 13 − ▢ = 5

13 − 5 = ____

The missing number is ____.

5. 7 + ▢ = 14

14 − 7 = ____

The missing number is ____.

Explain Your Thinking What related fact can you use to find the missing number in 11 − ____ = 5?

Practice

Find the missing number.

Whole	
13	
Part	**Part**
	4

1. $4 + \square = 13$

   Think $13 - 4 =$ ____

   The missing number is 9.

You can think about part-part-whole to find a missing number.

2. $\square + 5 = 14$ $14 - 5 =$ ____	3. $2 + \square = 11$ $11 - 2 =$ ____	4. $\square + 8 = 12$ $12 - 8 =$ ____
5. $13 - \square = 7$ $13 - 7 =$ ____	6. $15 - \square = 8$ $15 - 8 =$ ____	7. $\square + 8 = 13$ $13 - 8 =$ ____
8. $\square + 6 = 15$ $15 - 6 =$ ____	9. $8 + \square = 15$ $15 - 8 =$ ____	10. $9 + \square = 18$ $18 - 9 =$ ____
11. $9 - \square = 7$ $9 - 7 =$ ____	12. $14 - \square = 10$ $14 - 10 =$ ____	13. $\square + 8 = 17$ $17 - 8 =$ ____

Problem Solving ▶ Logical Thinking

Write the number.

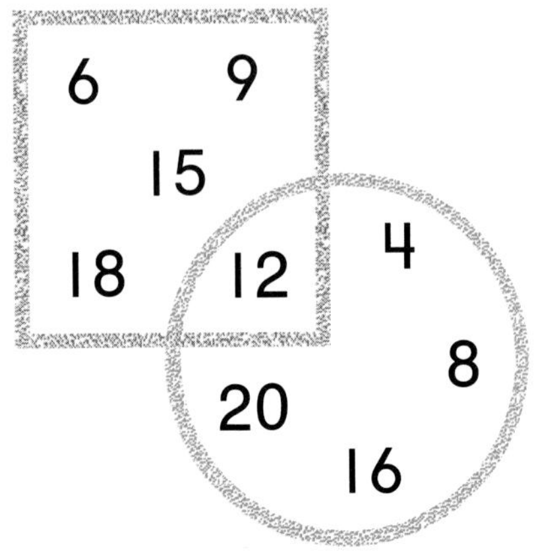

14. I am outside the circle. I am greater than 10. You say my name when you count by 5s.

    ____

15. I am in the circle. I am the sum of two of the other numbers. I am less than 15.

    ____

At Home Put up to 11 items in a bag. Ask your child to remove some and count them. Then have your child tell you how many are still in the bag.

Name ______________________________

Write a Number Sentence

 **Audio Tutor 1/9** Listen and Understand

Objective
Write number sentences to solve problems.

You can write a number sentence to solve a problem.

8 girls and 7 boys carry banners in the Fourth of July parade.

How many children are carrying banners?

UNDERSTAND

What do you know?

- 8 girls carry banners in the parade.
- 7 boys carry banners in the parade.

PLAN

You can write a number sentence.

Do you add or subtract?

add

SOLVE

Write an addition sentence.

8 + 7 = 15

15 children carry flags in the parade.

Think
I add 8 and 7.
The sum is 15.

LOOK BACK

Does your answer solve the problem?
Does your answer make sense?

Guided Practice

Write a number sentence to solve.

Draw or write to explain.

1. There are 12 fire trucks in the parade. 9 fire trucks have gone by. How many more fire trucks are the children waiting to see?

   Think
   12 is the whole.
   9 is one part. What is the other part?

   ____ − ____ = ____

   ____ fire trucks

2. In the band 7 pipers march in a row. 5 pipers march in another row. How many pipers march in the two rows?

   Think
   Do I need to find how many in all?

   ____ + ____ = ____

   ____ pipers

Practice

3. There are 16 cars in the parade. 7 cars have beeping horns. The other cars have music playing. How many cars have music playing?

   ____ − ____ = ____

   ____ cars

4. Mario makes 7 flags for his friends to wave at the parade. Juan makes 8 flags. How many flags did the boys make?

   ____ + ____ = ____

   ____ flags

Go on

Name ______________________

Mixed Problem Solving

Strategies
Draw a picture
Write a number sentence
Find a pattern

Solve.

Draw or write to explain.

1. There are 9 horns and 5 drums in the second grade band. How many instruments are in the band?

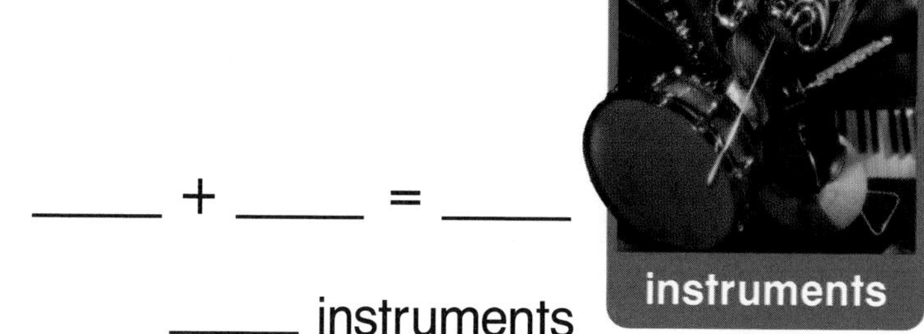

instruments

____ + ____ = ____

____ instruments

2. The children make a star pattern on their float. What color star comes next?

float

__________ star

3. There are 6 bicycles in the parade. 4 of the bicycles are decorated. How many bicycles are not decorated?

bicycle

____ bicycles

4. 10 people are riding unicycles. 4 of them are dressed as clowns. How many people on unicycles are not dressed as clowns?

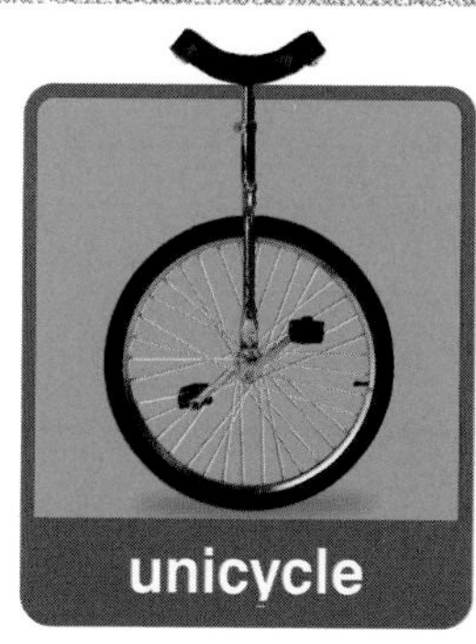

unicycle

____ people

At Home Ask your child to read his or her number sentence for Exercise 1 and explain how it solves the problem.

Problem Solving on Tests • **Listening Skills**

Open Response

Listen to your teacher read the problem.
Solve.

1. There are 16 people in costumes. 7 of them are dressed as clowns. The rest are dressed as animals. How many of the people are dressed as animals?

Show your work using pictures, numbers, or words.

_____ people

2. Write a story problem for this number sentence.

$12 - 5 = 7$

____

____

____

Multiple Choice

Listen to your teacher read the problem.
Choose the correct answer.

3. 8 ○ 16 ○ 18 ○ 26 ○

4. 76 ○ 16 ○ 8 ○ 2 ○

Education Place
See **eduplace.com/map** for more Test-Taking Tips.

Name ______________________________

Now Try This Variables

You can use a shape to stand for a number to solve a problem.

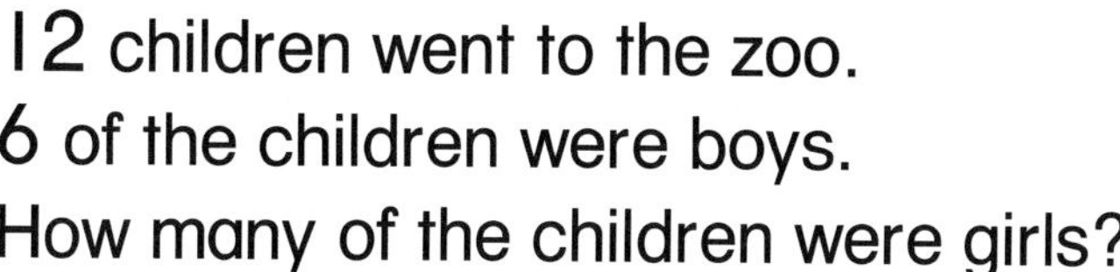

12 children went to the zoo.
6 of the children were boys.
How many of the children were girls?

Part	Part
6	
Whole 12	

We know that 12 is the total and 6 is one of the parts.
We can use a △ to stand for the missing part.
We can write $6 + \triangle = 12$ to solve the problem.

The △ stands for __6__ girls.

Think
6 and how many equal 12?

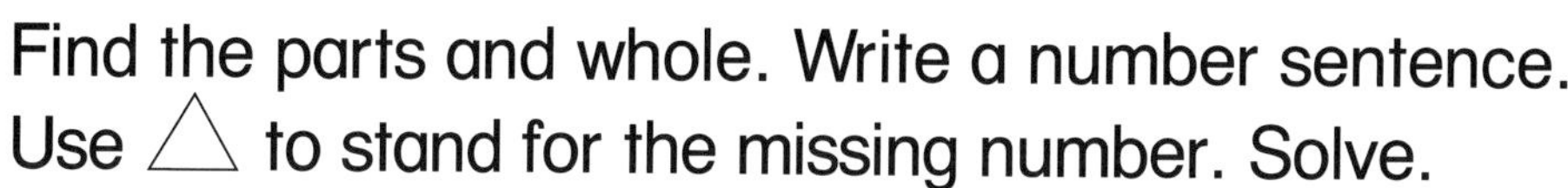

Find the parts and whole. Write a number sentence.
Use △ to stand for the missing number. Solve.

1. Sona counted 15 seals on a rock. 4 seals went underwater. How many seals were still on the rock?

   _____ + _____ = _____

   The △ stands for _____ seals.

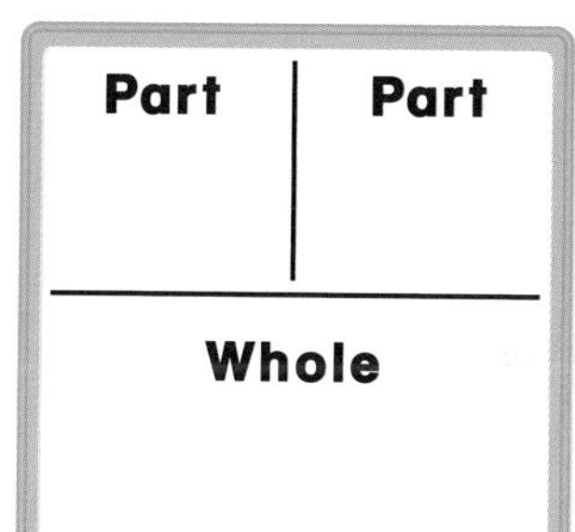

2. Sean saw 18 monkeys. Some of the monkeys were in a tree. 8 of the monkeys were on the ground. How many monkeys were on the ground?

   _____ + _____ = _____

   The △ stands for _____ monkeys.

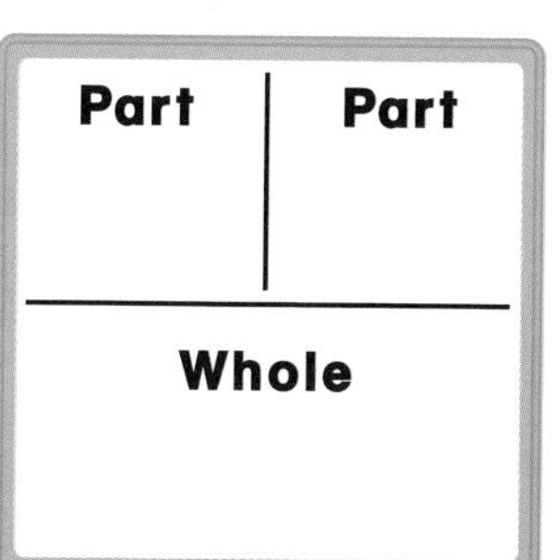

3. **Talk About It** Can you use another shape or letter to stand for a number? Why?

Problem Solving

Math Challenge

Clowning Around

Which hat belongs to each clown?

- Smiley's hat is not red.
- Happy's hat is next to the red hat.
- Grumpy's hat is all one color.

Write each clown's name under his hat.

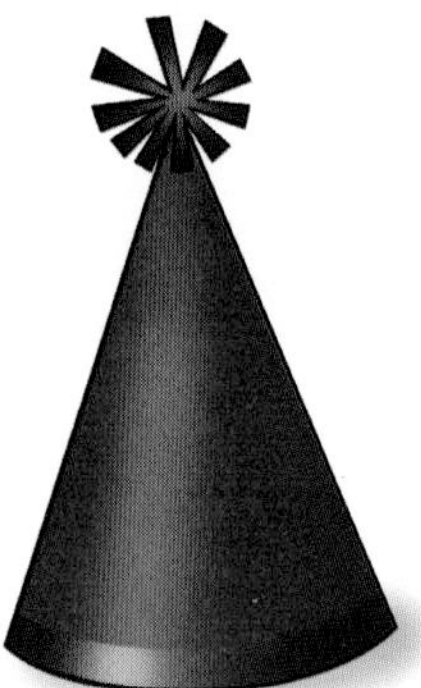

______ ______ ______

Key Topic Review

Addition

Add.

1. $8 + 8 =$ ______
2. $8 + 9 =$ ______
3. $9 + 8 =$ ______

4. $6 + 8$
5. $4 + 8$
6. $9 + 5$
7. $4 + 9$
8. $5 + 7$
9. $8 + 3$

Add.
Think about ways to make 10.

10. $6 + 4 + 9$
11. $5 + 5 + 5$
12. $8 + 0 + 3$
13. $1 + 9 + 4$
14. $2 + 8 + 3$
15. $2 + 7 + 0$

16. $5 + 5 + 0 =$ ______
17. $8 + 1 + 9 =$ ______
18. $2 + 7 + 8 =$ ______
19. $5 + 4 + 6 =$ ______

Name ______________________

Vocabulary

Complete the sentence.

1. You find the ______________ when you subtract.
2. A ______________ is a set of related facts.
3. You get a difference when you ______________.

difference
fact family
subtract

Concepts and Skills

Subtract.

4. $\begin{array}{r} 8 \\ -8 \\ \hline \end{array}$

5. $\begin{array}{r} 7 \\ -0 \\ \hline \end{array}$

6. $\begin{array}{r} 5 \\ -0 \\ \hline \end{array}$

7. $\begin{array}{r} 9 \\ -9 \\ \hline \end{array}$

Use the number line.
Count back to subtract.

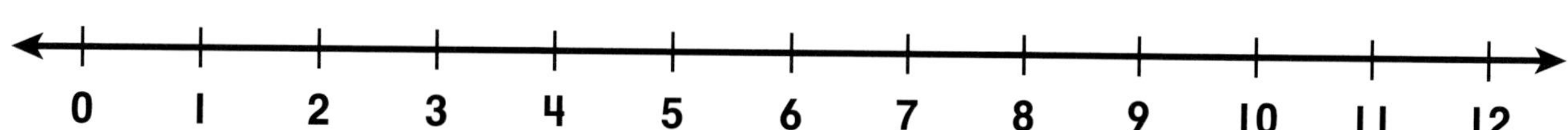

8. 10 − 3 = ______
9. 6 − 4 = ______
10. 12 − 9 = ______

Use the picture. Complete the number sentence.

11. How many more blue stars are there?

______ − ______ = ______

Add or subtract.

12. 10 + 2 = ______

    12 − ______ = 2

13. 9 + 4 = ______

    13 − 4 = ______

Chapter Review/Test

Circle the names for each number.

14. **11**   8 + 2   8 + 3   11 − 0   11 − 2

15. **7**   4 + 3   5 + 2   10 − 3   11 − 6

Complete the number sentences.

16. 7 + 4 = ______   11 − ______ = 4

______ + 7 = 11   11 − 4 = ______

17. ______ − 9 = 7   9 + ______ = 16

16 − 7 = ______   7 + ______ = 16

Problem Solving

Write a number sentence to solve.

18. There are 7 boys and 9 girls in the class. How many students are in the class?

______ + ______ = ______

______ students

19. There are 14 books on the shelf. 9 books are red. The other books are blue. How many blue books are on the shelf?

______ − ______ = ______

______ blue books

20. Zach has 12 cookies. He gives 8 to his friends. How many cookies does Zach have left?

______ − ______ = ______

______ cookies

Data, Graphing, and Probability

CHAPTER 4

INVESTIGATION

Use the tally chart to tell about the picture. Complete the chart. Then use the chart picture to tell as much as you can about field day.

Field Day Activities

Rope Tug	𝍸 𝍸
Cheering	
______	
______	

 Fun in the Sun

Look at page 75.
Use the tally chart to complete the pictograph.

Draw one  for each child.

Field Day Activities

Rope Tug	
Cheering	
____________	
____________	

Name ______________________________

Hands-On

Activity: Take a Survey

Objective
Use tally marks in a survey; use and compare data.

Vocabulary
survey
tally marks
data

What sport do your classmates like best?

Take a **survey** to find out.

Tally marks help you organize the **data**, or information, you collect.

Work Together

Take a survey with a friend.

Ask 10 classmates which sport they like best.
Make a tally mark on the chart for each answer.

𝍸 | stands for 6.

Favorite Sports

Soccer	
Baseball	
Basketball	

Use the data in your chart to answer the question.

1. Which sport is chosen most often? ______________
2. Which sport is chosen least often? ______________
3. Do more children choose soccer or basketball? ______________
4. **Talk About It** How does making tally marks help you keep track of your count?

Work Together

Which food do your classmates like best?
Take a survey to find out.

| stands for 1.
𝍸 stands for 5.

Ask 10 classmates.
Make a tally mark for each answer.

Favorite Lunch Foods

burger	
grilled cheese	
hot dog	

Use the data in the chart to answer the question.

1. How many children like grilled cheese best? ______ children

2. Which food is chosen most often? ____________

3. Which food is chosen least often? ____________

Complete the sentence to write a question about your chart.

4. How many more children like ____________ than like ____________?

5. Complete the number sentence to answer your question.

_____ − _____ = _____

6. **Talk About It** Look at the results of your survey. Which of the foods do you think is liked by the fewest children in your whole school? Explain your answer.

Go on

Name ____________________

On Your Own

Rick takes a survey of his class.
Megan takes a survey of her class.
They ask a question: **What is your favorite place to visit?**
Then they make tally charts.

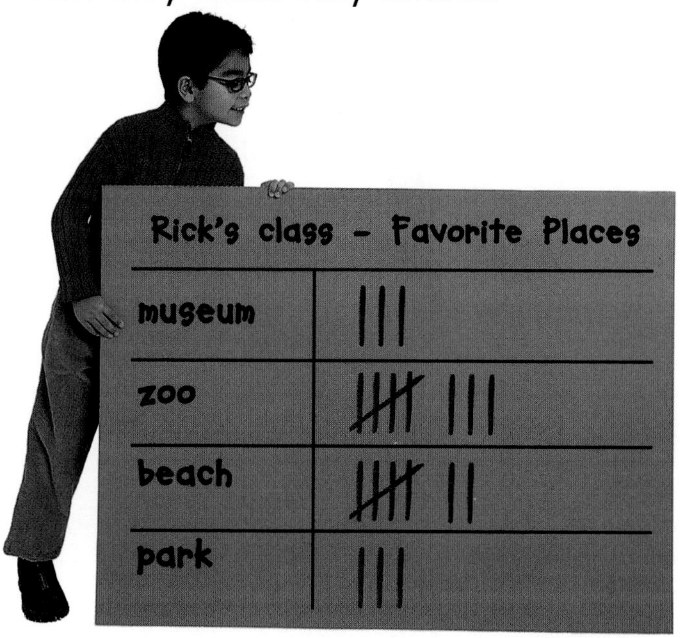

Use the data in both charts to answer the question.

1. In whose class do more children choose the beach?

   Megan's class

2. In whose class do more children choose the museum?

   ____

3. How many more children choose the zoo in Rick's class than in Megan's class?

   ______ children

4. How many fewer children choose the park in Megan's class than in Rick's class?

   ______ children

5. How many children are in Rick's survey?

   ______ children

6. How many children are in Megan's survey?

   ______ children

7. **Talk About It** Which place do you predict the fewest number of children in the whole school would choose as their favorite? Why?

At Home Make a chart like the one at the top of the page with your child. Then have your child survey family members about their favorite place to visit.

Now Try This Create a Survey

Step 1

Select a topic from the box or choose your own topic to complete the question in the chart.

What is your favorite ______?

Write the topic in the tally chart.

Step 2

Think of 3 answer choices.
Write them in the tally chart.

Step 3

Take your survey.
Complete the tally chart.

What is your favorite ______________?

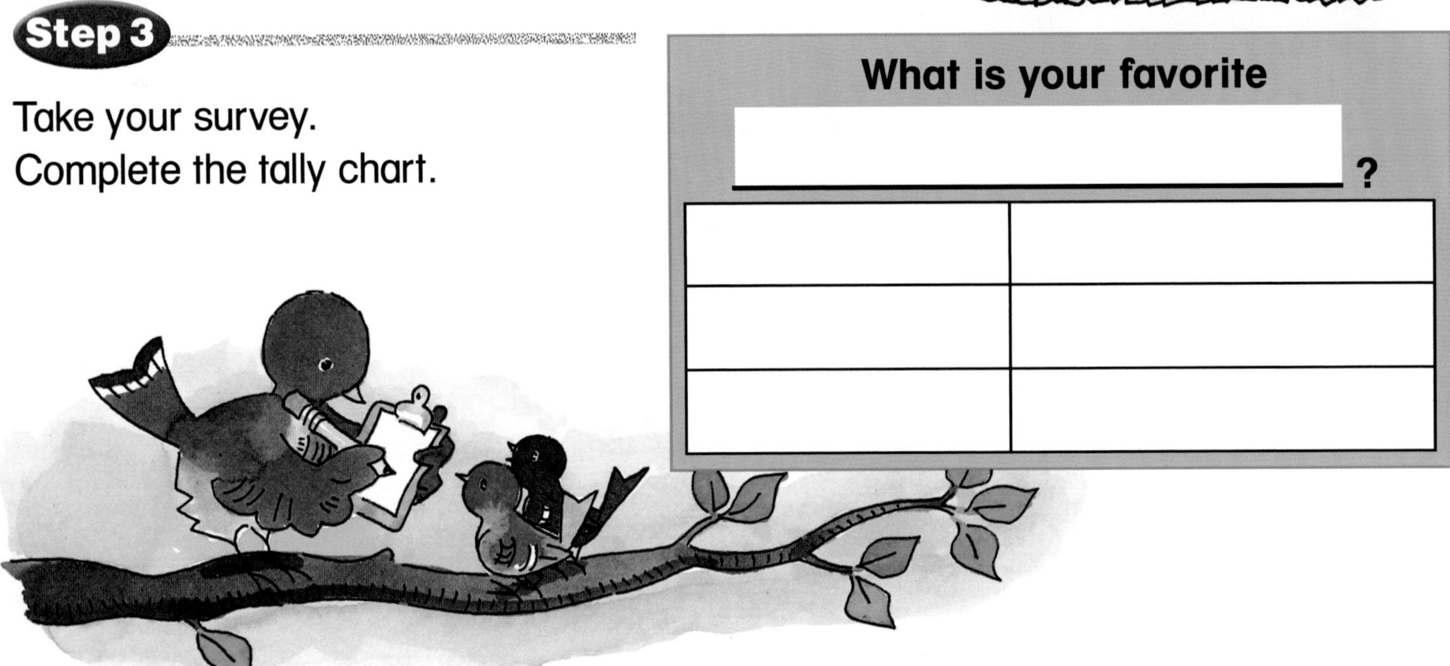

Use your tally chart.

1. Which answer is chosen most often? ______________

2. Write a question about your chart. Have a friend use your chart to answer the question.

____

____

____

3. **Talk About It** Describe something else your chart shows.

Name ______________________

Read a Pictograph

Objective
Use data in a pictograph.

Vocabulary
pictograph
symbols

A **pictograph** uses **symbols** to show information.

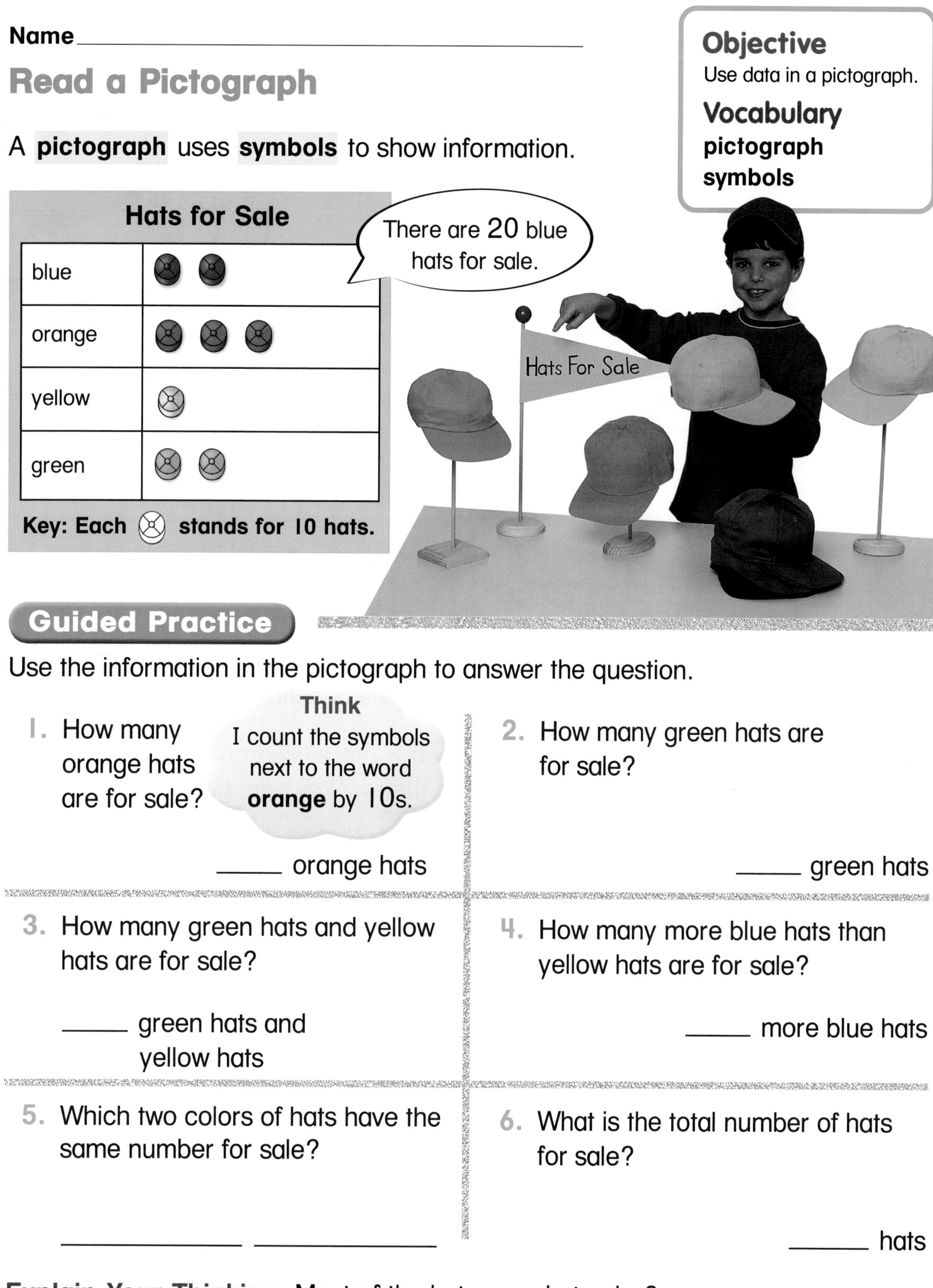

Hats for Sale

blue	
orange	
yellow	
green	

Key: Each (symbol) stands for 10 hats.

Guided Practice

Use the information in the pictograph to answer the question.

1. How many orange hats are for sale?

   Think
   I count the symbols next to the word **orange** by 10s.

   _____ orange hats

2. How many green hats are for sale?

   _____ green hats

3. How many green hats and yellow hats are for sale?

   _____ green hats and yellow hats

4. How many more blue hats than yellow hats are for sale?

   _____ more blue hats

5. Which two colors of hats have the same number for sale?

   __________ __________

6. What is the total number of hats for sale?

   _____ hats

Explain Your Thinking Most of the hats are what color? Explain how to find the answer without counting.

Practice

The tally chart shows what the children like best at the playground.

1. Use the tally chart to make a pictograph. Draw 1 ☺ for every 2 children.

Things Children Like

slide	swings	glider	monkey bars
卌 |	卌 卌	卌 |||	卌 |

Things Children Like

slide	☺ ☺ ☺
swings	
glider	
monkey bars	

Key: Each ☺ stands for 2 children.

Use the information in the pictograph to answer the question.

2. How many more children like using the glider than the slide?

_____ more children

3. If 2 more children say they like the monkey bars best, how many ☺ will you add to the pictograph?

_____ 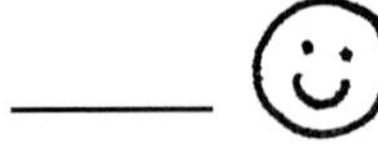

Problem Solving ▶ Data Sense

Use this pictograph.

4. How many playground toys are jump ropes?

_____ jump ropes

5. **Talk About It** How will you find the total number of playground toys?

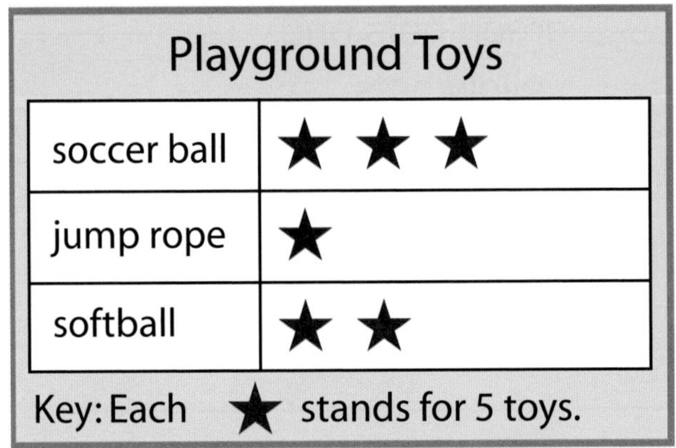

Playground Toys

soccer ball	★ ★ ★
jump rope	★
softball	★ ★

Key: Each ★ stands for 5 toys.

At Home Have your child tell you how he or she counts to find the number of soccer balls shown in the pictograph.

Hands-On

Name ______________________________

Activity: Make and Read Bar Graphs

Objective
Make and read a bar graph; compare data on a bar graph.

Vocabulary
bar graph

The tally chart shows how many children choose each snack on Field Day.

The **bar graph** shows the same data.

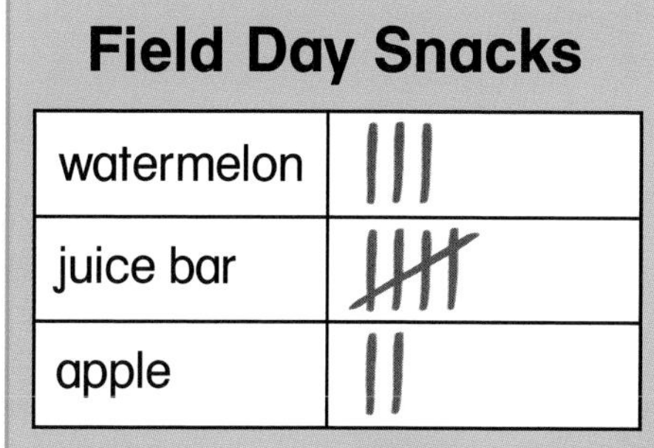

Field Day Snacks

watermelon	|||
juice bar	𝍸
apple	||

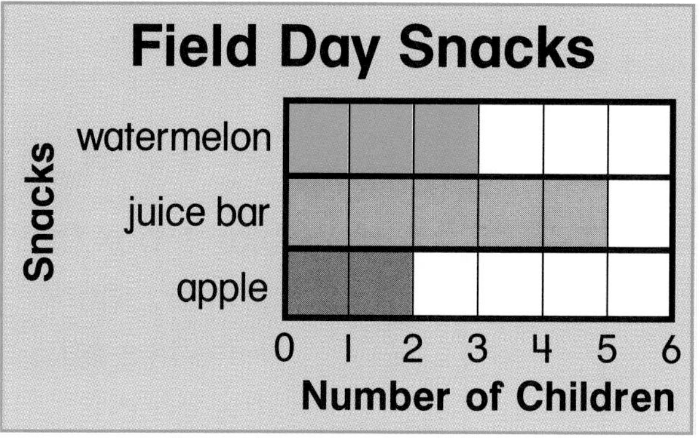

To read the bar graph, find the end of the bar. Then look at the number below the end of the bar.

Work Together

Use the bar graph to answer the question.

1. How many children choose watermelon?

   _____ children

2. How many children choose an apple?

   _____ children

3. **Talk About It** How many children choose snacks on Field Day? How do you know?

Work Together

1. Use the tally chart to complete the bar graph.

Favorite Snacks

Snack	Tally
cheese	𝍷𝍷𝍷
pretzels	𝍸
yogurt	𝍷𝍷

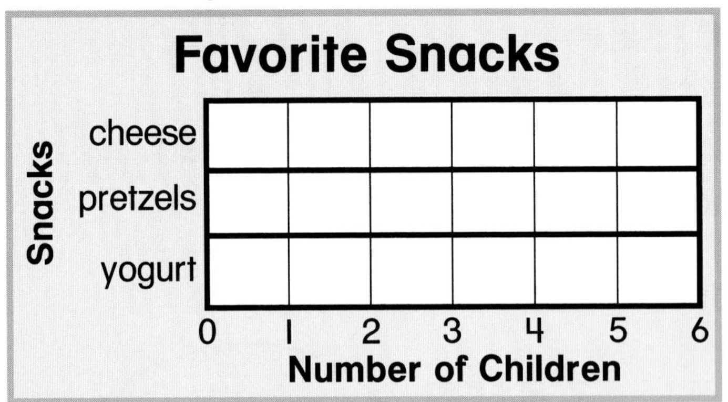

Use the tally chart or bar graph to answer the question.

2. Which snack is chosen most often? ____________

3. How many children choose their favorite snack? ______ children

Take a survey.

Ask 10 classmates to choose a favorite fruit.
Make a tally chart.
Then use the chart to make a bar graph.

Favorite Fruits

Fruit	Tally
apple	
orange	
banana	

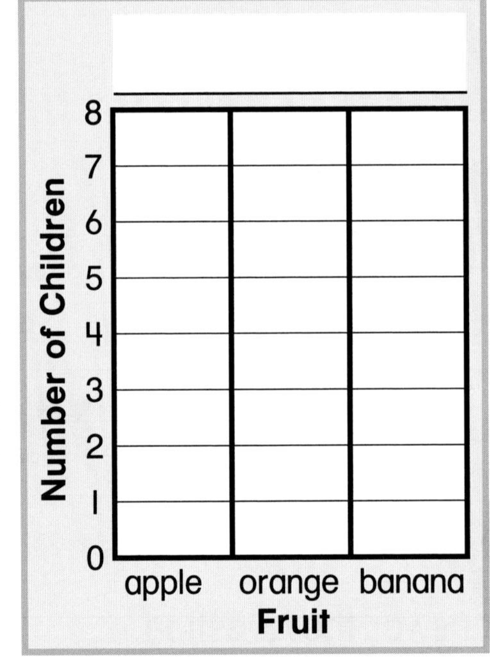

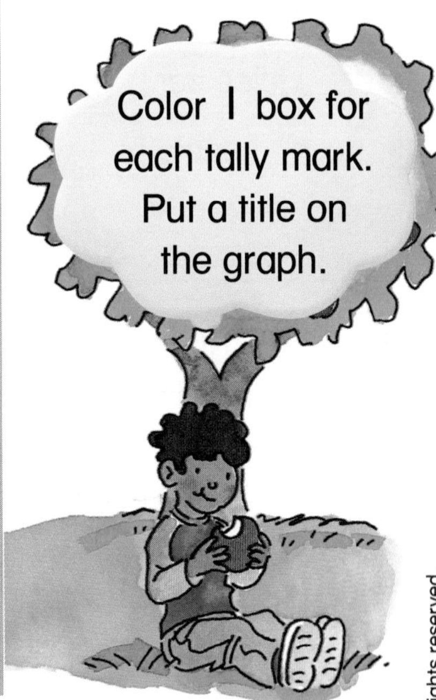

Use the tally chart or bar graph to answer the question.

4. Do more children choose oranges or apples?

____

5. Do fewer children choose oranges or bananas?

____

6. **Talk About It** For Exercise 5 did you use the tally chart or bar graph to answer the question? Why?

Go on

Name ______________________________

On Your Own

Annie sells 5 lemonades. She sells 2 more bottles of water than lemonade. Annie sells 3 juice boxes. She sells 1 more milk than juice box.

1. Color the bar graph to show what Annie sold.

Use the data above to answer the question.

2. How many more people buy water than buy juice boxes?

   ______ more people

3. What is the total number of drinks that Annie sells?

   ______ drinks

4. Which drink do the greatest number of people buy?

   ____

5. Which drink do the least number of people buy?

   ____

6. **Talk About It** Annie needs to buy more drinks to sell another day. Which drink should she buy the most of? Why?

On Your Own

Ella keeps a record of the number of drinks she sells.

Use her table to complete the bar graph.

Day of Week	Monday	Tuesday	Wednesday	Thursday	Friday
Drinks Sold	10	6	8	6	4

Be sure to label each bar.

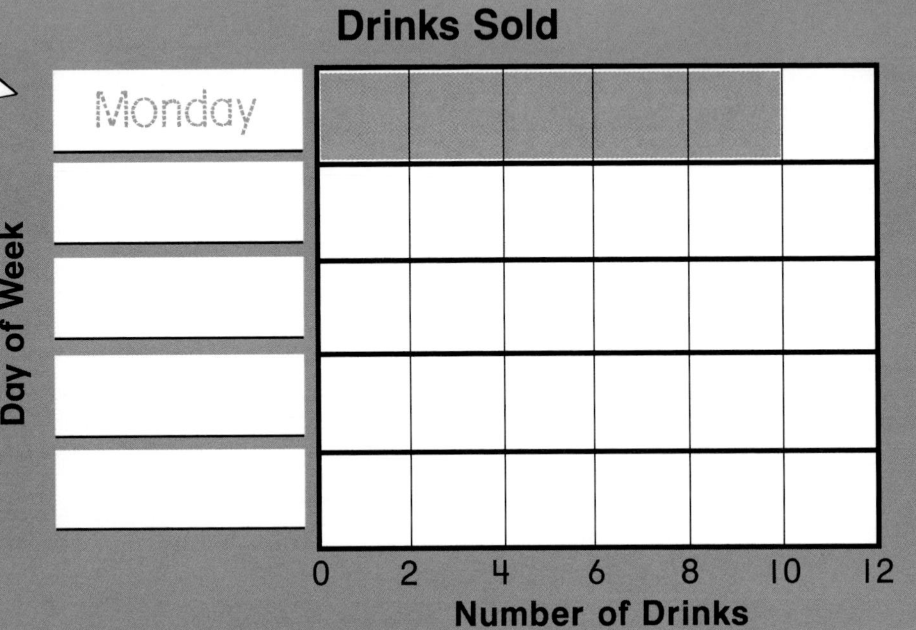

Color 1 box for every 2 drinks.

The space from 1 box to the next means 2 drinks.

Use the graph to answer the question.

1. On which day is the greatest number of drinks sold?

   ____

2. How many drinks are sold altogether on Monday and Friday?

   ______ drinks

3. How many more drinks are sold on Wednesday than Thursday?

   ______ more drinks

4. On which days are the same number of drinks sold?

   ____

   ____

5. **Talk About It** If Ella sells only 9 drinks on Monday, where would the bar on the graph end? Explain why.

At Home Have your child explain how he or she can use the bar graph on this page to find on which day the fewest number of drinks were sold.

Name ________________________________

Line Graphs

Objective
Read and make a line graph.

Vocabulary
line graph

Hands-On

You can describe data in different ways.

A **line graph** shows how something changes over time.

This line graph shows the number of children on the playground at different times of the day.

The greatest increase of children was from 2:00 to 3:00. That is when the school days ends.

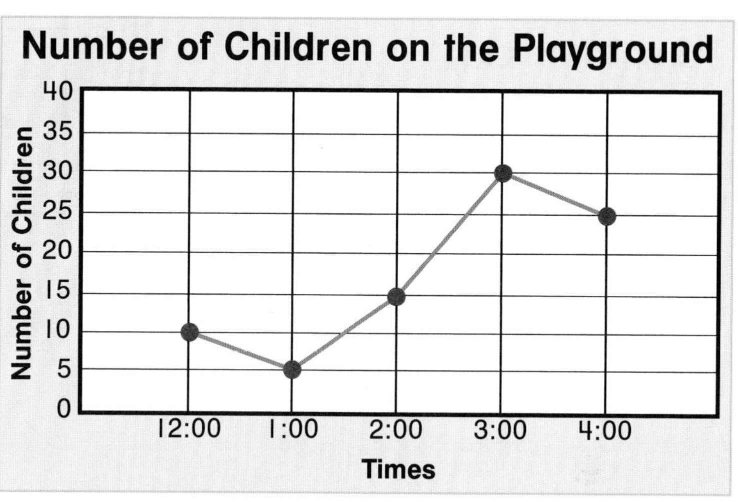

To read this line graph look at a time. Move up the line graph to the dot. Move left to find how many children were on the playground at that time.

Work Together

Use the line graph to answer the question.

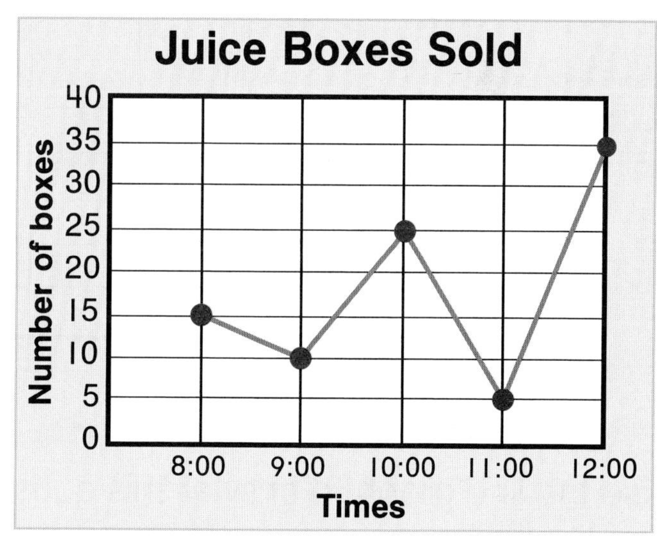

1. At what time were the most juice boxes sold? __________
2. At what time were the least juice boxes sold? __________
3. At what time were 25 juice boxes sold? __________
4. How many more juice boxes were sold at 10:00 than at 8:00?

   ______ juice boxes
5. **Talk About It** Describe the change in the number of juice boxes sold from 10:00 to 12:00.

Work Together

Use the line graph to answer the question.

1. How many children played basketball on Monday? ______

2. What day of the week did 5 children play basketball? ______

3. What two days had the same number of children playing basketball?

______ ______

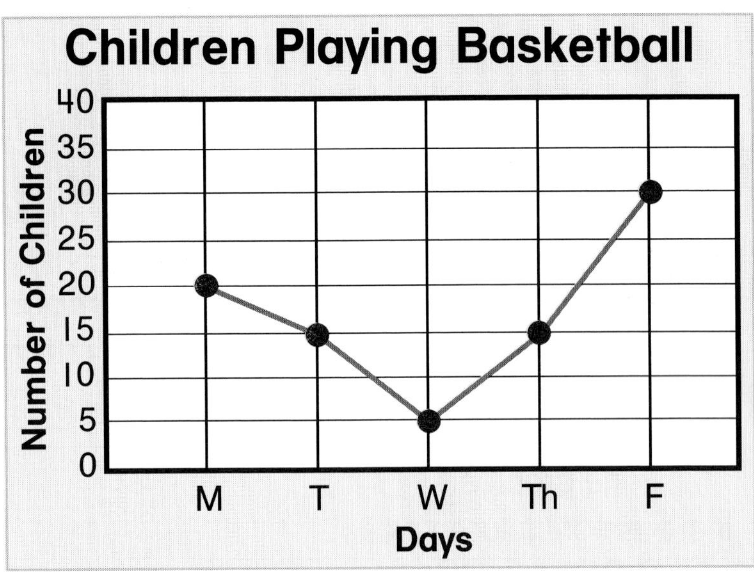

Make a line graph. Show how many children bring their lunch from home each day.

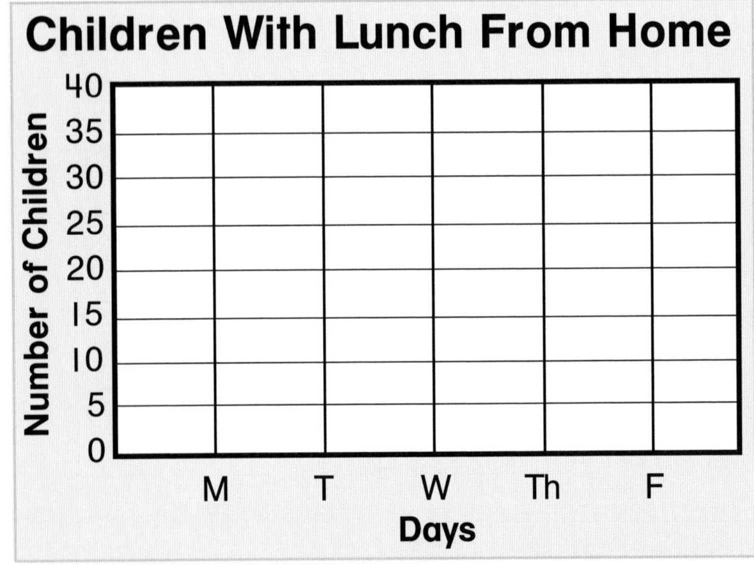

If the exact number is not on the line graph, I can mark my dot near where it would be.

Use the line graph to answer this question.

4. Which day do the most children bring their lunch from home?

______

5. **Talk About It** Describe how you use the graph to tell how many children bring their lunch from home on Friday.

At Home Ask your child to explain how the line graph would change if 5 more children brought their lunch from home on Wednesday.

Name ____________________

Graphing on a Coordinate Grid

 **Audio Tutor 1**/10 Listen and Understand

Use **ordered pairs** to find and name points on a **grid.**

Objective
Locate and identify points on a grid.

Vocabulary
ordered pairs
grid

This grid shows where things are in a classroom. What object is at (4, 5)?

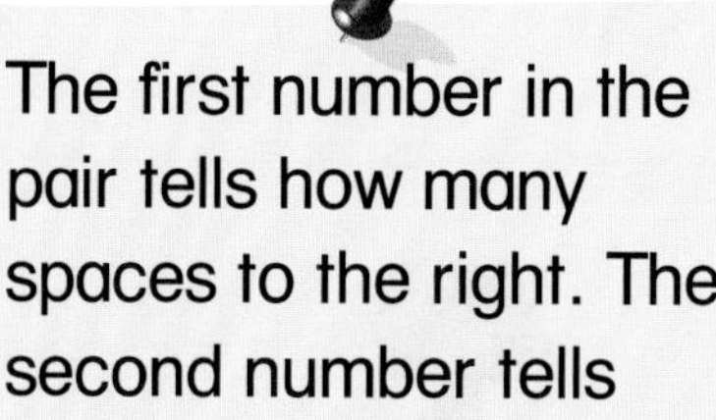

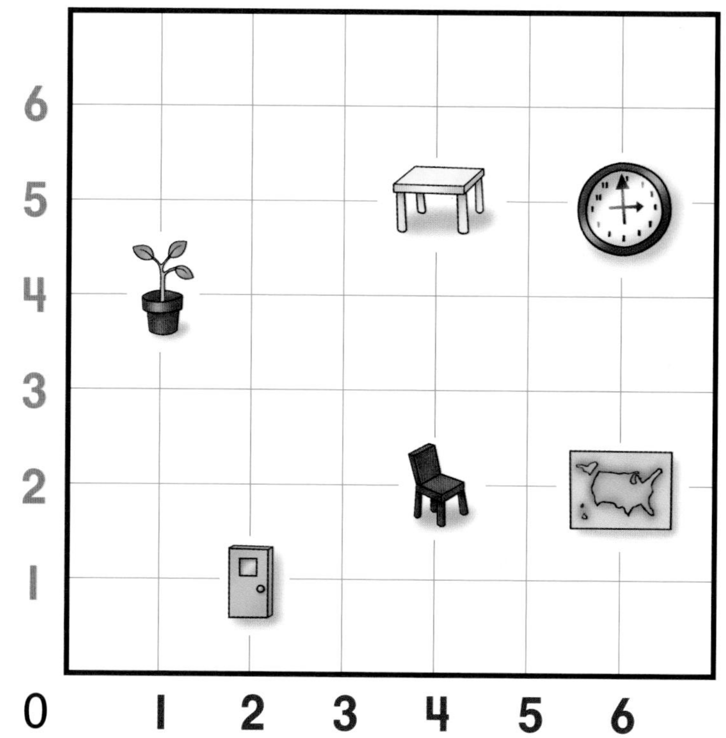

- Step 1: Always start at 0.
- Step 2: Go 4 spaces to the right. →
- Step 3: Go up 5 spaces. ↑

The ___table___ is at (4, 5).

Guided Practice

Use the ordered pair.
First go right.
Then go up.
Write the name of what you find.

1. (4, 2) __________
2. (6, 2) __________
3. (6, 5) __________
4. Find the plant on the grid. Write the ordered pair.
   (____, ____)
5. Find the door on the grid. Write the ordered pair.
   (____, ____)

Explain Your Thinking Why are (4, 5) and (5, 4) different ordered pairs?

Extra Practice at eduplace.com/map

Practice

Remember
First move to the right.
Then move up.

Find the object on the grid.
Write the ordered pair.

1. (6, 5)

2. (____, ____)

3. (____, ____)

4. (____, ____)

5. (____, ____)

6.  (____, ____)

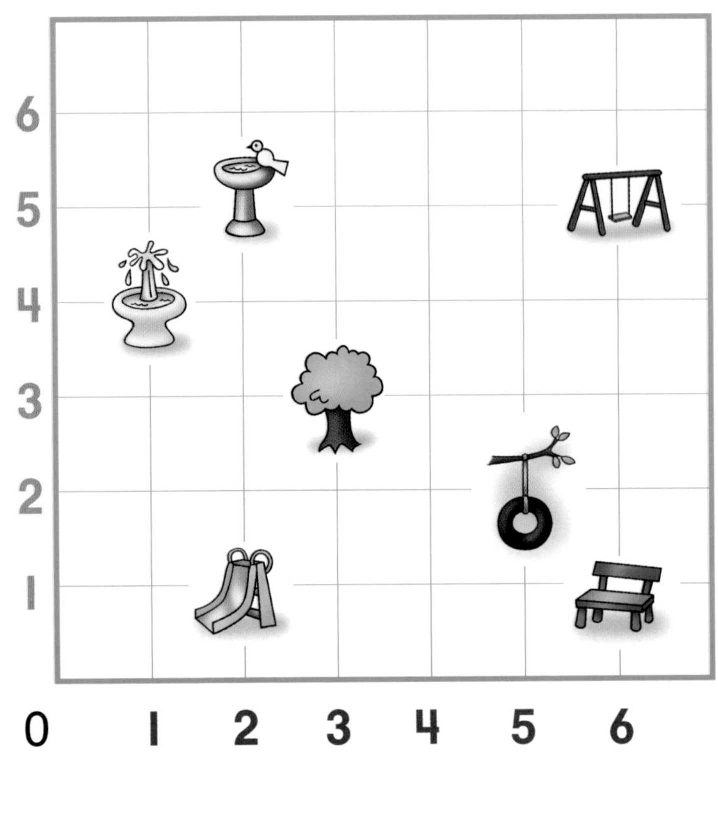

Problem Solving ▶ Spatial Sense

Use the grid above to solve.

7. Jessica goes from place to place on the playground. These ordered pairs show the places she visits in order from first to last.

   (2, 1), (6, 1), (6, 5), (2, 5), (2, 1)

   Draw lines to connect in order the places she visits. What shape is her path?

   ____

 **At Home** Use the grid above. Say an ordered pair. Have your child draw an object at this location on the grid. Repeat using different ordered pairs.

Name ______________________________

Activity: Make and Read Venn Diagrams

Objective
Read and make a Venn diagram.

Vocabulary
Venn diagram

Hands-On

This Venn diagram shows Fran's 6 friends.

One circle shows all her friends at school.
One circle shows all her friends in the neighborhood.
The names that are in both circles are her friends that are in the neighborhood and at school.

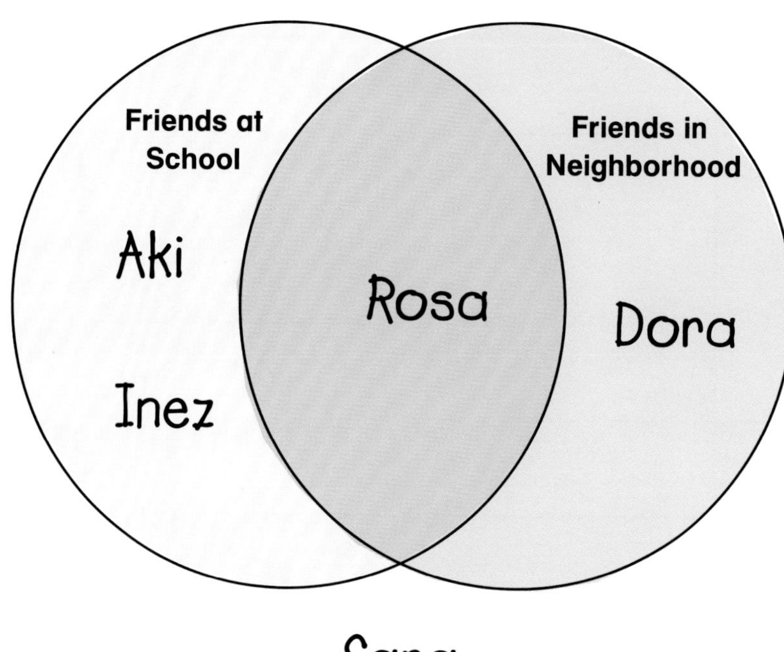

Sara

Work Together

Use the Venn diagram to answer the question.

> **Think**
> Which circle shows all the friends at school?

1. How many friends does Fran have at school? _____

2. How many friends does Fran have that go to her school and live in her neighborhood? _____

3. Sahil is Fran's new friend in the neighborhood. He goes to a different school than Fran. Write Sahil's name in the diagram.

4. **Talk About It** Why do you think Sara's name is not inside a circle?

Work Together

Ask 15 classmates if they like peanut butter, jelly, both, or neither. Write their names in the chart.

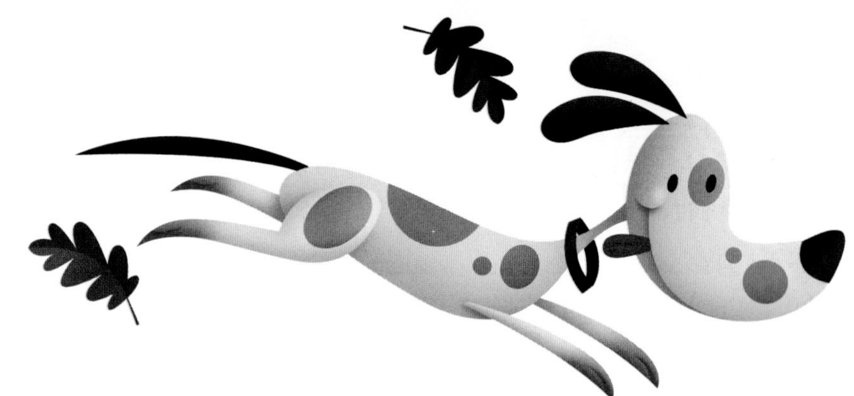

Peanut butter	Jelly	Both	Neither

Name ____________________

Use the chart to complete the Venn diagram.

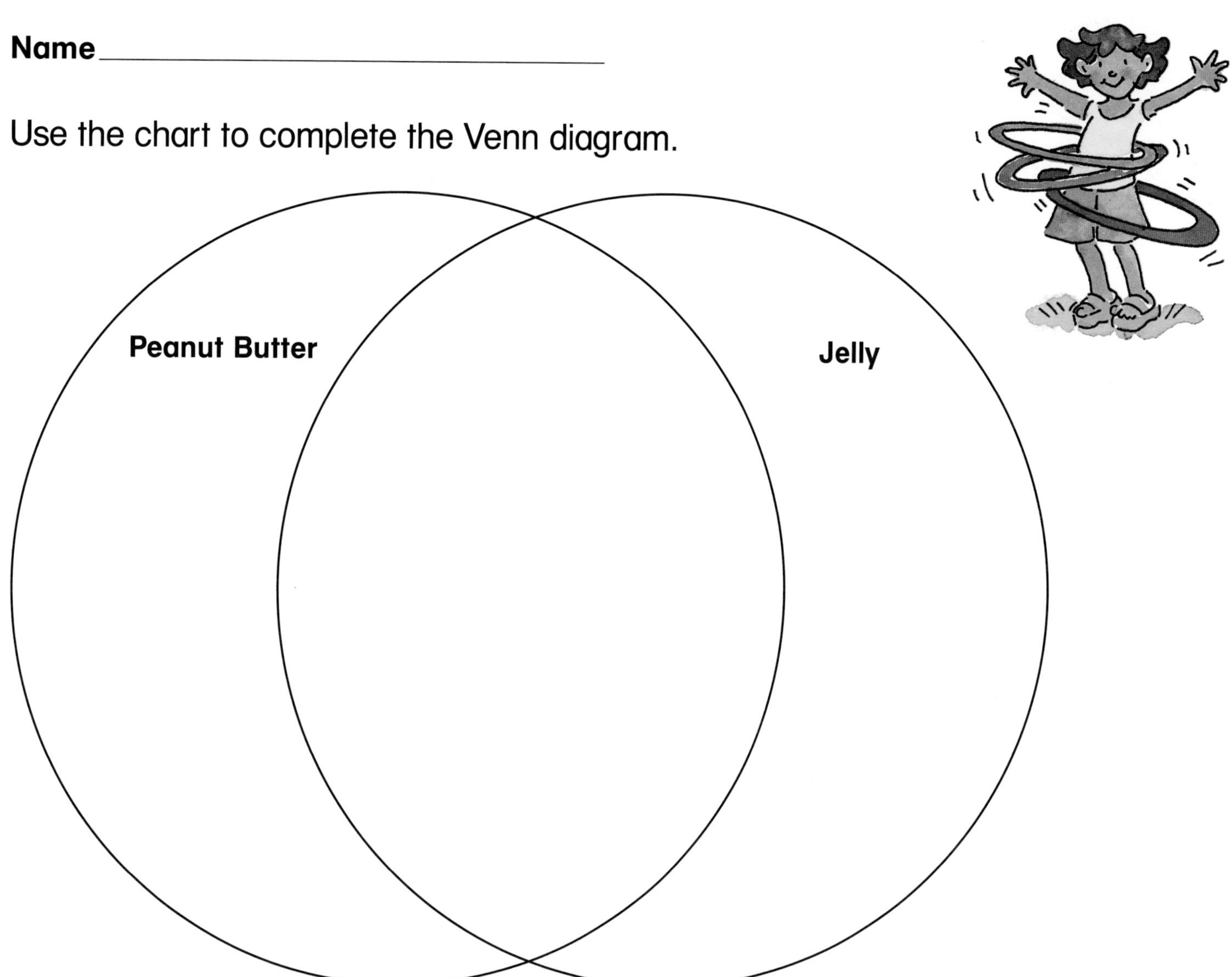

Use the Venn diagram to answer the question.

1. How many people like peanut butter? _____

2. How many people liked both peanut butter and jelly? _____

3. Where did you place the names of children who did not like peanut butter or jelly? Why?

____

____

4. **Talk About It** What if you wanted to add bread to your survey? How could you change your Venn diagram to show the results?

Quick Check

Use the data to answer the question.

Favorite Games

Rope Tug	☺ ☺ ☺
Ring Toss	☺
Musical Chairs	☺ ☺

Key: Each ☺ stands for 2 votes.

1. How many more children choose the Rope Tug than the Ring Toss?

_____ children

2. How many children choose apple juice and orange juice?

_____ children

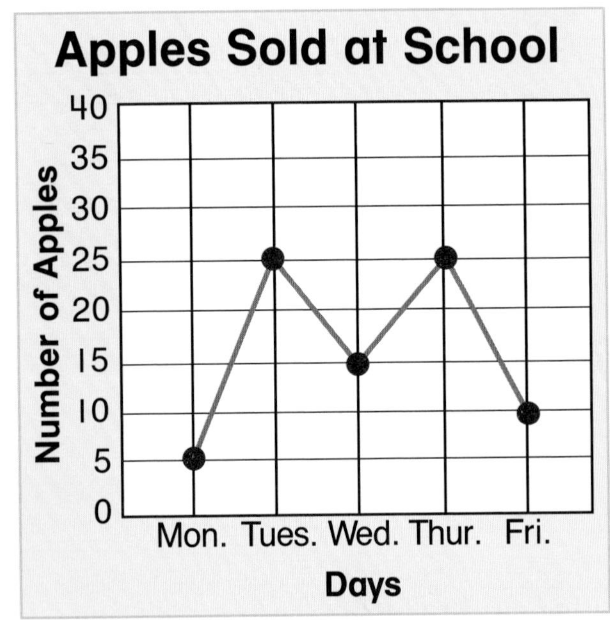

3. How many apples are sold on Wednesday?

_____ apples

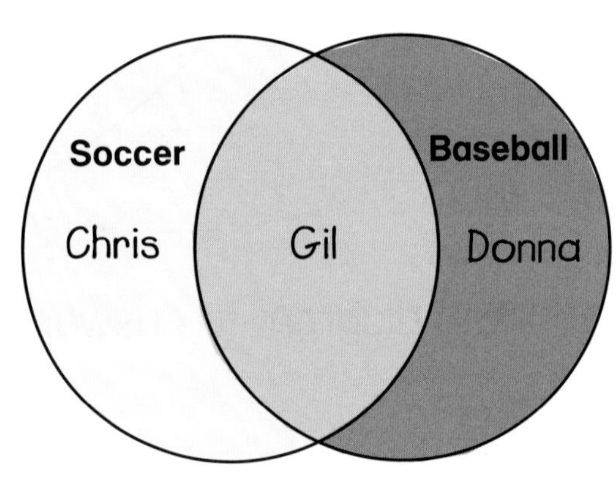

4. Who plays soccer and baseball?

____

Find the object on the grid.
Write the ordered pair.

5.  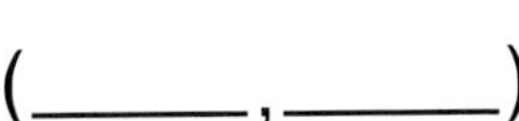 (_____,_____)

6.  (_____,_____)

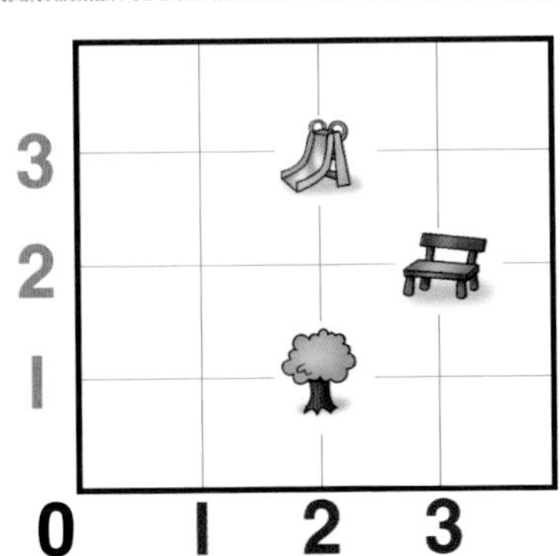

Name ______________________________

Activity: More, Less, and Equally Likely

 **Audio Tutor 1**/12 Listen and Understand

> **Objective**
> Determine if an event is more likely, less likely, or equally likely to happen.
>
> **Vocabulary**
> **more likely** **certain**
> **less likely** **probable**
> **equally likely**
> **impossible**

Hands-On

Sometimes you can tell if an event is **more likely, less likely,** or **equally likely** to happen.

How likely is it that Trey will get a instead of a ?

Trey returns the cube to the bag after each pick.

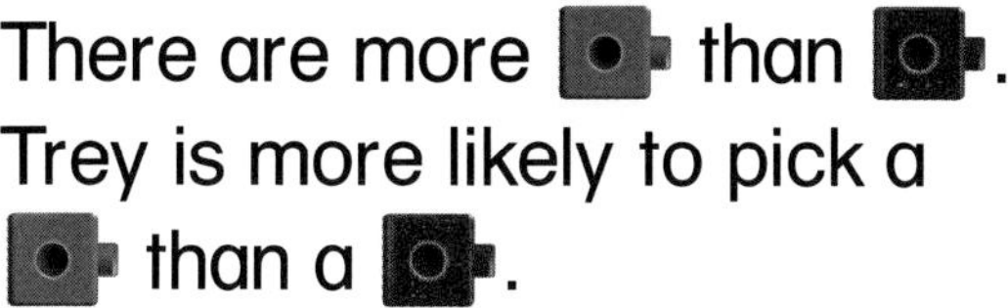
There are more than .
Trey is more likely to pick a than a .

Trey picks a cube out of the bag.
He records the color in the tally chart.
Trey does this 10 times.

Colors Picked	
blue	|||| ||
red	|||

Work Together

Tell how likely it is the event will happen.

1. 5 and 5 are in a bag.
How likely are you to pick a instead of a ?

more likely   less likely   equally likely

2. Place 5 and 5 in a bag.

Follow these steps 10 times to complete the tally chart.

1. Pick a cube.
2. Record the color.
3. Return the cube to the bag.

Colors Picked	
blue	
red	

3. **Talk About It** What do you think your answers will be if you repeat Exercise 2 ten more times? Why?

On Your Own

Tell how likely it is the event will happen. Then follow the steps 10 times to complete the tally chart.

Steps
1. Pick a cube.
2. Record the color in the tally chart.
3. Return the cube to the bag.

1. 6 [green cube] and 4 [orange cube] are in a bag. How likely are you to pick a [green cube] instead of a [orange cube]?

more likely   less likely   equally likely

2. Place 6 [green cube] and 4 [orange cube] in a bag.

Colors Picked	
green	
orange	

3. 3 [green cube] and 7 [orange cube] are in a bag. How likely are you to pick a [green cube] instead of a [orange cube]?

more likely   less likely   equally likely

4. Place 3 [green cube] and 7 [orange cube] in a bag.

Colors Picked	
green	
orange	

Look at the bag of cubes.
How likely are you to pick a [cube] instead of a [cube]?

5.

more likely

less likely

equally likely

6.

more likely

less likely

equally likely

7.

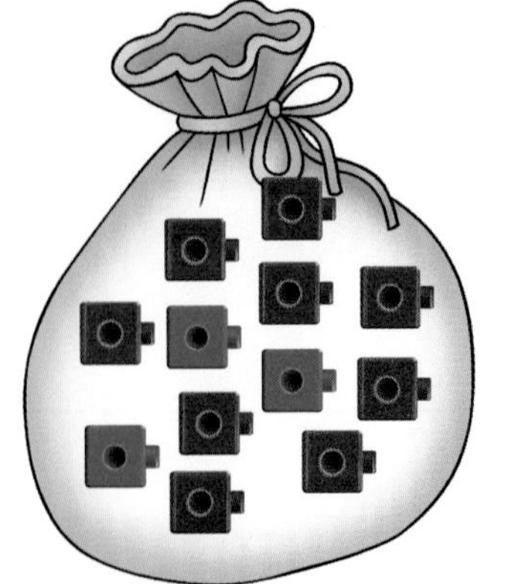

more likely

less likely

equally likely

8.

more likely

less likely

equally likely

Go on

Name ______________________________

An event that is **certain** will happen.

An event that is **probable** is likely to happen.

An event that is **impossible** will never happen.

Work Together

Look at the bag of 7 cubes.
Write **certain**, **probable**, or **impossible** to describe the event.

1. You will pick a purple cube. ____________
2. You will pick a cube. ____________
3. You will pick a yellow cube. ____________

Put the cubes shown above in a paper bag.
Follow these steps 10 times.

1. Pick one cube.
2. Record the color.
3. Return the cube to the bag.

Colors Picked	
blue	
yellow	
purple	

On Your Own

Look at the bag of cubes. Circle the correct event.

4. Which event is certain?

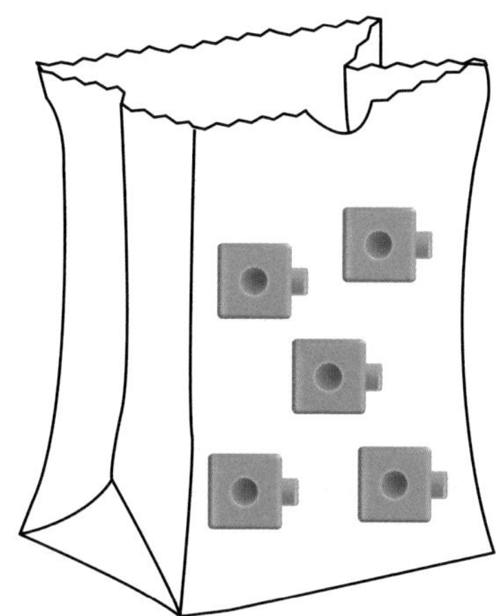

I will pick a green cube.

I will pick a red cube.

5. Which event is probable?

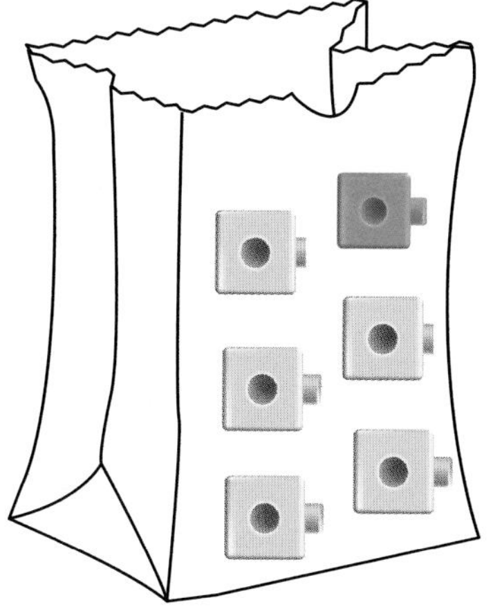

I will pick a green cube.

I will pick a yellow cube.

At Home Present your child with an event such as those in this lesson. Ask if the event is more likely, less likely, or equally likely to happen than another.

Now Try This Fair and Unfair

The games you play should be fair. Each player should have the same chance of winning.

Three children play a game with a spinner. Each child chooses a color. 1 point is scored each time the spinner stops on that color.

This spinner is **fair**.

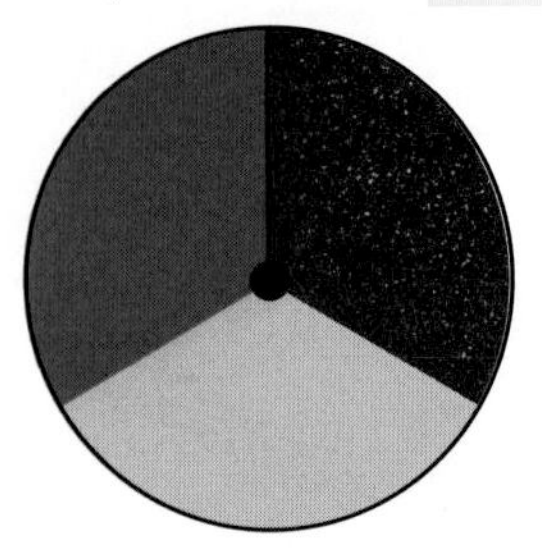

This spinner is fair.

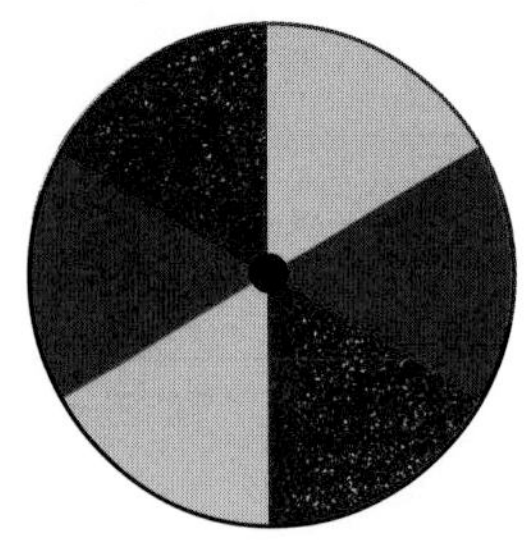

This spinner is **unfair**.

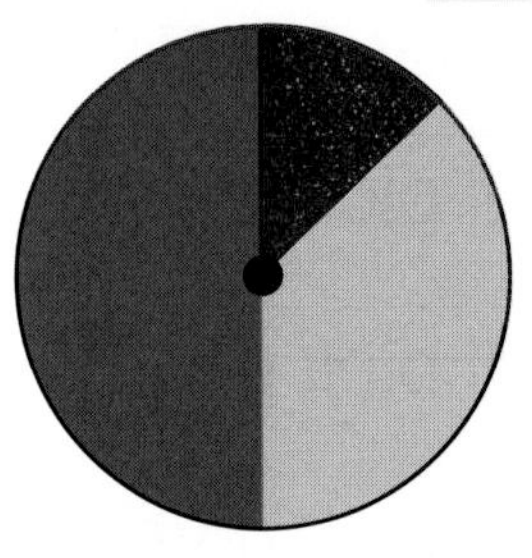

Look at the spinner.
Write **fair** or **unfair** to describe the spinner.

1. Three children play.

____

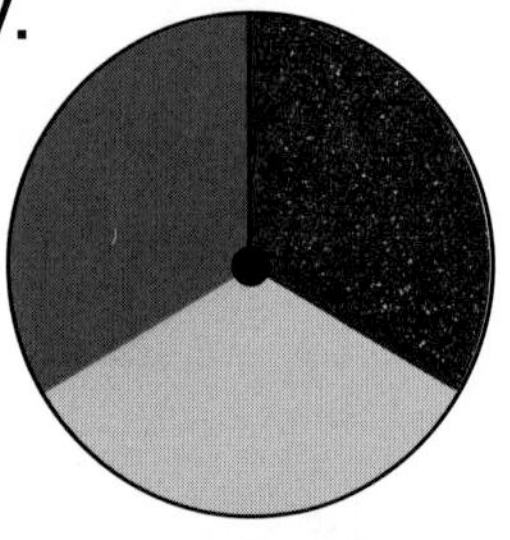

2. Two children play.

____

3. Four children play.

____

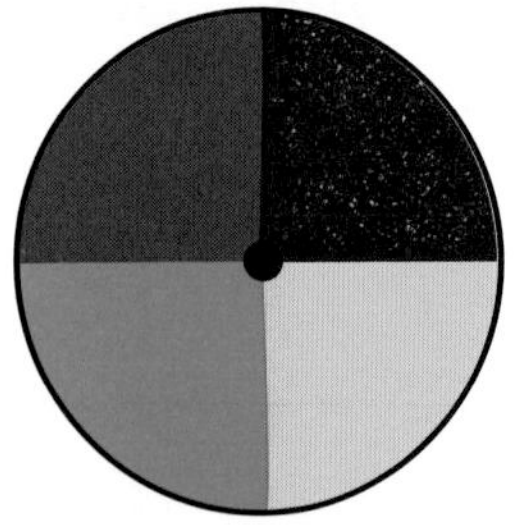

4. Three children play.

____

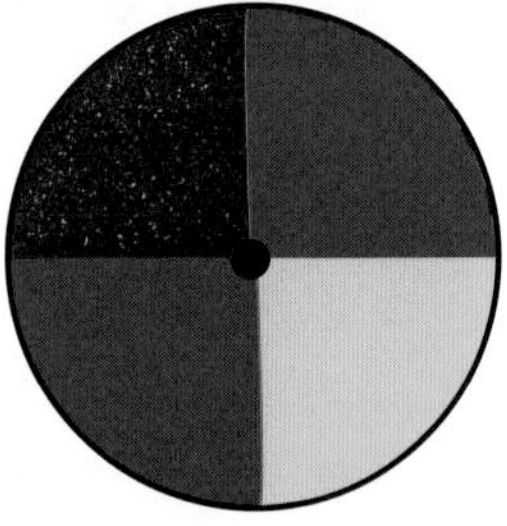

5. Two children play.

____

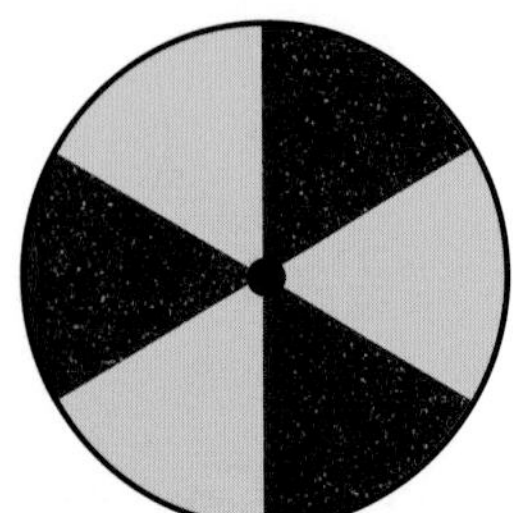

6. Four children play.

____

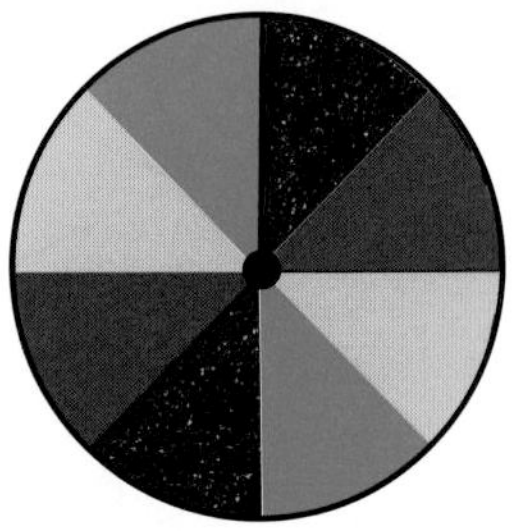

7. **Talk About It** When is a spinner a fair spinner?

Name ______________________

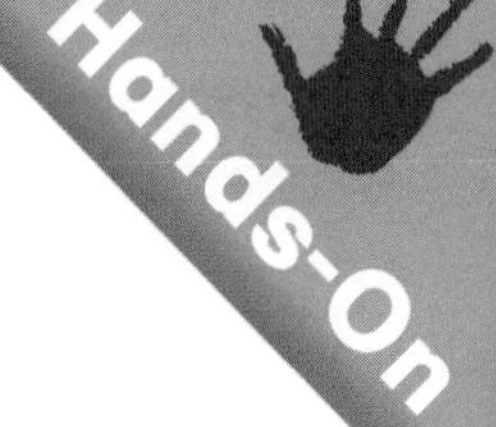

Activity: Predicting Outcomes

Objective
Predict and record the outcome of an event.

Vocabulary
predict outcome

Sometimes you can **predict** the **outcome** of an event. This means you can tell what will most likely happen.

Work Together

1. Predict what the outcome will be when you use this spinner.

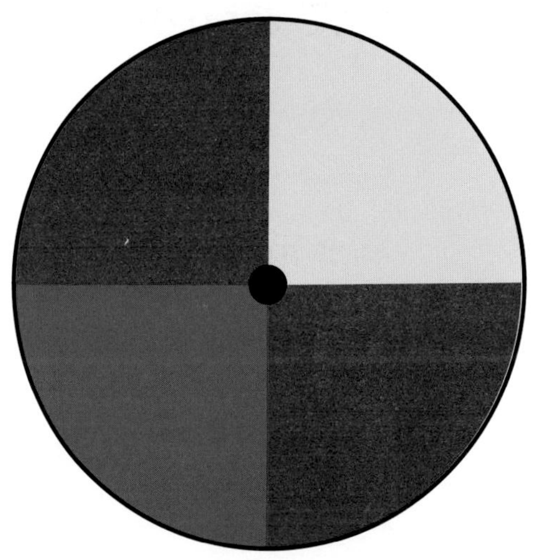

- Most of the spinner is red.
- The spinner will point to red most often.

2. Use a paper clip and a pencil.
Spin 10 times.
Record each spin on the tally chart.
Which color did you land on most often?

____

Spins	
Red	
Yellow	
Blue	

3. **Talk About It** What do you predict will happen if you spin another 10 times? If you spin another 50 times? Explain your prediction.

On Your Own

Use the spinner below.

1. Predict the color the spinner will land on most often. ____________

2. Use a paper clip and pencil.
Spin 10 times. Record your spins in the tally chart.

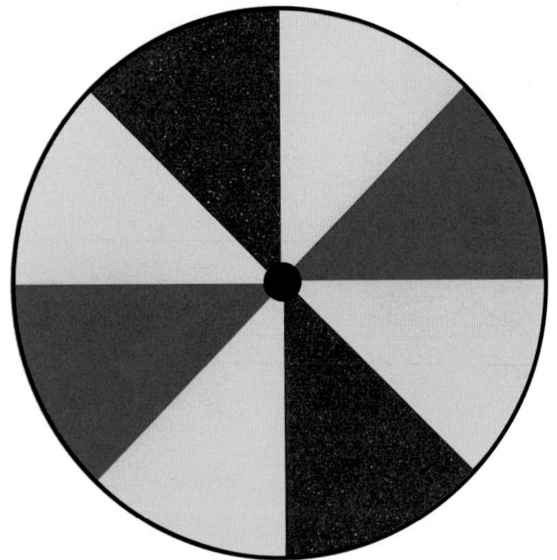

Spins

Red	
Yellow	
Blue	

3. Which color did you land on most often? ____________

Use the spinner below.

4. Predict the color the spinner will land on most often. ____________

5. Spin 25 times. Record each spin in the tally chart.

Spins

Red	
Yellow	
Blue	

6. Which color did you land on most often? ____________

7. **Talk About It** Can you always correctly predict the outcome of an event? Why?

At Home Continue the experiments with your child. Find out if the color landed on the most remains the same.

Name ______________________________

Use a Graph

Objective
Use data in a graph to solve a problem.

You can use data in a graph to solve a problem.

Use the data to add.

Each child chooses one Field Day event. How many children choose the rope tug and ball throw events?

Find the data in the bar graph. Then add.

Think
6 children are in the rope tug and 8 children are in the ball throw.

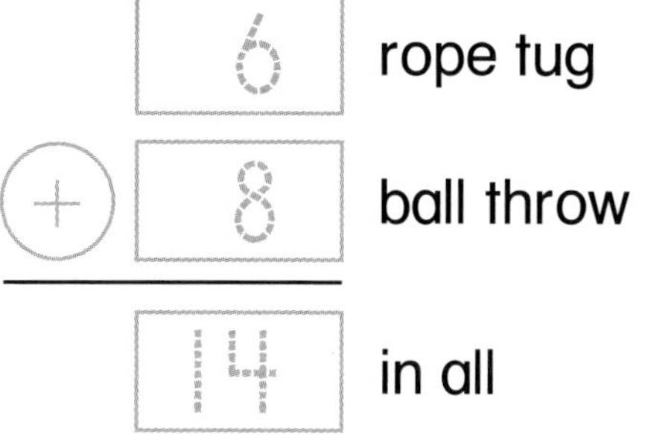

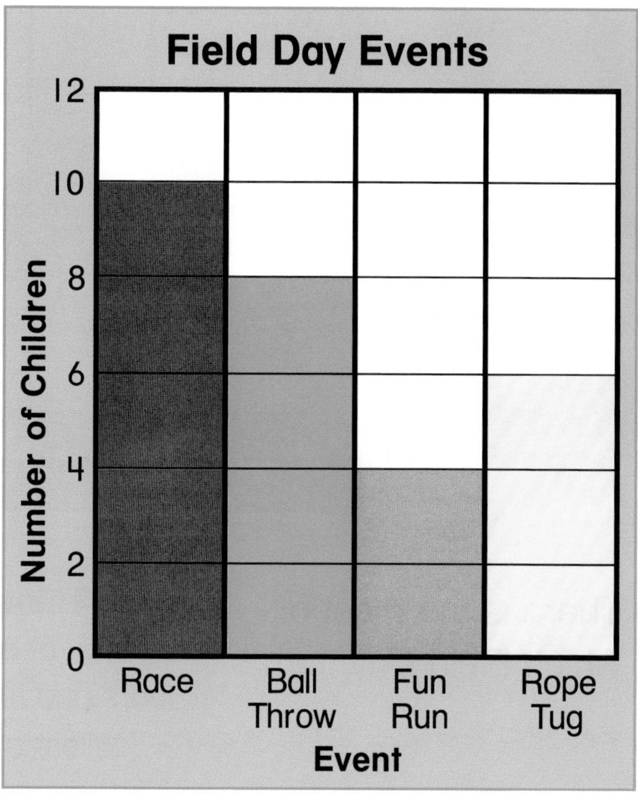

Use the data to compare.

How many more children choose the race than the fun run?

Find the data in the bar graph.

Think
10 children are in the race and 4 children are in the fun run.

Subtract to compare.

10  4 = 

______ more children

Guided Practice

Use data in the graph to solve.

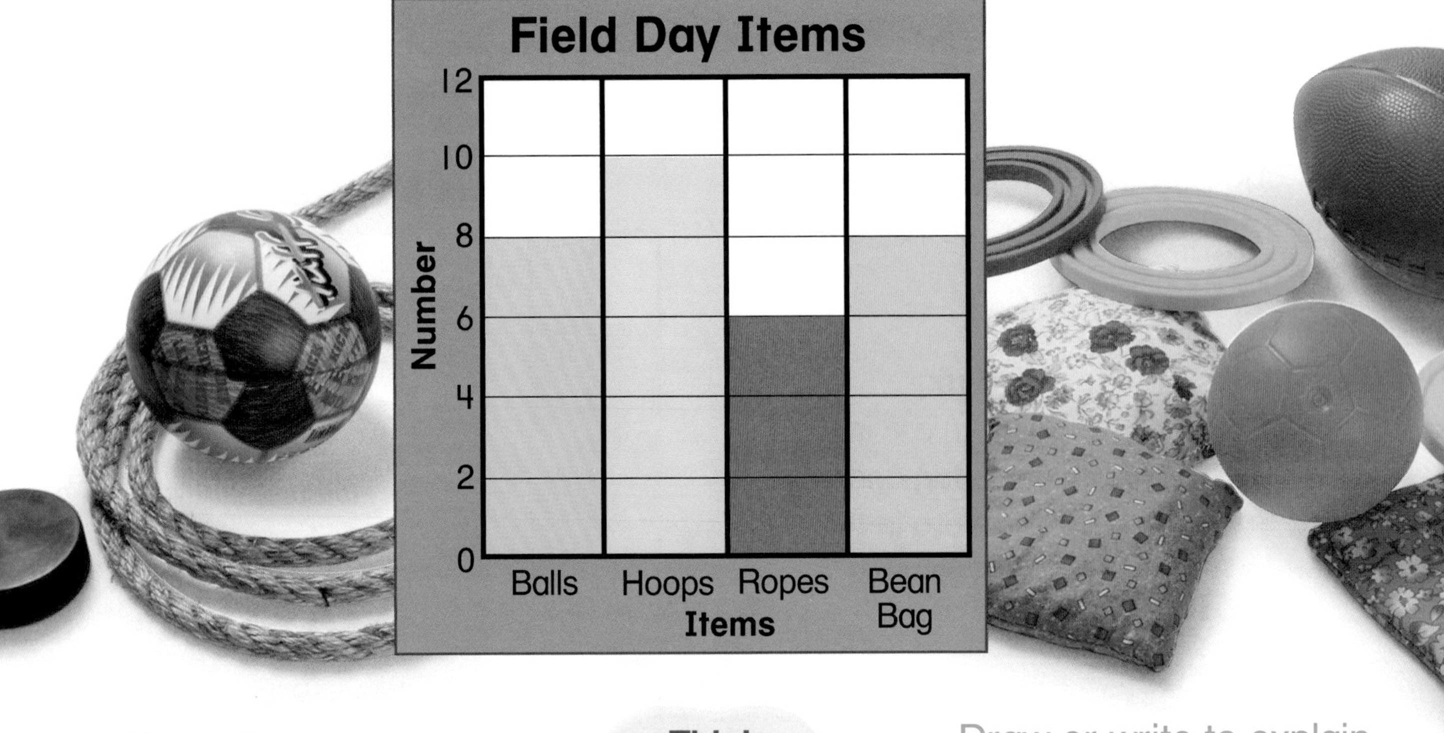

1. There is the most of which Field Day item?

Think
I look at all the bars and find the tallest one.

Draw or write to explain.

hoops

2. How many more bean bags than ropes does the class have for Field Day?

Think
I find the numbers on the graph. Then I subtract.

_____ bean bags

Practice

3. The class has the same number of which items?

____

____

4. How many more hoops than ropes does the class have?

_____ more

Go on

Name ____________________

Mixed Problem Solving

Strategies
Use Models to Act It Out
Write a Number Sentence
Draw a Picture

Solve.
Use the data in the graph.

Draw or write to explain.

1. How many hockey cards and basketball cards does Dan have altogether?

basketball

____ hockey and basketball cards

2. How many fewer football cards than basketball cards does Dan have?

football

____ football cards

3. Dan gets 2 more hockey cards. How many hockey cards does Dan have now?

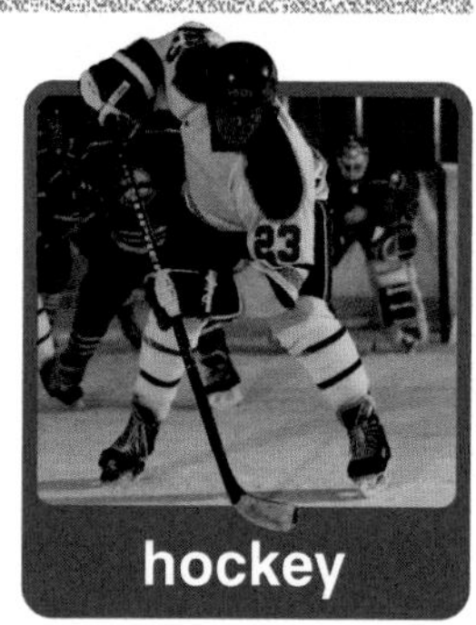
hockey

____ hockey cards

At Home Ask your child how the graph above would change if Dan had 2 more football cards.

Problem Solving on Tests • Listening Skills

Open Response

Listen to your teacher.
Solve.

Show your work using pictures, numbers, or words.

1. Jill makes a bar graph. It shows that 12 of her friends like math. 6 friends like science. 4 friends like reading. Color to show what her graph looks like.

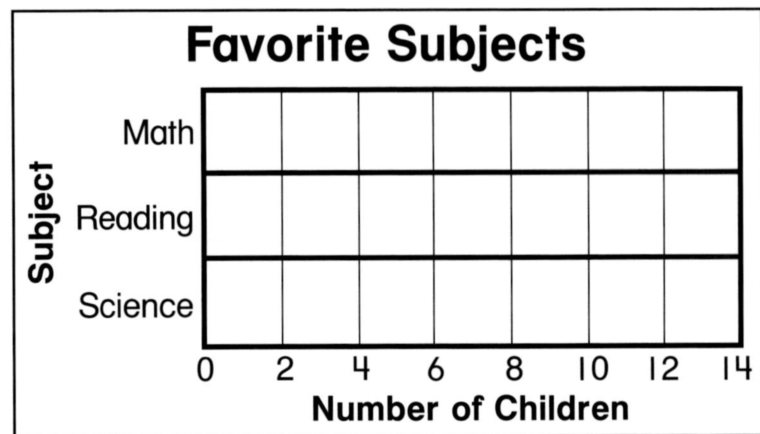

2. Look back at Exercise 1. How many more children like math than reading?

_____ children

Multiple Choice

Listen to your teacher.
Choose the correct answer.

3. 2 ○ 4 ○ 6 ○ 8 ○

4.

 ○ 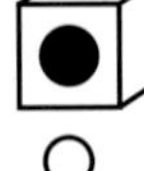 ○  ○ 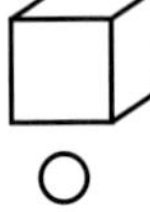 ○

Education Place
See **eduplace.com/map** for more Test-Taking Tips.

Name ___________________________

Now Try This Dressing Up!

Wesley has a red and blue shirt. He has yellow, green, and orange pants.

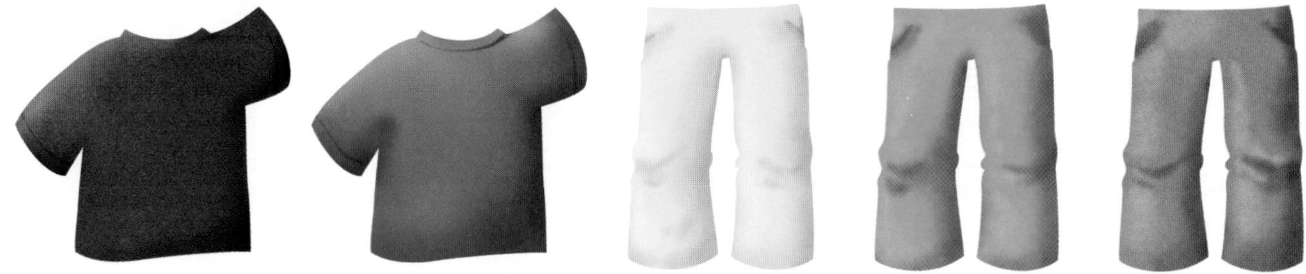

Color the shirts and pants to show all the combinations of clothes that Wesley can wear.

How many combinations of shirts and pants can Wesley wear? _____

Problem Solving

Math Challenge

Delicious Data

Maya took a survey. She wanted to know if people liked eggs, muffins, or fruit best for breakfast. She made a bar graph from the data she collected.

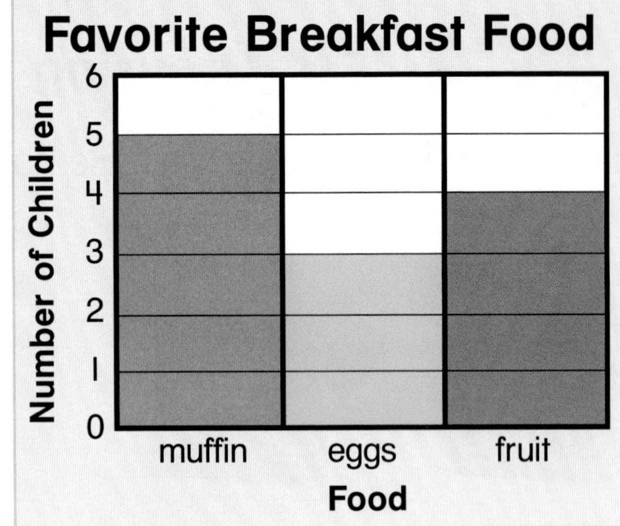

Circle the sentences that are true about the data. Cross out the sentences that are false.

1. Most of the people liked muffins.
   Most of the people liked fruit.

2. One more person liked fruit than eggs.
   One more person liked fruit than muffins.

3. The least number of people liked fruit.
   The least number of people liked eggs.

4. Maya surveyed 10 people.
   Maya surveyed 12 people.

WEEKLY WR READER eduplace.com/map

Key Topic Review

Addition and Subtraction

Add.

1. $7 + 8$
2. $9 + 7$
3. $8 + 4$
4. $6 + 7$
5. $8 + 9$
6. $9 + 5$

Subtract.

7. $13 - 5$
8. $18 - 9$
9. $14 - 8$
10. $17 - 8$
11. $15 - 7$
12. $16 - 8$

Extra Practice at eduplace.com/map

Name ______________________________

Chapter Review/Test

Vocabulary

Match.

1. **ordered pairs**
2. **survey**
3. **impossible**

collect data on a question

will never happen

number pairs you use on a grid

Concepts and Skills

Use the data to answer the question.

4. How many children play soccer?

_______ children

5. How many more children play tennis than piano?

_______ more children

After-School Activities

tennis	☺ ☺ ☺
soccer	☺ ☺ ☺ ☺
piano	☺ ☺

Key: Each ☺ stands for 2 children.

Find the object on the grid.
Write the ordered pair.

6. (_____, _____)

7.  (_____, _____)

8.  (_____, _____)

Chapter Review/Test

Use the data to answer the question.

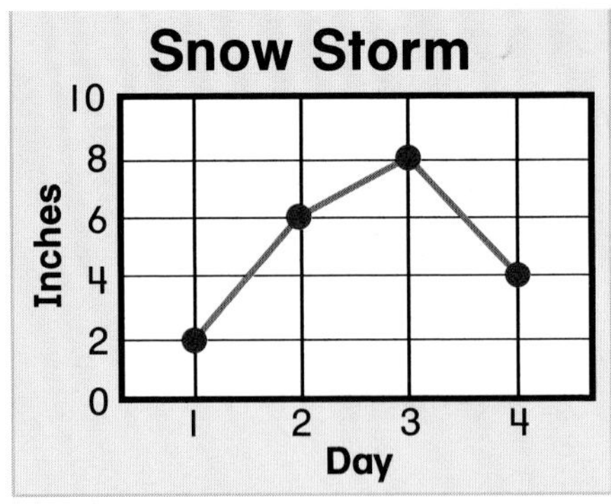

9. On which day did the most snow fall? ___________

10. How much more snow fell on Day 2 than on Day 1? ___________

Look at the bag of cubes.
How likely are you to pick a [cube] instead of a [cube]?

11. 

more likely

less likely

equally likely

12. 

more likely

less likely

equally likely

Look at the Venn diagram.
Use the data to answer the question.

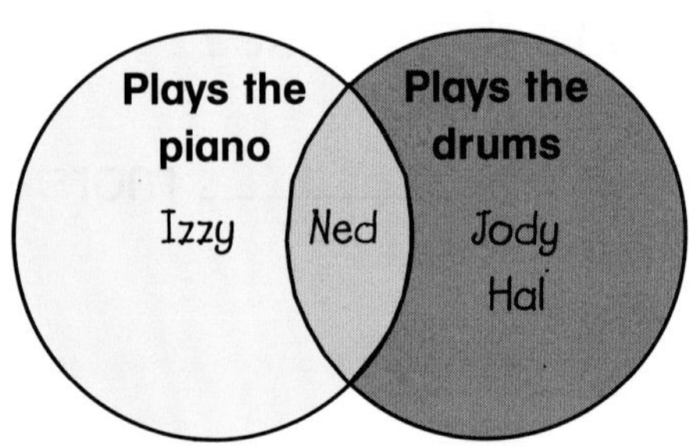

13. Who plays the drums and the piano?

____

Problem Solving

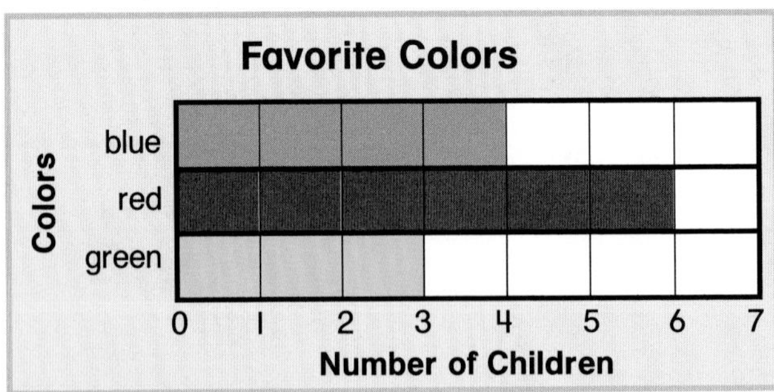

Use data in the graph to solve.

Draw or write to explain.

14. How many children choose their favorite color?

_____ children

15. How many more children like red than green?

_____ children

Enrichment

Name ______________________________

Number Puzzles

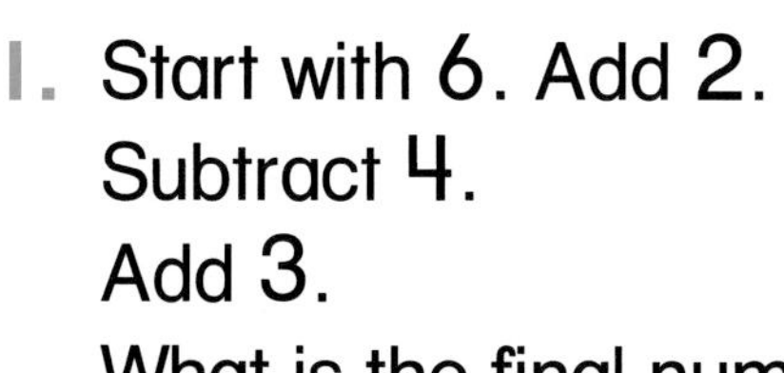

Read each puzzle.
Find the final number.
Write the number sentences to show your work.

Draw or write to explain.

1. Start with 6. Add 2.
   Subtract 4.
   Add 3.
   What is the final number? ____

2. Start with 14. Subtract 7.
   Subtract 3.
   Double the number.
   What is the final number? ____

3. Start with 15. Subtract 5.
   Add 6.
   Subtract 10.
   What is the final number? ____

4. Start with 8. Add 2.
   Subtract 6.
   Add 10.
   What is the final number? ____

Write Your Own

Write your own number puzzle.
Share it with a friend.

____

____

____

Education Place
Visit **eduplace.com/map** for brain teasers.

Calculator Number Hunt

Use a .

Find a number to add or subtract to complete the number sentence.

Write + or − .

Then write a number that completes the number sentence.

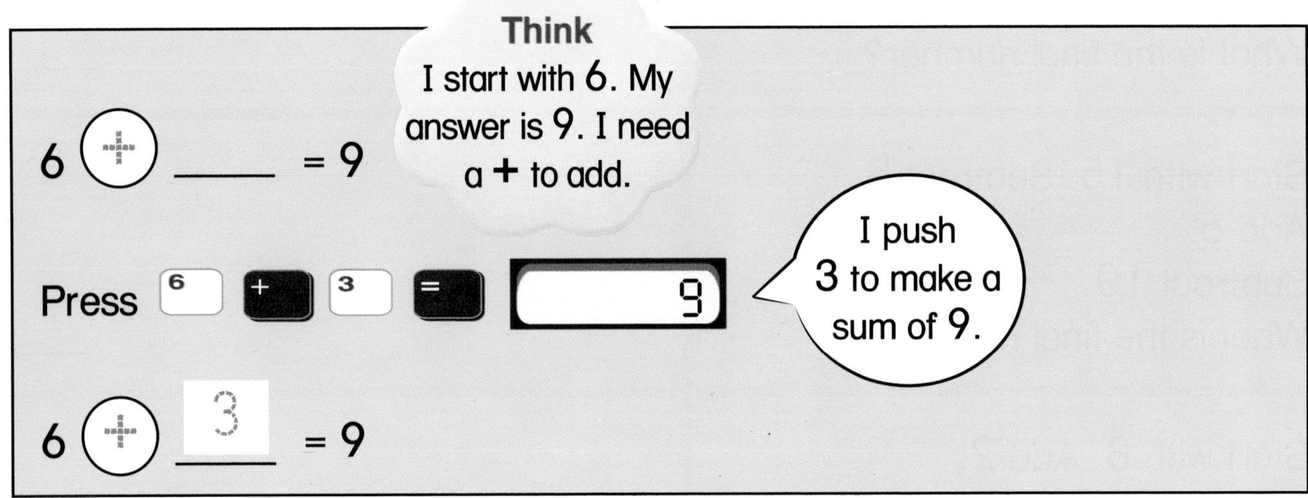

Complete the number sentence.

1. 8 ◯ ____ = 12
2. 2 ◯ ____ = 2
3. 15 ◯ ____ = 8
4. 6 ◯ ____ = 15
5. 14 ◯ ____ = 9
6. 18 ◯ ____ = 9

Talk About It How do you know if you should add or subtract?

Name ____________________

Vocabulary

Complete the sentence.

greater than
less than
survey

1. 14 is ____________ 11.

2. 4 is ____________ 8.

Concepts and Skills

Use the number line.
Complete the sentence.

30 31 32 33 34 35 36 37 38 39 40

3. 36 is one more than _____.

4. 32 is one less than _____.

Circle a group of ten. Then circle the best estimate.

5. 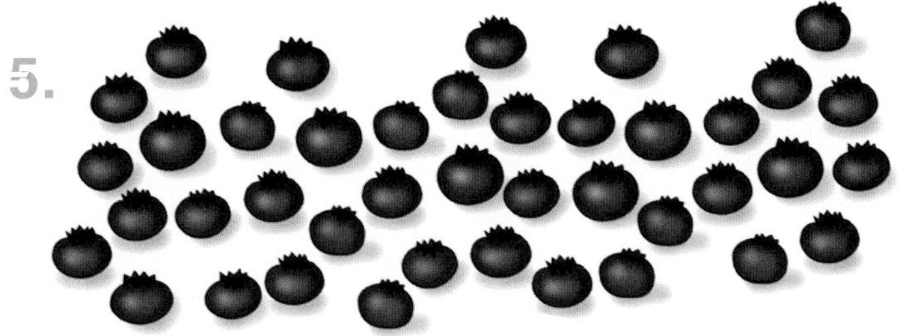

about 40 about 50

Add or subtract.

6. $\begin{array}{r} 8 \\ 4 \\ +\ 2 \\ \hline \end{array}$

7. $\begin{array}{r} 9 \\ -\ 4 \\ \hline \end{array}$

Complete the number sentences for the fact family.

8. 15 − ____ = 7 15 − 7 = ____

____ + 8 = 15 8 + ____ = 15

Use the data to answer the question.

9. How many pretzels were sold on Thursday?

____ pretzels

10. How many more pretzels were sold on Monday than Tuesday?

____ pretzels

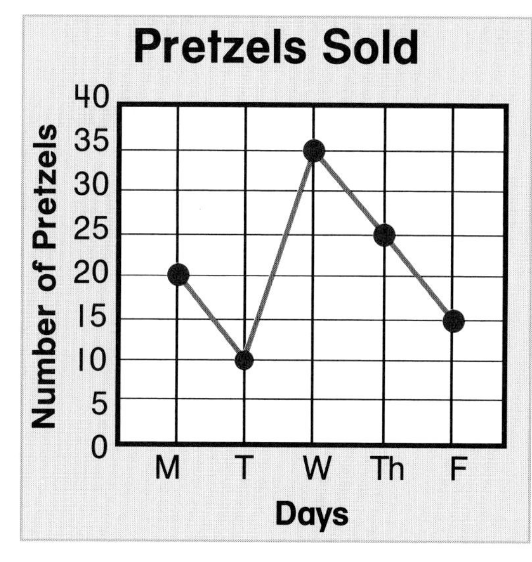

Unit 1 Test

Look at the graph.

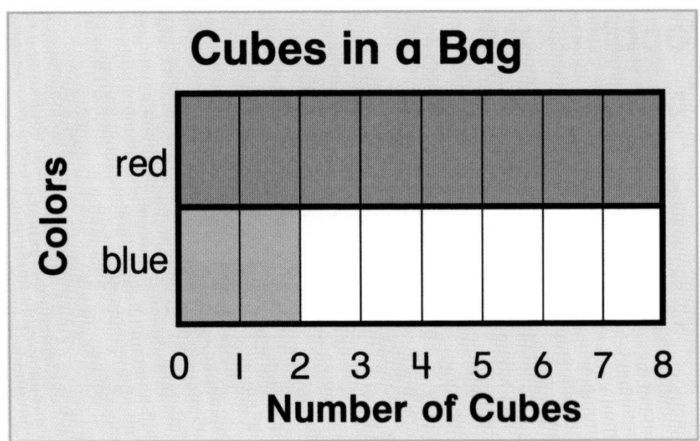

11. How likely are you to pick a red cube instead of a blue cube?

more likely   less likely   equally likely

Use the data in the graph to solve.

12. How many blue cubes are in the bag? _____ blue cubes

13. How many cubes are in the bag altogether? _____ cubes

Problem Solving

The park map is on a grid.
Find the object on the grid.
Circle the ordered pair.

14.    (4, 2)   (2, 4)

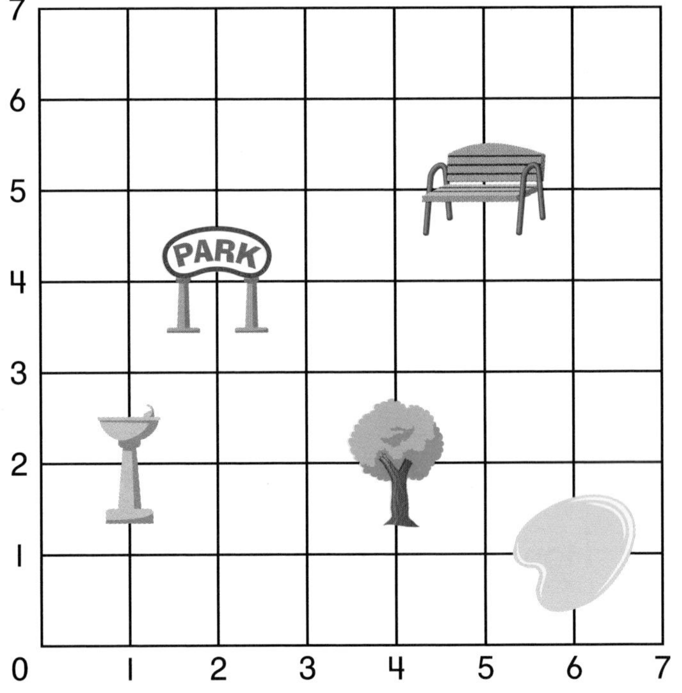

Use the park map.
Circle the more reasonable answer.

15. The dog runs from the PARK to the fountain. The cat runs from the PARK to the pond. Which runs farther?

dog   cat

Name________________________

Cumulative Test Prep

Test-Taking Tips

Read carefully to be sure you know what each question is asking.

Check to be sure you answered every question.

Multiple Choice

Fill in the ○ for the correct answer.

1. What is another name for 9 + 5?

   16 ○ 15 ○ 14 ○ 13 ○

2. Find the sum.

   9 + 5 + 1

   15 ○ 16 ○ 17 ○ 18 ○

3. Mark the related number sentence for 7 + 6 = 13.

   ○ 7 + 7 = 14
   ○ 13 − 8 = 5
   ○ 6 + 6 = 12
   ○ 13 − 7 = 6

4. Mark the number that comes just before 43.

   41 ○ 42 ○ 43 ○ 44 ○

Multiple Choice

Fill in the ○ for the correct answer. If the correct answer is not here, choose NH.

5. Ian has 9 pennies. He finds 2 more. How many pennies does he have?

11	12	13	NH
○	○	○	○

6. Mark the number shown here.

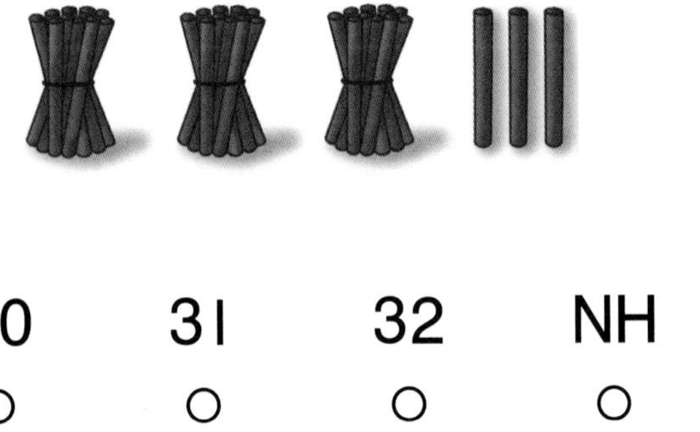

30	31	32	NH
○	○	○	○

7. Mark the number that completes the number sentence.

$$8 + \blacksquare = 15$$

6	7	8	NH
○	○	○	○

Open Response

Solve.

8. Pilar won 8 prizes. Kwan won 5 prizes. How many fewer prizes did Kwan win? Complete the number sentence.

_____ − _____ = _____

Use the pictograph to answer questions 9 and 10.

Games We Play

Game	Players
Hide and Seek	☺
Pop-the-Balloon	☺ ☺ ☺ ☺
Ring Toss	☺ ☺

Key: Each ☺ stands for two players.

9. Which game has the greatest number of players?

____

10. How many more players play Pop-the-Balloon than Ring Toss?

_____ more

Education Place
Look for Cumulative Test Prep
eduplace.com/map for more practice.

READING MATH

Going Bananas

Look back at the story to answer these questions.

● **1.** Look at page 6. How many peanuts would Hanna the elephant get if each bag had 2 peanuts rather than 5 peanuts?

▲ **2.** Which animal's lunch could be written as 1 ten and 2 ones?

☆ **3.** Look at page 7. What if Charlie gave 2 bananas to each of the other animals? Count backwards by 2 to see how many bananas he would have left.

▲ **4.** What animal would you like to feed at the zoo? What would you feed it? How would you count it?

Answers
1. 14 **2.** Tommy the Tortoise **3.** 2 **4.** Answers will vary.

Reading Strategies

● Cause and Effect
☆ Sequence of Events
▲ Noting Details
▲ Question

UNIT 2

What's for Lunch?

written by **Cindy Carlone**
illustrated by **Sheila Bailey**

Charlie the Monkey helps Mr. Lou feed the animals at the zoo. Bananas, peanuts, cabbage, meat, and fish are what animals like to eat.

How many boxes are on the cart?

1, 2, ___, ___, ___

"Mr. Lou," Charlie started to say,
"Why did we have bananas today?
Momma Seal, Rory, Tommy, and Hanna—
not one of them wanted to eat a banana!"

Mr. Lou smiled and held up the bunch.
"I wonder what monkeys are having for lunch."
Then Charlie smiled. "Oh, now I see!
Hooray! These bananas are meant for me!"

Count the number of bananas that Charlie gets.

1, 2, 3, 4, 5, ___, ___, ___, ___, ___

Hanna the Elephant also says no
to bananas—they just don't help elephants grow!
"Hay and carrots are fun to munch,
but peanuts are better, especially for lunch."

Count the number of peanuts Hanna gets by 5s.

5, 10, 15, 20, ____, ____, ____

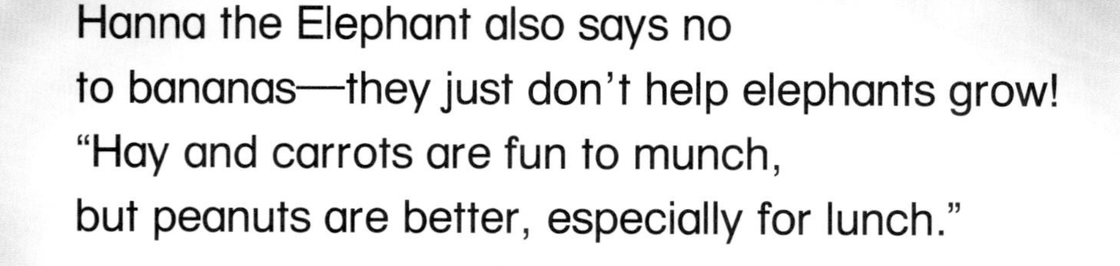

Momma Seal is the first to get lunch.
"Would you like a banana from this bunch?"
"Oh no, Charlie, that is not my wish.
What I want are some great-big fish."

Count the fish by 2s.

2, ____, ____

Charlie tosses bananas through the door
to Rory the Lion, who starts to roar.
"Bananas are fine, but lions don't eat them.
We'd rather have steaks—you just can't beat them!"

Count the number of steaks by 2s.

2, 4, ___, ___, ___

Tommy the Tortoise is next to be fed.
He sees the bananas, then shakes his head.
"When I'm hungry, Charlie, what I like to eat
are cabbages and greens—but nothing sweet."

Count the number of cabbages that Tommy eats by 2s.

2, 4, 6, ___, ___, ___

Numbers Through 100

From the Read-Aloud Anthology

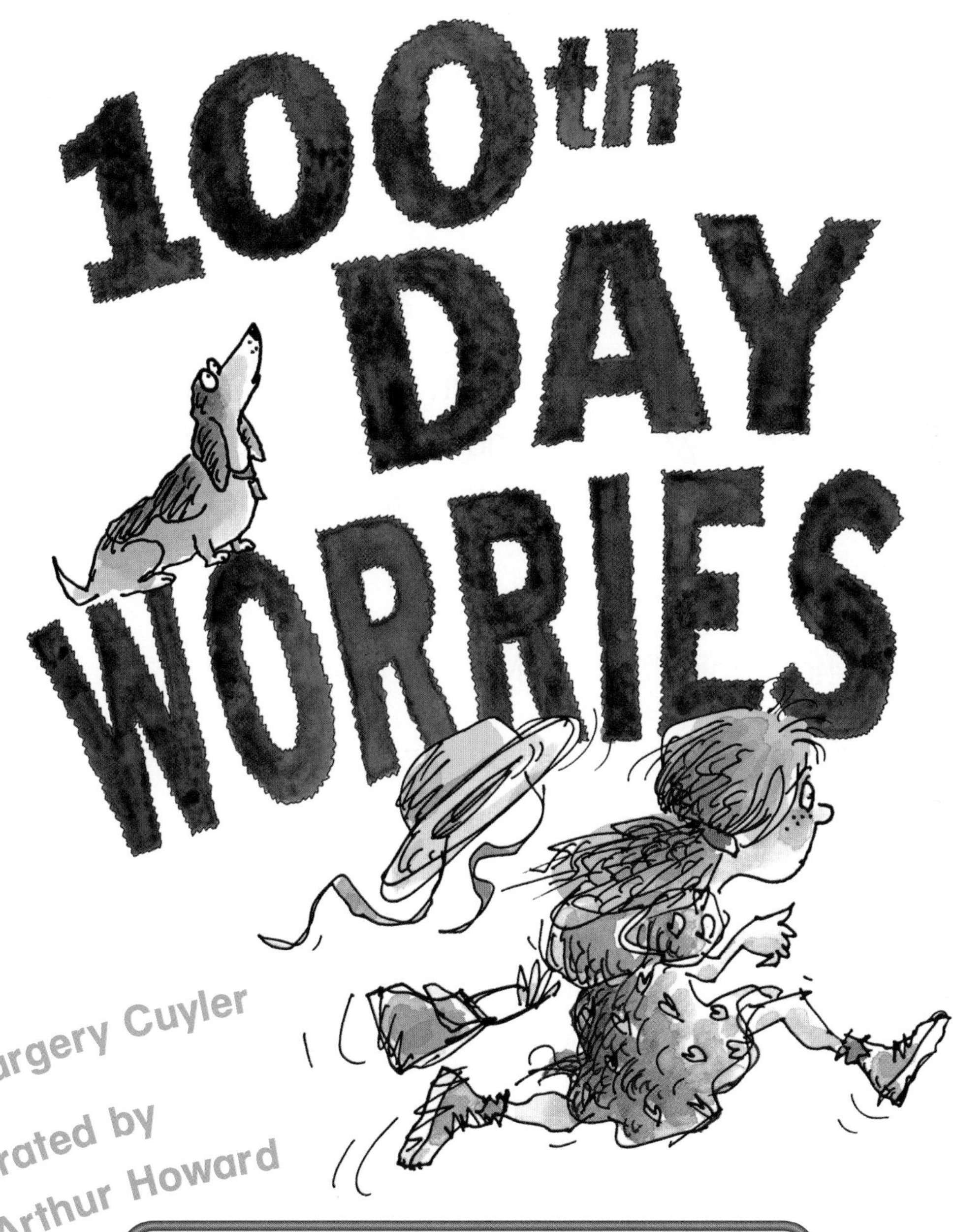

Access Prior Knowledge

This story will help you review

- Sorting and classifying
- Ways to make 10
- Grouping and counting

After story hour, Mr. Martin said it was time to put their 100 things out in the hall. "What did you bring, Jessica?" he asked.

"Here are 10 ribbons from my dad," she said.

"10?" asked Mr. Martin.

"And 10 screws from my mom," said Jessica.

The other kids came over to look.

"And 10 erasers from my brother and 10 beads from my sister," said Jessica.

"Pretty," said Anita.

"And here are 10 buttons from my father, and 10 pennies and 10 nickels from my mother, and 10 barrettes from my sister, and 10 rocks from my brother's iguana's aquarium," said Jessica.

"Cool," said Leslie.

"And what's this?" asked Mr. Martin.

"It's 10 kisses from my mom," said Jessica. "See?"

"I brought in 100 things my family gave me," said Jessica. "Is that okay?"

"Wow!" said Mr. Martin. "I've seen a lot of great collections for the 100th day of school, but this one—"

Jessica swallowed.

"This one is really special," said Mr. Martin. "You've brought in ...100 bits of love!"

Name ______________________

Think
3 red,
2 green, 2 yellow,
2 purple, and
1 striped

Work with a partner.
Use the picture of Jessica's collection on page 119c.
Complete the number sentence to describe the group of 10.

1. ribbons by color 3 + 2 + 2 + 2 + 1 = 10

2. screws by size ____ + ____ + ____ + ____ = 10

3. buttons by color ____ + ____ + ____ = 10

Write how many of each thing.
Count by 10s.
Write how many in all.

4. ____ screws, ____ buttons, ____ barrettes,

____ rocks, ____ kisses, ____ ribbons,

____ pennies, ____ nickels ____ in all

5. **Create and Solve** Think of 10 different small things such as grains of rice, beads, push pins, and so on. Draw 10 of each thing. Count by 10s to check that your collection shows 100.

Dear Family,

My class is starting Unit 2. I will be learning about place value, patterns, and numbers to 100. These pages show some of what I will learn and have activities for us to do together.

From, ______________________

Vocabulary

These are some words I will use in this unit.

digit Any of the symbols 0, 1, 2, 3, 4, 5, 6, 7, 8, 9

ordinal numbers Numbers used to show order or position

1st, 2nd, 3rd... are ordinal numbers.

even number A number where you make groups of two and have none left over

8 is an even number.

repeating pattern A pattern that has a part that is repeated over and over again

1 2 3 1 2 3 1 2 3
(1 2 3 is the pattern unit that repeats)

odd number A number where you make groups of two and have one left over

7 is an odd number.

growing pattern A pattern that increases or decreases by the same amount

5 10 15 20 25 30
(Add 5 to get the next number.)

Some other words I will use are **just before**, **just after**, **between**, **pattern unit**, and **place value.**

Vocabulary Activity

Let's work together to complete these sentences.

1. 9 is an ______________ number.

2. 4th is an example of an ______________ number.

How To find the value of a digit

To find the value of a digit, find the value of the place it is in.

Find the value of the digits in 72.

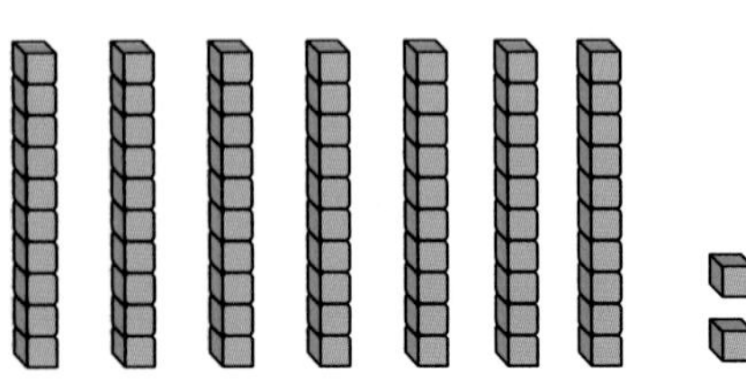

72

Tens	Ones
7	2

The number 72 has two digits, 7 and 2.

7 tens and 2 ones

The value of 7 tens is 70.   70 + 2   The value of 2 ones is 2.

 Literature

These books link to the math in this unit. We can look for them at the library.

Spunky Monkeys on Parade
by Stuart J. Murphy
Illustrated by Lynne Cravath
(HarperCollins, 1999)

One Hundred Hungry Ants
by Elinor J. Pinczes

mama provi and the pot of rice
by Sylvia Rosa-Casanova

Education Place

We can visit *Education Place* at

eduplace.com/maf

for the Math Lingo game, *e*•Glossary, and more games and activities to do together.

Place Value

INVESTIGATION

Find groups of 10 on the page.
Find groups with less than 10.
How many ways can you write the number of all things?

THE HOBBY HOUSE

DeAngelo rides to the Hobby House. He travels 9 blocks. Circle the path DeAngelo takes.

blue path orange path red path

Can you find another path with 9 blocks?

Start

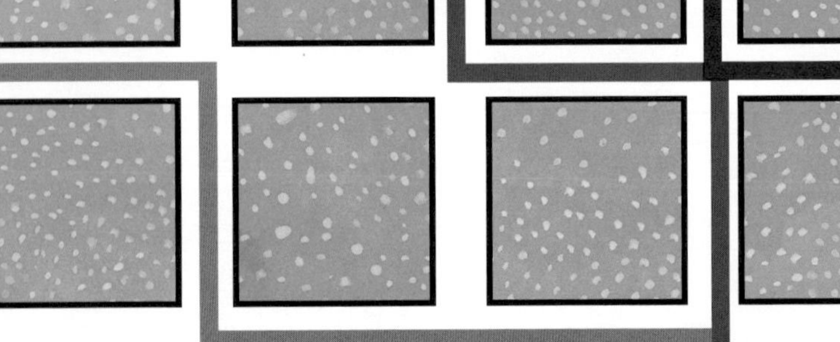

⊢ 1 Block ⊣

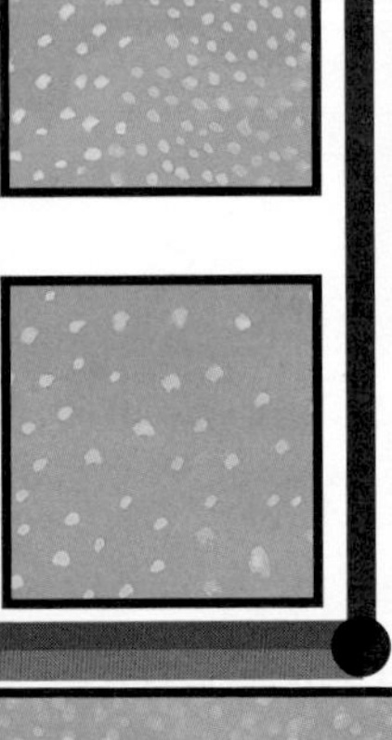

Talk About It Is the path DeAngelo took the shortest route? Why or why not?

End

Name ____________________________________

Tens Through 100

You can show a number using **tens**.
Count by tens to find the **value**.

Objective
Count, read, and write tens.

Vocabulary
tens
value

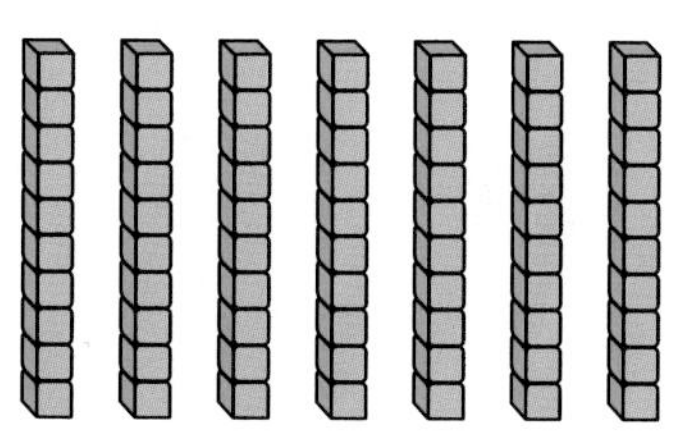

7 **tens** = 70

Guided Practice

Write the number of tens.
Then write the value.

1. Think: I count by tens to find the value.

_____ tens
_____
thirty

2. 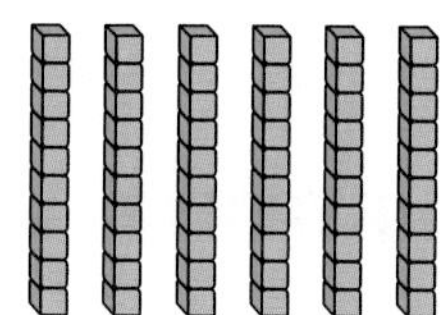

_____ tens
_____
forty

3. 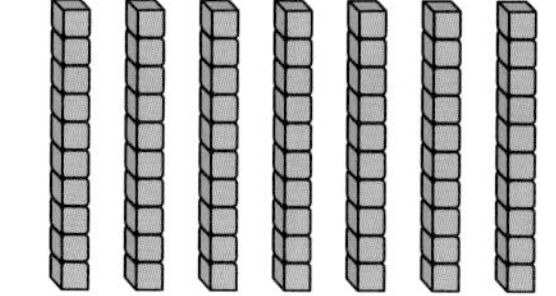

_____ tens
_____
fifty

4. 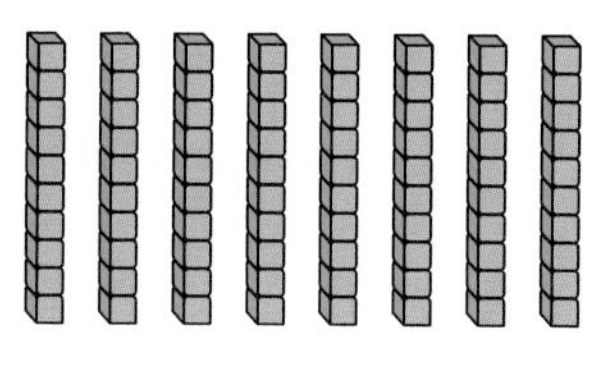

_____ tens
_____
sixty

5. 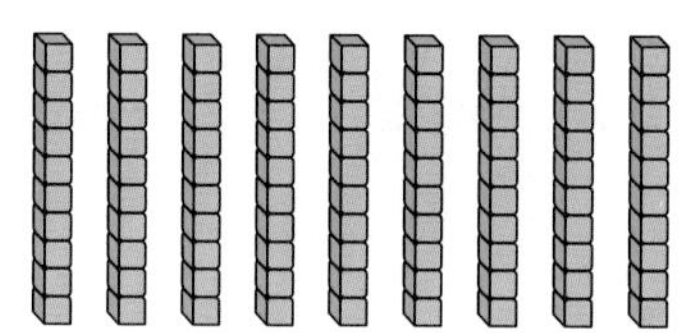

_____ tens
_____
seventy

6. 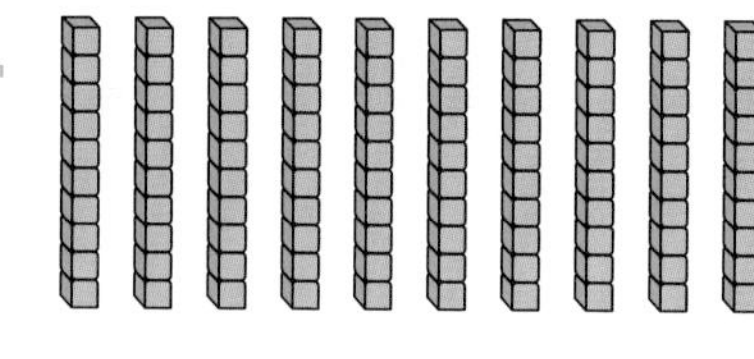

_____ tens
_____
eighty

7. _____ tens
_____
ninety

8. _____ tens
_____
one hundred

Explain Your Thinking What pattern do you see in the numbers you wrote above?

Practice

Remember
Think 10 more when you count by tens.

Write the number of tens.
Then write the value.

1. 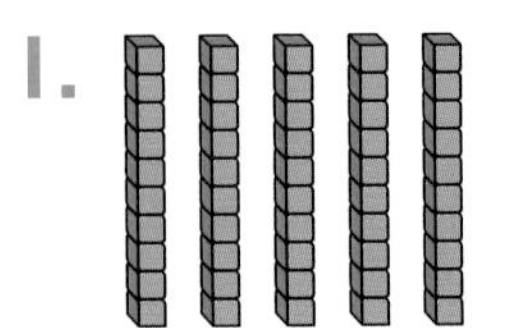

5 tens

50

fifty

2. 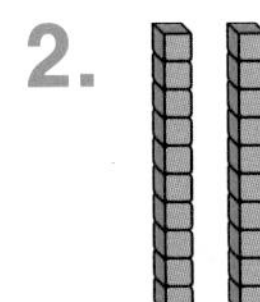

_____ tens

_____

twenty

3. 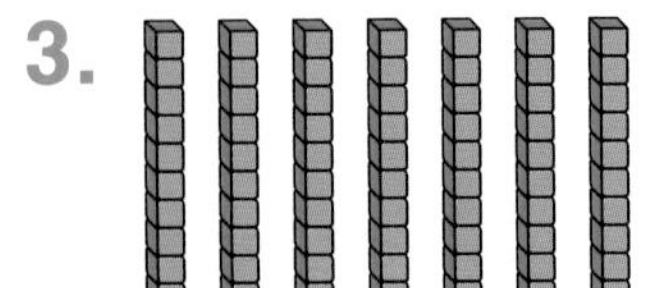

_____ tens

_____

seventy

4. _____ tens

_____

ninety

5. 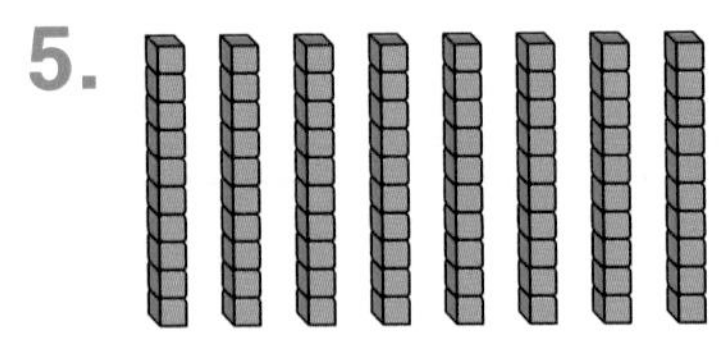

_____ tens

_____

eighty

6. 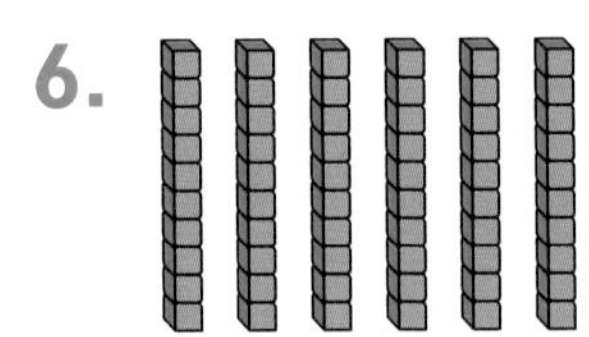

_____ tens

_____

sixty

7. Write the missing numbers.

100 90 _____ _____ 60 50 _____ _____ _____ 10

Algebra Readiness ▶ Patterns

8. Continue the pattern.

22	32	42	_____	_____	_____

9. **Talk About It** Describe the pattern.

At Home Say numbers that are less than one hundred. Ask your child how many tens are in each number.

Name ______________________________

Tens and Ones to 100

You can show a number using tens and **ones**.

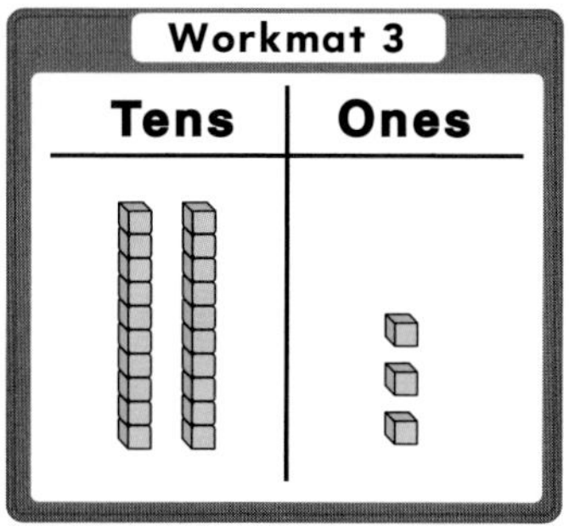

Objective
Use tens and ones models to show numbers to 100.

Vocabulary
ones

Workmat 3

Tens	Ones
2	3

23

twenty-three

Guided Practice

Complete the chart.

	Count how many.	Write the tens and ones.	Write the number.
1.	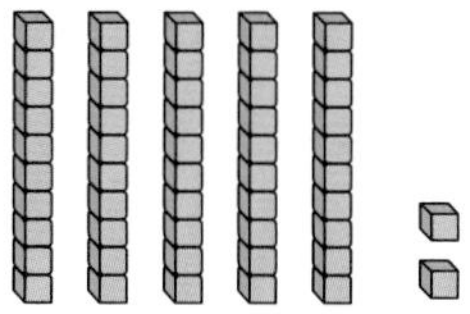	Tens / Ones	______ fifty-two
2.	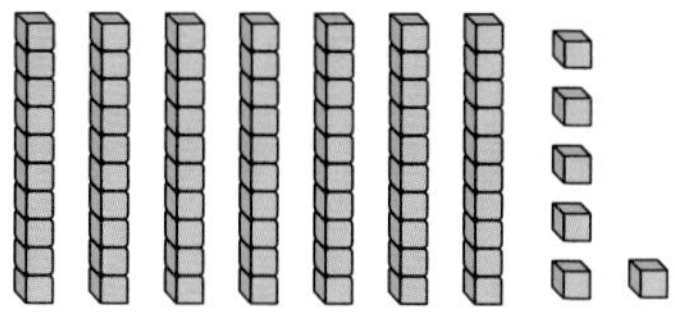	Tens / Ones	______ seventy-six
3.	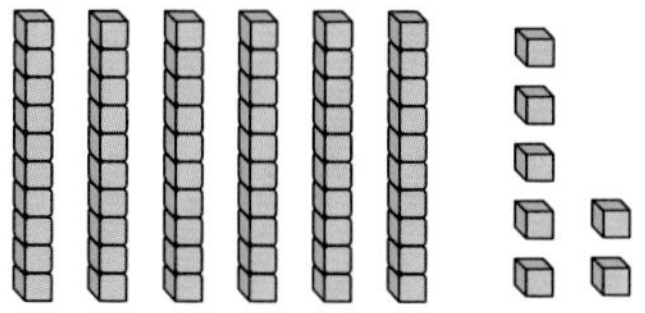	Tens / Ones	______ sixty-seven
4.	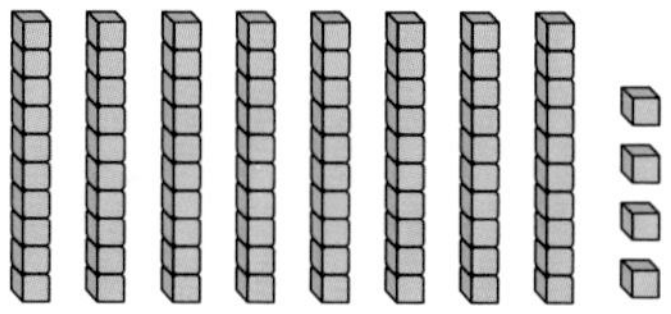	Tens / Ones	______ eighty-four

Explain Your Thinking How is 76 different from 67?

Practice

Complete the chart.

	Count how many.	Write the tens and ones.	Write the number.
1.		Tens: 4, Ones: 3	43 forty-three
2.		Tens: ___ Ones: ___	___ thirty-five
3.		Tens: ___ Ones: ___	___ ninety
4.		Tens: ___ Ones: ___	___ eighty-seven

Problem Solving ▶ Reasoning

5. Kayla counts her stickers. She puts them in 3 groups of ten and has 2 stickers left over. How many stickers does Kayla have?

Draw or write to explain.

_____ stickers

At Home Use bundles of 10 objects such as toothpicks and some loose toothpicks. Say a number such as 45. Ask your child to show you the number and say how many tens and ones.

Name ________________________________

Identify Place Value

 **Audio Tutor 1**/13 Listen and Understand

Objective
Identify the value of the tens and ones digits of numbers.

Vocabulary
digit
place

To find the value of a **digit**,
find the value of the **place** it is in.

Find the value of each digit in 78.

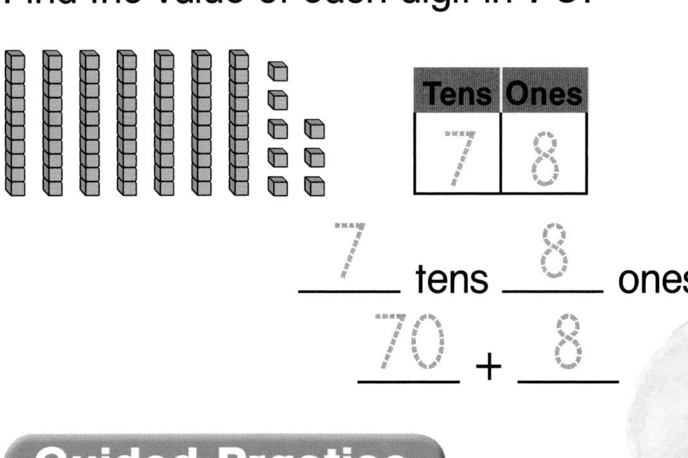

Tens	Ones
7	8

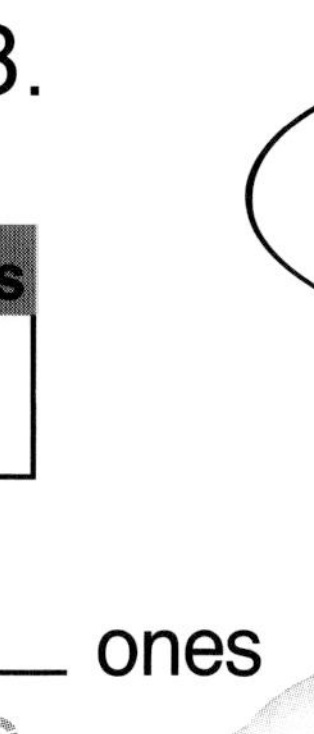

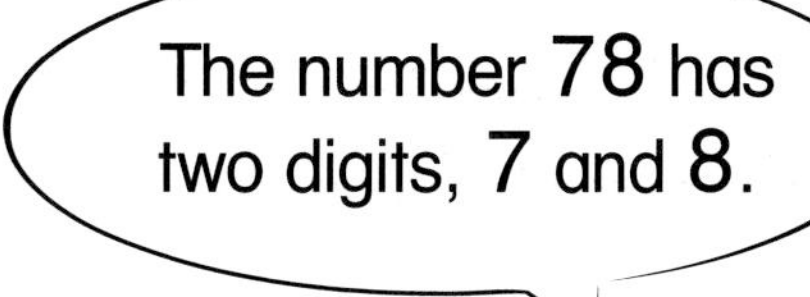

7 tens 8 ones

70 + 8

Guided Practice

Complete the chart.

	Count how many.	Write the tens and ones.	Write the values.	Write the number.
1.		______ tens ______ ones	______ + ______	______
2.		______ tens ______ ones	______ + ______	______

Circle the value of the red digit.

3. 63
60 6

4. 94
40 4

5. 19
1 10

Explain Your Thinking Why does the digit 0 have a value of 0 in the number 40?

Practice

Remember
To find the value of a digit, find the value of its place.

Complete the chart.

	Count how many.	Write the tens and ones.	Write the values.	Write the number.
1.		3 tens 1 ones	30 + 1	31
2.		____ tens ____ ones	____ + ____	____
3.		____ tens ____ ones	____ + ____	____

Circle the value of the red digit.

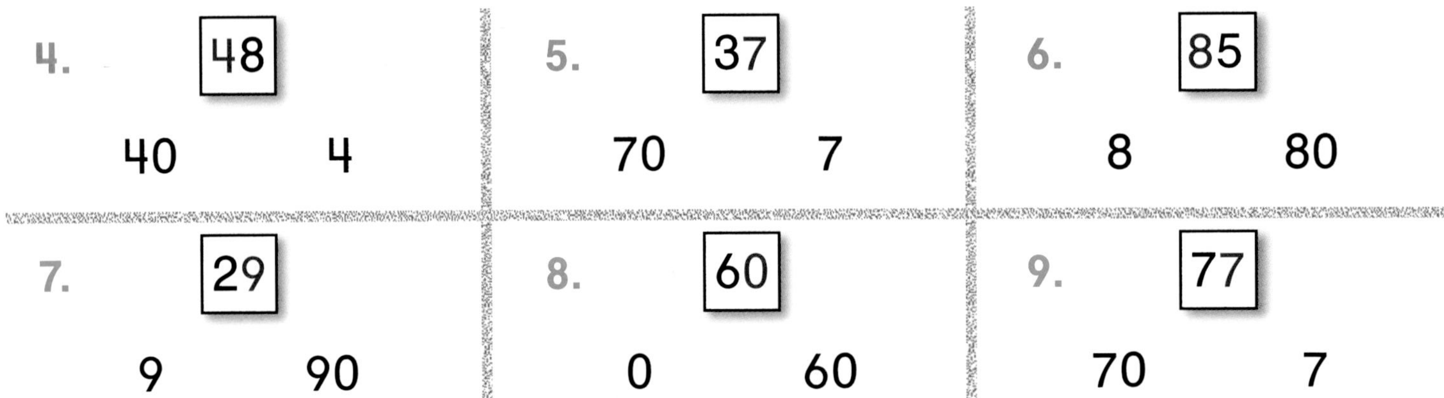

4. 48 — 40 4

5. 37 — 70 7

6. 85 — 8 80

7. 29 — 9 90

8. 60 — 0 60

9. 77 — 70 7

Problem Solving ▶ Number Sense

10. I have more ones than tens.
The value of my tens digit is 70.
What two numbers could I be? ______ or ______

11. **Talk About It** Explain how you decided what numbers fit the clues.

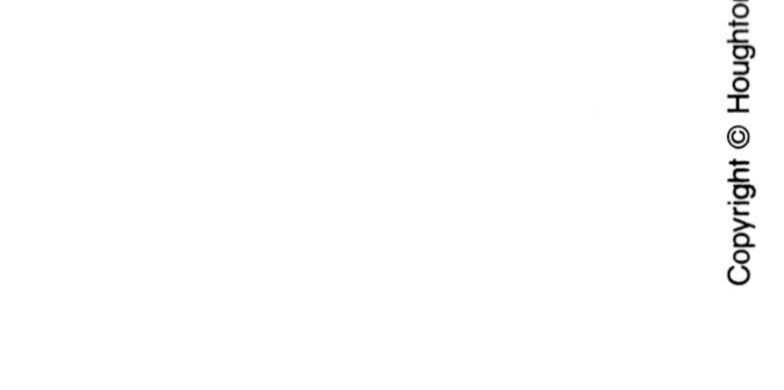

At Home Ask your child how many tens and ones there are in two-digit numbers such as 39 and 52.

Game

Activity

Name ______________________

Color to Match

1 Player

What You Need: crayons

56	red
41	orange
28	dark blue
35	brown
77	green
69	light blue
83	yellow
94	purple

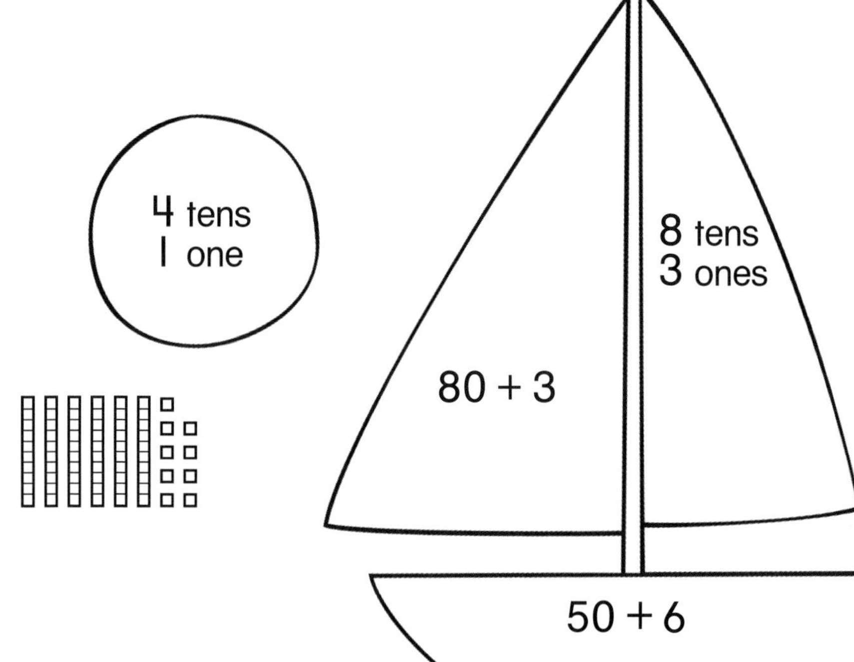

60 + 9

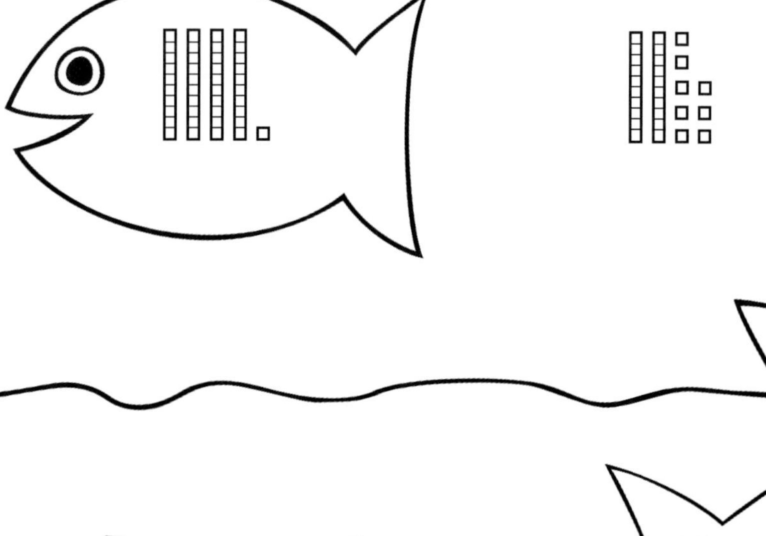

70 + 7

9 tens
4 ones

3 tens
5 ones

Quick Check

Write the number of tens.
Then write the value.

1. ______ tens

______
sixty

2. 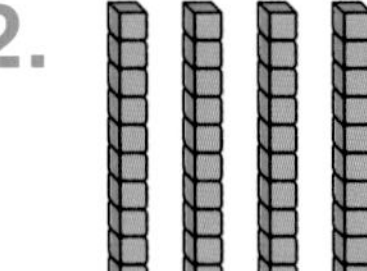 ______ tens

______
forty

Complete the charts.

	Count how many.	Write the tens and ones.	Write the number.
3.		Tens / Ones	______ forty-nine
4.		Tens / Ones	______ seventy-five

	Count how many.	Write the tens and ones.	Write the value of each digit.	Write the number.
5.		______ tens ______ ones	______ + ______	______
6.		______ tens ______ ones	______ + ______	______

Circle the value of the red digit.

7. 

4 40

8. 85

50 5

9. 78

7 70

Name ____________________

Different Ways to Show Numbers

 **Audio Tutor 1/14 Listen and Understand**

Objective
Show numbers in different forms — words, models, and expanded form.

You can show a number in different ways.
These are some ways to show 34.

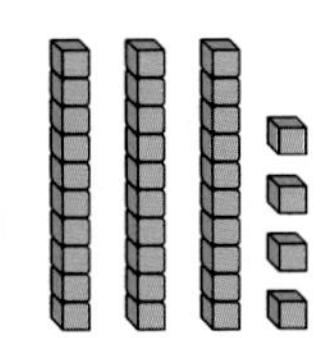	  	3 tens 4 ones	30 + 4

Guided Practice

Circle a way to show the number.

Think
I know that the number 31 has 3 tens.

1. **31** 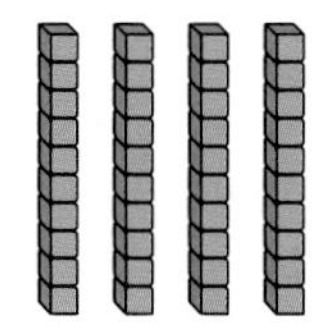 3 tens 1 one

2. **54** 50 + 4 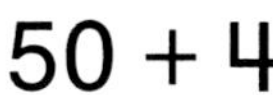     

3. **60** 60 + 10 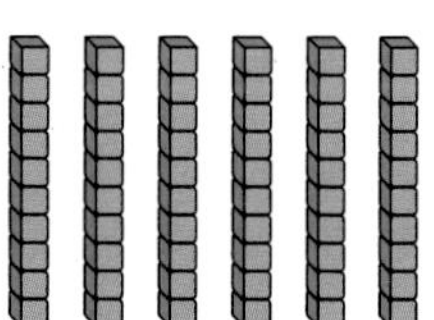

4. **29**    9 tens 2 ones

5. **57** 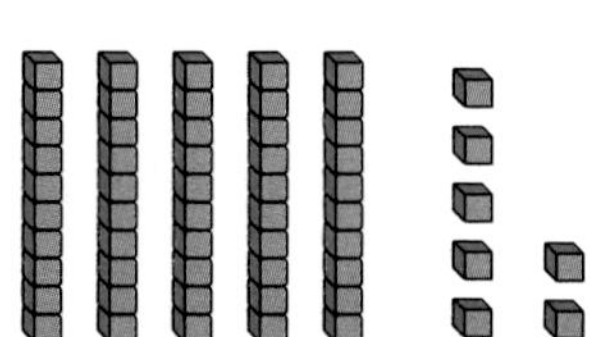 5 tens 2 ones

Explain Your Thinking In what other way can you show the number 57?

Practice

Remember
Think about how many tens and ones are in the number.

Circle two ways to show the number.

1. 72 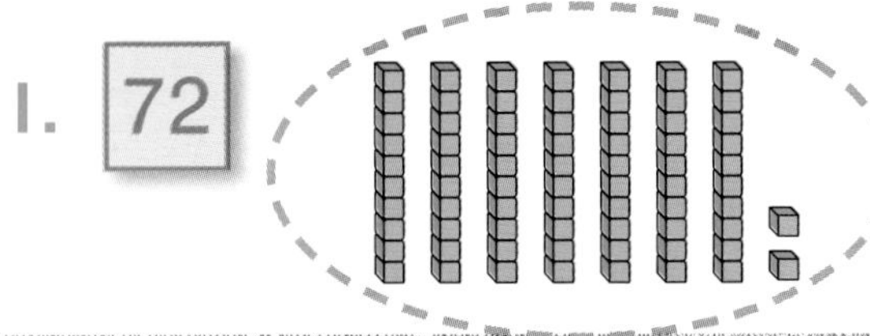 2 tens 7 ones 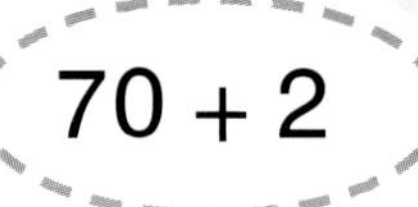 70 + 2

2. 33 3 tens 3 ones 30 + 3   

3. 67 7 tens 6 ones 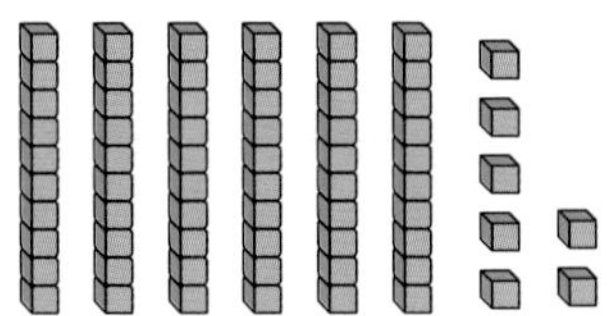 60 + 7

4. 28  20 + 30  

5. 56 50 + 6 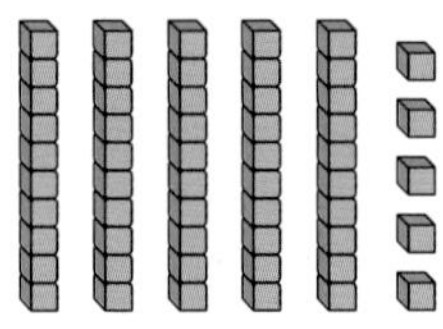 5 tens 6 ones

6. 43 4 + 30 4 tens 3 ones 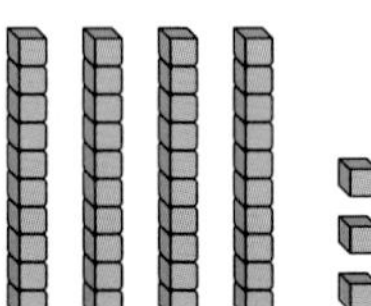

Problem Solving ▶ Number Sense

7. Show the number 42 in two different ways.

At Home Ask your child to draw two ways to show the number 35.

Name ________________________________

Compare Two-Digit Numbers

 **Audio Tutor 1**/15 Listen and Understand

Objective
Compare two-digit numbers using the symbols >, <, or =.

Vocabulary
greater than
less than
equal to

Use these symbols to compare numbers.

> greater than
< less than
= equal to

Compare 34 and 25.
First compare tens.

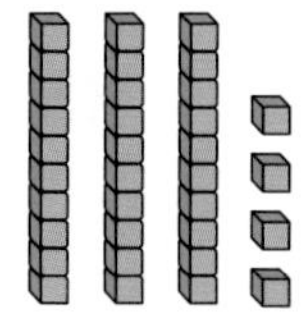 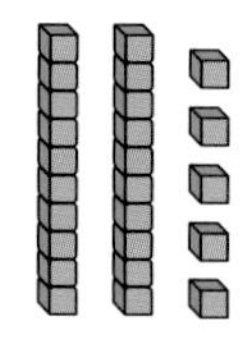

34 25

3 tens is greater than 2 tens.
34 is **greater than** 25.
$34 > 25$

Compare 45 and 46.
First compare tens. If the tens are the same, compare the ones.

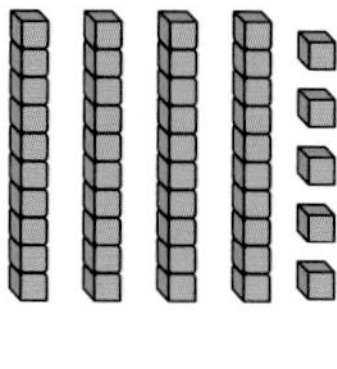 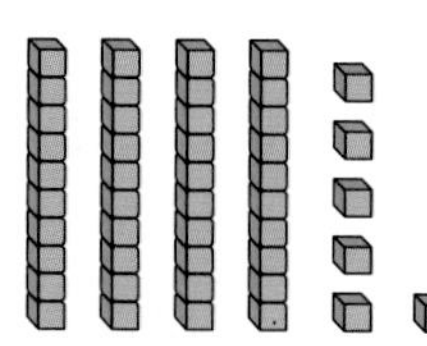

45 46

5 ones is less than 6 ones.
45 is **less than** 46.
$45 < 46$

Guided Practice

Write the numbers.
Compare.
Write **>**, **<**, or **=**.

Think
The tens and ones are the same.

1. 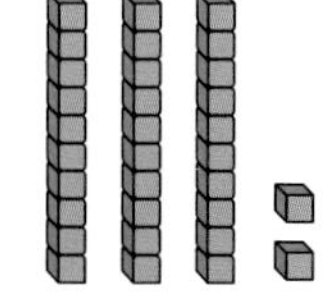 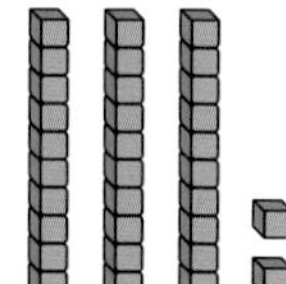

32 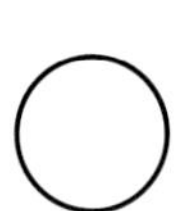 32

2. 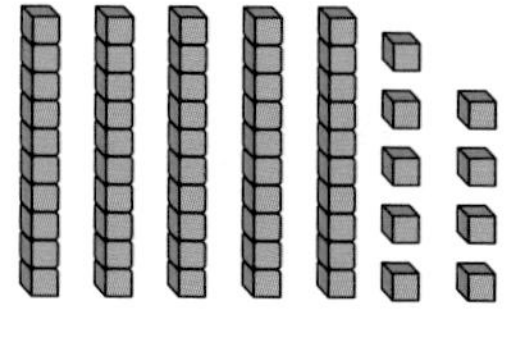

____ 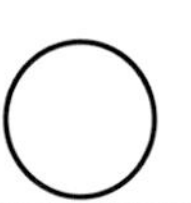 ____

Write **>**, **<**, or **=**.

3. 87 ◯ 68

4. 65 ◯ 59

5. 19 ◯ 41

Explain Your Thinking Did you need to compare the ones in Exercise 5? Why?

Practice

First compare the tens. Then, if you need to, compare the ones.

Write the numbers. Compare.
Write >, <, or =.

1. 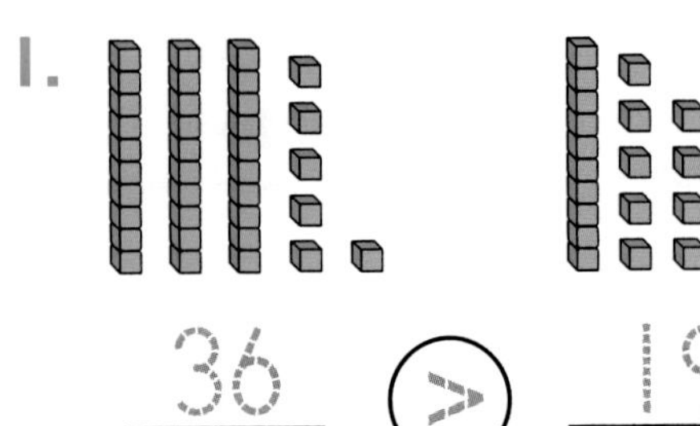

36 (>) 19

2. 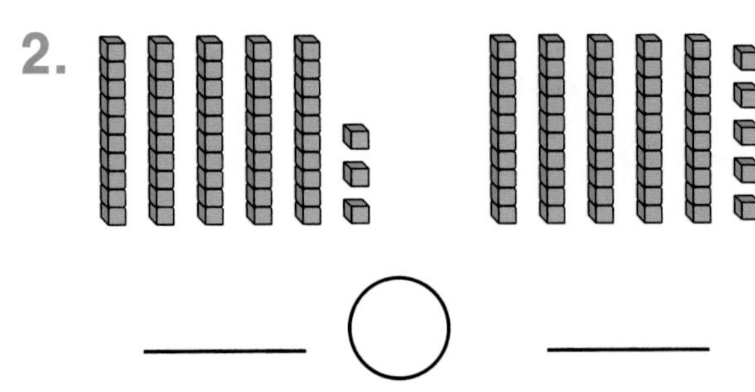

____ ○ ____

Write >, <, or =.

3. 53 ○ 53
4. 62 ○ 57
5. 85 ○ 88
6. 24 ○ 29
7. 89 ○ 95
8. 52 ○ 35
9. 43 ○ 24
10. 23 ○ 19
11. 18 ○ 61
12. 55 ○ 45
13. 81 ○ 81
14. 92 ○ 59

Problem Solving ▶ Number Sense

15. Shawn has 3 dimes and 5 pennies. Laura has 3 dimes and 8 pennies. Who has more money?

Draw or write to explain.

__________ has more money.

At Home Have your child choose two numbers between 10 and 100 and tell which number is greater.

Name ____________________

Reasonable Answers

Objective
Tell if an answer is reasonable and explain the answer.

Problem Solving

Choose the most reasonable answer.

Alex can hold 8 crayons in one hand. Rosa can hold more.

About how many crayons can Rosa hold in one hand?

4 crayons

14 crayons

44 crayons

THINK

Do I need to add or subtract?

What choices could be the answer?

Which number is the reasonable answer?

DECIDE

Neither. I need to find a number that is greater than 8.

14 or 44

I know that 4 does not make sense because it is less than 8.

14 is the most reasonable answer because it would be too hard to hold 44 crayons in one hand.

Rosa can hold about 14 crayons in one hand.

Guided Practice

Circle the most reasonable answer.

Draw or write to explain.

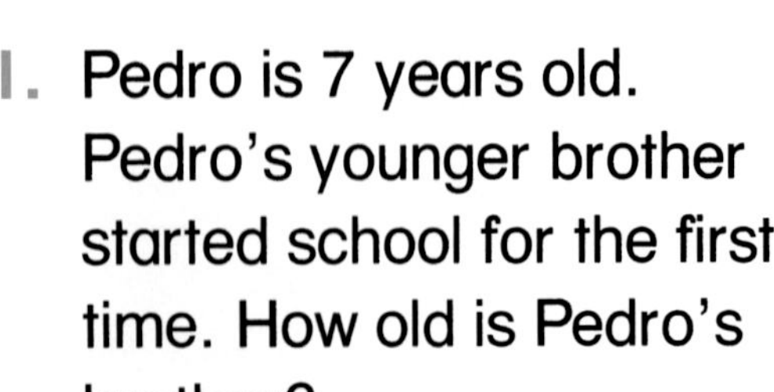

1. Pedro is 7 years old. Pedro's younger brother started school for the first time. How old is Pedro's brother?

Think
How old are you when you start school?

1 year old 5 years old 44 years old

2. Cara and Jamal collect baseball cards. Jamal has 28 cards. Cara has a few more cards than Jamal. About how many cards could she have?

Think
I look for a number a little greater than 28.

10 cards 31 cards 80 cards

Practice

3. Last year in Ms. Roy's first-grade class there were 20 children. This year she has more children. How many children does she have in her class?

18 children 24 children 84 children

4. Sally buys two model cars. She puts them on a shelf with the rest of her collection. How many model cars does she have now?

1 model 3 models 10 models

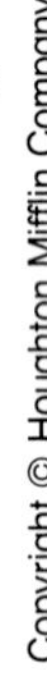

At Home Ask your child to explain why the answers he or she chose are reasonable.

Name ____________________

Now Try This What Is Equal?

Use these symbols to compare numbers.

= equal to
≠ not equal to

Write the numbers.
Compare.
Write = or ≠.

1\. 3 tens 2 ones 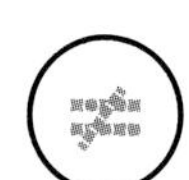

32 ≠ 23

2\. 5 tens 1 one   40 + 8

____ ◯ ____

3\. 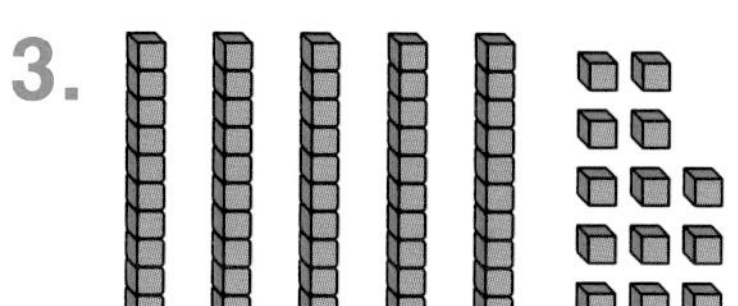 60 + 3

____ ◯ ____

4\. 70 + 7 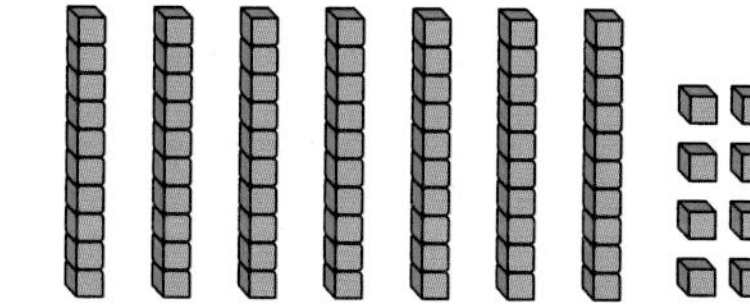

____ ◯ ____

5\. 70 + 9   8 tens 3 ones

____ ◯ ____

6\. 9 tens 6 ones   60 + 9

____ ◯ ____

7\. **Write About It** Write numbers in different ways for your friend to compare using = and ≠.

____

____

Activity

Math Challenge

Tile Artist

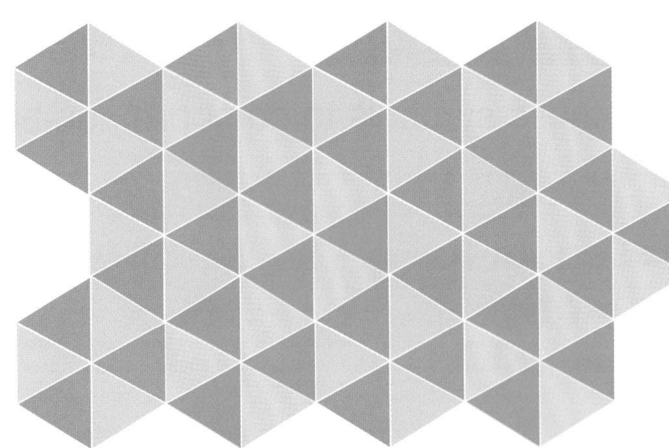

A tessellation is a group of shapes that fit together to make a pattern.

This tessellation is made using tiles on a kitchen floor.

Use ▲ to make a tessellation. Then trace.

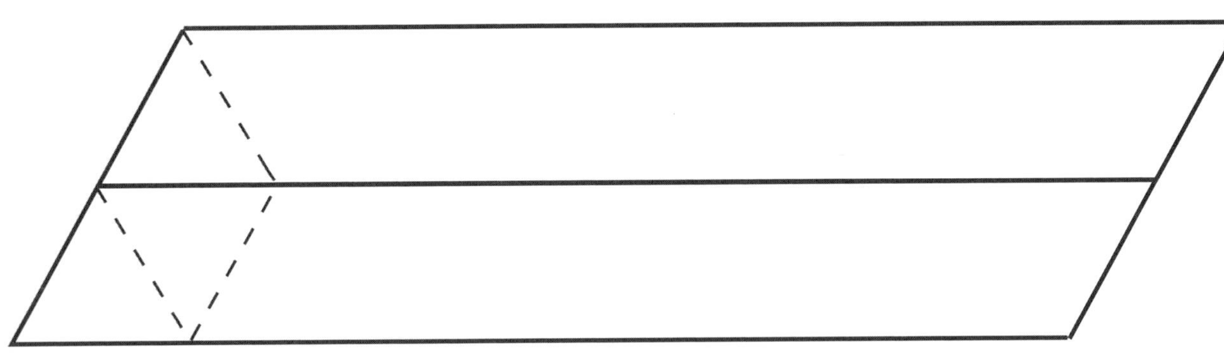

How many triangles does it take to cover this section? _____ triangles

Color your triangles to make a pattern.

Key Topic Review

Facts

Add or subtract.

1. 6 − 4 = _____
2. 3 + 5 = _____
3. 11 − 6 = _____
4. 9 − 8 = _____
5. 12 − 5 = _____
6. 10 + 4 = _____
7. 4 + 7 = _____
8. 12 − 3 = _____
9. 6 + 6 = _____
10. 17 − 9 = _____
11. 7 + 9 = _____
12. 13 − 7 = _____

Extra Practice at eduplace.com/map

Name ____________________

Chapter Review/Test

Vocabulary

Use the word in a sentence.

1. **tens** ______________________________

____

2. **equal to** ______________________________

____

Concepts and Skills

Write the number of tens. Then write the value.

3. ____ tens

____ fifty

4. 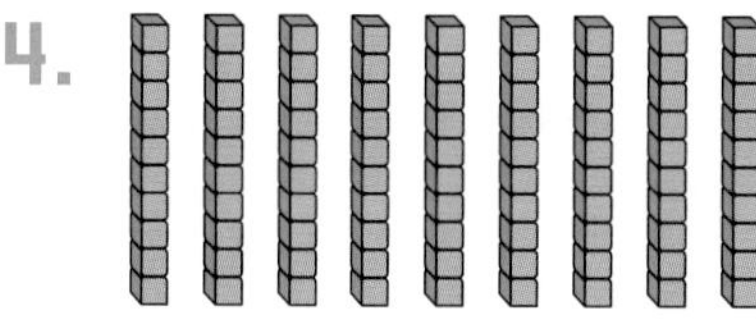

____ tens

____ ninety

Write the tens and ones. Write the number.

5. 5 tens 4 ones

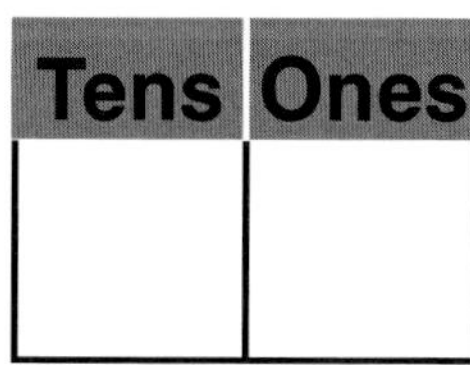

____ fifty-four

6. 3 tens 8 ones

Tens	Ones

____ thirty-eight

Complete the chart.

	Count how many.	Write the tens and ones.	Write the value of each digit.	Write the number.
7.		____ tens ____ ones	____ + ____	____
8.		____ tens ____ ones	____ + ____	____

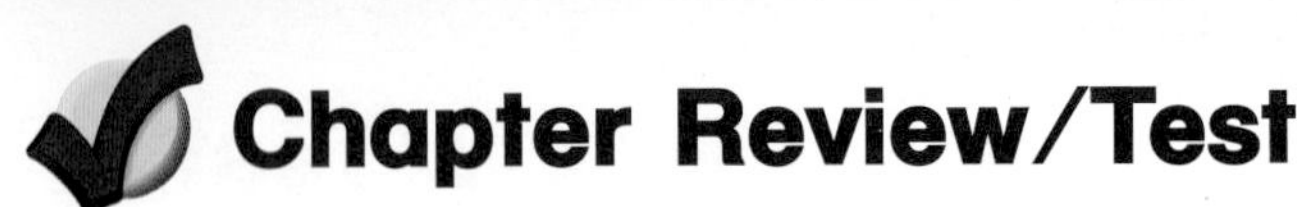

Chapter Review/Test

Circle the value of the red digit.

9.  25

50   5

10. 81

80   8

Circle two ways to show the number.

11. 57

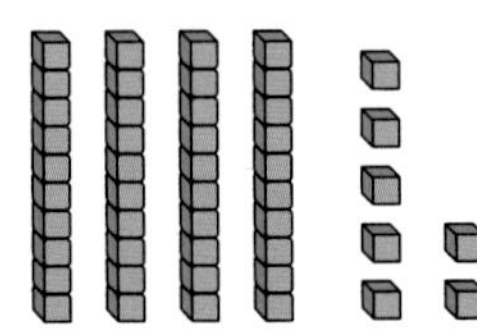

50 + 7

5 tens 7 ones

12. 18

10 + 8

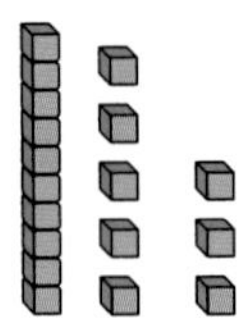

1 + 80

Compare the numbers.
Write >, <, or =.

13. 76 ◯ 67

14. 36 ◯ 46

Problem Solving

Circle the most reasonable answer.

15. Mr. Lee and Mrs. Joy collect pins. Mr. Lee has about 50 pins. Mrs. Joy has almost the same number of pins as Mr. Lee. About how many pins does she have?

Draw or write to explain.

60 pins   41 pins   47 pins

CHAPTER 6

Number Concepts and Patterns

INVESTIGATION

What are the different ways you can count the groups in this picture?

People Using Math

Alvin Ailey

Alvin was born in Texas and moved to Los Angeles with his mother. He began dancing in high school. After dancing for several years, Alvin formed his own dance company and performed all over the world. Alvin created more than 75 ballets during his lifetime.

In 1988, he was given a lifetime achievement award by the President of the United States. Even today, his dance company continues to travel all over the world.

Alvin Ailey had many dancers in his company.

Draw a picture of 16 dancers. Circle each group of ten. Tell how many tens and ones are in your group of dancers.

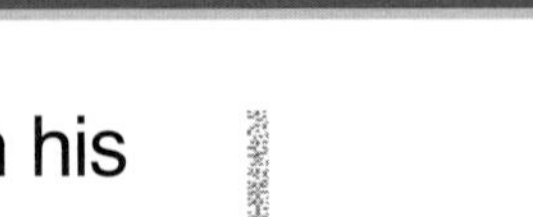

Draw or write to explain.

_____ ten _____ ones

_____ dancers

Name ______________________

Even and Odd Numbers

 **Audio Tutor 1/16** Listen and Understand

Objective
Identify even and odd numbers.

Vocabulary
even **odd**

Hands-On

Make groups of two to find if a number is **even** or **odd**.

A number is even when there are none left over.

8 is an even number.

A number is odd when there is one left over.

11 is an odd number.

Use cubes or draw dots.
Make groups of two to show the number.
Circle **even** or **odd**.

Think
When I make groups of 2 with 15 I have one left over.

1.  15 even odd
2.  26 even odd   
3.  13 even odd 
4.  12 even odd
5.  21 even odd

Explain Your Thinking When you make groups of two, can you ever have more than one left over? Why?

Practice

Remember
You can make groups of 2 to tell if a number is even or odd.

Use cubes or draw dots.
Make groups of two to show the number.
Circle **even** or **odd**.

1. 21 even odd
2. 18 even odd
3. 14 even odd
4. 22 even odd
5. 16 even odd
6. 25 even odd
7. 7 even odd
8. 17 even odd
9. 19 even odd
10. 20 even odd
11. 5 even odd
12. 23 even odd

Algebra Readiness ▶ Patterns

13. Color the even numbers .

Color the odd numbers .

1	2	3	4	5	6	7	8	9	10
11	12	13	14	15	16	17	18	19	20

14. Write the next even number. ______

Write the next odd number. ______

15. **Talk About It** Is 68 even or odd? Tell how you know.

At Home Put a number of small items, such as buttons, on a table. Ask your child to make groups of two and tell you if the number is odd or even.

Hands-On

Name ______________________________

Activity: Skip Counting

 **Audio Tutor 1**/17 Listen and Understand

Objective
Skip count by 2s, 3s, 4s, 5s, and 10s.

Vocabulary
hundred chart

Skip counting on a **hundred chart** shows different number patterns.

Work Together

Use the hundred chart.

1. Count by 2s.
   Color the numbers.
2. Count by 5s.
   Circle the numbers.
3. Count by 3s.
   Put an X on the numbers.
4. **Talk About It**
   What patterns do you see in the hundred chart?

1	2	3	4	5	6	7	8	9	10
11	12	13	14	15	16	17	18	19	20
21	22	23	24	25	26	27	28	29	30
31	32	33	34	35	36	37	38	39	40
41	42	43	44	45	46	47	48	49	50
51	52	53	54	55	56	57	58	59	60
61	62	63	64	65	66	67	68	69	70
71	72	73	74	75	76	77	78	79	80
81	82	83	84	85	86	87	88	89	90
91	92	93	94	95	96	97	98	99	100

Follow the pattern.
Write the missing numbers.

5. 32, 34, 36, ____, 40, ____
6. 12, 16, 20, ____, ____, 32
7. 12, 15, 18, ____, ____, 27
8. 50, 55, 60, ____, 70, ____
9. 48, 46, 44, ____, 40, ____
10. 98, 96, 94, ____, ____, 88

Talk About It Which is faster, counting by 2s or 5s to 100? Why?

Extra Practice at eduplace.com/map

On Your Own

When you count by ones or skip count, the numbers follow patterns.

Use the hundred chart.
Write the missing numbers.

1	2		4					9	10
11	12			15			18		
21		23	24		26				
	32			35		37		39	
41			44				48		50
		53		55				59	
			64						
	72			75		77		79	
81			84		86				
91	92				96		98	99	100

1. Count by 5s.
   Circle the numbers.

2. Count by 10s.
   Put an X on the numbers.

3. **Talk About It** What patterns do you see?

Follow the pattern. Write the missing numbers.

4. 50, 60, 70, ____, 90, ____

5. 45, 50, 55, ____, ____, 70

6. 100, 90, 80, ____, 60, ____

7. 90, 85, 80, ____, ____, 65

8. Which three boxes continue the pattern? Circle the answer.

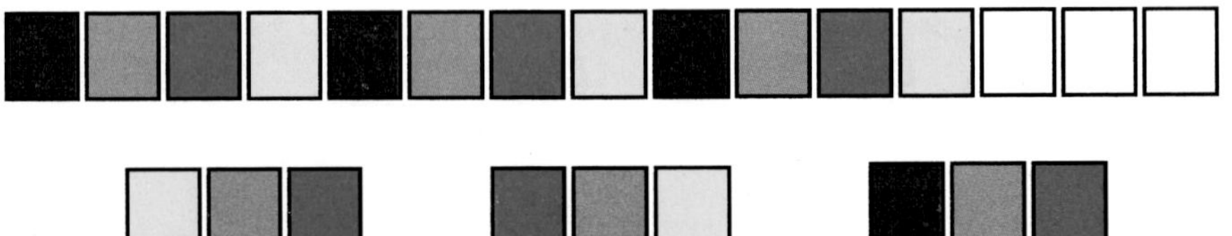

At Home Together with your child practice counting forward and backward by 1s, 2s, 5s, and 10s on the hundred chart.

Name ______________________

Order Two-Digit Numbers to 100

Objective
Order whole numbers.

Vocabulary
just before
between
just after

A number line can help you find the position of a number.

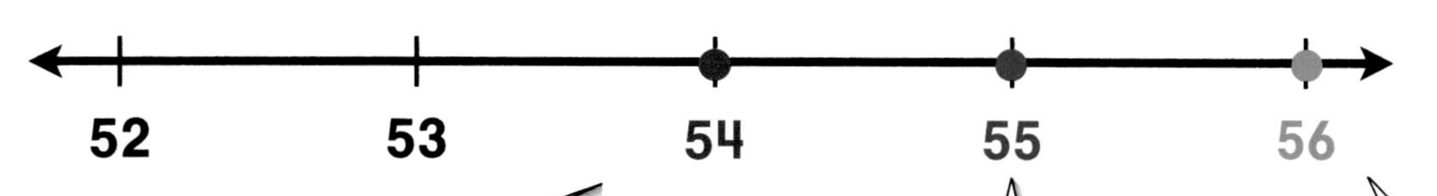

54 is **just before** 55.

55 is **between** 54 and 56.

56 is **just after** 55.

Guided Practice

Use the number line.

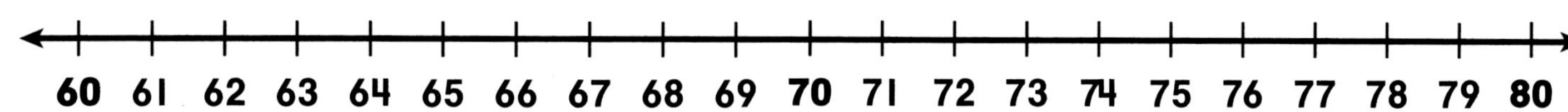

Write the number that comes just after.

1. 63, ______

Think
I find 63. Then I look for the number that comes just after it.

2. 79, ______
3. 69, ______

Write the number that comes just before.

4. ______, 65
5. ______, 70
6. ______, 73
7. ______, 68

Write the number that comes between.

8. 68, ______, 70
9. 72, ______, 74
10. 76, ______, 78

Write the missing numbers.

11. 63, 64, 65, ______, ______, 68, ______, 70, ______, 72, ______
12. 80, 79, 78, ______, ______, ______, ______, 73, 72, ______

Explain Your Thinking What numbers come before 66 but after 62? How did you use the number line to find the answer?

Practice

Remember
A number line can help you find a number that comes just before, between, or just after.

Use the number line.

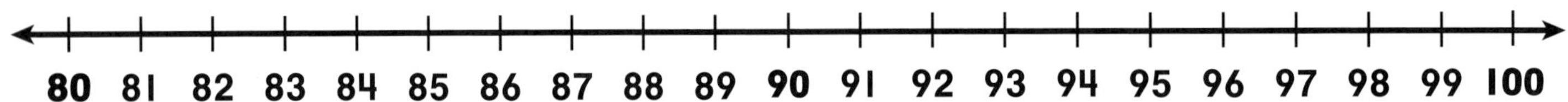

Write the number that comes just after.

1. 90, 91
2. 99, ____
3. 95, ____
4. 81, ____

Write the number that comes just before.

5. ____, 94
6. ____, 100
7. ____, 90
8. ____, 83

Write the number that comes between.

9. 85, ____, 87
10. 96, ____, 98
11. 89, ____, 91

Write the missing numbers.

12. 85, 86, 87, ____, ____, ____, ____, 92, ____, ____, 95
13. 99, 98, 97, ____, ____, 94, ____, ____, ____, ____, 89

Problem Solving ▶ Logical Thinking

14. I am a number between 71 and 75. I am an odd number. What number am I?

Draw or write to explain.

I am ____.

At Home Say a number between 50 and 100. Ask your child to tell you the numbers that come just before and just after.

Name ______________________________

Ordinal Numbers

Objective
Use ordinal numbers.

Vocabulary
ordinal numbers

Ordinal numbers tell you the position of people or things.

Guided Practice

Use the picture.
Circle the answer.

1. You are just in front of the 4th child in line. What place are you in line?

   5th 3rd 8th

   Think
   I know 3rd comes before 4th.

2. You are just behind the 15th child in line. What place are you in line?

   14th 15th 16th

3. You are just before the 20th child. What place are you in line?

   16th 19th 20th

4. You are just after the 14th child. What place are you in line?

   15th 16th 17th

Explain Your Thinking How many children are in front of the 12th child? Tell how you know.

Practice

You can use ordinal numbers to tell where people or things are.

Use the picture.
Circle the answer.

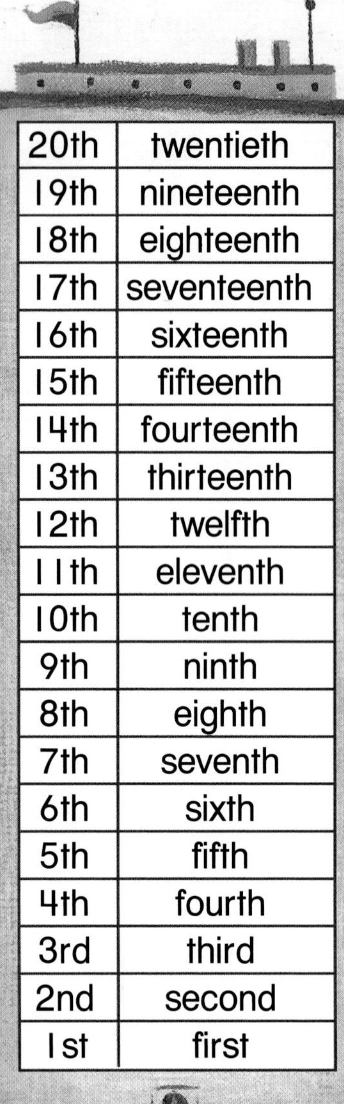

20th	twentieth
19th	nineteenth
18th	eighteenth
17th	seventeenth
16th	sixteenth
15th	fifteenth
14th	fourteenth
13th	thirteenth
12th	twelfth
11th	eleventh
10th	tenth
9th	ninth
8th	eighth
7th	seventh
6th	sixth
5th	fifth
4th	fourth
3rd	third
2nd	second
1st	first

1. Which floor is just above the fourteenth floor?

   13th　　14th　　 15th

2. Which floor is just below the 3rd floor?

   second　　third　　sixth

3. Which floor is between the 15th and 17th floor?

   14th　　18th　　16th

4. Which floor is just below the top floor?

   second　　tenth　　nineteenth

5. Which floor is two floors above the fourth floor?

   second　　fifth　　sixth

Reading Math ▶ Vocabulary

Use the words in the box.
Complete the sentence.

between
above
below
top
bottom

6. The third floor is __________ the second floor.

7. The __________ floor is the first floor.

8. The twentieth floor is the __________ floor.

9. The sixth floor is __________ the seventh floor.

10. The eleventh floor is __________ the tenth and twelfth floors.

Go on

Name ____________________

Now Try This — Ordinal Numbers to 100th

If you know these numbers for counting by tens,

twenty	thirty	forty	fifty	sixty	seventy	eighty	ninety
20	30	40	50	60	70	80	90

and these ordinal numbers,

first	second	third	fourth	fifth	sixth	seventh	eighth	ninth
1st	2nd	3rd	4th	5th	6th	7th	8th	9th

then you can name ordinal numbers up to 100th.
Just follow the pattern.

Delete "y" then add -ieth.

Use the ordinal numbers first through ninth.

twentieth	twenty-first	twenty-second	twenty-third	twenty-fourth
20th	21st	22nd	23rd	24th

Draw lines to match.

1. 40th — eightieth
2. 90th — fortieth
3. 60th — fiftieth
4. 50th — ninetieth
5. 80th — sixtieth

6. 26th — fifty-third
7. 53rd — thirty-fifth
8. 92nd — twenty-sixth
9. 35th — seventy-first
10. 71st — ninety-second

At Home Place up to 20 small objects in a line. Point to objects randomly and have your child tell you where they are in the line using ordinal numbers.

Quick Check

Use cubes or draw dots.
Make groups of two to show the number.
Circle **even** or **odd**.

1. 27 even odd

2. 23 even odd

Use the hundred chart.
Follow the pattern.
Write the missing numbers.

3. 64, 66, 68, _____, 72, _____

4. 100, 95, 90, _____, 80, _____

5. 36, 39, 42, _____, _____, 51

1	2	3	4	5	6	7	8	9	10
11	12	13	14	15	16	17	18	19	20
21	22	23	24	25	26	27	28	29	30
31	32	33	34	35	36	37	38	39	40
41	42	43	44	45	46	47	48	49	50
51	52	53	54	55	56	57	58	59	60
61	62	63	64	65	66	67	68	69	70
71	72	73	74	75	76	77	78	79	80
81	82	83	84	85	86	87	88	89	90
91	92	93	94	95	96	97	98	99	100

Use the number line.

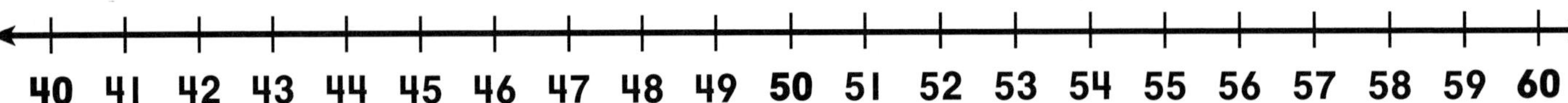

Write the number that comes just after.

6. 53, _____

7. 49, _____

Write the number that comes just before.

8. _____, 41

9. _____, 60

Write the number that comes between.

10. 48, _____, 50

11. 40, _____, 42

12. 45, _____, 47

13. Use the picture.
Circle the 2nd child in line.

Name ______________________

Repeating and Growing Patterns

Audio Tutor 1/18 Listen and Understand

> **Objective**
> Extend, describe, and create repeating and growing patterns.
>
> **Vocabulary**
> **repeating pattern**
> **pattern unit**
> **growing pattern**

A **repeating pattern** has a **pattern unit** that repeats over and over again.

What is the next number?

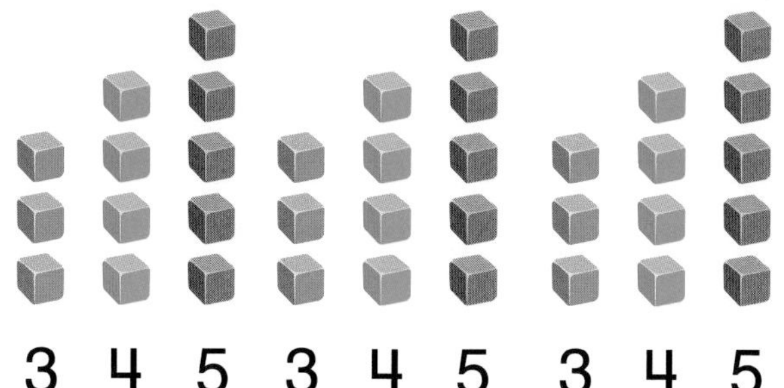

3 4 5 3 4 5 3 4 5

3, 4, 5 keeps repeating.

3

A **growing pattern** can get bigger in the same way over and over again. What is the next number?

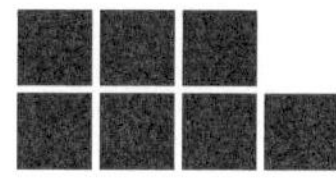

1 3 5 7

2 is added to get the next number.

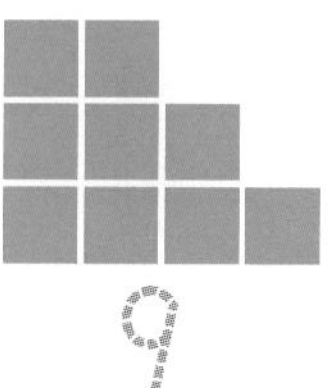

9

Guided Practice

Draw the next picture to continue the pattern. Write the numbers.

1.         

1 2 2 ____ ____ ____ ____ ____ ____ ____ ____

2.  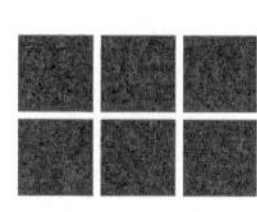 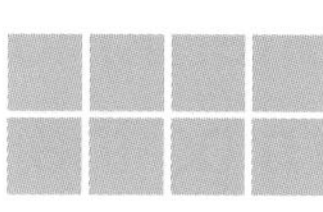

2 4 ____ ____ ____

Explain Your Thinking How are growing patterns different from repeating patterns?

Practice

Remember
A repeating pattern repeats a part over and over. In a growing pattern each part gets bigger than the last.

Draw the next picture to continue the pattern. Write the numbers.

1.    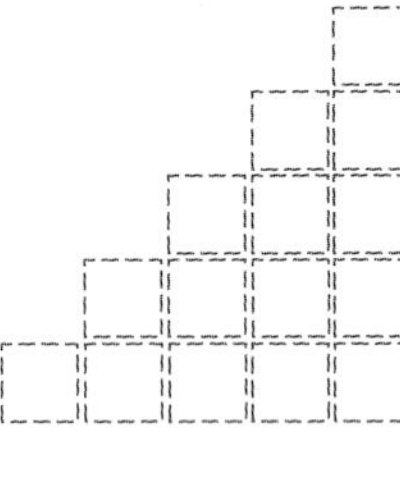

1 ___3___ ___6___ ___10___ ___15___

2. 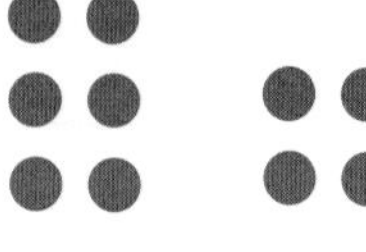  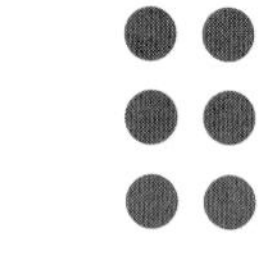 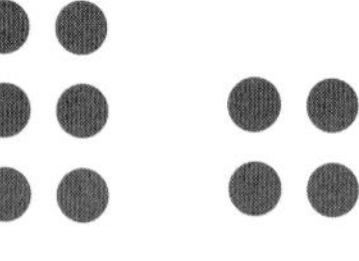  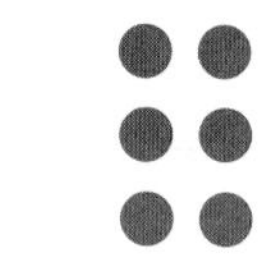  

___6___ ____ ____ ____ ____ ____ ____ ____ ____ ____

3. 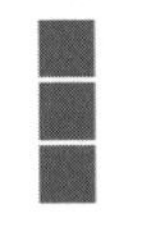 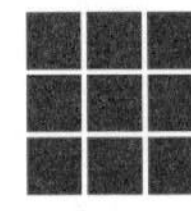 

___3___ ____ ____ ____ ____

Write the numbers to continue the pattern.

4. 3 1 6 3 1 6 3 1 6 ____ ____

5. 5 10 15 20 25 30 35 40 ____ ____

Problem Solving ▶ Visual Thinking

6. Circle the letter pattern that has the same type of repeating pattern as the shapes.

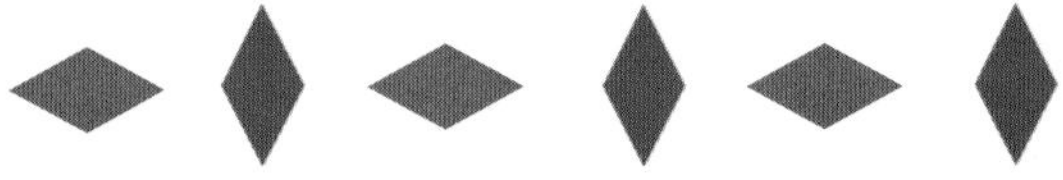

A B A B A B A B C A B C A B C

At Home Help your child draw shape patterns to match the patterns in exercise 6.

Name ___________________________

Find a Pattern

 **Audio Tutor 1**/19 Listen and Understand

Objective
Use patterns to solve problems.

Problem Solving

Some lightbulbs are sold in packs of 3. There are 3 bulbs in one pack. There are 6 bulbs in two packs. There are 9 bulbs in three packs. How many bulbs are in five packs?

UNDERSTAND

What do you know?

- The bulbs are sold in packs.
- One pack has 3 bulbs.
- Two packs have 6 bulbs.
- Three packs have 9 bulbs.

PLAN

Make a table to help you find a pattern.

Number of Packs	1	2	3	4	5
Number of Bulbs	3	6	9		

This is a growing pattern.

SOLVE

Extend the pattern to find the answer.

Number of Packs	1	2	3	4	5
Number of Bulbs	3	6	9	12	15

Count by 3s until you reach 5 packs.

There are 15 bulbs in 5 packs.

LOOK BACK

Did you answer the question?
How do you know your answer makes sense?

Guided Practice

Look for the pattern.
Then solve.

1. Each child sells 2 tickets. How many tickets do 6 children sell?

Think I can skip count by 2s.

Children	1	2	3	4	5	6
Tickets	2	4	6			

_____ tickets

2. Each bug costume costs $5 to make. How much does it cost to make 5 bug costumes?

Think What is the pattern?

Costumes	1	2	3	4	5
Cost	$5	$10	$15		

$ _____

Practice

3. Each flower costume has 3 buttons. How many buttons are on 7 costumes?

Costumes	1	2	3	4	5	6	7
Buttons	3	6	9				

_____ buttons

4. There are 10 chairs in each row. How many chairs are in 5 rows?

Rows	1	2	3	4	5
Chairs	10	20	30		

_____ chairs

Name ____________________

Mixed Problem Solving

Strategies
Write a Number Sentence
Find a Pattern
Draw a Picture

Solve.

Draw or write to explain.

1. 4 children collect tickets at each door. There are 5 doors. How many children are needed to collect tickets?

Doors	1	2	3	4	5
Children	4	8	12		

ticket

_____ children

2. In the orchestra there are 5 people in each row. There are 6 rows. How many people are there?

Rows	1	2	3	4	5	6
People	5	10	15			

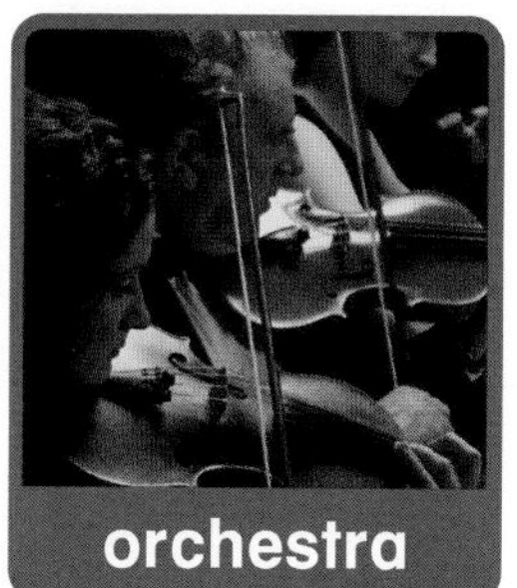
orchestra

_____ people

3. Juan's class made 5 masks on Monday. On Tuesday they made 8 more masks. How many masks did Juan's class make?

mask

_____ masks

4. **Multistep** There are 16 people on stage when the curtain opens. 7 people leave. 1 person comes on stage. How many people are on stage now?

stage

_____ people

 **At Home** Choose a food that comes in a pack; for example, a package of butter. Then make a table to figure out how many sticks of butter you would have if you had 3 packs.

Problem Solving on Tests • Listening Skills

Open Response

Listen to your teacher read the problem.
Solve.

1. Animal crackers are sold in packs. There are 10 crackers in one pack. How many crackers are in five packs?

Packs	1	2	3	4	5
Animal Crackers	10	20	30		

Show your work, using pictures, numbers, or words.

______ crackers

2. Each day Mr. Johnson walks 3 miles. How many miles does he walk in 6 days?

Days	1	2	3	4	5	6
Miles	3	6	9			

______ miles

Multiple Choice

Listen to your teacher read the problem.
Choose the correct answer.

■ ▲ ● ■ ▲ ● ■ ▲ ● __?__

3. 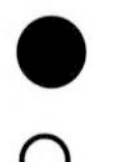 ○  ○  ○ ○

4. 26 ○ 28 ○ 30 ○ 35 ○

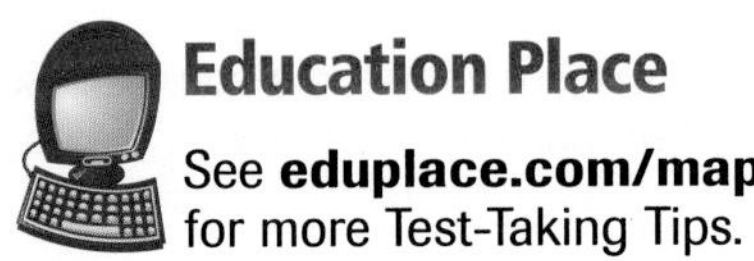
Education Place
See **eduplace.com/map** for more Test-Taking Tips.

Name ______________________________

Now Try This Translating Patterns

Susan and Peter made the same kind of pattern.
Susan made her pattern with apples.

Peter made his pattern with letters.

A B A B A B A B

Use numbers to show the pattern another way.

1.         

____ ____ ____ ____ ____ ____ ____ ____ ____

Use colors to show the pattern another way.

2.         

____ ____ ____ ____ ____ ____ ____ ____ ____

Use shapes to show the pattern another way.

3.         

____ ____ ____ ____ ____ ____ ____ ____ ____

4. **Talk About It** How can you use sound to make the same kind of pattern in Exercise 3?

____

Problem Solving

Social Studies Connection
Give Me a Lift

The escalator was invented in 1891. It began as a ride at an amusement park at Coney Island.

A group of friends ride up an escalator. Who is the 3rd person to reach the top?

____

WEEKLY WR READER eduplace.com/map

Key Topic Review

Pictograph

Use the pictograph to answer the question.

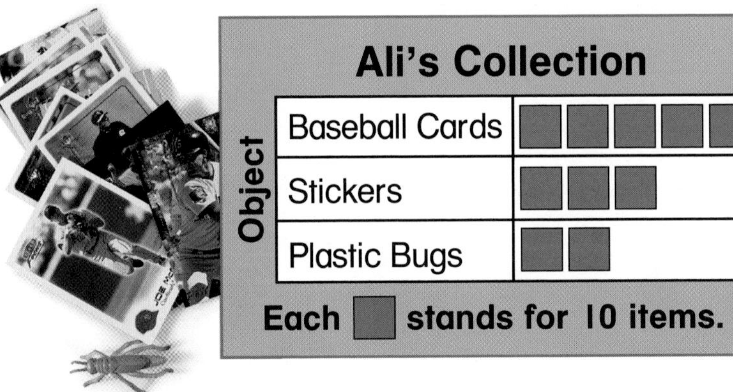

Ali's Collection

Object	
Baseball Cards	■ ■ ■ ■ ■
Stickers	■ ■ ■
Plastic Bugs	■ ■

Each ■ stands for 10 items.

1. How many stickers does Ali have?

   ______ stickers

2. How many stickers and bugs does Ali have altogether?

   ______ stickers and bugs

3. How many more baseball cards than bugs does she have?

   ______ baseball cards

4. Which of her collections has the most items?

   ____

5. Which collection has the fewest items?

   ____

6. How many items does she have in all?

   ____

Extra Practice at eduplace.com/map

Name ____________________

Vocabulary

Write the word that completes the sentence.

even
pattern
ordinal

1. You can use __________ numbers to tell you the positions of people or things.

2. A number is __________ when you make groups of two and have none left over.

Concepts and Skills

Draw dots. Make groups of two to show the number. Circle **even** or **odd**.

3. 13

even odd

4. 16

even odd

5. 17

even odd

6. 12

even odd

Use the hundred chart.
Follow the patterns.
Write the missing numbers.

1	2	3	4	5	6	7	8	9	10
11	12	13	14	15	16	17	18	19	20
21	22	23	24	25	26	27	28	29	30
31	32	33	34	35	36	37	38	39	40
41	42	43	44	45	46	47	48	49	50
51	52	53	54	55	56	57	58	59	60
61	62	63	64	65	66	67	68	69	70
71	72	73	74	75	76	77	78	79	80
81	82	83	84	85	86	87	88	89	90
91	92	93	94	95	96	97	98	99	100

7. 12, 22, ______, 42, ______, 62

8. 55, 60, ______, 70, 75, ______

9. 46, 49, 52, ______, ______, 61

10. 59, 49, ______, ______, 19, 9

Chapter Review/Test

Use the number line.

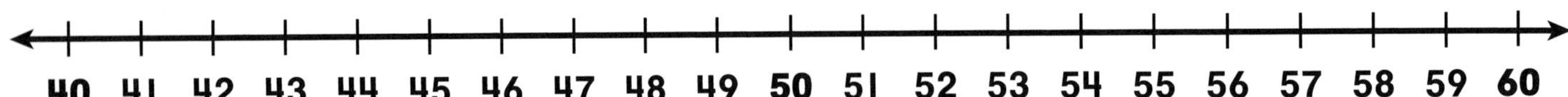

Write the number that comes just after.

11. 53, ____ 12. 49, ____ 13. 56, ____

Write the number that comes just before.

14. ____, 60 15. ____, 56 16. ____, 43

Use the picture. Circle the answer.

17. Which child is last in line?

10th 14th 1st

18. Which child is in between the 5th and the 7th child?

8th 10th 6th

Draw the next picture to continue the pattern.
Write the numbers.

19.     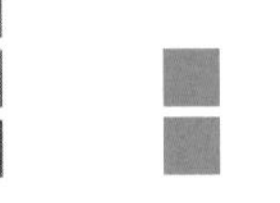

____ ____ ____ ____ ____ ____ ____ ____ ____ | ____

Problem Solving

Look for the pattern. Then solve.

20. There are 3 flowers on each necklace. How many flowers are in 6 necklaces?

Necklaces	1	2	3	4	5	6
Flowers	3	6	9			

____ flowers

Enrichment

Name ____________________

Addition and Subtraction Patterns

You can make number patterns by adding or subtracting.

Add or subtract to continue each pattern.

1. 46th 50th 54th 58th _____ _____

What is the pattern? ____________

2. 60th 55th 50th 45th _____ _____

What is the pattern? ____________

3.

Start	+4	−1	+4	−1	+4	−1
6	10	9				

What is the pattern? ____________

4.

Start	−	+	−	+	−	+
35	30	32	27	29	24	26

What is the pattern? ____________

Write Your Own

Write your own pattern with addition and subtraction.
Ask a friend to continue the pattern.

____

____

Education Place
Visit **eduplace.com/map** for brain teasers.

Calculator
Hop, Skip, and Jump

Use a calculator to count forward and backward by different numbers.

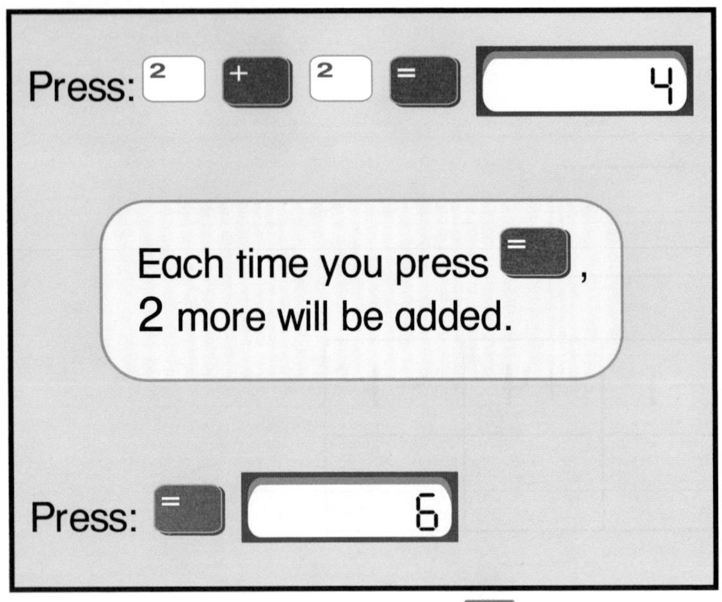

1	2	3	4	5	6	7	8	9	10
11	12	13	14	15	16	17	18	19	20
21	22	23	24	25	26	27	28	29	30
31	32	33	34	35	36	37	38	39	40
41	42	43	44	45	46	47	48	49	50
51	52	53	54	55	56	57	58	59	60
61	62	63	64	65	66	67	68	69	70
71	72	73	74	75	76	77	78	79	80
81	82	83	84	85	86	87	88	89	90
91	92	93	94	95	96	97	98	99	100

Use the hundred chart, a calculator, and a yellow, a blue, and a red crayon.

1. Color **99** yellow.
   Press 9 9 − 3 =
   Keep pressing = to count back by 3s. Color the numbers yellow as you count back.

2. Circle **6** in blue.
   Press 6 + 6 =. Keep pressing = to count by 6s. Circle the numbers in blue as you count.

3. Which numbers are colored yellow and circled?

   ____

   ____

4. Put a red **X** on **4**.
   Press 4 + 4 =. Keep pressing = to count by 4s. Put a red **X** on the numbers as you count.

5. Which numbers are in all three patterns?

   _____ _____ _____ _____ _____ _____ _____ _____

Name ______________________

Unit 2 Test

Vocabulary

Complete the sentence.

even
odd
ordinal numbers

1. A number is __________ when you make groups of 2 and there is one left over.
2. 32 is an __________ number.
3. Ninth and sixteenth are examples of __________.

Concepts and Skills

Compare the numbers. Write >, <, or =.

4. 56 ◯ 68
5. 28 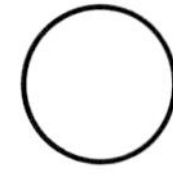 28
6. 92 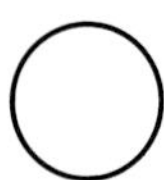 84

Use the picture.
Circle the answer.

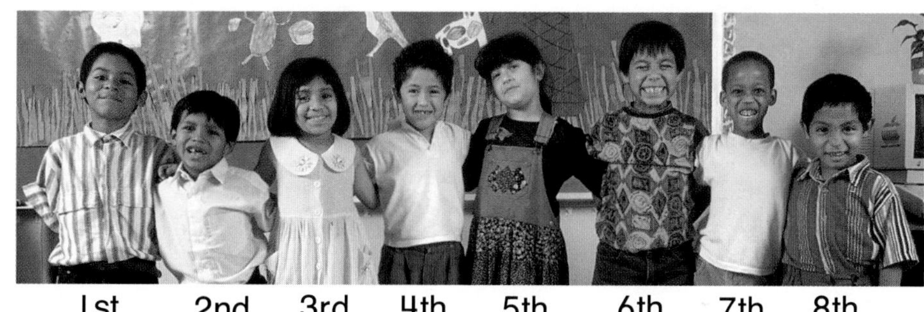

1st 2nd 3rd 4th 5th 6th 7th 8th

7. Which child is in front of the 7th child in line?

eleventh fifth sixth

8. Which child is behind the fourth child in line?

5th 3rd 6th

Draw dots. Make groups of two to show the number.
Circle even or odd.

9. 15 even odd

10. 14 even odd

Unit 2 Test

Use the hundred chart.
Write the missing numbers.

1	2	3	4	5	6	7	8	9	10
11	12	13	14	15	16	17	18	19	20
21	22	23	24	25	26	27	28	29	30
31	32	33	34	35	36	37	38	39	40
41	42	43	44	45	46	47	48	49	50
51	52	53	54	55	56	57	58	59	60
61	62	63	64	65	66	67	68	69	70
71	72	73	74	75	76	77	78	79	80
81	82	83	84	85	86	87	88	89	90
91	92	93	94	95	96	97	98	99	100

11. 68 67 _____ 65 _____ 63

12. 56 59 62 _____ _____ 71

Problem Solving

Circle the most reasonable answer.

Draw or write to explain.

13. Keon has 58 stamps. Samara has a few more stamps. About how many stamps does she have?

50 stamps   61 stamps   100 stamps

14. Dillon is 8 years old. He and his older sister go to the same school. How old is Dillon's sister?

25 years old   2 years old   12 years old

Look for the pattern. Then solve.

15. There are 2 apples in each bag. How many apples are in 5 bags?

Bags	1	2	3	4	5
Apples	2	4	6		

_____ apples

Name________________________

Test-Taking Tips

Read every answer before you make your choice.

If a problem is difficult, skip it and go on to the next. Remember to go back to it when you have finished the others.

Multiple Choice

Fill in the ○ for the correct answer.

1. Find the number that belongs in the box.

   14 − ■ = 6

   ○ 7 ○ 8 ○ 9 ○ 10

2. What is another way to show 53?

   ○ 5 tens and 5 ones

   ○ 30 + 5

   ○ 5 tens and 3 ones

   ○ 50 + 30

3. What number comes just after 54?

   ○ 50 ○ 52 ○ 53 ○ 55

4. Mark the related number sentence for 8 + 4 = 12.

   ○ 8 + 8 = 16

   ○ 12 − 6 = 6

   ○ 4 + 4 = 8

   ○ 12 − 4 = 8

Multiple Choice

Fill in the ○ for the correct answer. If the correct answer is not here, choose N.

5. Compare. What makes the following true?

25  18

$>$	$<$	$=$	N
○	○	○	○

6. Which date comes between the thirteenth and fifteenth of May?

12th	14th	16th	N
○	○	○	○

7. Which number is even?

5	9	15	N
○	○	○	○

Open Response

Solve.

8. Berto has 11 flags. His sister Adela has 8 flags. How many more flags does Berto have? Write a number sentence to solve.

_______________ flags

9. Write the next 3 numbers in the pattern. Explain how you found the numbers.

30 34 38 _____ _____ _____

____

____

10. Leslie buys postcards on her trip to Florida. 1 postcard costs 10¢. How much do 4 postcards cost?

Postcards	1	2	3	4
Cost	10¢			

_______ ¢

Education Place
Look for Cumulative Test Prep at **eduplace.com/map** for more practice.

READING MATH

Shape Up

Look back at the story to answer these questions.

△ **1.** Start at page 2. Count how many times you can find the green circle robot in the story.

● **2.** Look back at the story. What do you see in the story that has symmetry?

★ **3.** Look at page 6. Can you make a new pattern using the members of the shape family? Draw it on another piece of paper.

☆ **4.** Draw your own shape family. What shapes do you have?

Answers
1. 7 **2.** Answers will vary. Possible answers: picnic table, sandwich, cookie **3.** Check children's drawings. **4.** Check children's drawings.

Reading Strategies

△ Noting Details
● Categorize and Classify
★ Predict
☆ Summarize

UNIT 3

A Picnic in Space

written by Meish Goldish
illustrated by Russell Benfanti

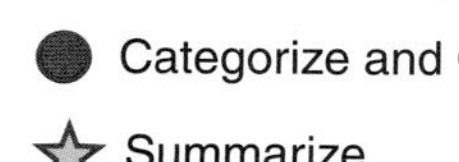

The Robots are having a picnic.
All of the family is there.
Do you know each robot's shape —
Circle, triangle, rectangle, or square?

Papa is a ______. Mama is a ______.

Brother is a ______. Sister is a ______.

The picnic is almost over!
Papa thanks everyone who came.
How many robots do you see?
Count the shapes that are the same.

How many circles? squares?

triangles? rectangles?

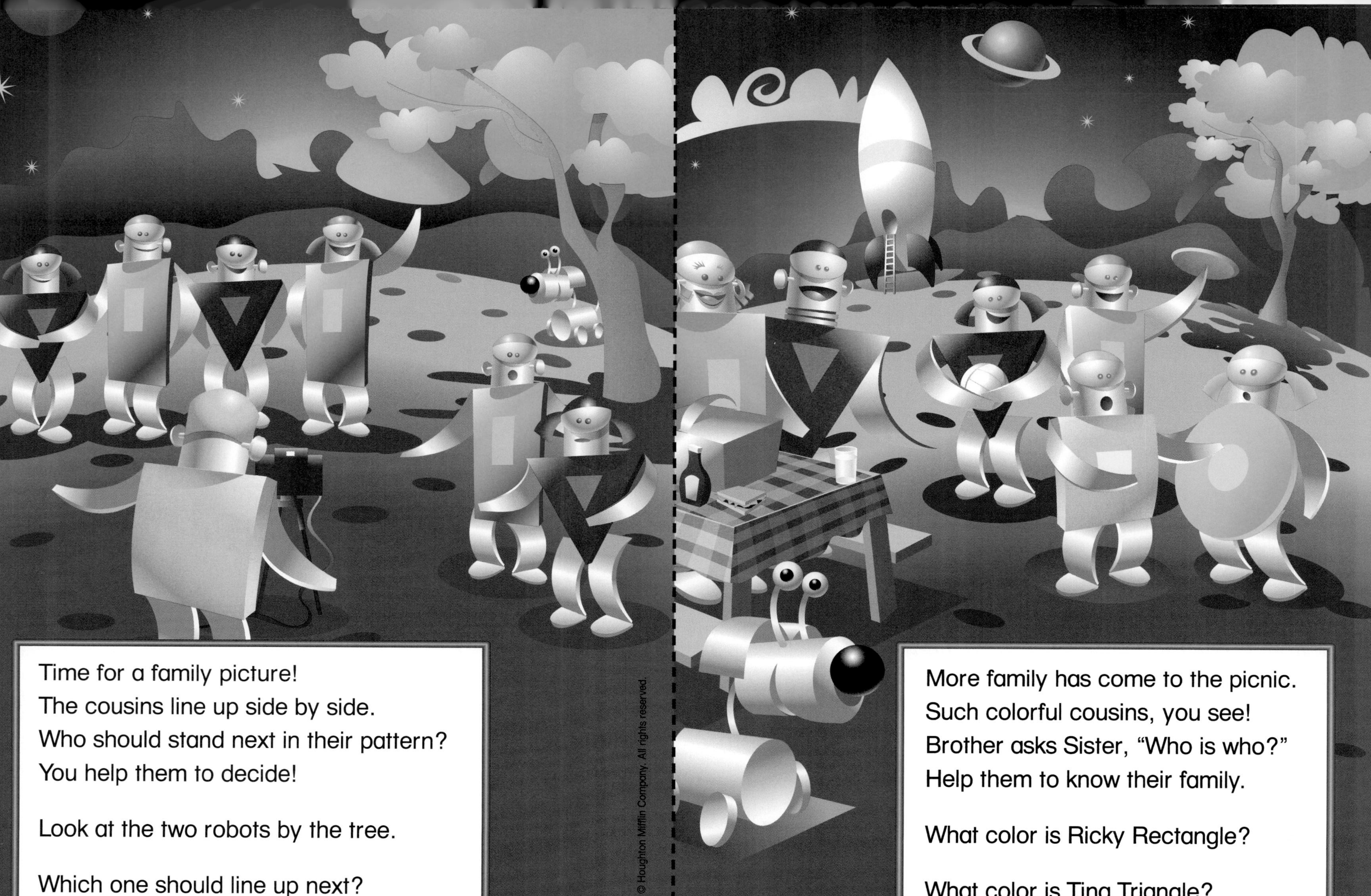

Time for a family picture!
The cousins line up side by side.
Who should stand next in their pattern?
You help them to decide!

Look at the two robots by the tree.

Which one should line up next?

More family has come to the picnic.
Such colorful cousins, you see!
Brother asks Sister, “Who is who?”
Help them to know their family.

What color is Ricky Rectangle?

What color is Tina Triangle?

Aunt Circle and Uncle Square are here.
They've brought good things to eat.
Each one has its very own shape.
I bet they all taste sweet!

Name the shape of each food.

Mama is ready to serve,
But why is she wearing a frown?
She can't find the sandwiches or lemonade.
Should she look left, right, up, or down?

For the sandwiches, she should look ________.

For the lemonade, she should look ________.

UNIT 3

Geometry and Fractions

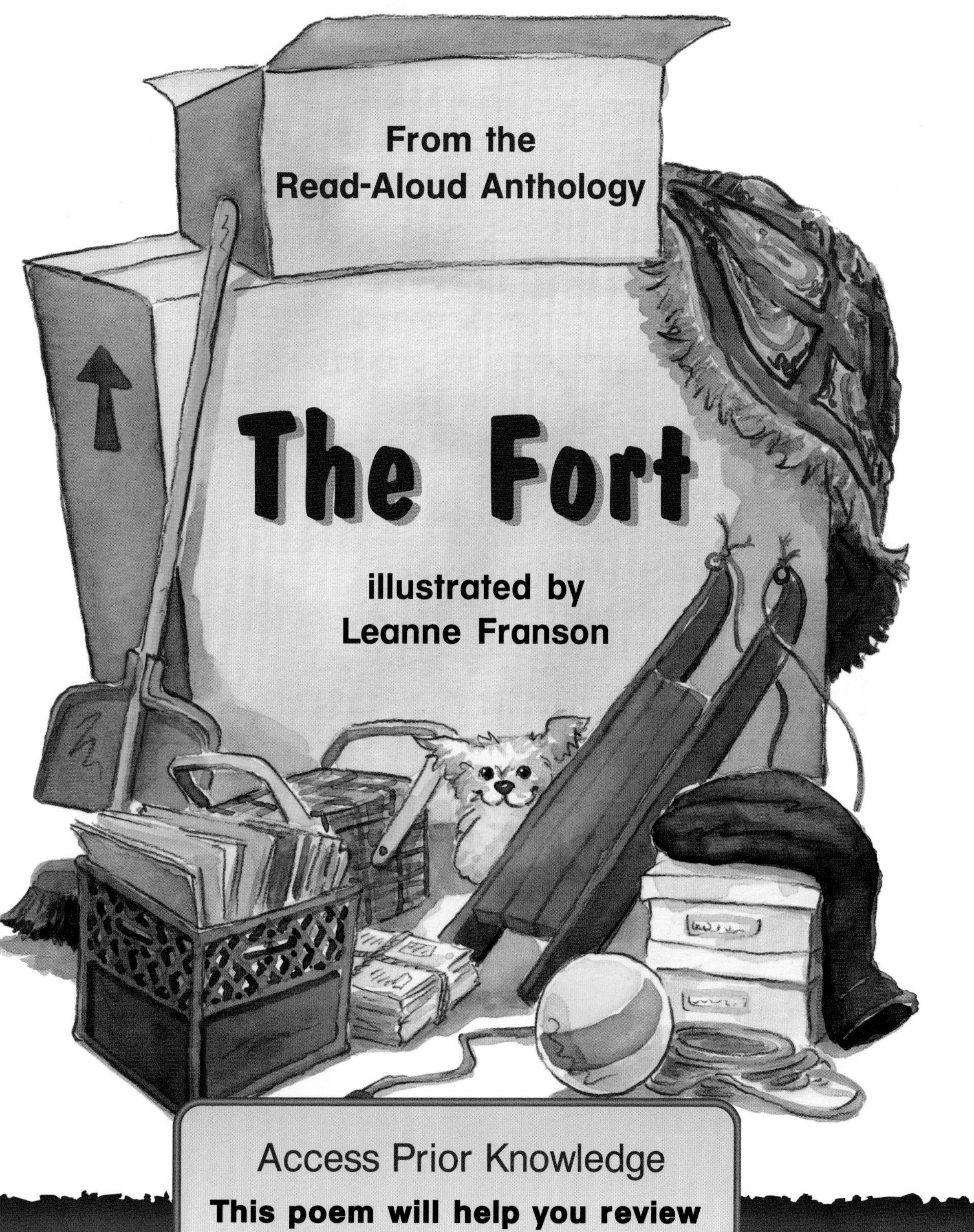

Access Prior Knowledge

This poem will help you review

- Plane shapes
- Solid shapes

What can we do on a rainy day?
We can build a fort inside and play!

We'll ask Mom and Dad for things we can use,
There are so many choices, which should I choose?

The sides of the box are wide and tall.
The faces are rectangles—this should be our wall!

Now we need windows, some round and some square.
And windows that open to let in fresh air!

A tent is perfect to add to our fort,
It's shaped like a triangle, with a pole for support.

This fort is perfect, now our work is all done.
It's finally time to have some fun!

Our friends can come over; they can bring all their toys!
This fort has plenty of room for both the girls and the boys.

Literature Activity

Name ______________________________

Word Bank	
straight round side corner face	circle rectangle triangle square

Use the picture on page 175c.
Find the object.
Write a sentence to describe the object.
Use some words from the word bank.

1. toy truck tire

Think
What shapes do I see?

____

____

2. picture frame

____

____

3. wall clock

____

____

4. **Create Your Own** This box is a rectangular prism. Decorate the box to look like a fort. Include some rectangles, triangles, and circles in your drawing.

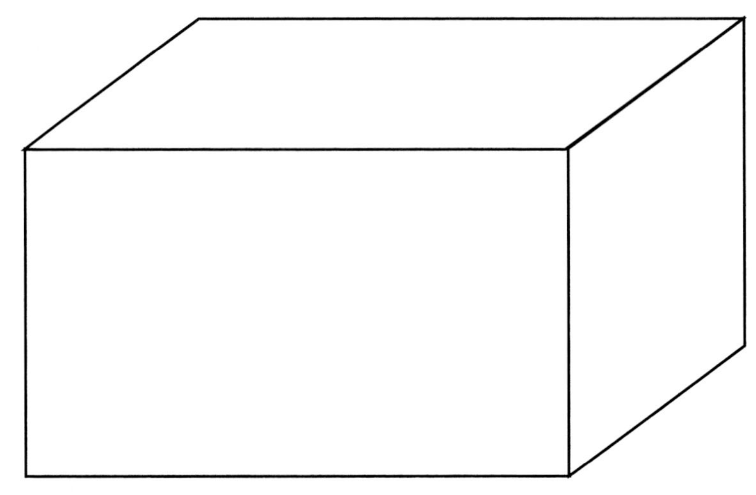

Dear Family,

My class is starting Unit 3. I will be learning about plane shapes, solid shapes, and fractions. These pages show some of what I will learn and have an activity for us to do together.

From, ______________________

Vocabulary

These are some words I will use in this unit.

vertex; vertices

The point where two sides meet.

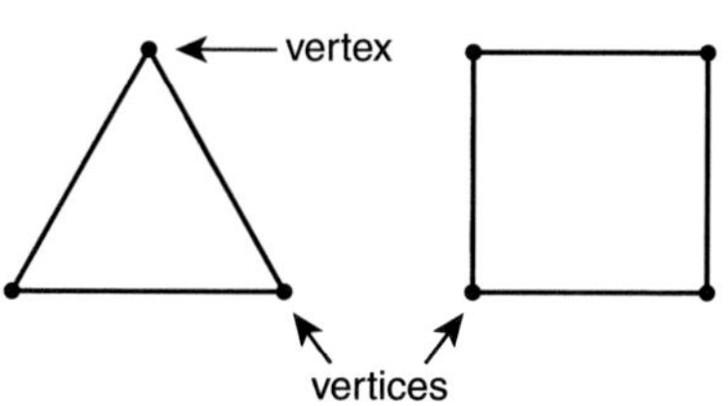

line of symmetry A line that separates a shape into two matching parts

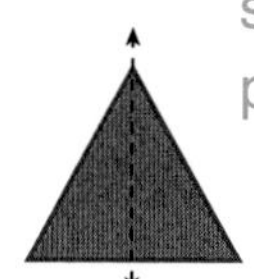

congruent Shapes that are the same size and shape

solid shapes Shapes that are not flat

edge An edge is where two faces meet.

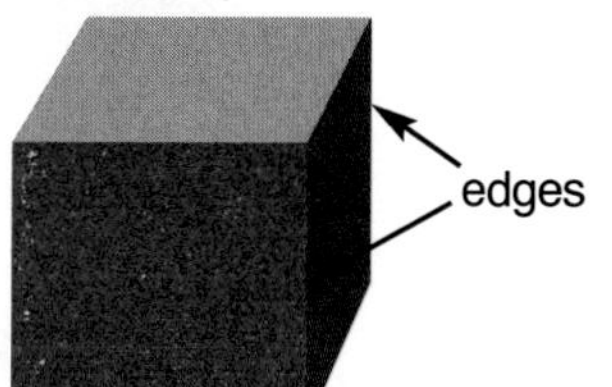

face A face is the flat surface of a solid shape

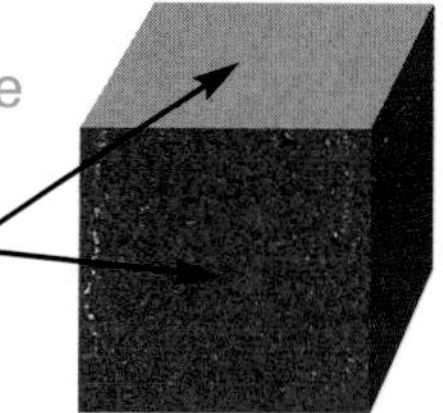

Some other words I will use are **slide**, **flip**, **turn**, **fraction**, **plane shapes**, **cone**, **cube**, **sphere**, **sides**, **unit fraction**, and **whole.**

Vocabulary Activity

Let's work together to complete these sentences.

1. Shapes that are the same shape and size are ______________.

2. A cylinder is a ______________.

How To use fractions to name part of a whole or a set

These two examples show what I will be learning.

What part is green?

There are 4 fourths.

1 fourth is green.

$\frac{1}{4}$ is green.

What part of the set is yellow?

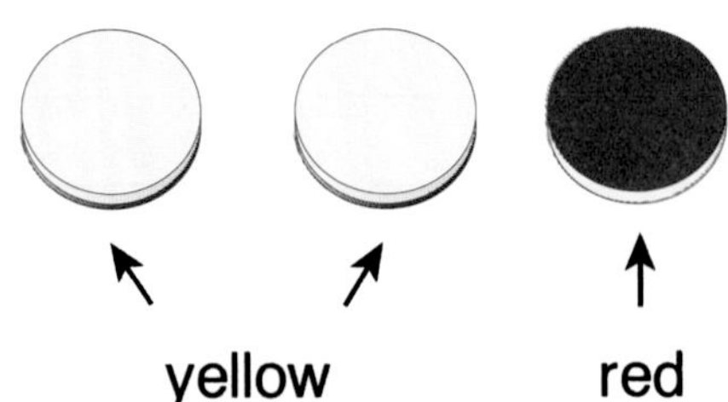

2 yellow counters

3 counters in all

$\frac{2}{3}$ of the counters are yellow.

Literature

These books link to the math in this unit. We can look for them at the library.

Inchworm and a Half
by Elinor J. Pinczes
Illustrated by Randall Enos
(Houghton Mifflin, 2001)

Shape
by Henry Pluckrose

Education Place

We can visit *Education Place* at

eduplace.com/maf

for the Math Lingo game, e•Glossary, and more games and activities to do together.

CHAPTER 7

Plane Shapes

INVESTIGATION

What patterns do you see?

Royal Patterns

Show each story with pattern blocks.

Name ____________________

Sides and Vertices of Plane Shapes

Objective
Identify, classify, and describe plane shapes.

Vocabulary
names of plane shapes
sides
vertex/vertices

Plane shapes have sides and vertices.

triangle

vertex → side

3 sides and 3 vertices

rectangle

side → vertices

4 sides and 4 vertices

circle

0 sides and 0 vertices

pentagon

5 sides and 5 vertices

hexagon

6 sides and 6 vertices

Guided Practice

1. Circle the rectangles.

Think
A square is a rectangle with all the sides the same length.

2. Circle the pentagons.

Write the name of the shape.
Write the number of sides and vertices.

3. ____________

____ sides and ____ vertices

4. ____ sides

____________ ____ vertices

Connect the red dots and name the shape.

5. ____________

Explain Your Thinking Compare the number of sides and vertices in each shape. What did you find?

Extra Help at **eduplace.com/map**

Practice

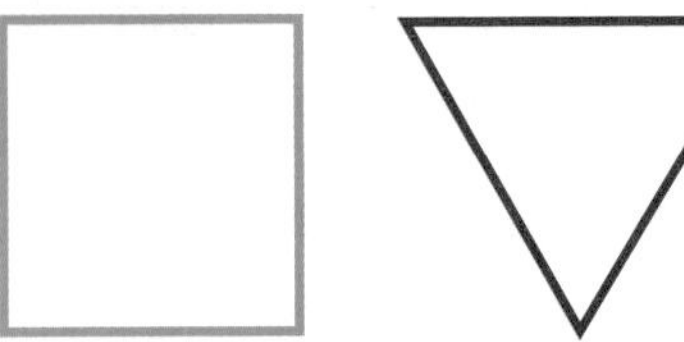

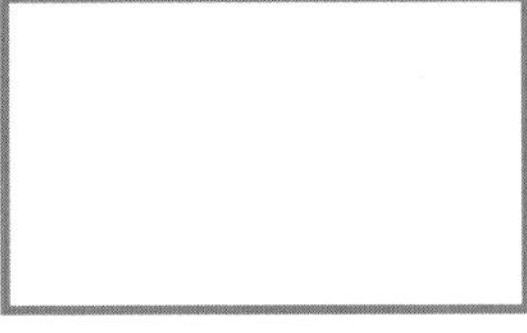

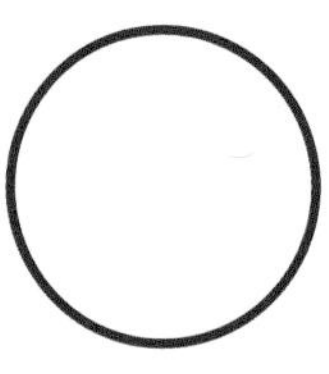

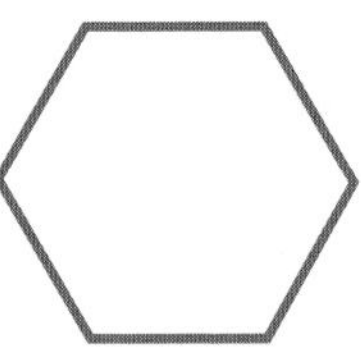

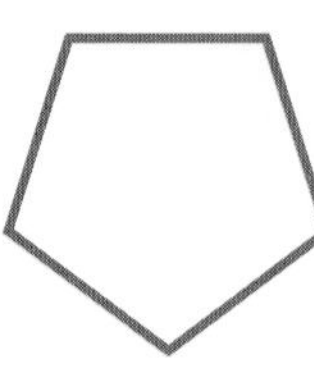

square triangle rectangle circle hexagon pentagon

Draw the shape.

1. 4 sides 4 vertices

2. 3 sides 3 vertices

3. 4 equal sides 4 vertices

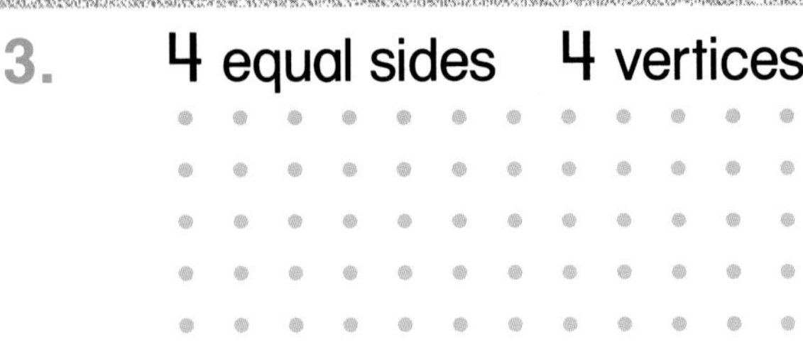

4. 5 sides 5 vertices

Problem Solving ▶ Reasoning

Write the name of the shape.
Write two reasons for your answer.

5. 

triangle

It has 3 sides.

It has 3 vertices.

6. 

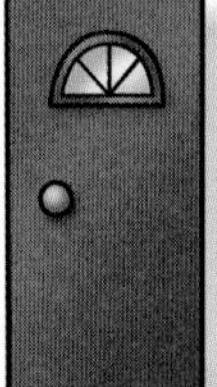

____

____

____

7. 

____

____

____

8. 

____

____

____

At Home Draw several shapes for your child and ask him or her to identify the number of sides and vertices.

Name ____________________

Angles

Where two sides of a shape meet at a vertex, there is an **angle**.

Objective
Identify and classify angles.

Vocabulary
acute angle
obtuse angle
right angle

This is a **right angle**.

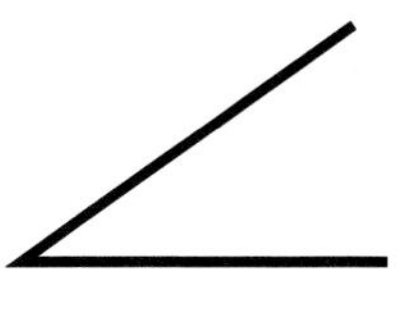

An **acute angle** is less than a right angle.

An **obtuse angle** is greater than a right angle.

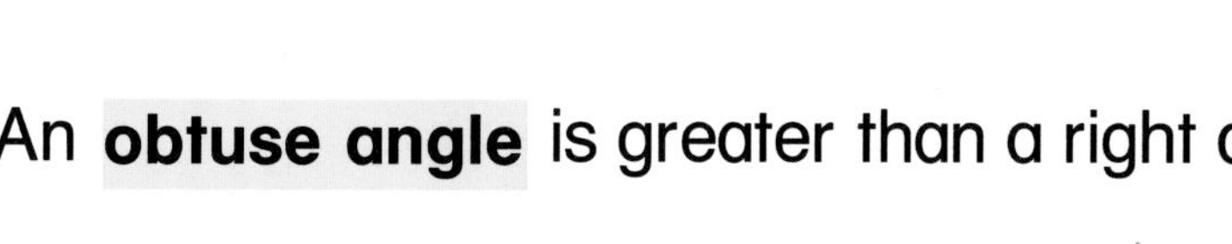

Work Together

Work with a partner.

Use a ▪ to find the kind of angle in the shape. Line up the corner of the block so it touches the vertex and one side of the shape.

This angle is a right angle.

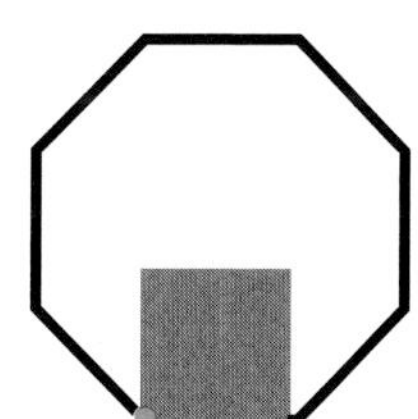

This angle is an obtuse angle.

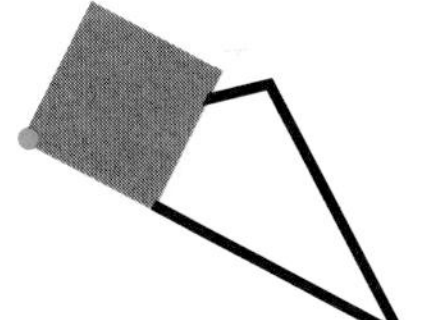

This angle is an acute angle.

Use a ▪. Name the angle. Write **acute**, **obtuse**, or **right**.

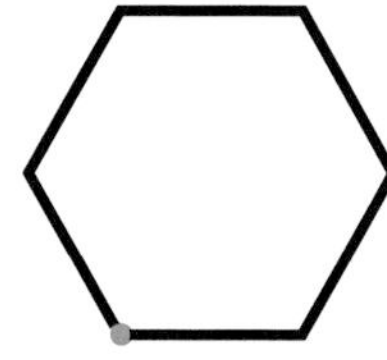

____

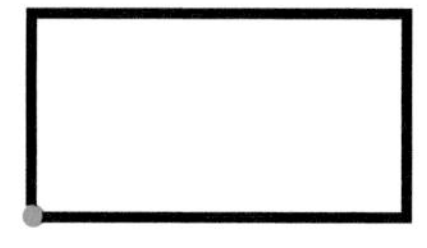

____

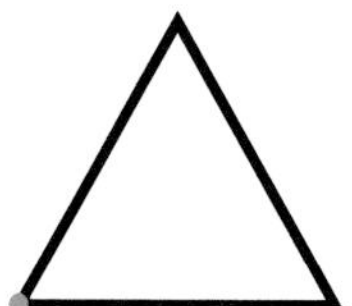

____

Talk About It What kind of angles does your desk have?

On Your Own

Trace a pattern block that shows the angle.
Color the two sides that meet to form the angle.

1. acute 

2. right 

3. obtuse 

Look at the angle.
Write **obtuse, acute,** or **right.**

4. obtuse

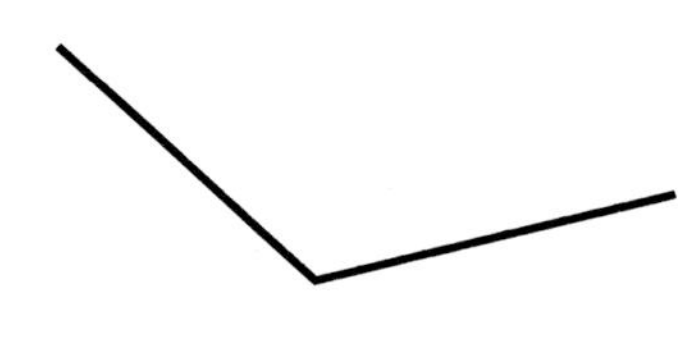

5. ______

6. ______

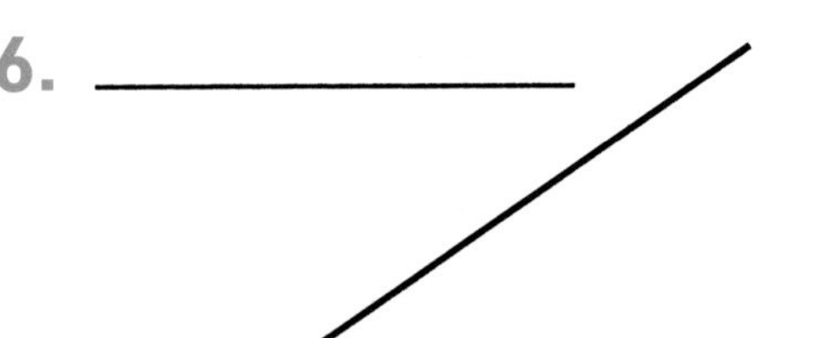

7. ______

8. ______

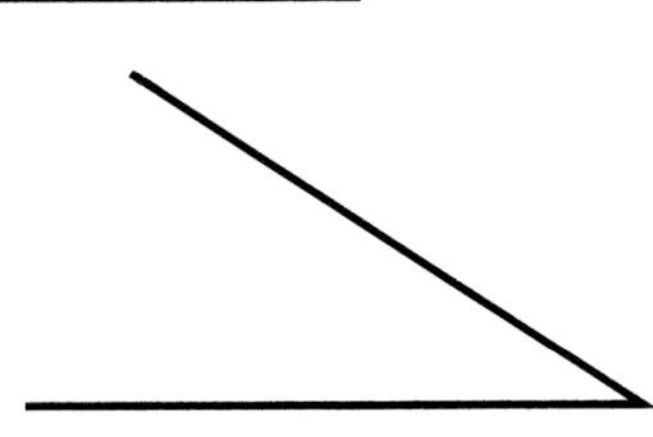

9. ______

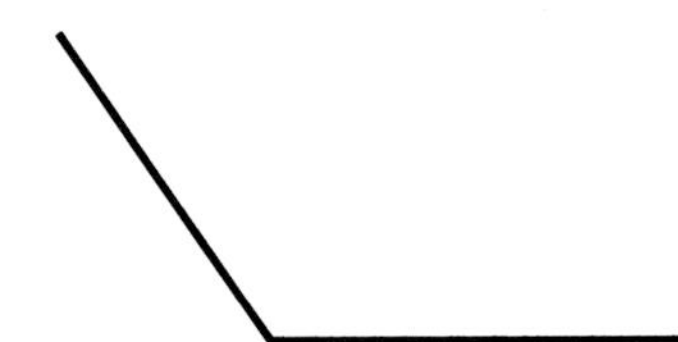

Problem Solving  Reasoning

10. Look at the two shapes.
How are they the same?
How are they different?

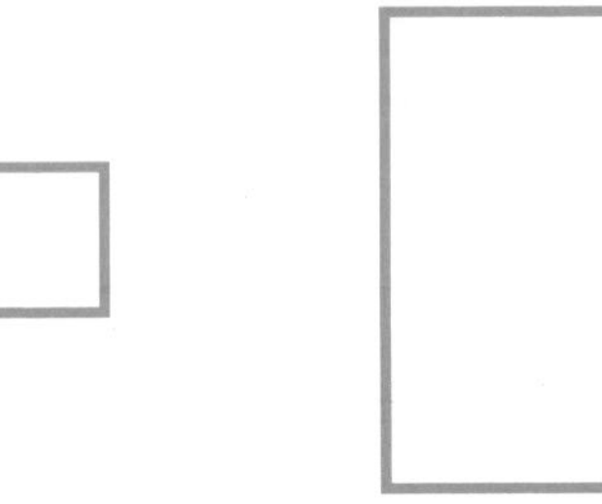

Draw or write to explain.

______

______

______

______

At Home Ask your child to find things with acute, obtuse, and right angles in your home.

Name ______________________________

Quadrilaterals

A shape with 4 sides is a **quadrilateral**.

These quadrilaterals are also **parallelograms**. Parallelograms have opposite sides that are the same distance apart.

The blue sides are the same distance apart.

The green sides are the same distance apart.

Objective
Identify a quadrilateral, parallelogram, rhombus, and trapezoid.

Vocabulary
quadrilateral
parallelogram
rhombus
trapezoid

A **rhombus** is a special type of parallelogram. All 4 sides are the same length.

A **trapezoid** is another kind of quadrilateral. Only one pair of opposite sides are the same distance apart.

Only the blue sides are the same distance apart.

Guided Practice

1. Draw a circle around every rhombus.

Think
All 4 sides are the same length.

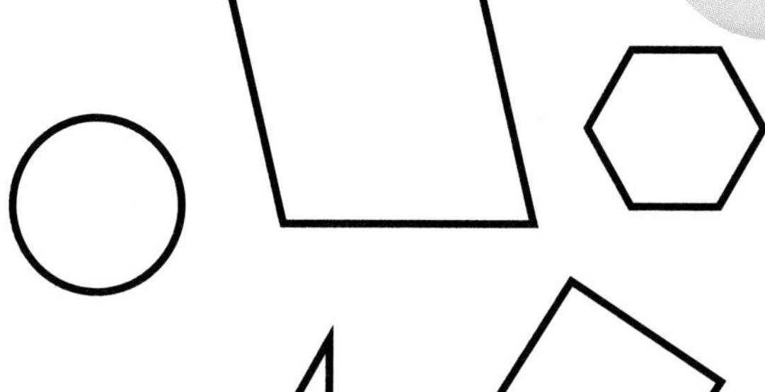

2. Draw a circle around every trapezoid.

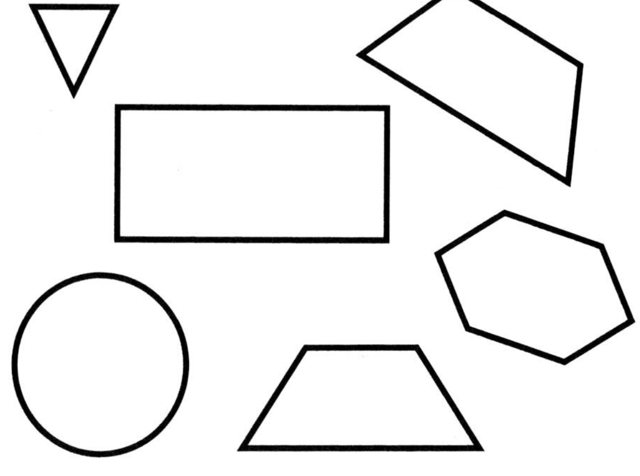

Practice

A quadrilateral has 4 sides.

1. Draw a circle around every quadrilateral.

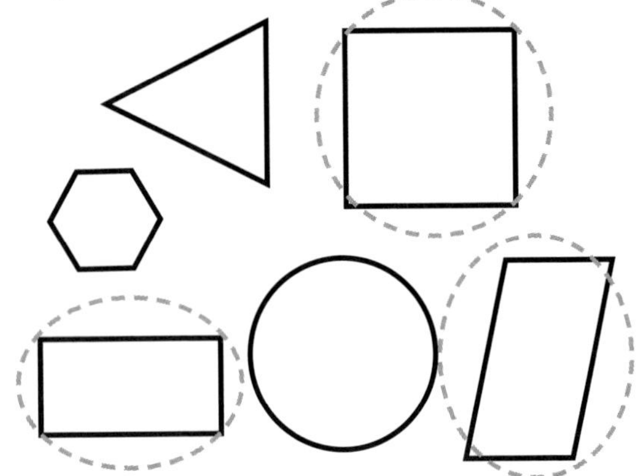

2. Draw a circle around every parallelogram.

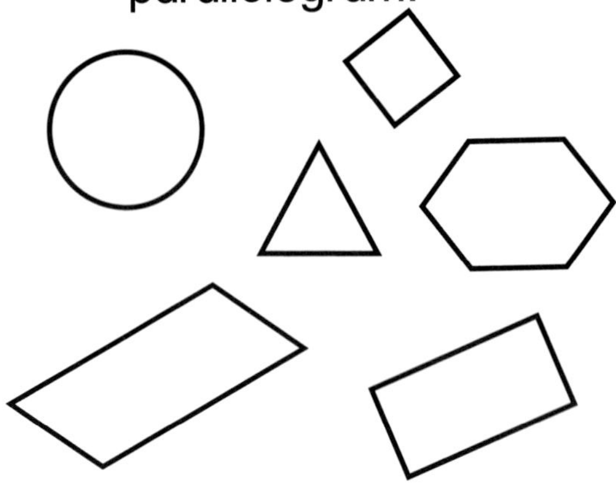

3. Draw a circle around every trapezoid.

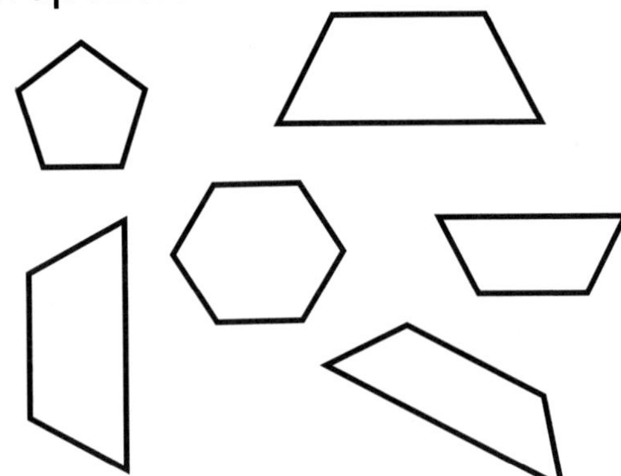

4. Draw a circle around every rhombus.

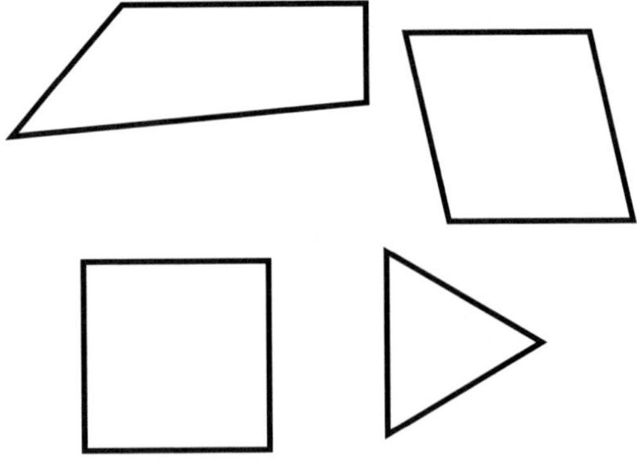

5. **Write About It** Is a square a rhombus? Why?

____

____

Problem Solving ▶ Logical Thinking

6. Circle the shape that matches the clues.

   It is a quadrilateral.
   It is a parallelogram.
   All of its angles are right angles.
   All sides are the same length.

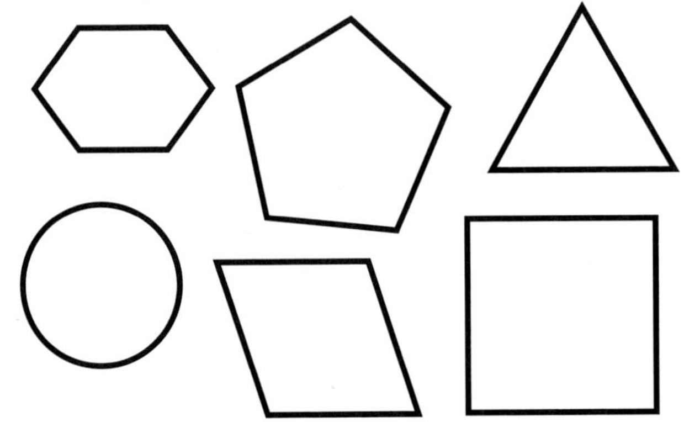

At Home Ask your child to draw a trapezoid and a rhombus.

Name ______________________________

Hands-On

Combine and Separate Shapes

You can take shapes apart and put them together to make new shapes.

Objective
Use pattern blocks to combine and separate shapes.

Use these blocks.

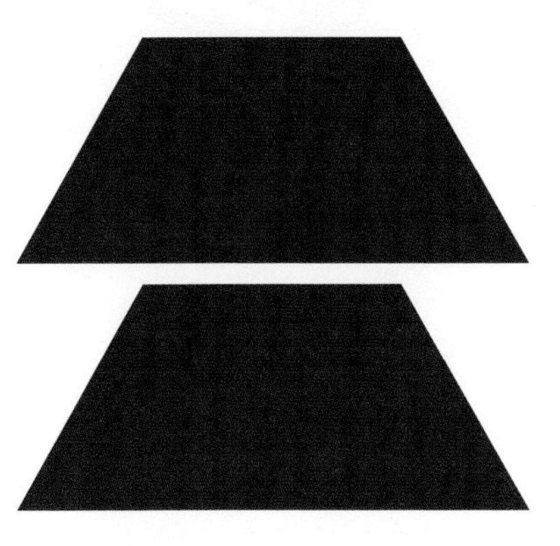

Make this shape.
Trace the blocks.

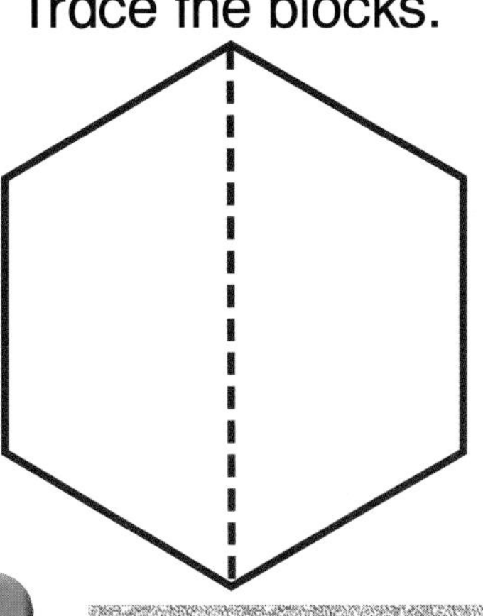

Use the same blocks.
Make this shape.
Trace the blocks.

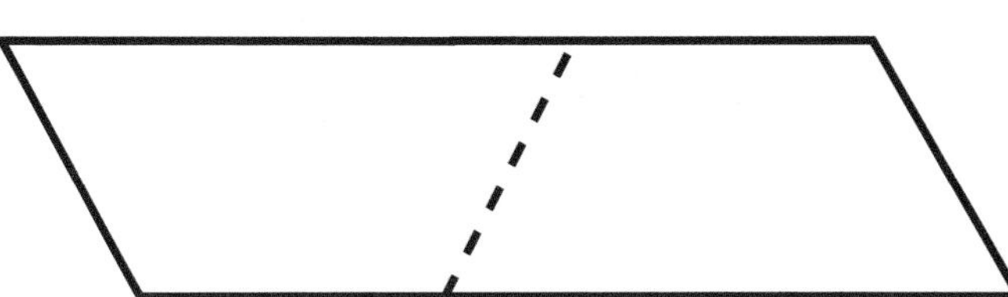

Guided Practice

Use pattern blocks. Make Shape A.
Then make Shape B. Trace the blocks.

	Use these blocks.	Shape A	Shape B
1.	4		
2.	2 1		

Explain Your Thinking What other blocks could you use to make Shape A in Exercise 2?

Use pattern blocks to make Shape A.
Then, change the blocks to make a new shape.
Trace the blocks.

	Use these blocks.	Shape A	New Shape
1.	1 (rhombus), 2 (triangle)		
2.	1 (trapezoid), 3 (triangle)		
3.	1 (trapezoid), 2 (rhombus)		

Name ______________________

Problem Solving ▶ Reasoning

1. Work with a partner.
   Use pattern blocks to fill the shape.

2. How many of each shape did you use?

3. Trace this shape on another piece of paper.
   Cut the shape on the dashed line.
   Use the two triangles to make a new shape.
   Draw the shape you make.

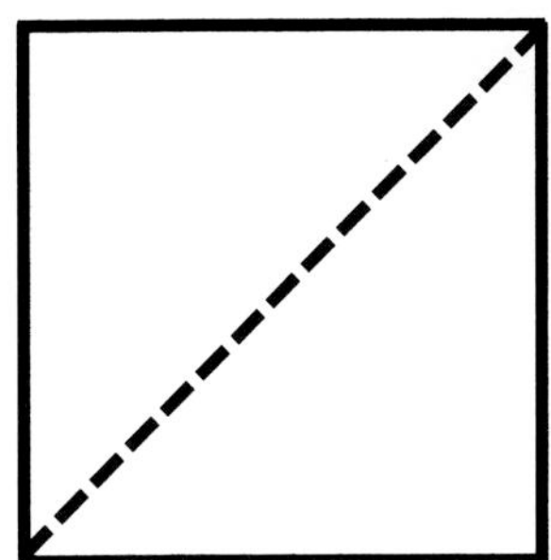

4. **Talk About It** Did everyone use the same number of each shape in Problem 1? Why?

At Home Ask your child to name other shapes he or she could use to make the shape in Exercise 1.

Quick Check

Circle the shapes that match the name.

1. quadrilateral

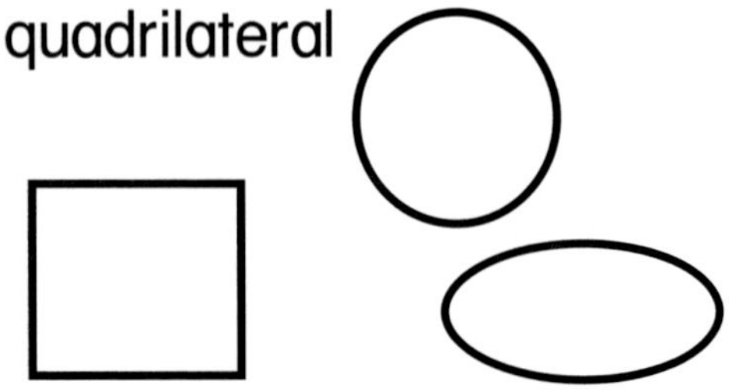

2. trapezoid

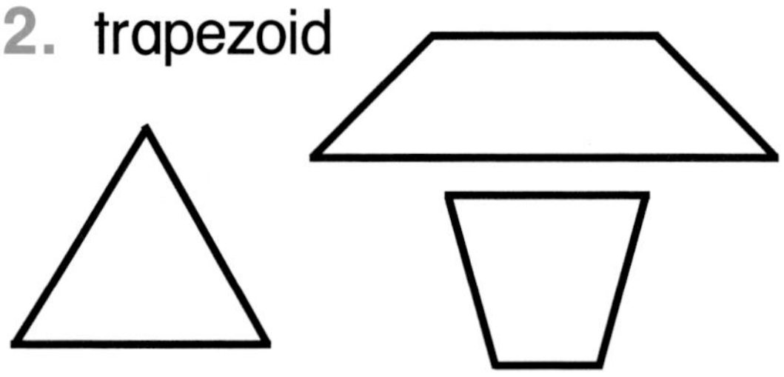

Write the name of the shape.
Write two reasons for your answer.

3.

____

____

____

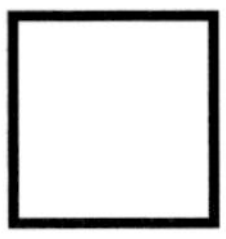

4.

____

____

____

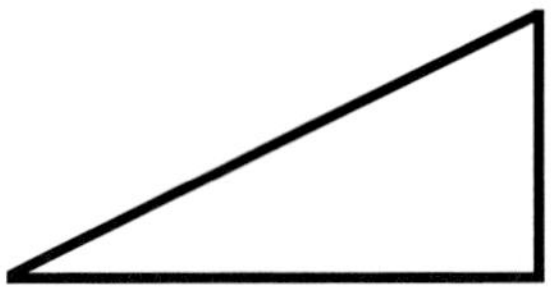

5. Look at the angle.
Write **acute, obtuse,** or **right**.

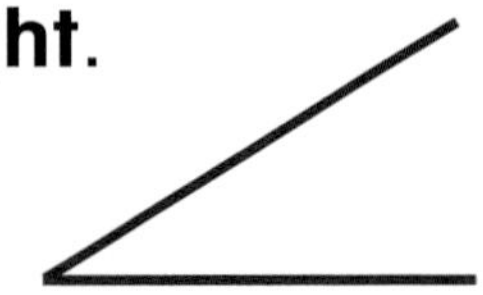

_______________ angle

Use the pattern blocks to make Shape A.
Then, change the blocks to make a new shape. Trace the blocks.

	Use these blocks.	Shape A	New Shape
6.	1 1		

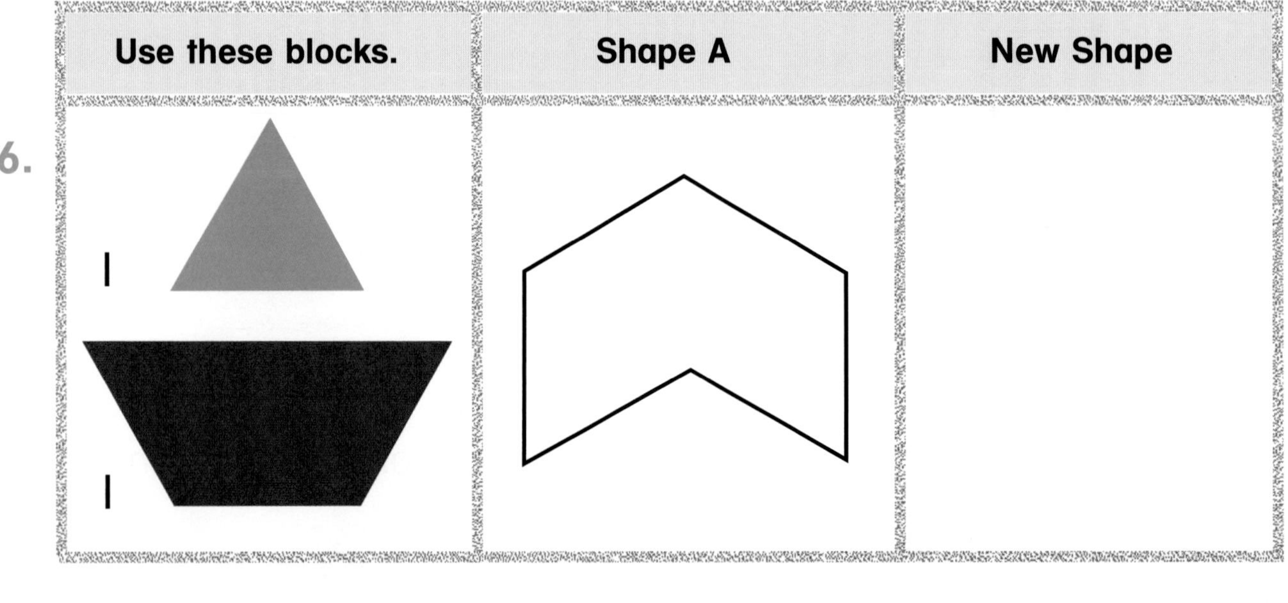

Facts Practice, see page 669.

Name ______________________________

Congruent Shapes

Objective
Identify congruent shapes.
Vocabulary
congruent

Shapes are **congruent** if they are the same size and the same shape.

These are congruent shapes.

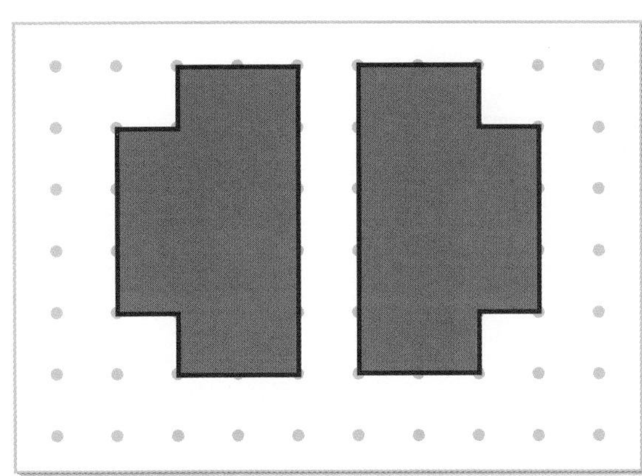

These are not congruent shapes.

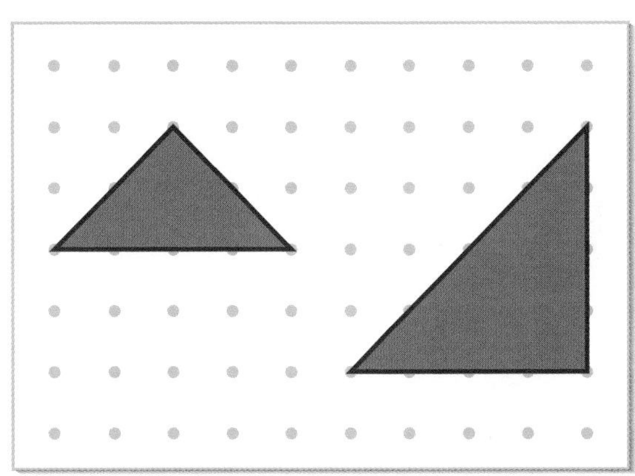

Guided Practice

Circle the shape that is congruent to the first shape.

Think
A congruent shape has the same size and shape as the first shape.

1. 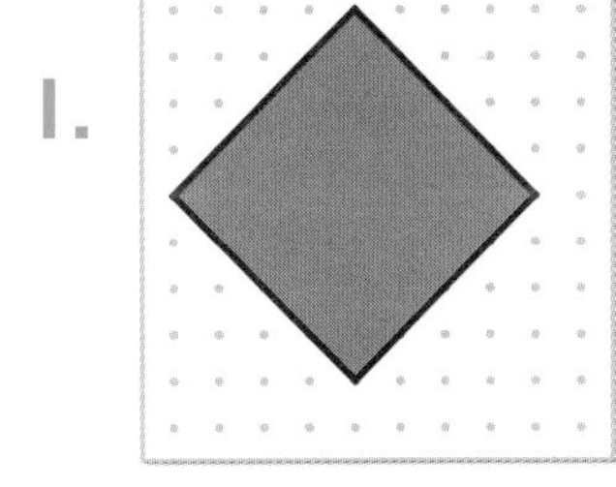 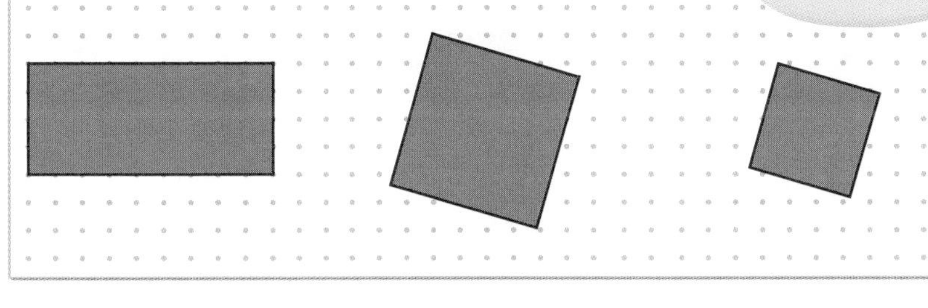

2. 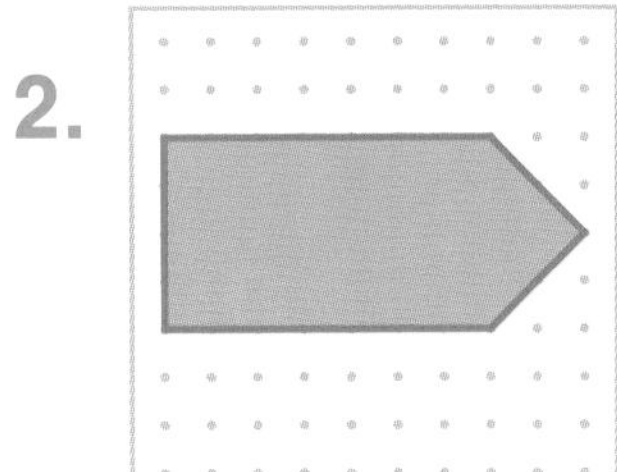 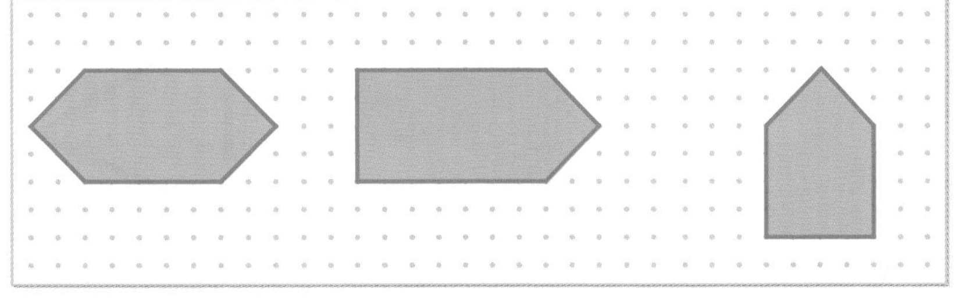

3. 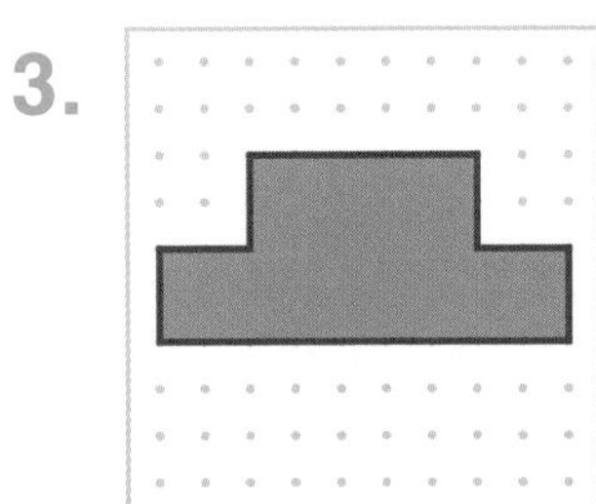 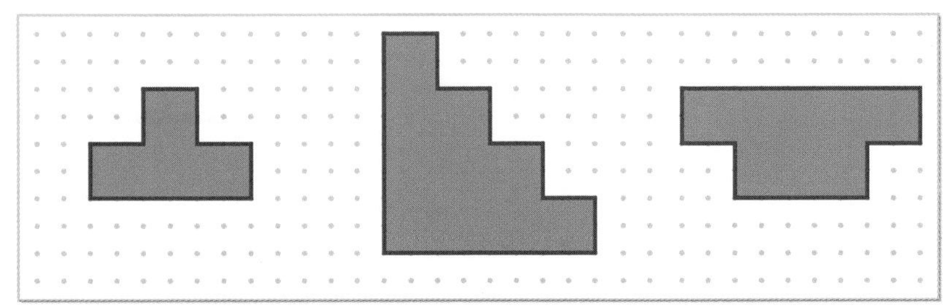

Explain Your Thinking Are two squares always congruent? Why?

Practice

Remember
Congruent shapes are the same size and shape.

Circle the shape that is congruent to the first shape.

1.

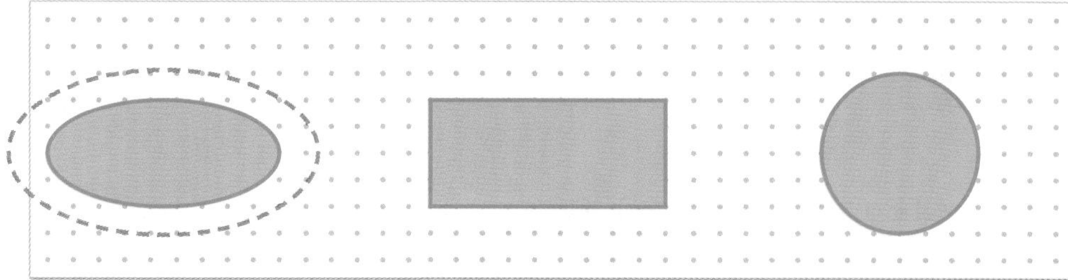

2.

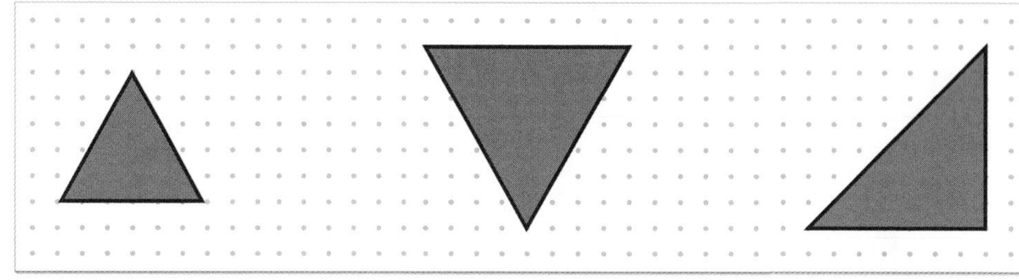

3.

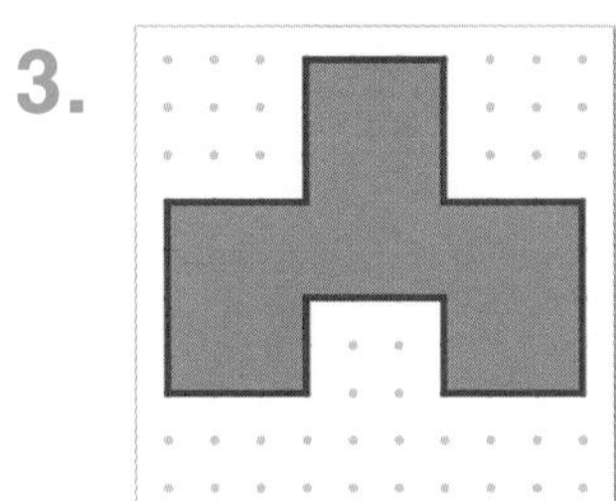

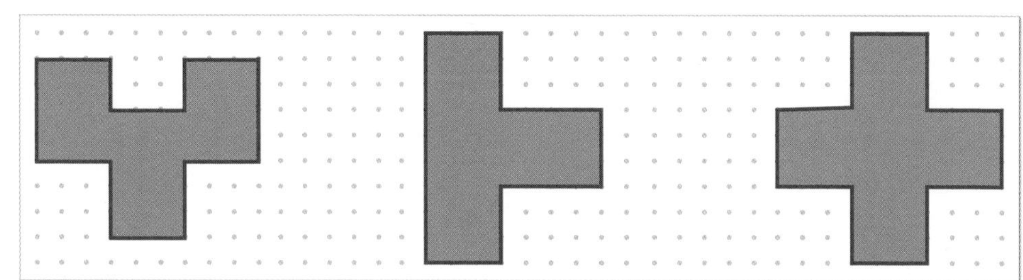

Problem Solving ▶ Visual Thinking

Draw a congruent shape.

4.

5.

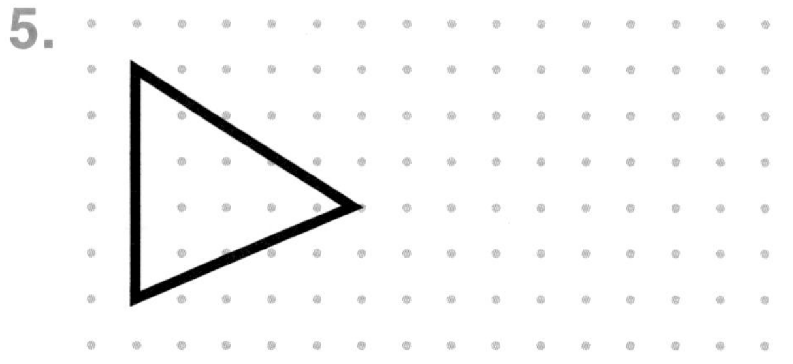

6.

7.

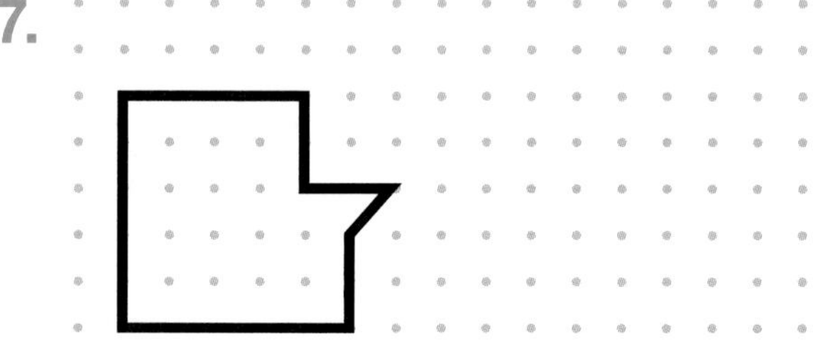

At Home Ask your child to explain why each shape is congruent to the first shape in Exercises 1–3.

Hands-On

Name ______________________________

Activity: Symmetry

Objective
Identify and draw lines of symmetry.

Vocabulary
line of symmetry
symmetry

Shapes with **symmetry** have two matching parts.

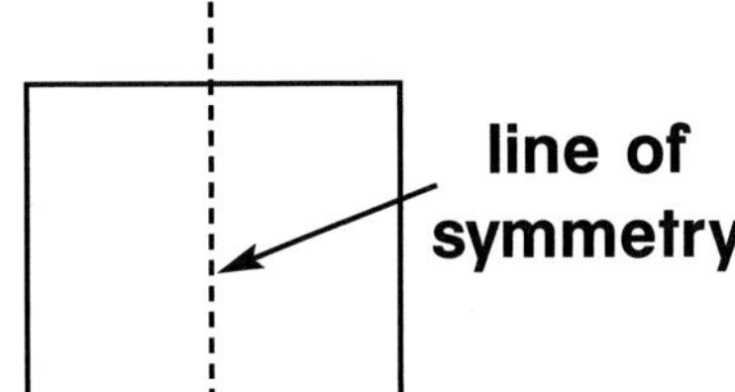

This shape does not have symmetry.

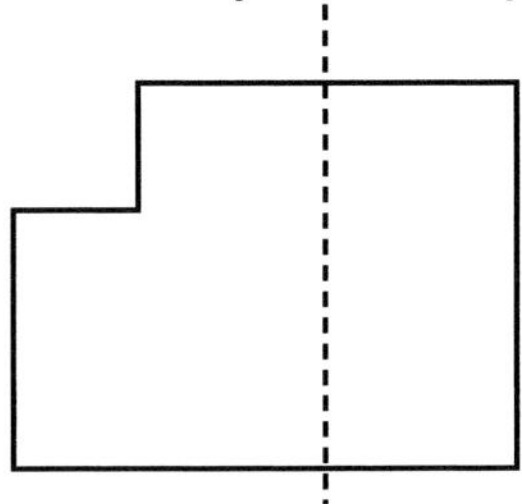

If a shape can be folded so that the two parts match, the shape has symmetry.

Work Together

Use the Shapes and Symmetry page (LT16).
Cut out the shapes.
Fold each shape to see if it has symmetry.
Glue each shape in the correct column.

Symmetry	No Symmetry

Make a shape of your own and glue it in the correct column.

Work Together

Circle the letter or shape if it has a line of symmetry.
Draw the line.

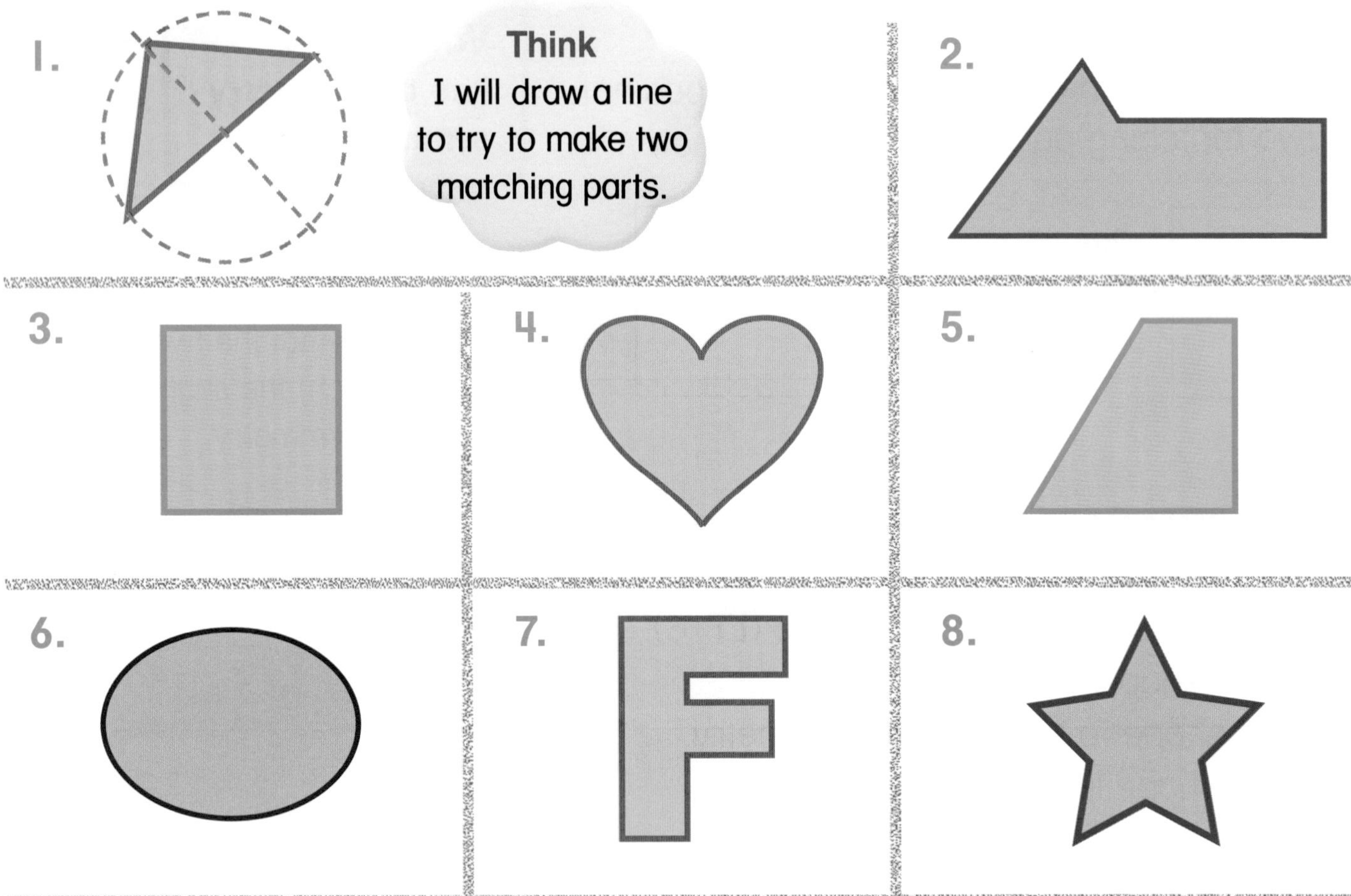

Draw a part that will match when the figure is folded on the dashed line.

9.

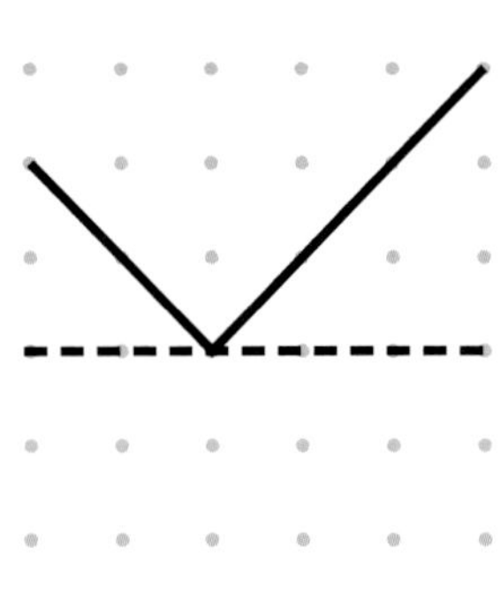

10. Draw your own.

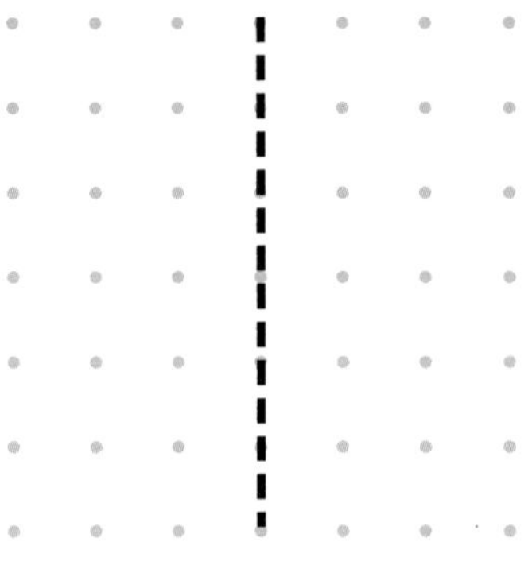

11. **Talk About It** How does folding a shape help show there is a line of symmetry?

On Your Own

Remember
Shapes with a line of symmetry have matching parts.

Circle the letter or shape if it has a line of symmetry. Draw the line.

1. C	2.	3. 4
4. V	5. 9	6. A
7. t	8. 8	9. B
10. $	11. G	12. *

13. **Talk About It** Every shape that has a line of symmetry has two congruent parts. Does every shape with two congruent parts have a line of symmetry? Trace these shapes to help you answer the question.

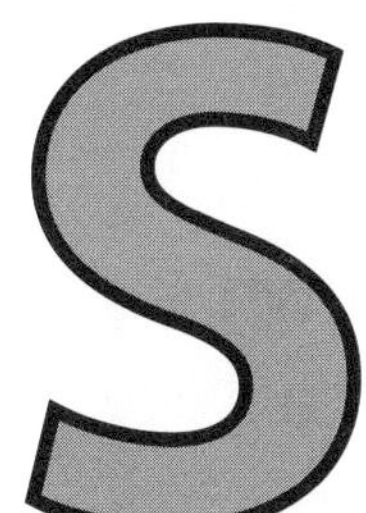

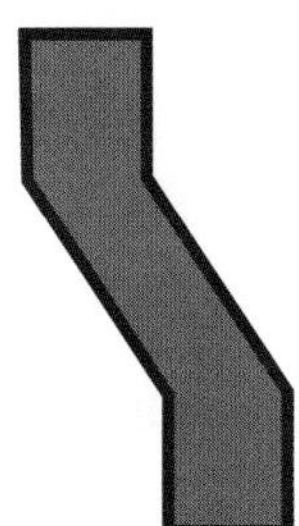

Now Try This Rotational Symmetry

Some shapes can be turned and look the same.
They have **rotational symmetry**.

Use the Shapes and Symmetry page (LT16).

1. Cut out the circle.
   Place it on top of this circle.

   Now turn the circle.
   When it is turned it looks the same.
   It has rotational symmetry.

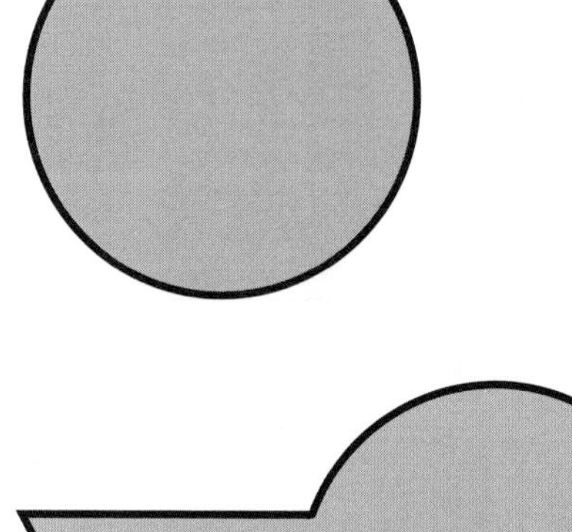

2. Cut out this figure.
   Place it on top of the figure on this page.
   Turn the figure.
   When it is turned it does not look the same.
   It does not have rotational symmetry.

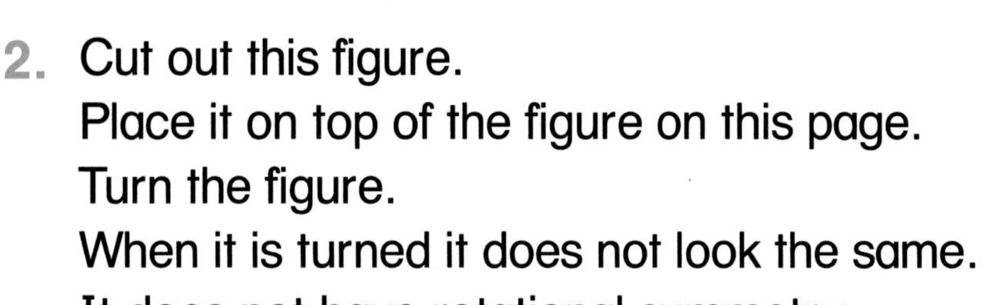

Cut out the rest of the figures on the Shapes and Symmetry page.
Use the drawings below to see if the figure has rotational symmetry.
Write yes or no.

1. 

   ____

2. 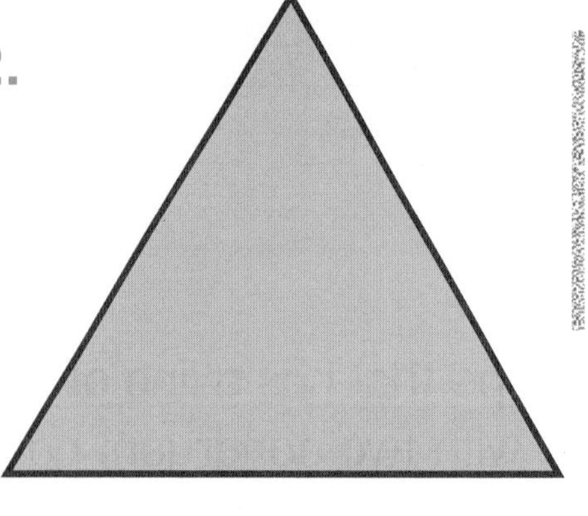

   ____

3. 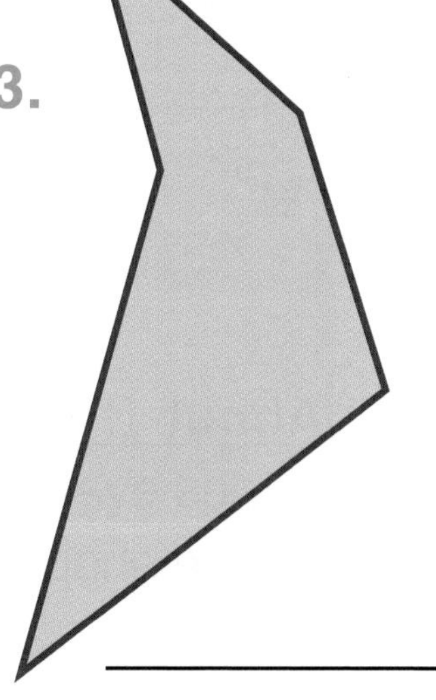

   ____

4. **Write About It** What capital letters can you turn upside down and they look exactly the same? Do these letters have rotational symmetry? How do you know?

Draw or Write to Explain.

Hands-On

Name ______________________________

Slides, Flips, and Turns

 **Audio Tutor 1**/21 Listen and Understand

Objective
Identify slides, flips, and turns.

Vocabulary
slide **flip** **turn**

You can move shapes in different ways.
Put [trapezoid] on the first shape.

Slide the shape.
Trace to show the move.

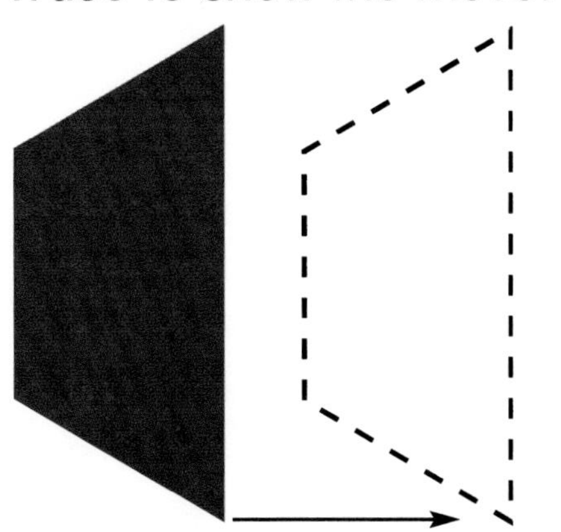

Pick up the shape and **flip** it.
Trace to show the move.

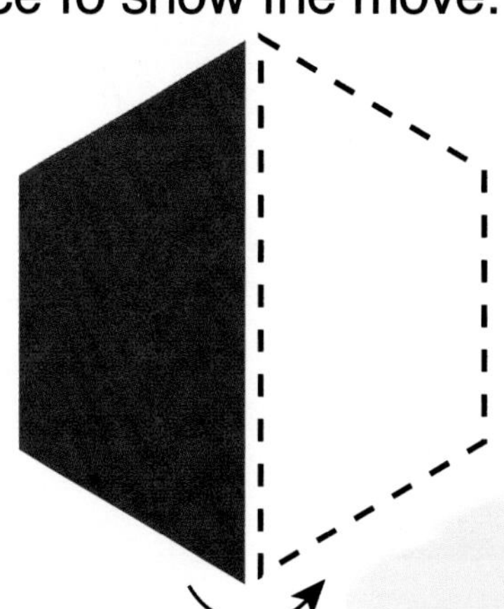

Think
of a shape flipping over a line.

Turn the shape.
Trace to show the move.

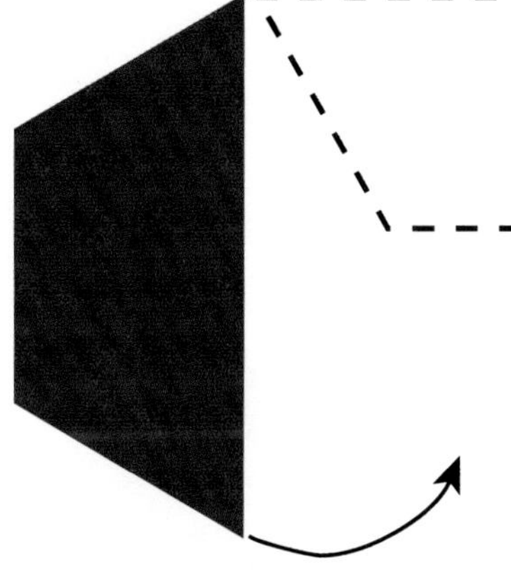

Guided Practice

Move the shape.
Trace to show the move.

Think
I can pick up the shape and flip it.

1. flip

2. slide

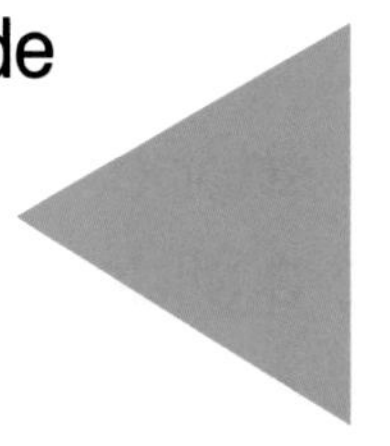

Explain Your Thinking How are a slide and a flip different? How are they the same?

Practice

Remember
You can move shapes in different ways.

Move the shape.
Trace to show the move.

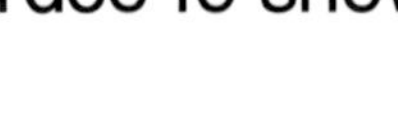

1. flip

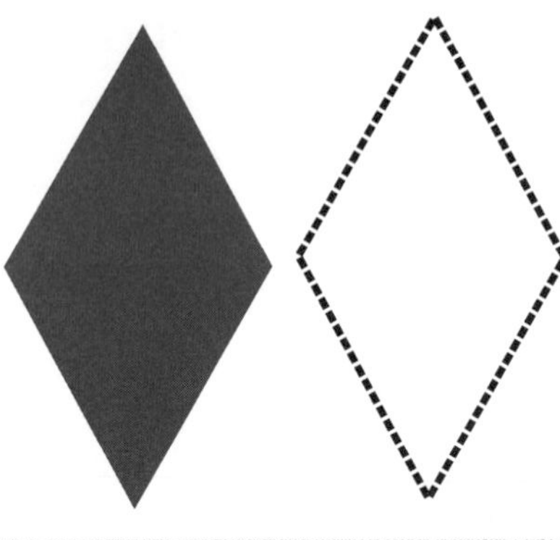

2. slide

3. turn

4. flip

5. turn

6. slide

Problem Solving ▶ Visual Thinking

7. Look at the shape.
Do you see a slide, flip, or turn? How do you know?

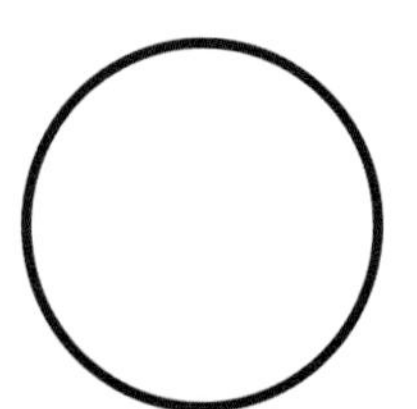

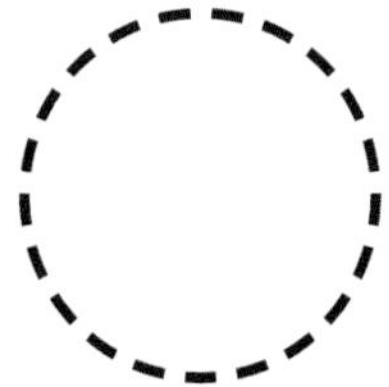

Draw or write to explain.

____

____

____

____

At Home Ask your child to show you how to slide, flip, and turn an envelope.

Problem Solving

Name________________________________

Find a Pattern

Objective
Identify and create geometric patterns.

Kia is making this belt for her teacher. She is not finished. Help Kia by naming the rest of the shapes in the pattern.

● ■ ■ ● ■ ■ ● ■ ■ ● ■ ■ ● ___ ___ ___ ___ ___ ___ ___ ___

UNDERSTAND

What do you know?

- The pattern is made with two shapes.
- The pattern repeats.

PLAN

What is the pattern?

Circle the pattern unit.

SOLVE

Continue the pattern on the belt.

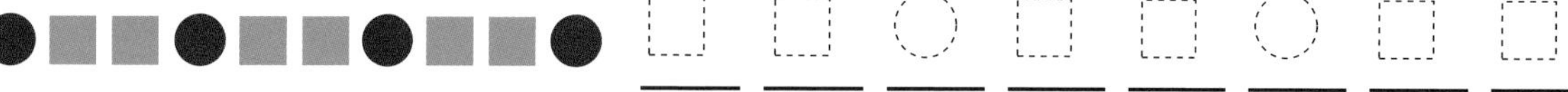

LOOK BACK

Say the pattern.
Do the shapes you drew extend the pattern?

Remember:
▶ Understand
▶ Plan
▶ Solve
▶ Look Back

Guided Practice

Draw the three shapes that come next in the pattern.

1. Mike saw this pattern on a folder.

Draw or write to explain.

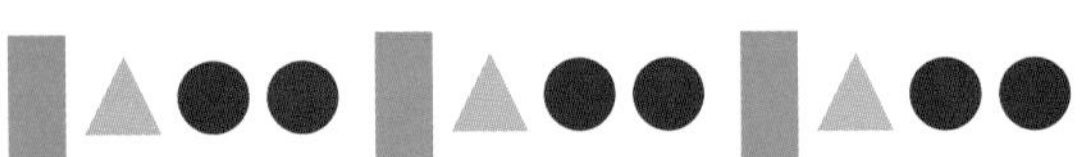

Think
The pattern unit is triangle, triangle, circle, circle.

2. Jenna saw this pattern on a cup.

Think
What is the pattern?

Practice

3. Gabe saw this pattern on a hat.

4. Rita saw this pattern on a poster.

5. Philipe saw this pattern on a shirt.

Go on

Name ____________________

Strategies
Draw a Picture
Write a Number Sentence
Find a Pattern

Mixed Problem Solving

Solve.

Draw or write to explain.

1. Tanya draws a pattern for a quilt. Draw the shape that will come next.

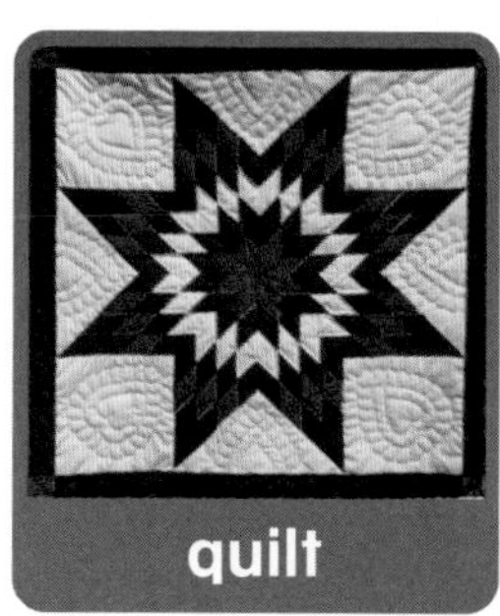
quilt

2. A bookcase has 2 shelves. Each shelf has 8 candles. How many candles are in the bookcase?

candles

_____ candles

3. Linda saw this pattern on a Navajo rug. Draw the next three shapes in the pattern.

Navajo rug

4. **Multistep** Carl has 6 green balloons and 4 red balloons. Three green balloons break. How many balloons does he have now?

balloons

_____ balloons

At Home Create a pattern using objects at home. Ask your child to name the pattern unit.

Problem Solving on Tests • Listening Skills

Open Response

Listen to your teacher read the problem. Solve.

1. Draw a square.
   Then draw a circle inside the square.

Show your work using pictures, numbers, or words.

2. Look at the pattern. Draw the two shapes that will come next.

______ ______

Multiple Choice

Listen to your teacher read the problem.
Choose the correct answer.

3.

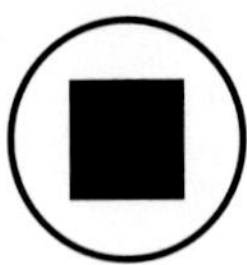 ○  ○  ○  ○

4.

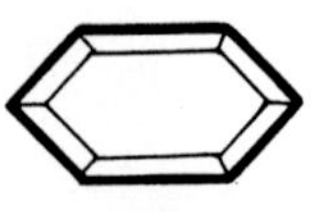 ○ 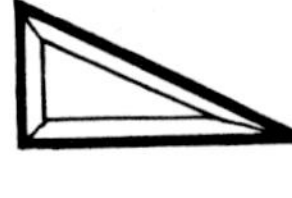 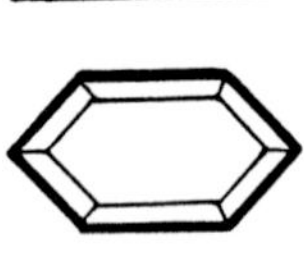 ○  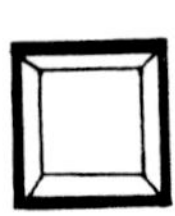 ○ 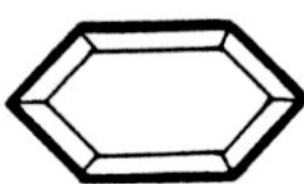 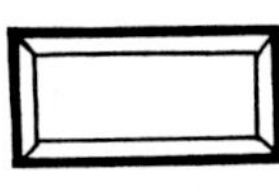 ○

Now Try This Curves and Angles

These are **curves.** They are not straight.

These are **angles.** The lines are straight and meet at a point or vertex.

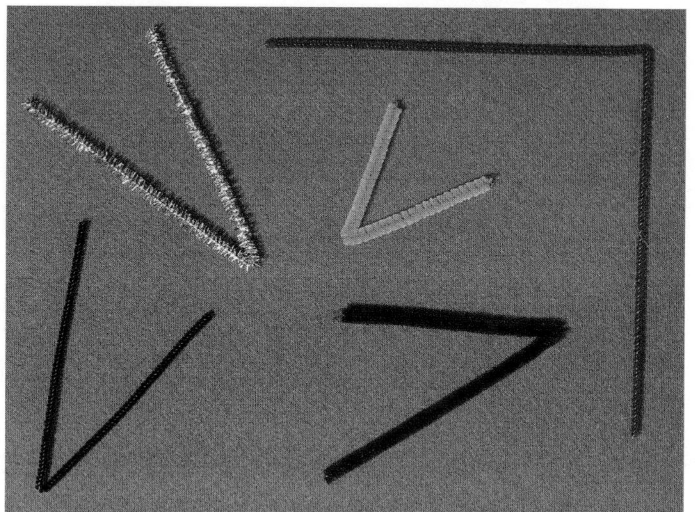

Write **true** or **false**.

1. This is an angle.

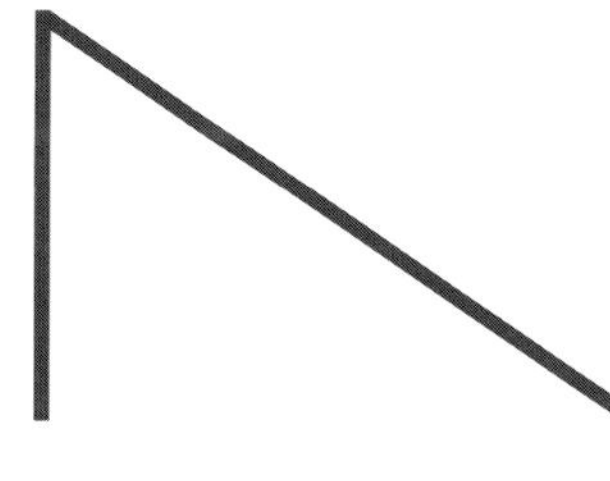

____

2. This is an angle.

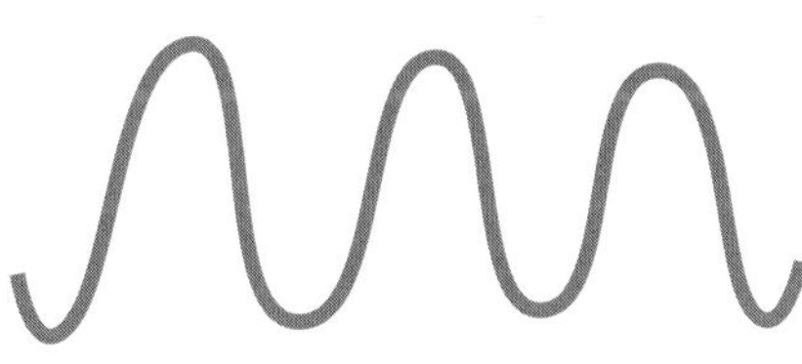

____

3. This is an angle.

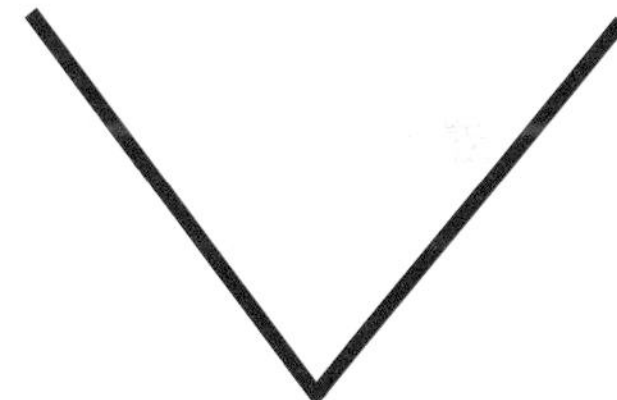

____

4. This is a curve.

____

5. This is a curve.

____

6. This is a curve.

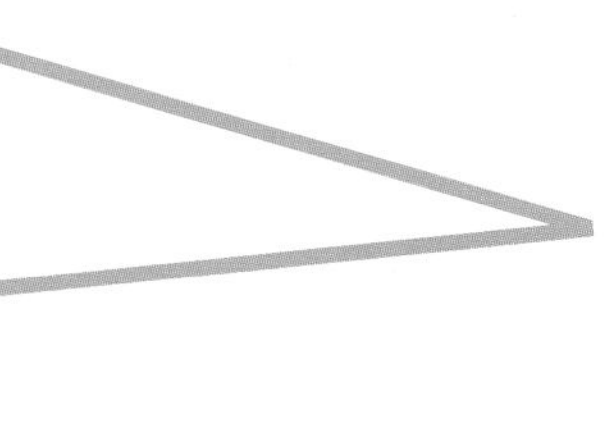

____

Problem Solving

Social Studies Connection

Flag Figure Activity

Togo

Puerto Rico

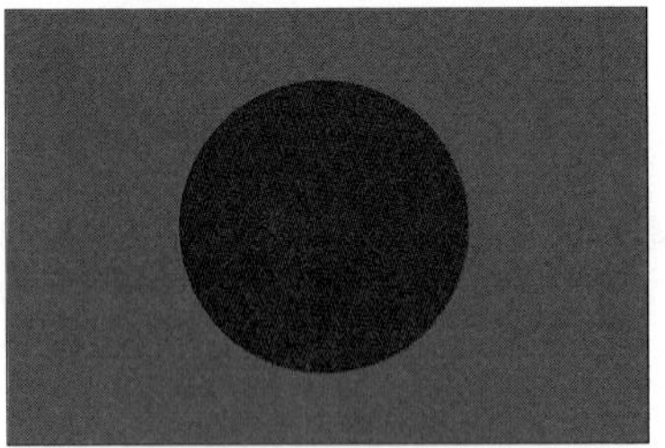
Bangladesh

Flags have shapes and colors that can mean many things.
Look at these flags from other countries.

Talk About It What shapes do you see?

WEEKLY WR READER eduplace.com/map

Key Topic Review

Ordering Numbers

Use the number line.
Complete the sentence.

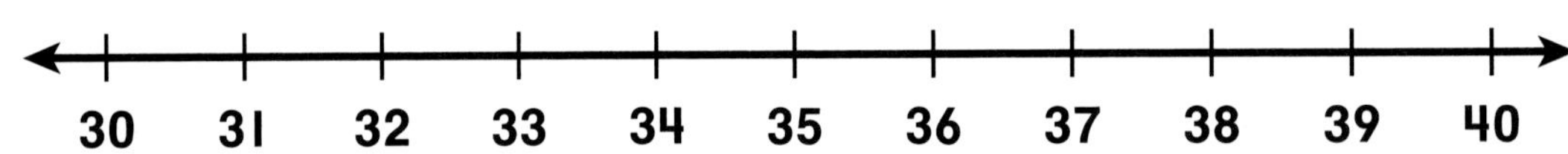

1. 31 is just before ______
2. 39 is just after ______
3. 34 is just before ______
4. 32 is just after ______
5. 35 is one more than ______
6. 39 is one less than ______
7. 40 is one more than ______
8. 37 is one less than ______

Count forward.
Write the missing numbers.

9. 31, 32, ______, ______, 35

Count backwards.
Write the missing numbers.

10. 40, ______, 38, 37, ______

Extra Practice at **eduplace.com/map**

Name ____________________

Chapter Review/Test

Vocabulary

Complete the sentence.

vertex
congruent
line of symmetry

1. The place where two sides meet is the ____________.

2. ____________ shapes are the same size and the same shape.

3. I can draw a ____________________ if both parts are matching.

Concepts and Skills

Write the name of the shape.
Write two reasons for your answer.

4. ____________

____

____

Look at the angle.
Write **acute, obtuse,** or **right**.

5. ____________ angle

6. Draw a circle around every trapezoid.

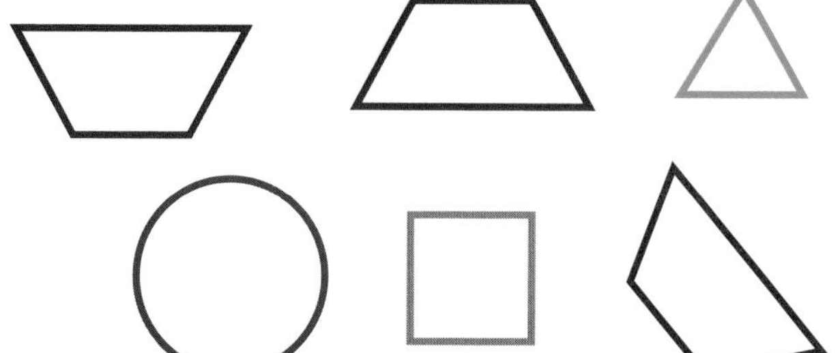

7. Draw a circle around every parallelogram.

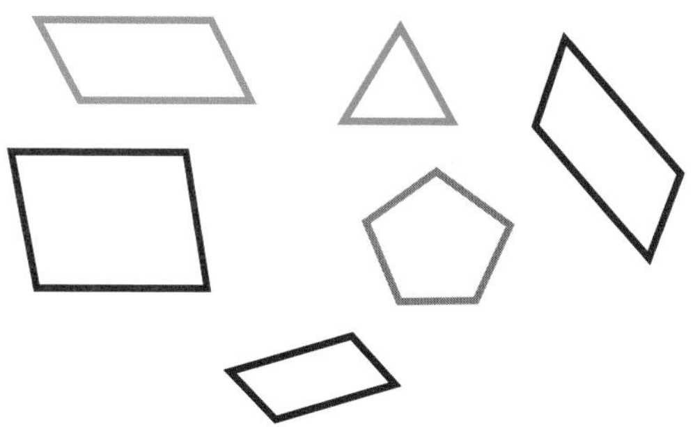

Circle the shape that is congruent to the first shape.

8. 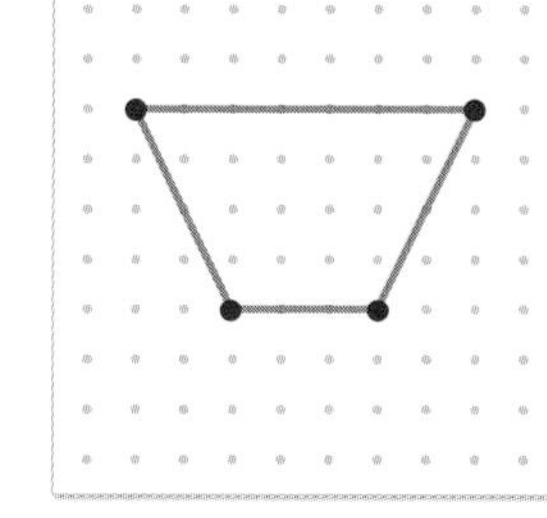

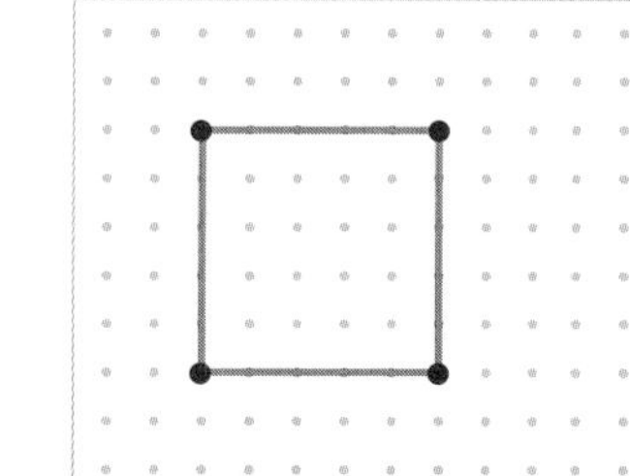

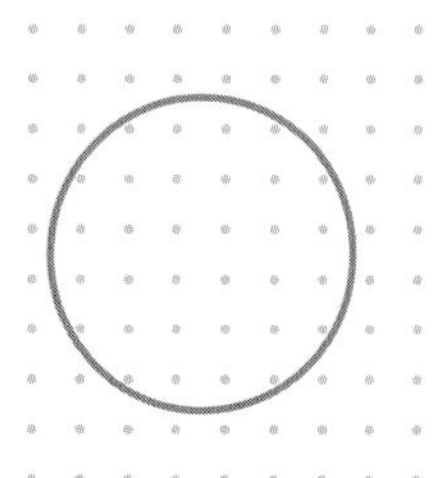

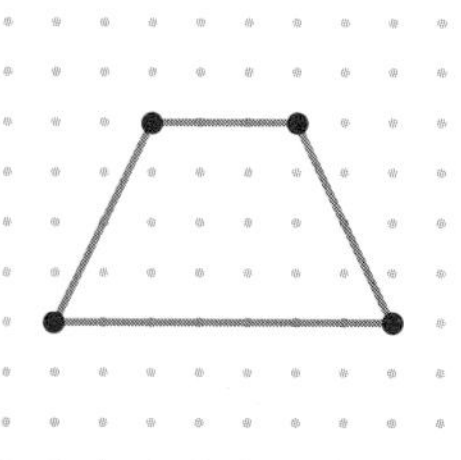

Chapter Review/Test

Circle the letters that have a line of symmetry.
Draw the line.

9. C

10. O

11. F

Use pattern blocks to make Shape A.
Then change the blocks to make a new shape. Trace the blocks.

12.

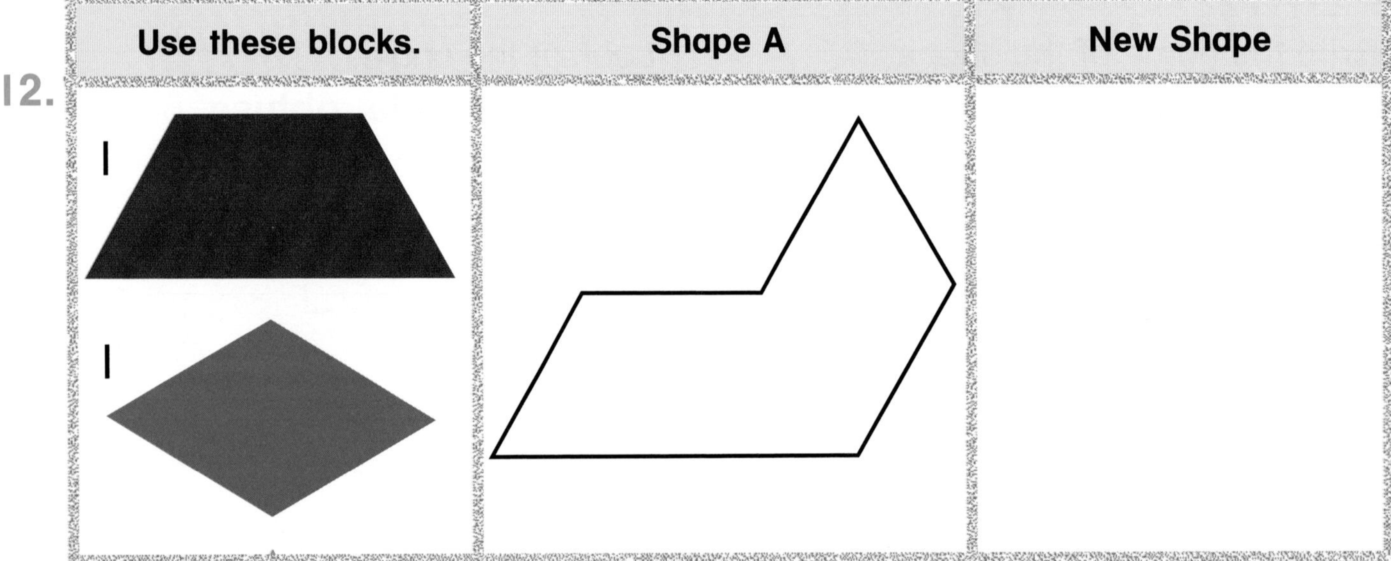

Use these blocks.	Shape A	New Shape
1 (trapezoid) 1 (rhombus)		

Move the shape.
Trace to show the move.

13. turn

14. flip

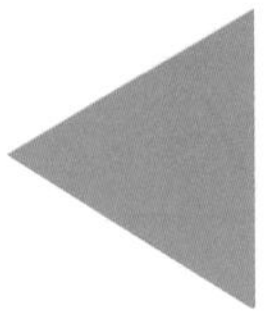

Problem Solving

Draw the three shapes that come next in the pattern.

15. Shannon saw this pattern on a cup.

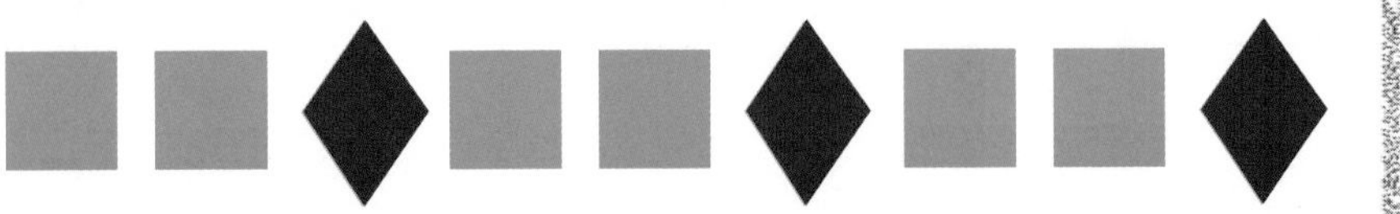

Solid Shapes

CHAPTER 8

INVESTIGATION

What objects can you find in your classroom that have the same shapes as the ones in this picture?

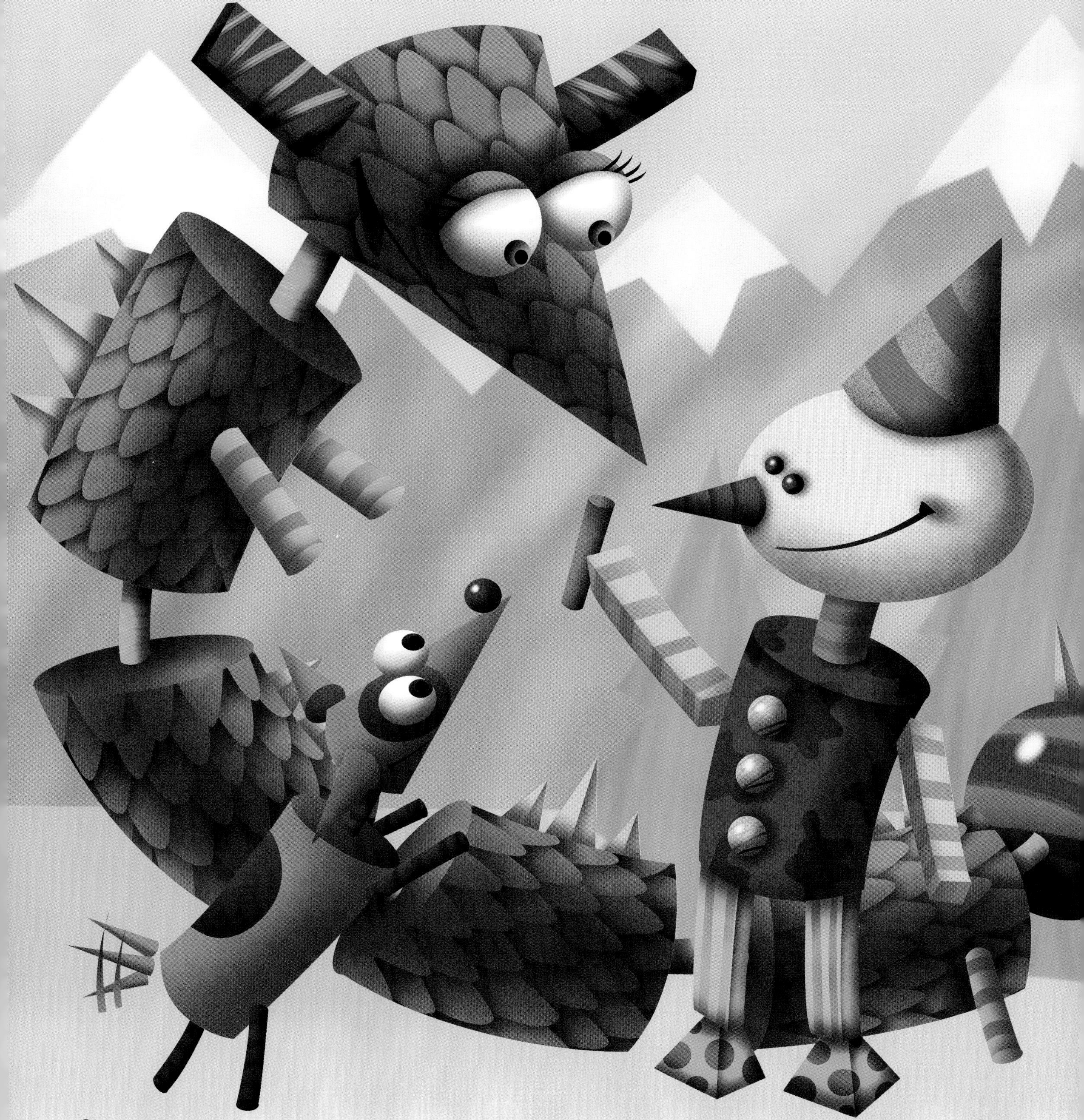

Toy Art

Draw a toy made of shapes.

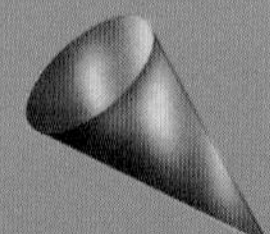

Name ______________________________

Identifying Solid Shapes

Objective
Identify solid shapes.

Vocabulary
names for solid shapes

rectangular prism **sphere** **square pyramid**

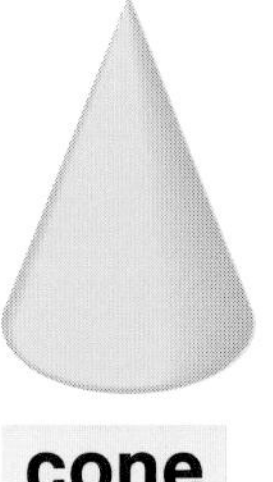

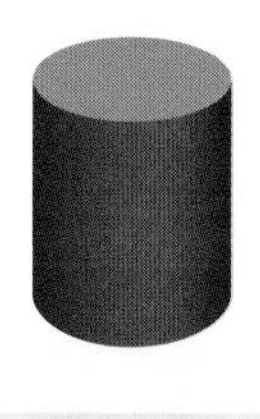

cone **cube** **cylinder**

Guided Practice

Write the name of the solid shape.
Circle the objects that are the same solid shape.

1.

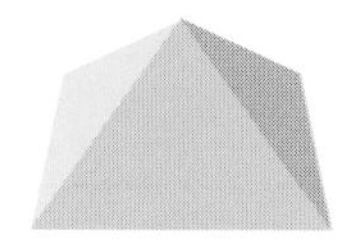

____

2.

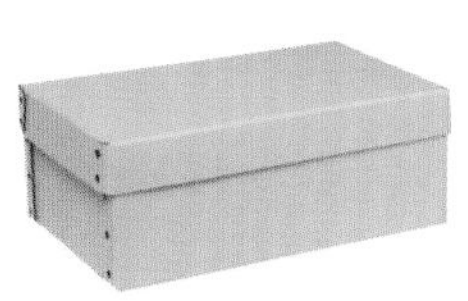
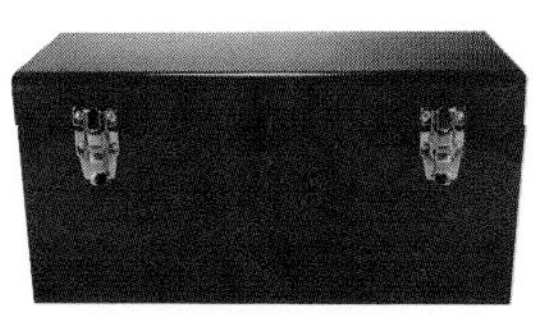

____

3.

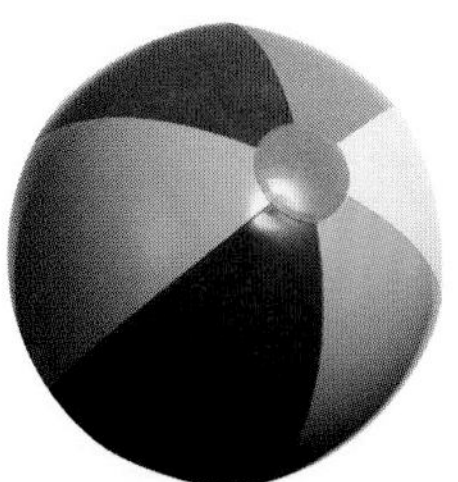

____

Explain Your Thinking Name some objects that are the same shape as a sphere.

Practice

Remember
Think about the shapes below to name each part.

Write the names of the two solid shapes in the picture.

   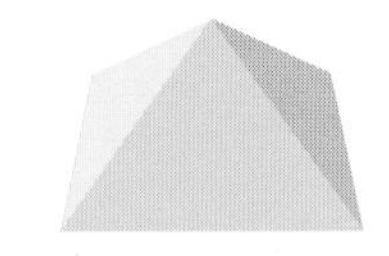 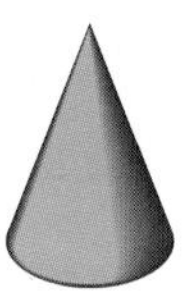

cube sphere rectangular prism cylinder square pyramid cone

1. 

sphere

cone

2. 

____

____

3. 

____

____

4. 

____

____

Problem Solving ▶ Visual Thinking

Write the number of [cube] used in each shape.

5. 

______

6. 

______

At Home Find objects in your home that are the same shapes as those named above. Ask your child to name the solid shapes.

Name ____________________

Faces, Edges, and Vertices

 Audio Tutor 1/22 Listen and Understand

Objective
Identify the faces, edges, and vertices of solid shapes.

Vocabulary
vertex **face**
vertices **edge**

You can describe solid shapes by the number of **faces,** **edges,** and **vertices.**

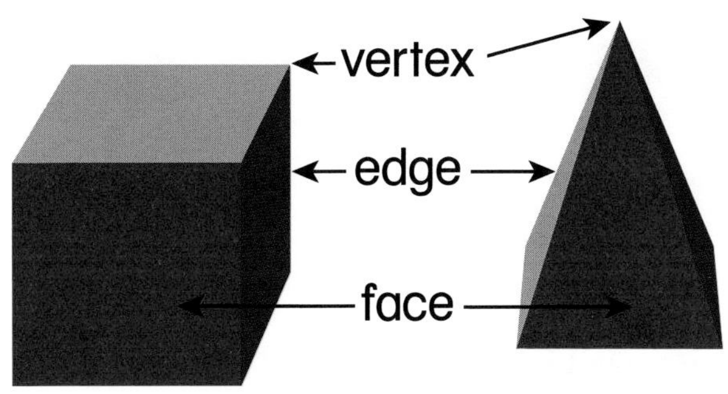

A **face** is a flat surface.
An **edge** is where 2 faces meet.
A **vertex** is the point where 3 or more edges meet.

Guided Practice

Use solid shapes to count the faces, edges, and vertices.

		Faces	Edges	Vertices
1.	cube	______	______	______
2.	sphere	______	______	______
3.	square pyramid	______	______	______
4.	cylinder	______	______	______
5.	rectangular prism	______	______	______
6.	cone	______	______	______

Explain Your Thinking How can you sort the solid shapes in Exercises 1–6 into two different groups?

Practice

Remember
There are faces, edges, and vertices you cannot see in the picture.

Circle the shapes that match the description.

1. 2 faces, 0 edges, 0 vertices

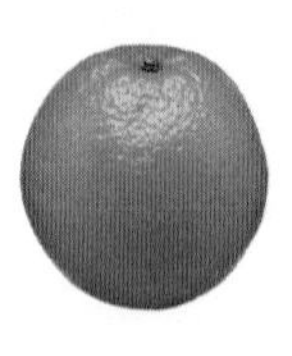

2. 6 faces, 12 edges, 8 vertices

3. 5 faces, 8 edges, 5 vertices

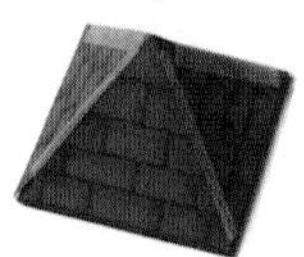

4. 1 face, 0 edges, 1 vertex

5. 0 faces, 0 edges, 0 vertices

6. 6 faces, 12 edges, 8 vertices

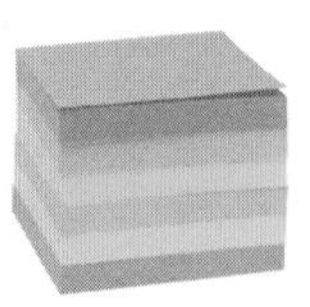

Problem Solving  Reasoning

Some solids slide.
Some solids roll.
Some solids stack.

7. Circle the solids that roll.
   Put an X on the solids that slide.
   Put a line under the solids that stack on top of each other.

8. **Talk About It** Which solids roll and slide? How do you know?

At Home Find objects in your home that slide, roll, or stack. Ask your child to show how they are alike and different.

Name ______________________

Activity: Plane Shapes on Solid Shapes

Hands-On

Objective
Make plane shapes from faces of solid shapes.

Some solid shapes have faces. You can trace around a face to make a plane shape.

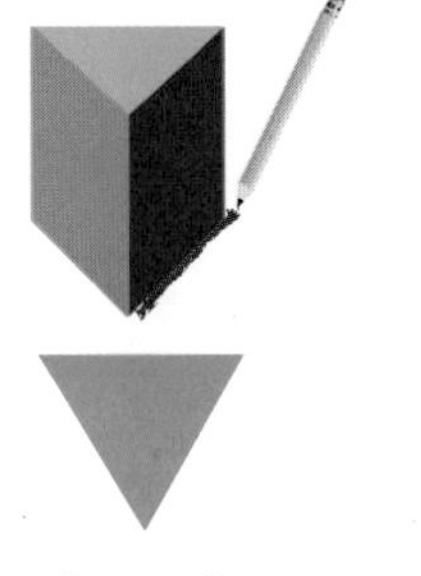

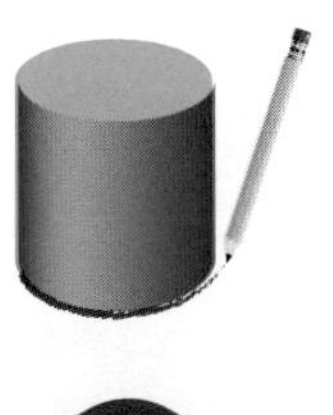

triangle   square   circle   rectangle

Work Together

Use the solid shape.
Trace the faces on a separate sheet of paper.
Circle the plane shape that matches a face.
Write the name of the plane shape.

Think
I can trace the face of the cube on another piece of paper.

1.  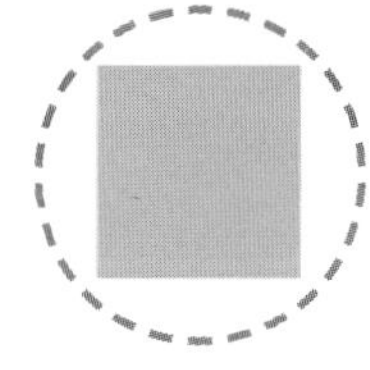   square

2.     ______________

3.   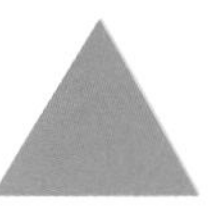  ______________

4.    ______________

5. **Talk About It** What solid shapes have more than one face? Exactly one face? Zero faces?

On Your Own

Draw the shapes you would make if you traced the faces of the object.

Remember
Some solid shapes have different shaped faces.

1\.

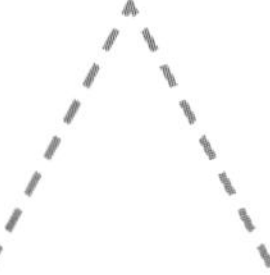

2\.

3\.

4\.

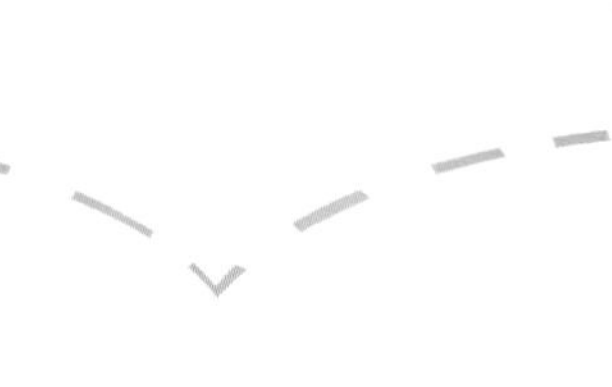

5\. **Write About It** What solid shapes could you trace to make this picture?

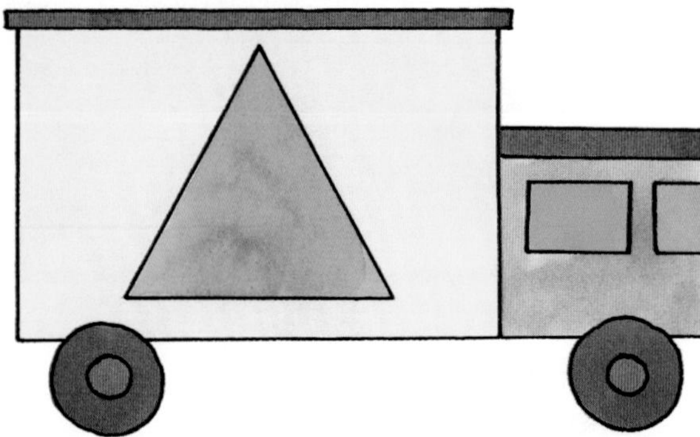

____

____

6\. What faces does a sphere have?

____

____

At Home Find objects that are solid figures. Have your child trace around the faces and name the plane shapes.

Go on

Name ______________________________

Now Try This **Make Solid Shapes**

Think
The straw is like an edge. The ball of clay is like a vertex.

Use straws and clay to make a cube.

Step 1

This makes one edge of a cube.

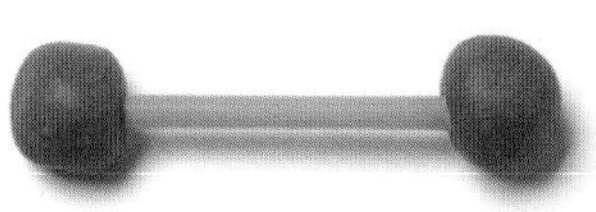

Step 2

This is one face of the cube.

Step 3

Make another face.

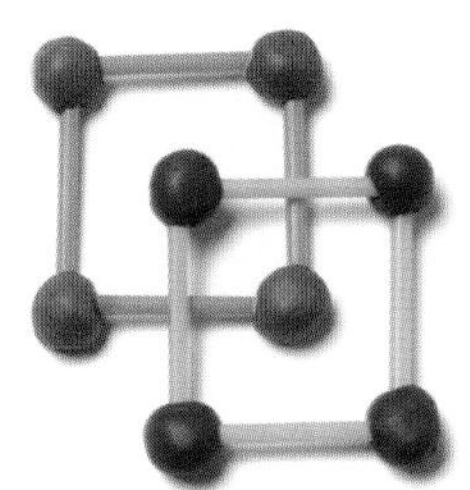

Step 4

Connect the faces to make the cube.

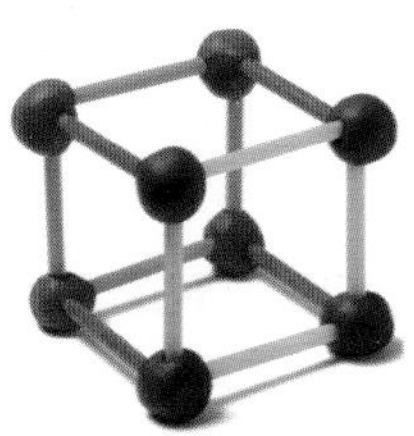

Use straws and clay to make the shape.
Write the number of faces, vertices, and edges.

1\.

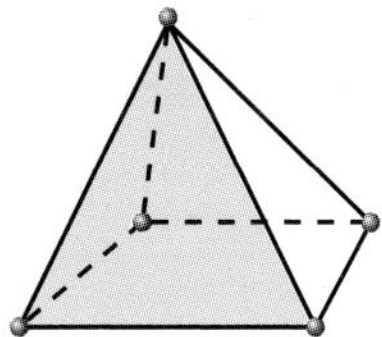

_____ triangle faces

_____ square face

_____ vertices

_____ edges

Build the blue face first. Cut straws to make shorter edges.

2\.

_____ rectangle faces

_____ vertices

_____ edges

3\. Write how many faces, edges, and vertices.

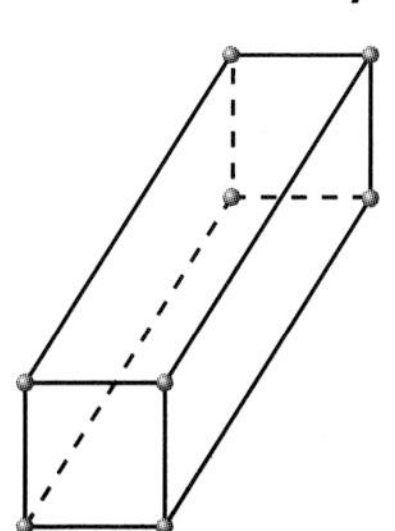

_____ square faces

_____ rectangular faces

_____ vertices

_____ edges

Quick Check

    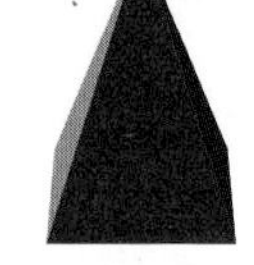 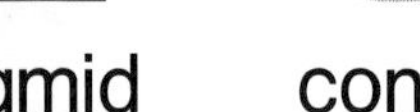

cube   sphere   rectangular prism   cylinder   pyramid   cone

Write the names of the two solid shapes in the picture.

1. 

____

____

2. 

____

____

Circle the shapes that match the number of faces, edges, and vertices.

3. 0 faces

   0 edges

   0 vertices

Draw the shapes you would make if you traced the faces of the solid shape.

4. 

Write how many faces, edges, and vertices.

5. 

_____ square faces

_____ vertices

_____ edges

Facts Practice, see page 669.

Name ________________________________

Classify and Compare Solid Shapes

Objective
Classify and compare solid shapes.

Audio Tutor 1/23 Listen and Understand

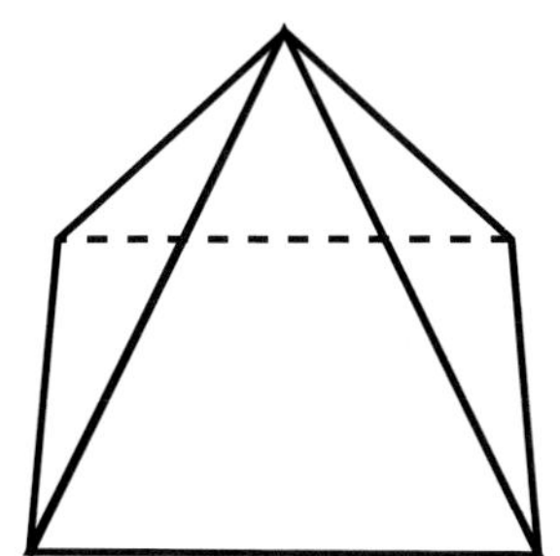

This is a square pyramid. It has __5__ faces.

Four of the faces are __triangles__.

The other face is a __square__.

A square pyramid has __5__ vertices.

A square pyramid has __8__ edges.

Guided Practice

Name the shape.
Write three reasons for your answer.

1. 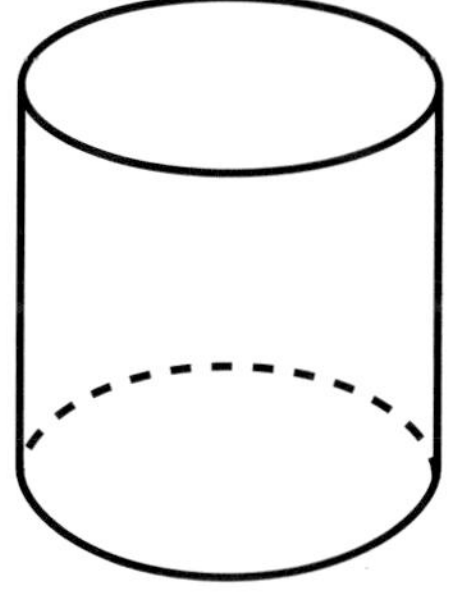

Think
This shape has two faces that are circles.

This is a ____________.

It has ____________

____

____

____

2. 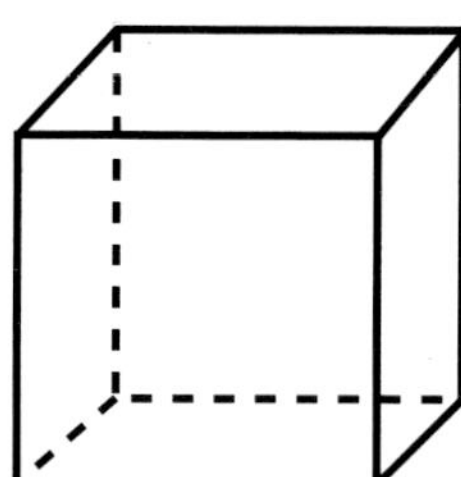

This is a ____________.

It has ____________

____

____

____

Explain Your Thinking How is a cylinder like a cone?

Extra Help at **eduplace.com/map**

Practice

Write how the pair is alike or different.
Count the faces, edges, and vertices.

	Alike	Different
1.	Both shapes roll.	A sphere has 0 faces. A cone has 1 face.
2.		
3.		
4.		

Problem Solving ▶ Visual Thinking

You can make a model of a solid shape.

5. Circle the one that makes a cylinder.

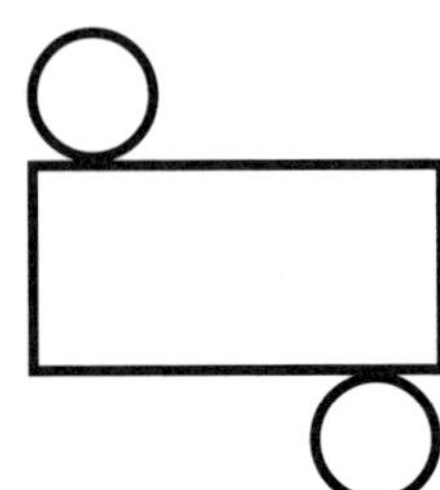

6. Put an X on the one that makes a cube.

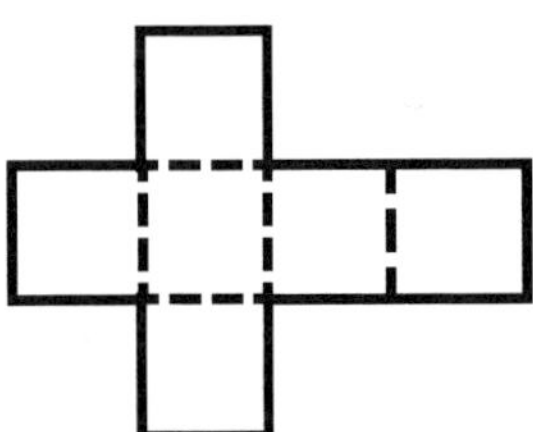

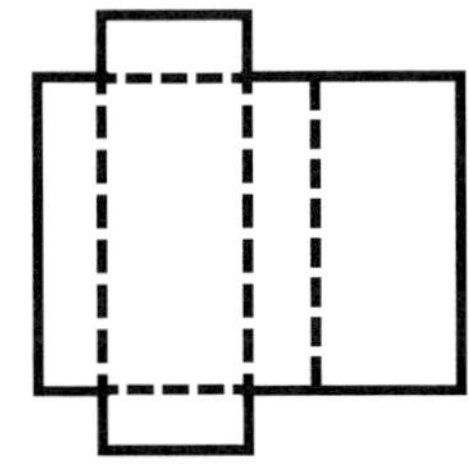

At Home Take your child on a shape walk to find examples of the shapes studied in this lesson.

Name ___________________________

Logical Thinking

Audio Tutor 1/24 Listen and Understand

Objective
Use logical thinking to solve problems.

Sometimes you can use clues to solve problems.

The math club goes on a shape search. They find more than 5 but fewer than 8 of Marina's favorite shape. Look at the table. Which shape is Marina's favorite?

Shape Search

Shape	Number
sphere	9
cone	2
cube	4
cylinder	6

UNDERSTAND

What do you know?

- They found more than 5 of Marina's favorite shape.
- They found fewer than 8 of Marina's favorite shape.

PLAN

Use logical thinking and the clues in the problem.

The number found is greater than 5.

The number found is less than 8.

The shape has a number between 5 and 8.

SOLVE

Cross out each shape that does not match the clue.

~~sphere~~ 9 is greater than 8.

~~cone~~ 2 is less than 5.

~~cube~~ 4 is less than 5.

cylinder 6 is between 5 and 8.

Marina's favorite shape is a cylinder.

LOOK BACK

Did you answer the question?
Does your answer make sense?

Extra Help at eduplace.com/map

Guided Practice

The table shows the number of votes for snack. Use the clues to find each person's favorite snack. Cross out the snacks that do not match the clues.

Favorite Snacks

Raisins	6
Pretzels	17
Fruit	14
Crackers	11

1. Eli's favorite snack got more than 7 votes but fewer than 13 votes. What is Eli's favorite snack?

   Think Which snack got 8 to 12 votes?

   Raisins
   Pretzels
   Fruit
   Crackers

   ____

2. Jayne likes the snack that got more than 12 votes. It got an odd number of votes. Which snack does Jayne like?

   Think Which snack got an odd number of votes that is greater than 12?

   Raisins
   Pretzels
   Fruit
   Crackers

   ____

Practice

3. Lexi's favorite snack got fewer than 13 votes. It got an even number of votes. Which snack does Lexi like?

   Raisins
   Pretzels
   Fruit
   Crackers

   ____

4. Sue's favorite snack got more than 12 votes. It did not get the most votes. What is Sue's favorite snack?

   Raisins
   Pretzels
   Fruit
   Crackers

   ____

Go on

Name ______________________________

Mixed Problem Solving

Strategies
Use Logical Thinking
Write a Number Sentence

Favorite Sphere-Shaped Fruit	
orange	11
grapefruit	14
globe grapes	6
cantaloupe	9

Use the table. Solve.

Draw or write to explain.

1. Jonah likes the fruit that got more votes than cantaloupe. It got an odd number of votes. Which fruit does he like?

____

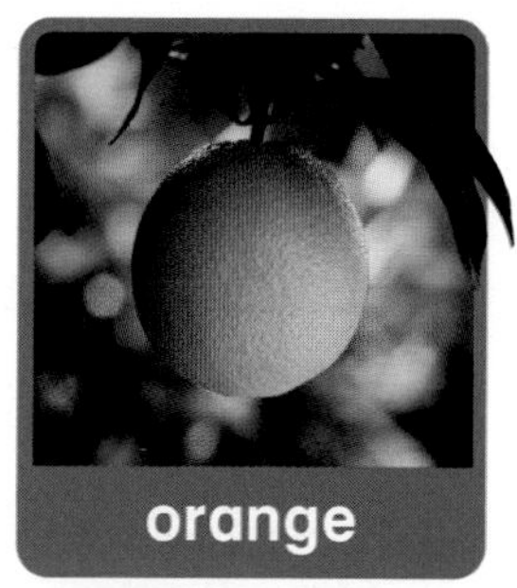

2. How many votes do globe grapes and cantaloupe have altogether?

______ votes

3. How many more votes did grapefruit get than globe grapes?

______ more votes

globe grapes

4. **Multistep** How many more votes than grapefruit did globe grapes and cantaloupe get?

______ more vote

At Home Ask your child to explain how he or she used clues to solve the problems in this lesson.

Problem Solving on Tests • Listening Skills

Open Response

Listen to your teacher read the problem.
Solve.

1. Yanni has 12 different toys. He closes his eyes and pulls out a toy with 2 faces and 0 vertices. It can roll. What shape is the toy?

Show your work using pictures, numbers, or words.

______

2. Emma builds a shape train out of blocks. She uses 1 rectangular prism, 2 cylinders, and 4 spheres. How many faces are on the blocks in the train?

______ faces

Multiple Choice

Listen to your teacher read the problem.
Choose the correct answer.

3.  ○   ○  ○ 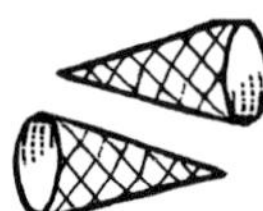 ○

4. 1 ○ 3 ○ 4 ○ 7 ○

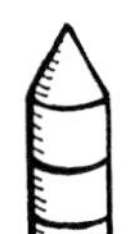 

Education Place
See **eduplace.com/map** for more Test-Taking Tips.

Name ____________________

Now Try This Shape Up!

Fill in the graph to show the number of each shape.

Solid Shapes on the Shelves

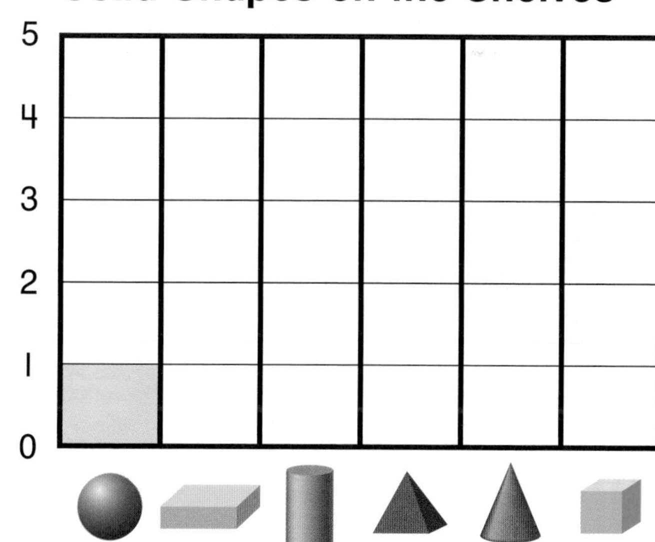

1. How many more cylinders than spheres are there? ____

2. If you were to trace the faces of all the cones, how many circles would be traced? ____

3. If you were to trace the faces of all the cylinders, how many circles would be traced? ____

4. What is one thing the graph shows?

____

____

5. **Write About It** Write a question about your graph. Ask a classmate to answer the question.

____

____

Activity

Art Connection

Shape Play

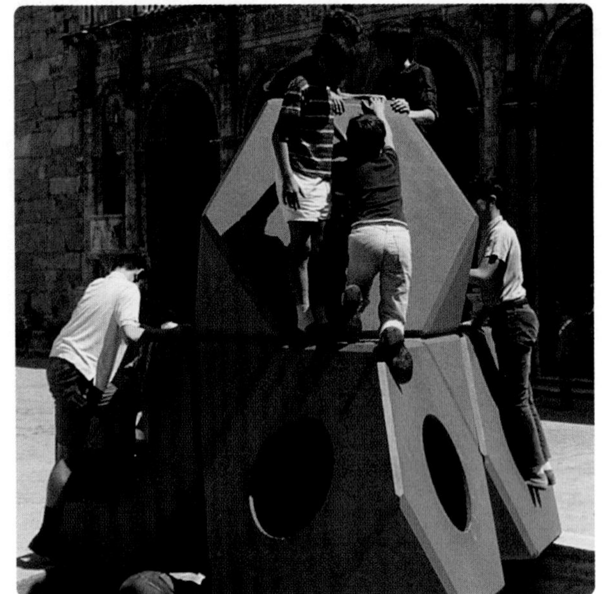

Isamu Noguchi was an artist.
He made many beautiful sculptures, including sculptures on which children can play.

This is one of his play sculptures called "Octetra." It is in Spoleto, Italy.

What plane shapes do you see on the solid shapes in the picture?

____

____

Key Topic Review

Place Value

Remember
> greater than
< less than
= equal to

Write the numbers.
Compare. Write >, <, or =.

1. 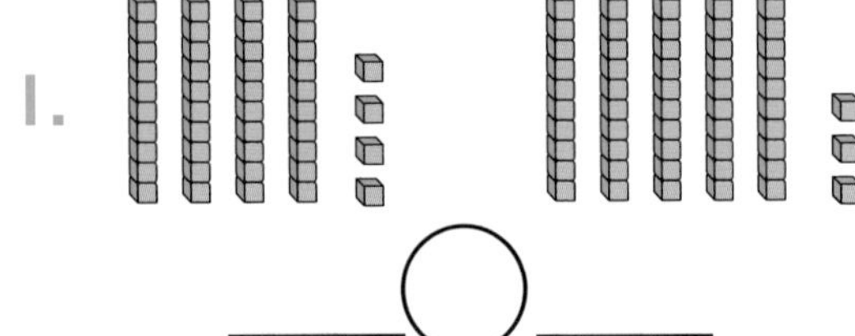

____ ◯ ____

2. 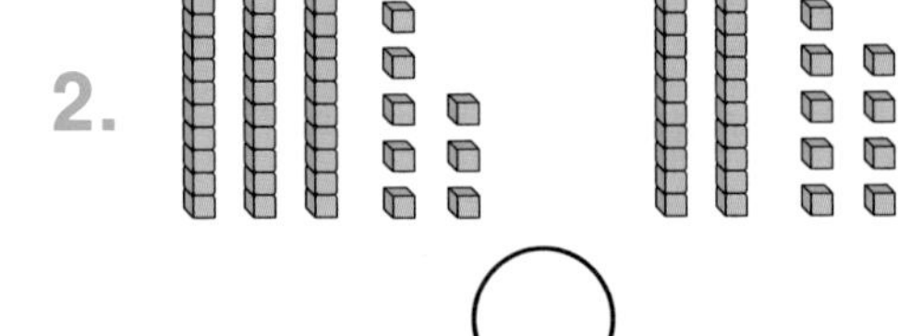

____ ◯ ____

Compare. Write >, <, or =.

3. 63 ◯ 72
4. 86 ◯ 68
5. 52 ◯ 49
6. 45 ◯ 54
7. 15 ◯ 13
8. 75 ◯ 75
9. 27 ◯ 23
10. 81 ◯ 91

Extra Practice at eduplace.com/map

Name ______________________

Chapter Review/Test

Vocabulary

Draw a line to match.

1. a flat surface — **edge**
2. where two faces meet — **face**
3. the point where 3 or more edges meet — **vertex**

Concepts and Skills

Write the names of the two solid shapes in the picture.

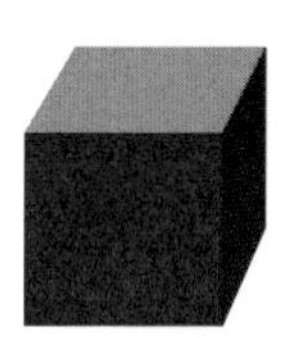
cube

sphere

cylinder

rectangular prism

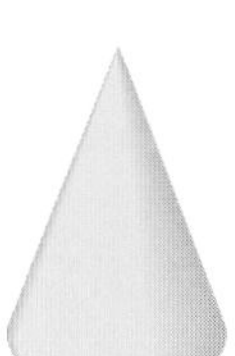
cone

square pyramid

4.  ______________ ______________

5.   ______________ ______________

Circle the shape that matches the description.

6. 2 faces, 0 edges, 0 vertices

7. 6 faces, 12 edges, 8 vertices

8. 0 faces, 0 edges, 0 vertices

9. 1 face, 0 edges, 1 vertex

Chapter Review/Test

Draw the shapes you would make
if you traced the faces of the solid shape.

10. 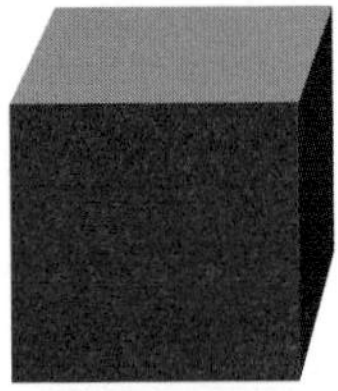

11. 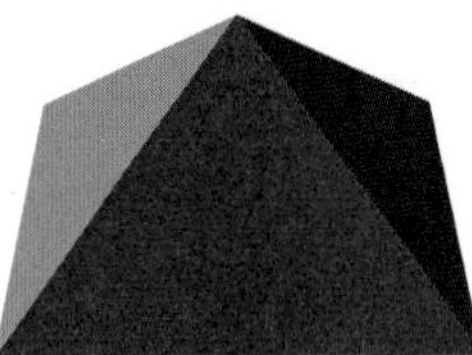

12. 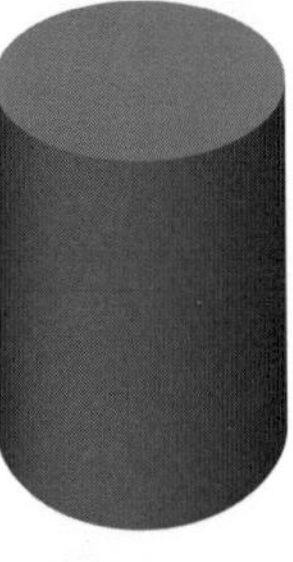

13. 

Write how the pair is alike or different.
Count the faces, edges, and vertices.

14. 

Alike	Different
____________	____________
____________	____________
____________	____________

Problem Solving

Use the table.
Solve.

Favorite Games	
Hide and Seek	15
Freeze Tag	6
Kickball	12
Hopscotch	8

15. Mindy's favorite game got more than 8 votes but less than 15 votes. What is her favorite game?

Hide and Seek　　Freeze Tag　　Kickball　　Hopscotch

Fractions

What do you see that is cut into halves?
What do you see that is cut into quarters?

CHAPTER 9

A Tasty Tale

Read the story.
Color the pictures to show the fractions in the story.
Draw fraction parts of foods on the table.

Luis likes to eat all of his lunch.

He eats the whole 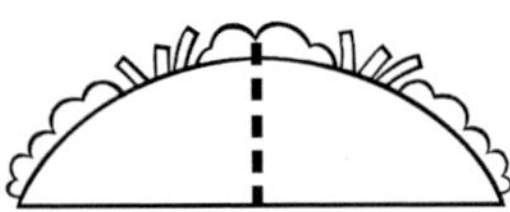. He drinks all of his 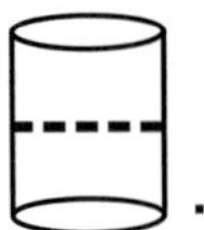.

Lin likes to eat one half of her lunch.

She eats one half of her 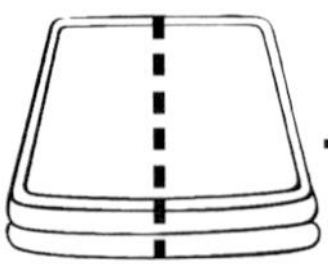. She drinks one half of her 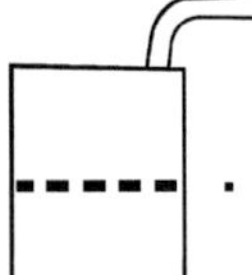.

One day, Luis shares his lunch with Lin.

They each eat one half of a 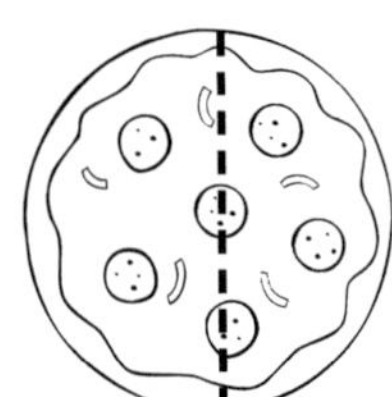 and one half of a .

Name ______________________________

Unit Fractions

> **Objective**
> Identify and write unit fractions.
>
> **Vocabulary**
> **denominator** **unit fraction**
> **fractions** **whole**
> **numerator**

Fractions name equal parts of a **whole**.
A **unit fraction** names one of the parts.

What part is orange?

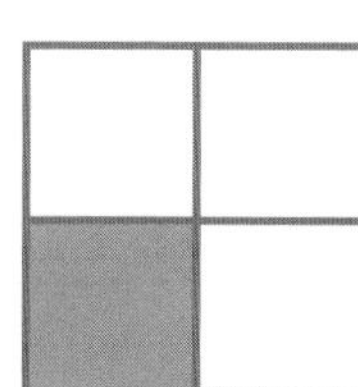

There are 4 fourths.

1 fourth is orange.

$\frac{1}{4}$ is orange.

This is how we write 1 fourth.

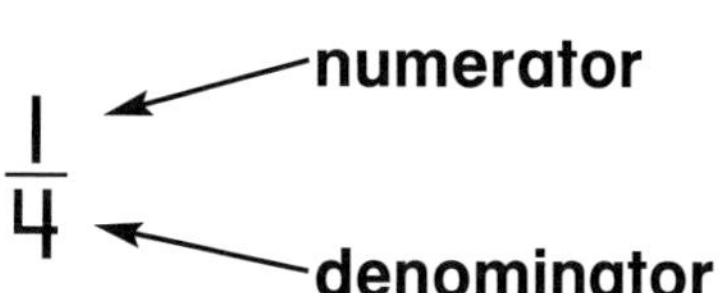

The **numerator** tells how many parts are shaded.

The **denominator** tells how many equal parts there are.

Guided Practice

Write the fraction for the shaded part.

1. 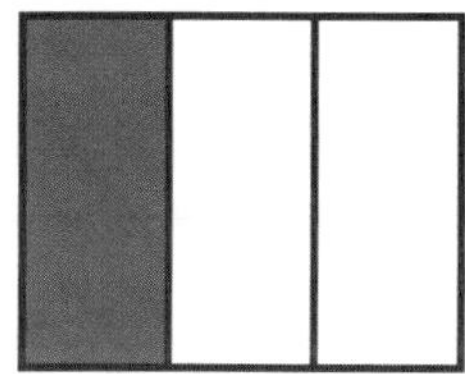 ______

Think
There are 3 equal parts. Each part is 1 third.

2. 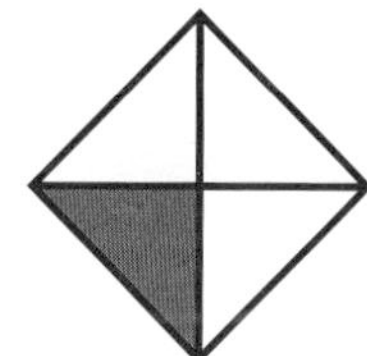 ______

3. 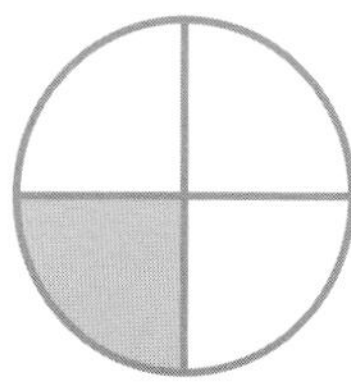 ______

4.  ______

5. 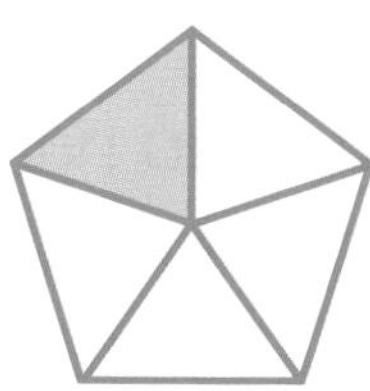 ______

Color to show the fraction.

6. $\frac{1}{8}$ 

7. $\frac{1}{10}$ 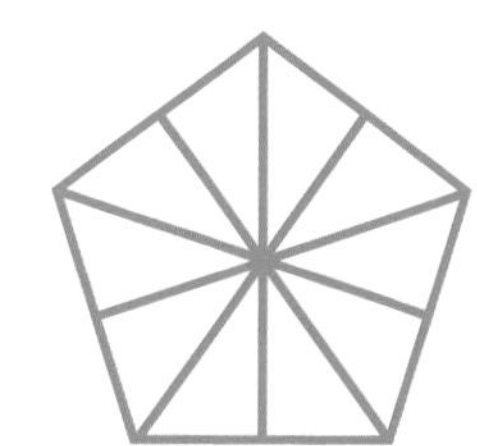

8. $\frac{1}{6}$ 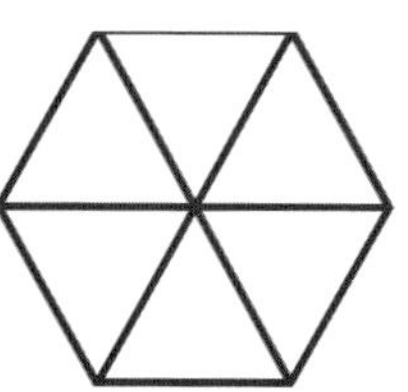

Explain Your Thinking What does the denominator mean in the fraction $\frac{1}{8}$?

Practice

Remember
The denominator of a fraction tells how many equal parts. The numerator tells how many parts are shaded.

Write the fraction for the shaded part.

1. 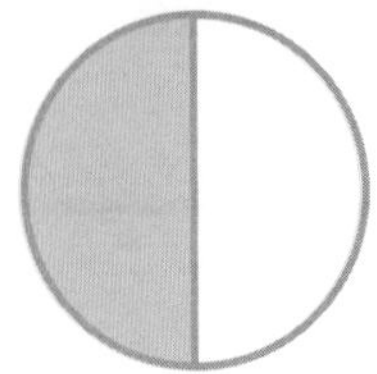 $\frac{1}{2}$

2.  ______

3. 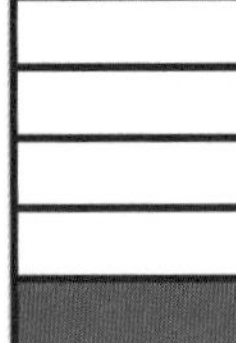 ______

4. 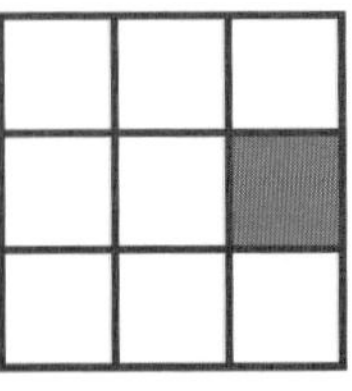 ______

5.  ______

6. 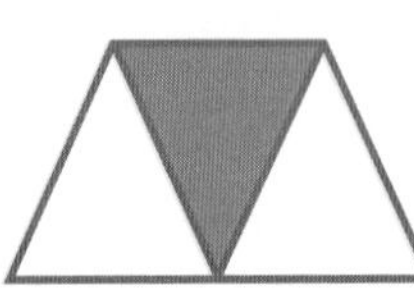 ______

Color to show one shaded part. Write the fraction.

7. 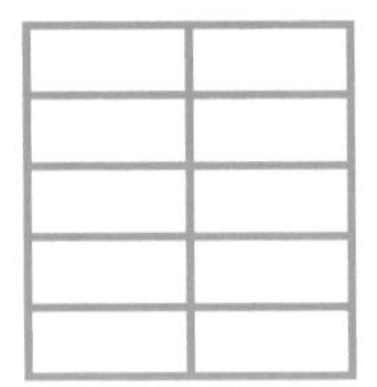 ______

8. 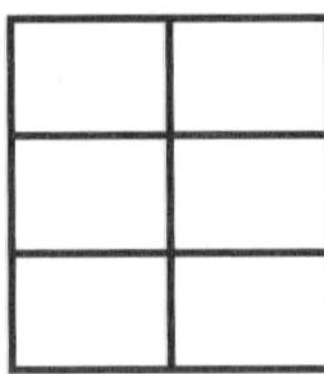 ______

9. 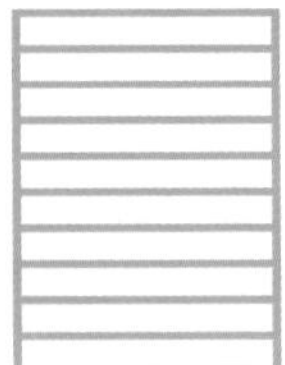 ______

Problem Solving  Reasoning

Draw and color to show the fraction.
Write the fraction.

10. Divide into halves. Color one half.

______

11. Divide into fourths. Color one fourth.

______

12. Divide into thirds. Color one third.

______

At Home Ask your child to fold towels or papers in halves, fourths, and thirds. Have him or her write the fraction for one of the equal parts.

Name ____________________

Other Fractions

Audio Tutor 1/25 Listen and Understand

Objective
Identify and write fractions.

Vocabulary
whole

Fractions can name more than one equal part of a whole.

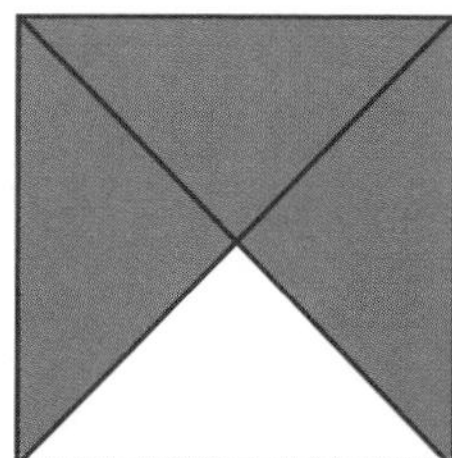

There are 4 equal parts.

3 parts are blue.

3 fourths are blue.

$\frac{3}{4}$ are blue.

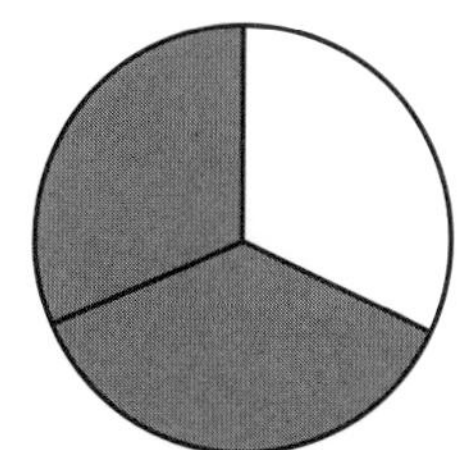

There are 3 equal parts.

2 parts are red.

2 thirds are red.

$\frac{2}{3}$ are red.

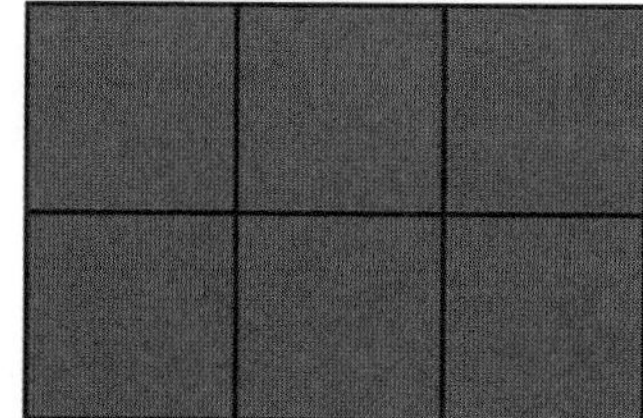

One **whole** is equal to 1.

The whole square is purple.

Six sixths are purple.

$\frac{6}{6}$ are purple. $\frac{6}{6} = 1$

Guided Practice

Write the fraction for the shaded parts.

1. 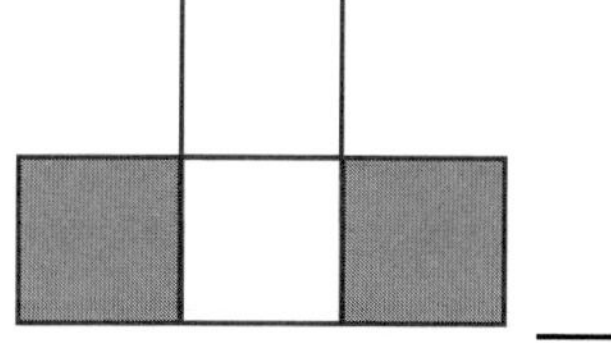 ______

Think
There are 4 equal parts. 2 fourths are shaded.

2. 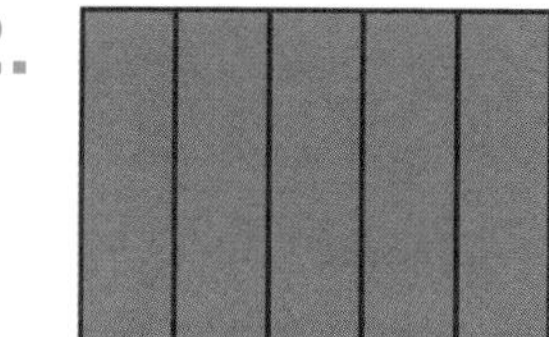 ______

3. 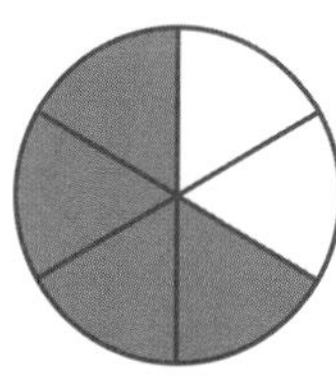 ______

4. 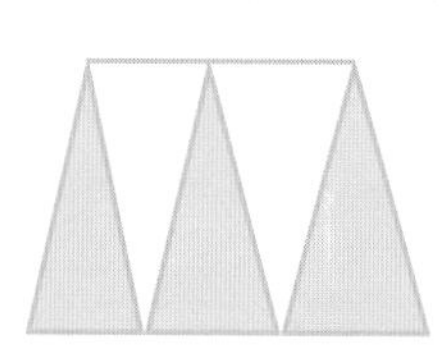 ______

5. 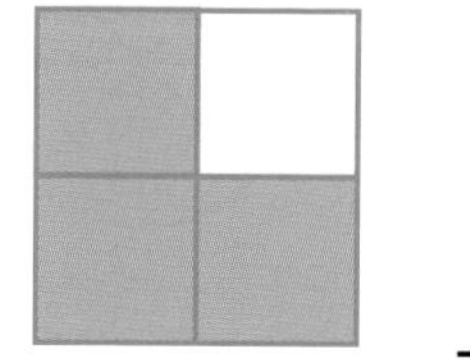 ______

Color to show the number of shaded parts.
Write the fraction for the shaded parts.

6. 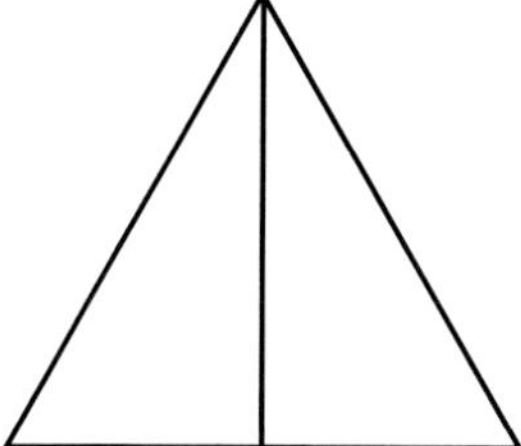

1 shaded part ______

7. 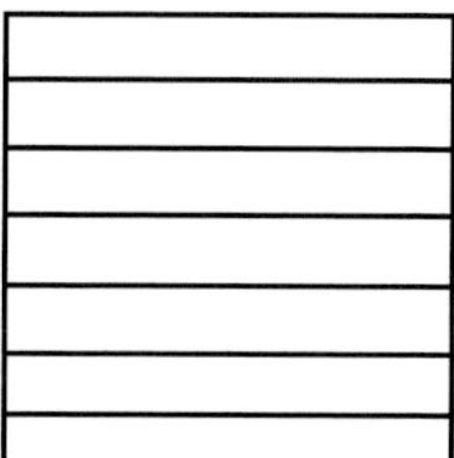

7 shaded parts ______

8. 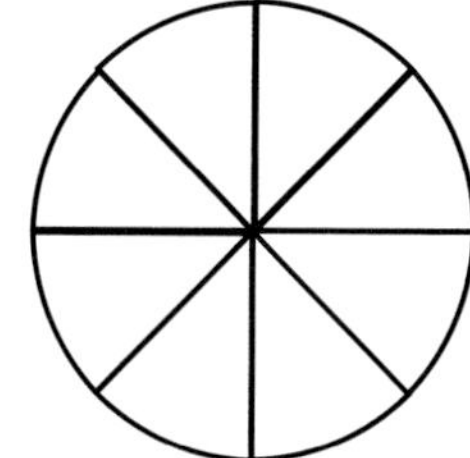

7 shaded parts ______

Explain Your Thinking What is the difference between the numerator and the denominator of a fraction?

Practice

Remember
Fractions can name part of a whole.

Write the fraction for the shaded parts.

1. 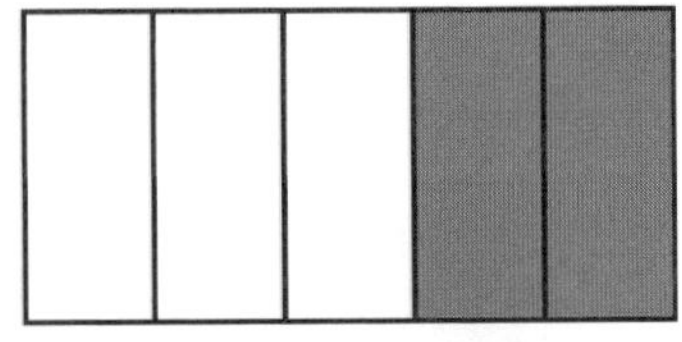 $\frac{2}{5}$

2. 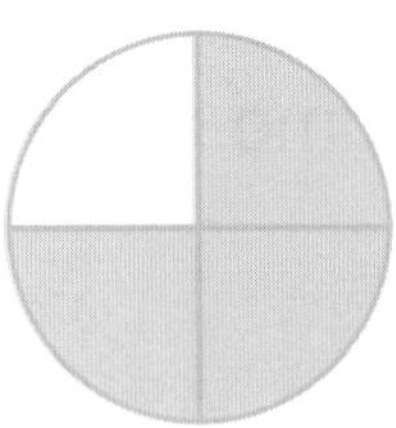 ______

3. ______

4. 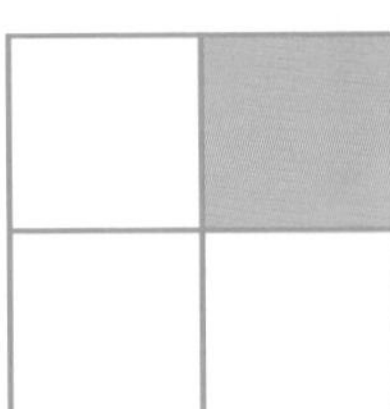 ______

5. 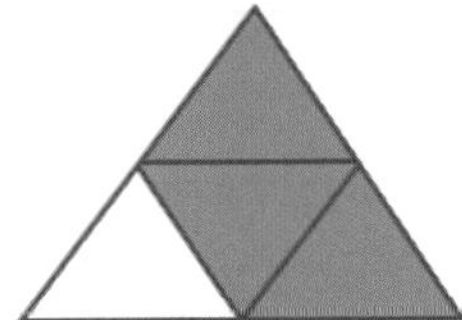 ______

6. 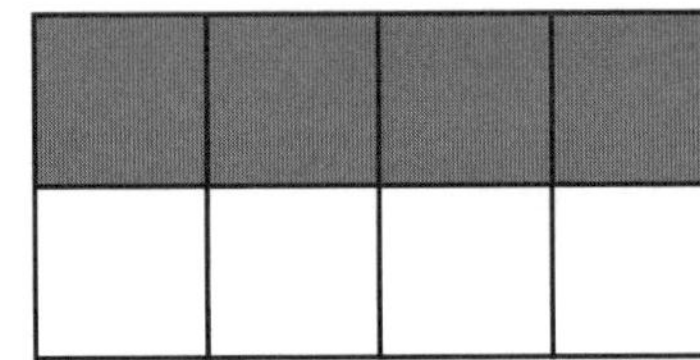 ______

Color to show the number of shaded parts.
Write the fraction for the shaded parts.

7. 8 shaded parts

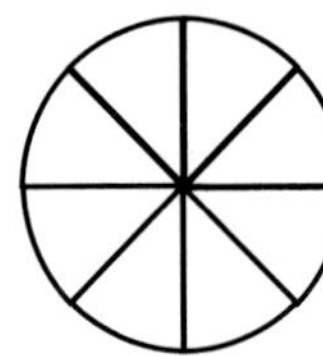 ______

8. 2 shaded parts

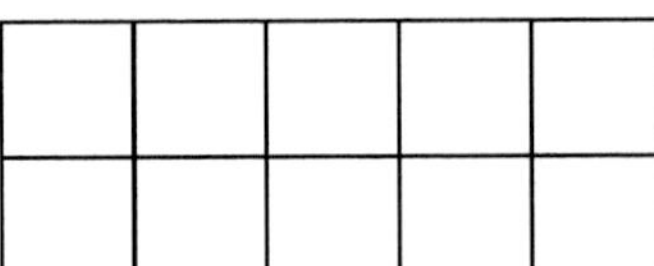 ______

Problem Solving  Number Sense

9. Look at the 2 wholes.
Each whole is 4 fourths.
Circle the fraction that names the orange parts.

 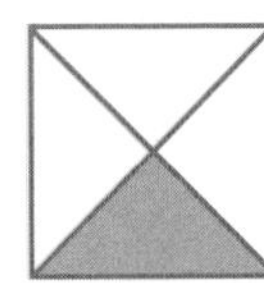

$\frac{1}{4}$ $\frac{3}{4}$ $\frac{5}{4}$

10. **Talk About It** Explain why you think the fraction you circled is correct.

At Home Choose several exercises above and ask your child what parts are not shaded. Then have him or her write the fraction.

Game Activity

Name ______________________________

Fraction Match

2 Players

What You Need: 16 counters for each player and Fraction Cards (LT23 and 24)

How to Play

1. Place the cards face down. Take turns. Pick one Fraction Card at a time.
2. Try to match the fraction on the card to a picture on the game board. Put a counter on the picture.
3. The first player to get 4 counters in a row or column wins.

Activity

Math Challenge
Funky Fractions

Look at these fractions.

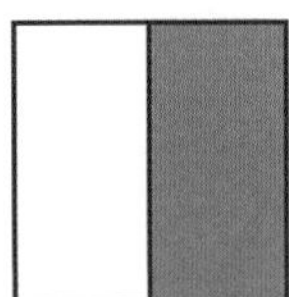

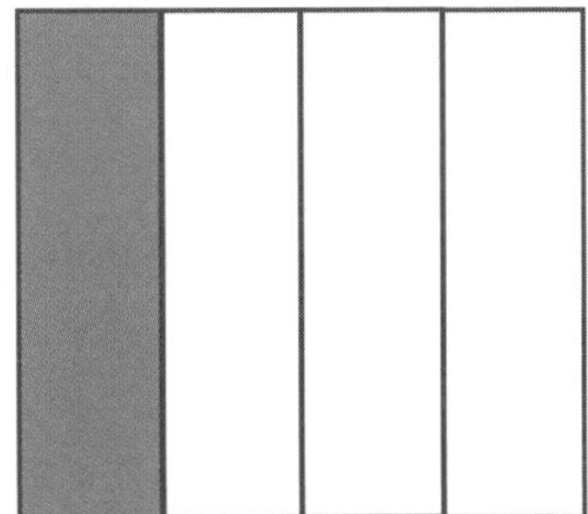

Write About It Is $\frac{1}{2}$ always greater than $\frac{1}{4}$? Why or why not?

____

____

Quick Check

Write the fraction for the shaded part.

1.

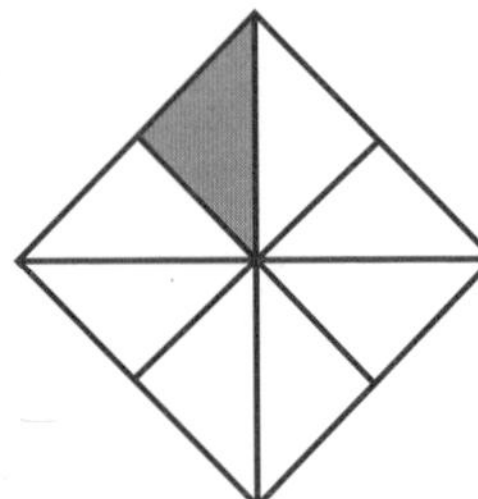

_____

2.

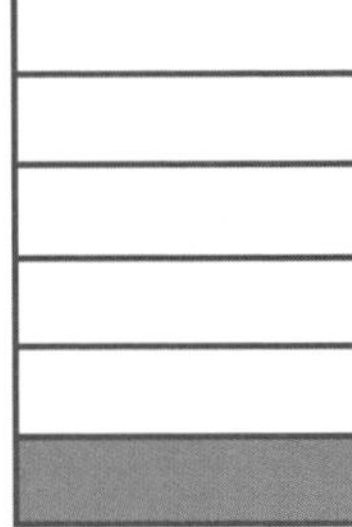

_____

Color to show the number of shaded parts.
Write the fraction for the shaded parts.

3. 3 shaded parts

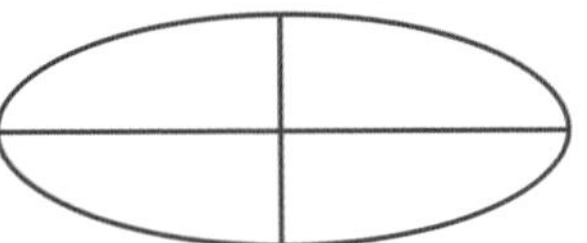

_____

4. 3 shaded parts

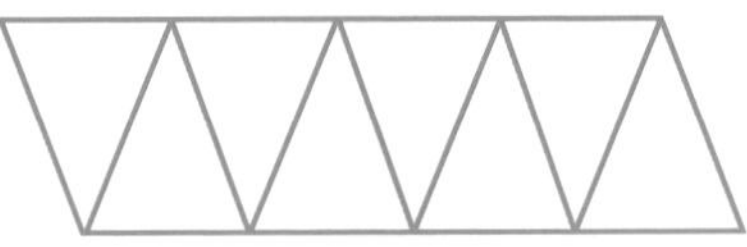

_____

Write the fraction for the shaded parts.

5.

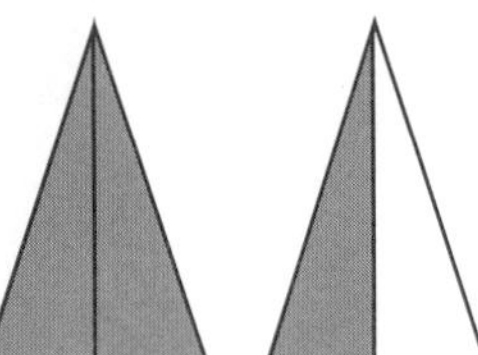

_____

6.

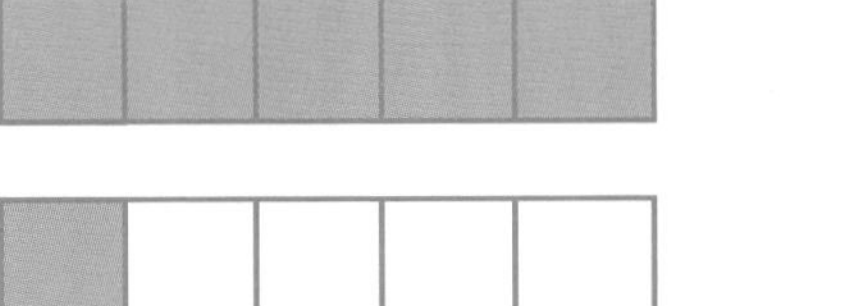

_____

Facts Practice, see page 671.

Name ______________________________

Comparing Fractions

 **Audio Tutor 1/27** Listen and Understand

Objective
Compare fractions using symbols

Vocabulary
greater than (>)
less than (<)

Use the symbols **>** and **<** to compare fractions.

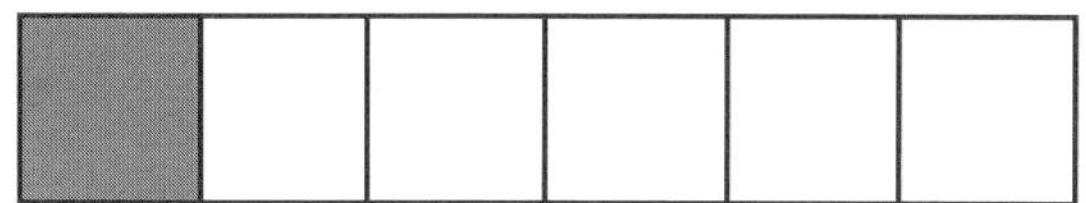

$\frac{1}{6}$ is shaded.

$\frac{1}{3}$ is shaded.

$\frac{1}{6}$ is **less than** $\frac{1}{3}$

$\frac{1}{6} < \frac{1}{3}$

$\frac{1}{3}$ is **greater than** $\frac{1}{6}$

$\frac{1}{3} > \frac{1}{6}$

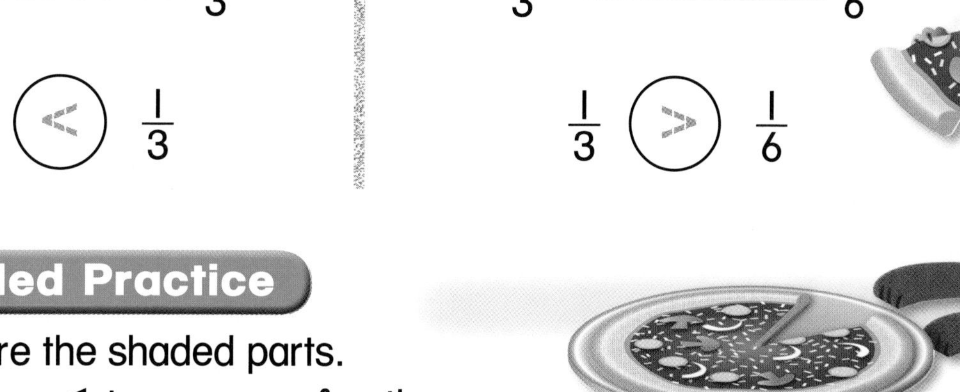

Guided Practice

Compare the shaded parts.
Write **>** or **<** to compare fractions.

1. 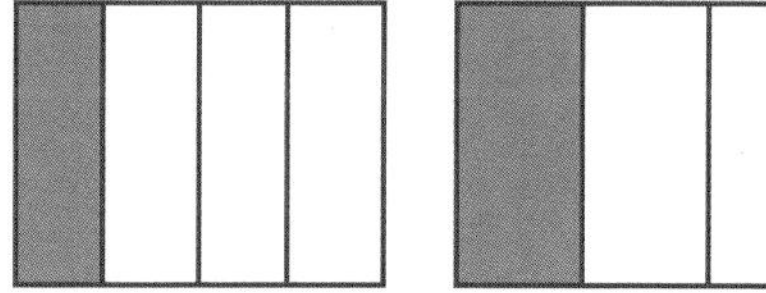

$\frac{1}{4}$ ◯ $\frac{1}{3}$

Think
$\frac{1}{4}$ is less than $\frac{1}{3}$.

2. 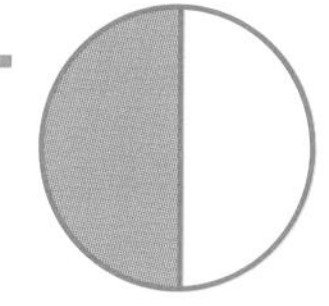 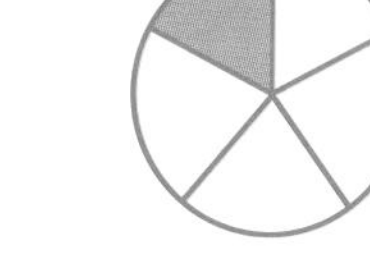

$\frac{1}{2}$ ◯ $\frac{1}{5}$

3. 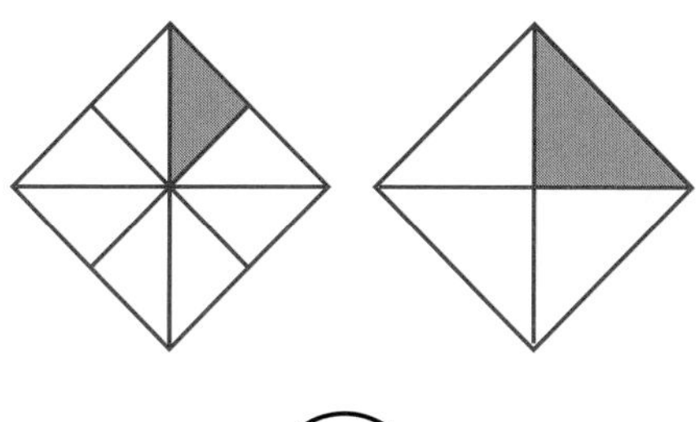

$\frac{1}{8}$ ◯ $\frac{1}{4}$

4. 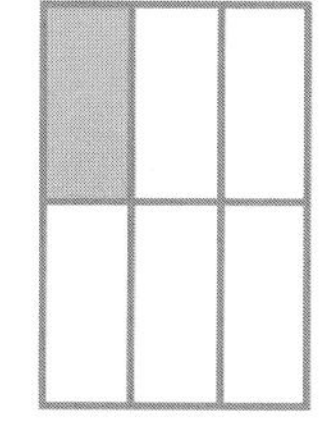 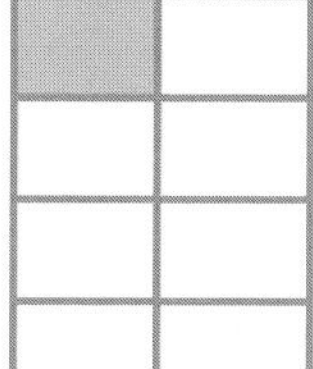

$\frac{1}{6}$ ◯ $\frac{1}{8}$

Explain Your Thinking Put $\frac{1}{2}$, $\frac{1}{3}$, and $\frac{1}{4}$ in order from least to greatest. How did you do it?

Remember
> greater than
< less than

Practice

Compare the shaded parts.
Write > or < to compare fractions.

1. 

$\frac{1}{3}$ (>) $\frac{1}{6}$

2. 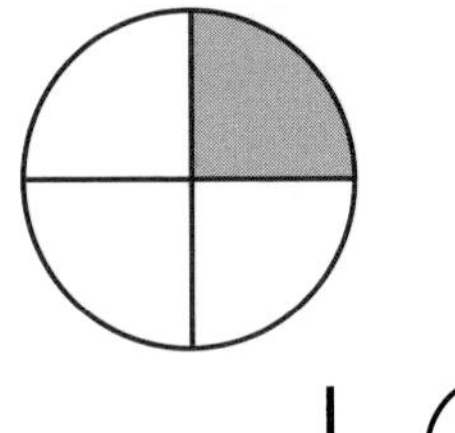

$\frac{1}{4}$ ◯ $\frac{1}{8}$

3. 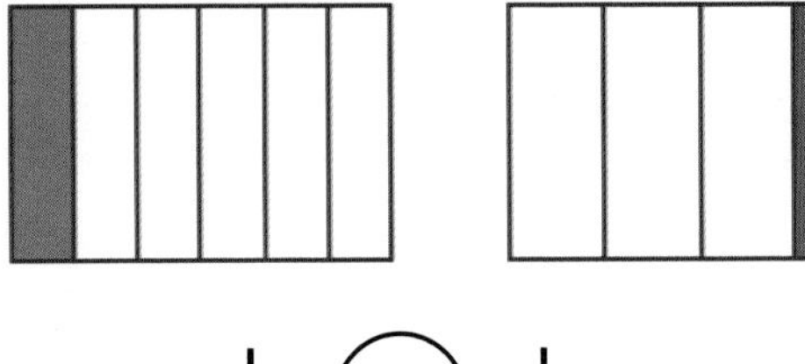

$\frac{1}{6}$ 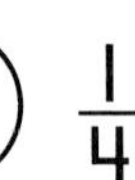 $\frac{1}{4}$

4. 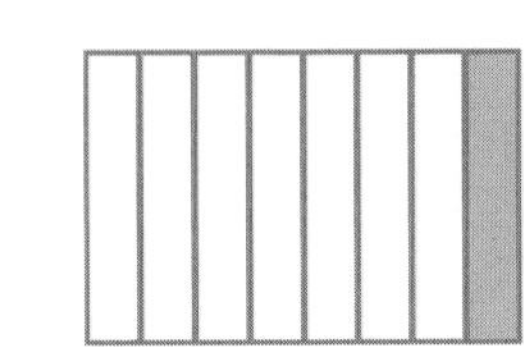 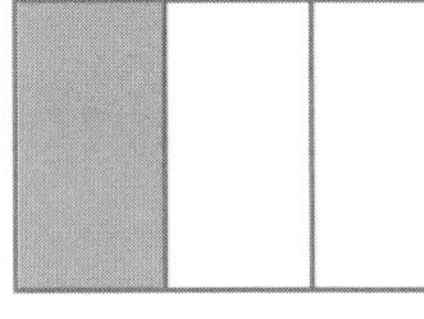

$\frac{1}{8}$ ◯ $\frac{1}{3}$

5. 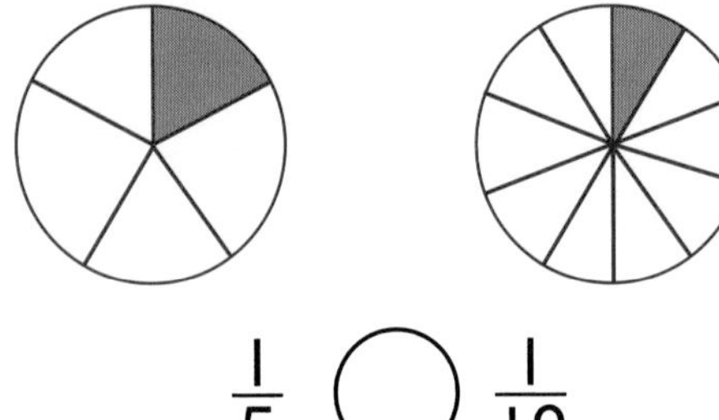

$\frac{1}{5}$ ◯ $\frac{1}{10}$

6. 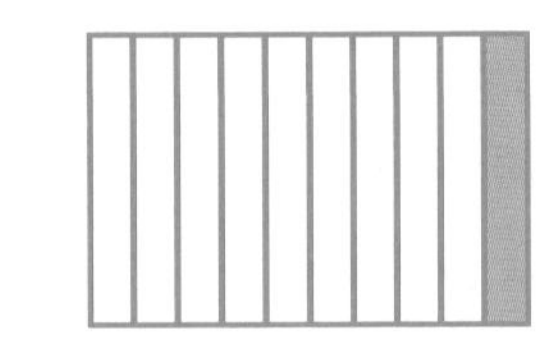

$\frac{1}{10}$ ◯ $\frac{1}{2}$

Problem Solving ▶ Visual Thinking

Circle the picture that matches the fraction.

7. More than $\frac{1}{2}$

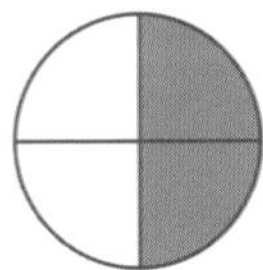 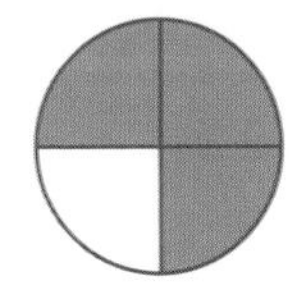 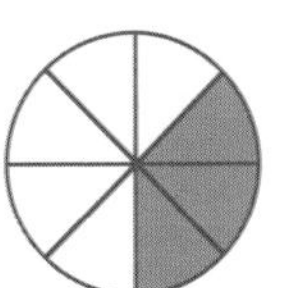

8. Less than $\frac{1}{2}$

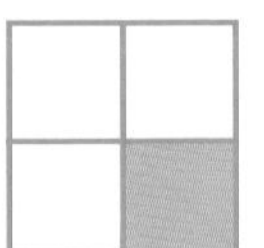 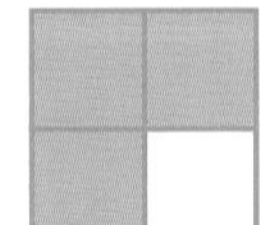 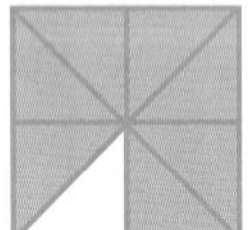

9. Equal to $\frac{1}{2}$

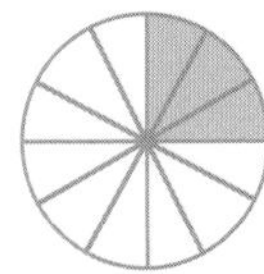 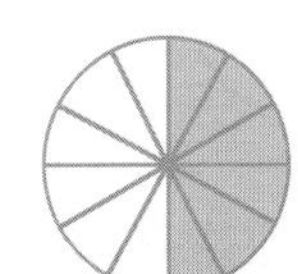 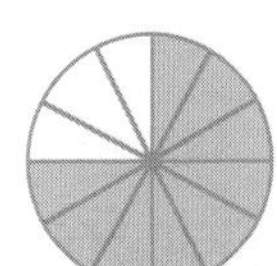

10. Equal to $\frac{1}{2}$

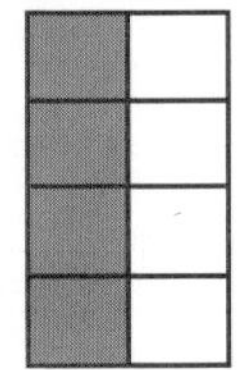 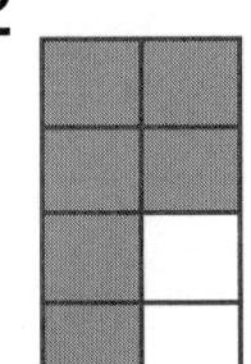 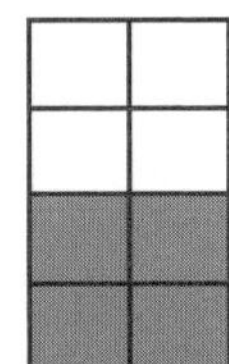

At Home Cut a piece of bread in half and another piece into fifths. Ask your child which is greater, $\frac{1}{2}$ or $\frac{1}{5}$. Ask him or her to explain why.

Name ______________________________

Fractions of a Set

 **Audio Tutor 1/28** Listen and Understand

Objective
Identify and write fractions that represent part of a group or set.

Fractions can name parts of a set.

1 red cube
3 cubes in all
$\frac{1}{3}$ of the cubes are red.

2 blue cubes
3 cubes in all
$\frac{2}{3}$ of the cubes are blue.

Guided Practice

Write a fraction for the parts of the set.

1.     

$\frac{\square \text{ blue}}{\square \text{ in all}}$ $\frac{\square \text{ yellow}}{\square \text{ in all}}$

Think
There are 4 circles in the set.
What part is blue?
What part is yellow?

2. 

$\frac{\square \text{ red}}{\square \text{ in all}}$ $\frac{\square \text{ blue}}{\square \text{ in all}}$

3. 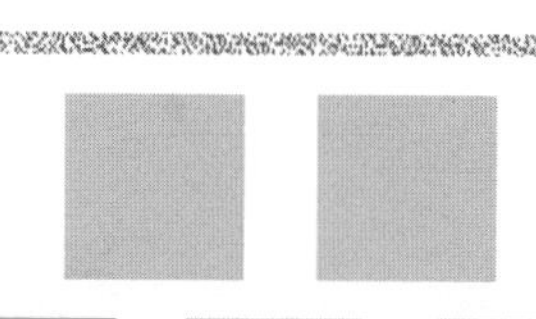

$\frac{\square \text{ yellow}}{\square \text{ in all}}$ $\frac{\square \text{ green}}{\square \text{ in all}}$

Explain Your Thinking There are 5 triangles. $\frac{3}{5}$ of the set is red. The rest are blue. What part of the set is blue? How do you know?

Extra Help at eduplace.com/map

Practice

Remember
The denominator tells how many parts in all.

Write a fraction for each color.

1. 

$\frac{1}{4}$ green $\frac{3}{4}$ yellow

2. 

_____ green _____ yellow

3. 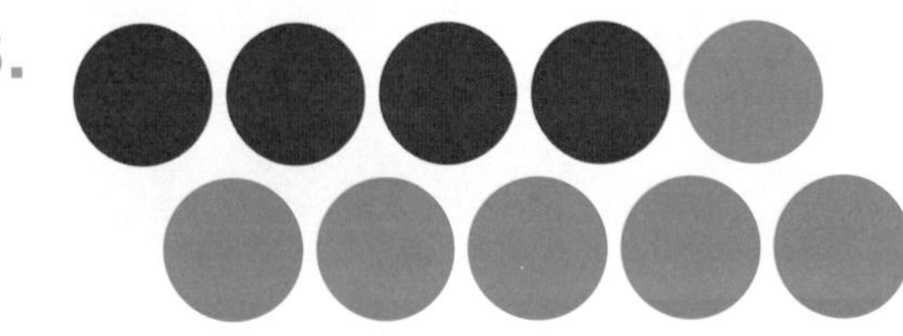

_____ blue _____ green

4. 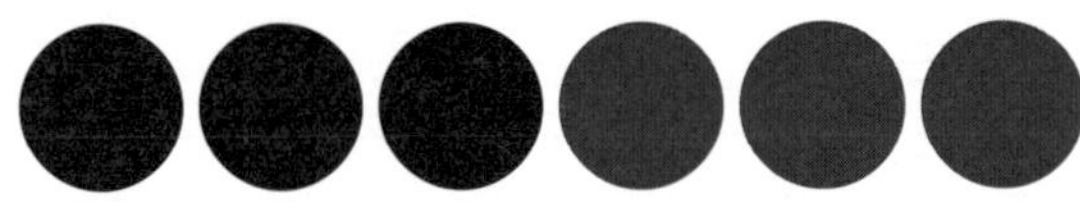

_____ red _____ blue

5. 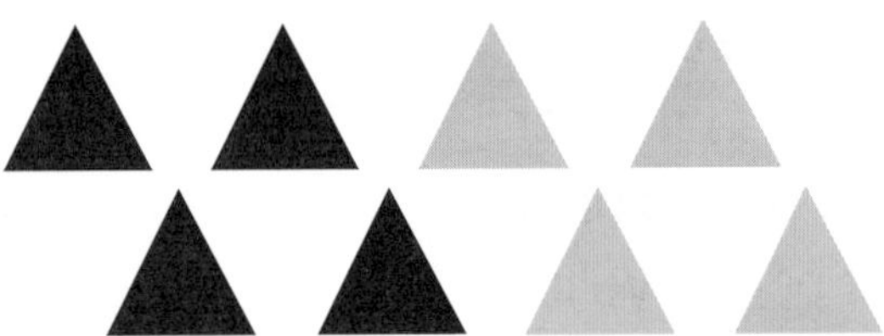

_____ red _____ yellow

6. 

_____ green _____ red

Problem Solving ▶ Number Sense

7. Color to show $\frac{2}{6}$ red.

Color to show $\frac{4}{6}$ blue.

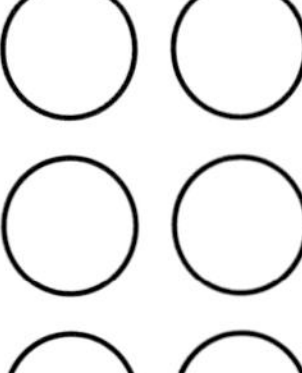

8. Color to show $\frac{5}{10}$ red.

Color to show $\frac{5}{10}$ blue.

At Home Place 6 to 10 pennies on the table. Ask your child to write a fraction for the pennies that are heads up and those that are tails up.

Problem Solving

Name ______________________________

Use a Picture

Objective
Solve problems using data from a picture.

Use a picture to solve a problem.

The sandwich is cut into 8 equal pieces.

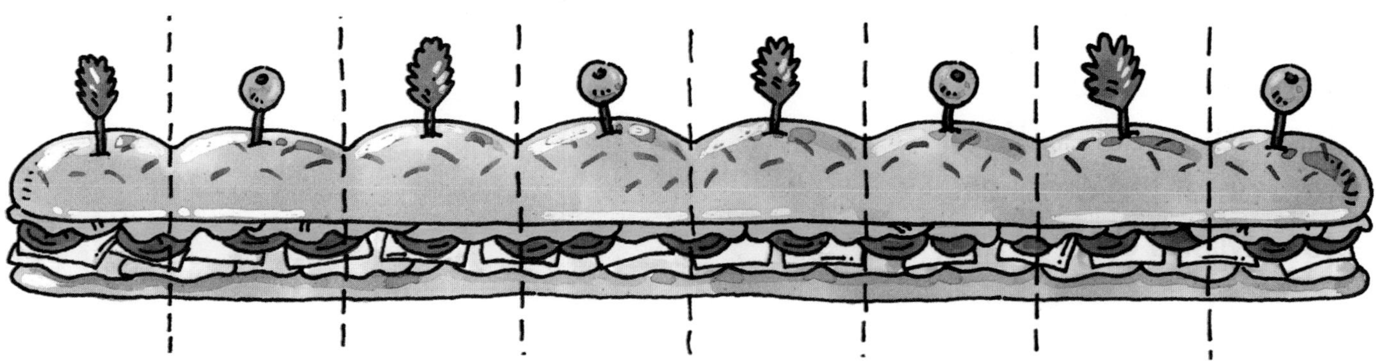

You can use a picture to find a fraction.

Chan eats 3 pieces of the sandwich.
What fraction of the sandwich does he eat?
Color the picture to show the fraction.

Think
How many pieces are in the whole sandwich? How many pieces does he eat?

[3] number of pieces Chan eats

[8] pieces in the whole sandwich

Chan eats $\frac{3}{8}$ of the sandwich.

You can use a picture to compare two fractions.

Sabrina eats $\frac{3}{8}$ of the sandwich.

Ty eats $\frac{2}{8}$ of the sandwich.

Who eats more, Sabrina or Ty?
Color the picture to show the fraction.

Think
Use the picture to find $\frac{3}{8}$. Use the picture to find $\frac{2}{8}$. Which is greater?

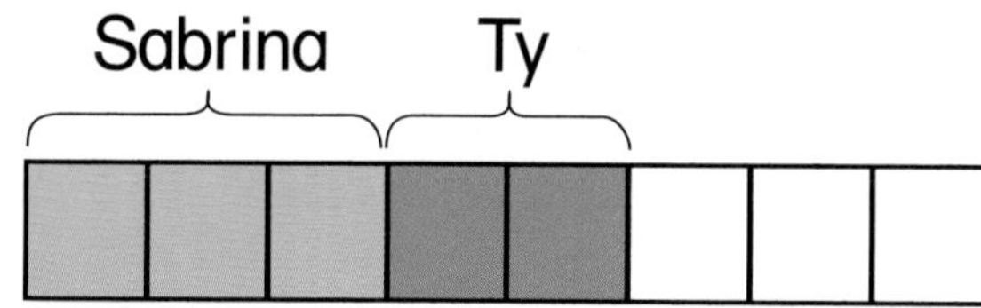

$\frac{3}{8}$ ◯ $\frac{2}{8}$

____________ eats more of the sandwich.

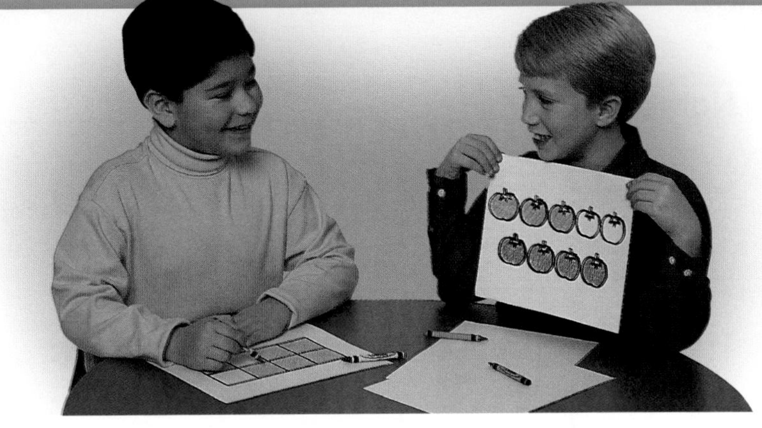

Guided Practice

Use the picture.
Color to solve the problem.

1. Misha eats 5 parts of this large cracker. What fraction of the cracker does Misha eat?

Think
There are 8 equal pieces in all.

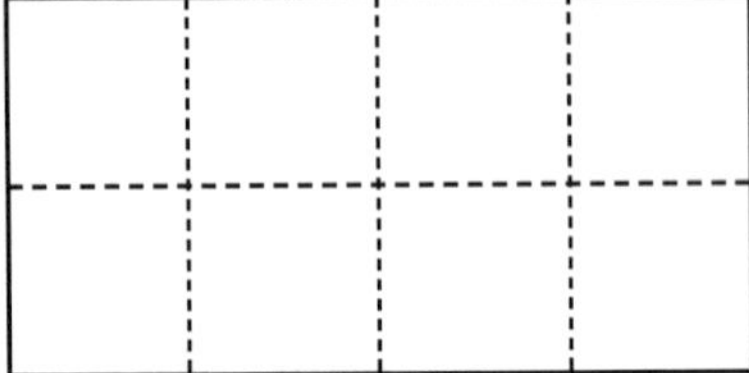

______

2. Anya eats $\frac{4}{9}$ of the tomatoes.

Deena eats $\frac{3}{9}$ of the tomatoes.

Who eats more tomatoes?

Think
Which is greater, $\frac{4}{9}$ or $\frac{3}{9}$?

______

Practice

3. Brian has 6 apples. Liza eats 1 apple. What fraction of the apples does Liza eat?

______

4. Debbie cuts a piece of clay into 10 equal pieces. She uses $\frac{3}{10}$ of the clay. How many pieces of clay are left?

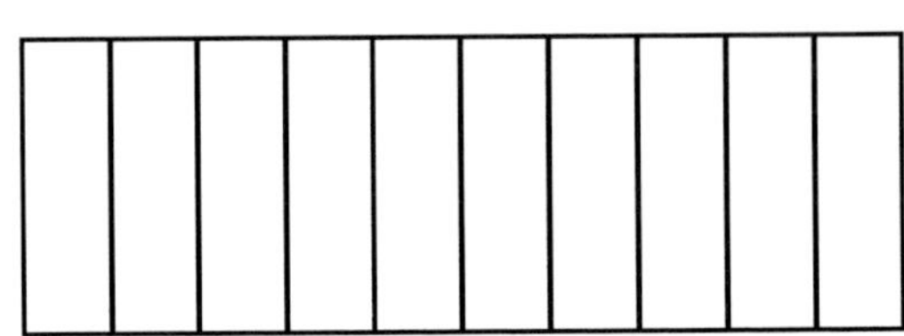

______ pieces

Go on

Name ________________________________

Mixed Problem Solving

Strategies
Draw a Picture
Use Models to Act It Out
Write a Number Sentence

Solve.

Draw or write to explain.

1. Max has 4 waffles.

   He eats $\frac{1}{2}$ of the waffles.

   How many waffles does he eat?

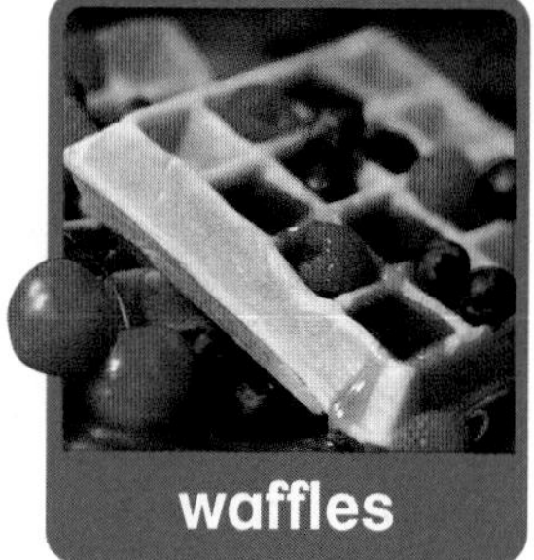
waffles

_____ waffles

2. Mary cuts a muffin into 3 equal pieces. She eats 2 pieces. What fraction of the muffin does she eat?

muffins

_____

3. Ty has 4 pancakes. He eats 1 pancake. Kendra eats 2 of the pancakes. What fraction of the pancakes are left?

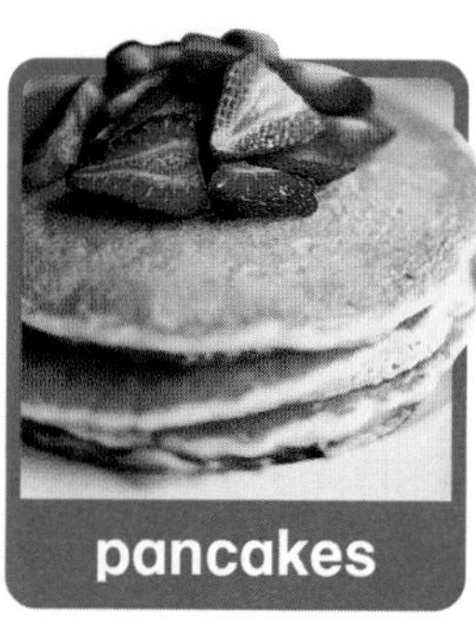
pancakes

_____

4. **Multistep** Jan buys a bagel. She cuts it in half. Then she cuts the pieces in half again. How many pieces of bagel does she have?

bagels

_____ pieces

At Home Share a snack with your child. Have him or her write the fraction for each part.

Problem Solving on Tests • **Listening Skills**

Open Response

Listen to your teacher read the problem.
Solve.

Show your work using pictures, numbers, or words.

1. The melon is cut into 8 equal slices. Three slices have blueberries on top. What fraction of the melon slices have blueberries? ______

2. What fraction of the melon slices do not have berries on top? ______

Multiple Choice

Listen to your teacher read the problem.
Choose the correct answer.

3. 5 ○ 6 ○ 7 ○ 11 ○

4. $\frac{1}{5}$ ○ $\frac{2}{5}$ ○ $\frac{3}{5}$ ○ $\frac{4}{5}$ ○

Education Place
See **eduplace.com/map** for Test-Taking Tips.

Name ______________________________

Now Try This Equivalent Fractions

Equivalent fractions name the same amount.

Look at the fraction strips below.

$\frac{1}{4}$	$\frac{1}{4}$	$\frac{1}{4}$	$\frac{1}{4}$

$\frac{1}{2}$	$\frac{1}{2}$

$\frac{1}{4}$ and $\frac{1}{4}$ is shaded. $\frac{1}{4}$ and $\frac{1}{4}$ equals $\frac{2}{4}$.

$\frac{2}{4}$ names the same amount as $\frac{1}{2}$.

$\frac{2}{4} = \frac{1}{2}$.

Color the fraction strip to name the same amount.
Write the **equivalent fraction**.

1.

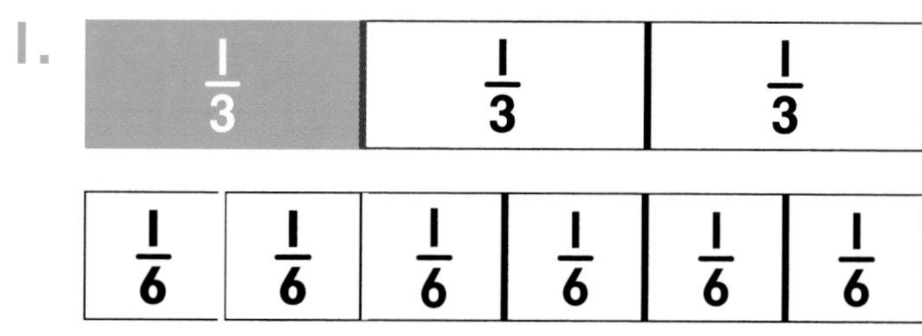

$\frac{1}{3} =$ ______

2.

$\frac{1}{4}$	$\frac{1}{4}$	$\frac{1}{4}$	$\frac{1}{4}$

$\frac{1}{8}$	$\frac{1}{8}$	$\frac{1}{8}$	$\frac{1}{8}$	$\frac{1}{8}$	$\frac{1}{8}$	$\frac{1}{8}$	$\frac{1}{8}$

$\frac{1}{4} =$ ______

3.

$\frac{1}{3}$	$\frac{1}{3}$	$\frac{1}{3}$

$\frac{1}{12}$	$\frac{1}{12}$	$\frac{1}{12}$	$\frac{1}{12}$	$\frac{1}{12}$	$\frac{1}{12}$	$\frac{1}{12}$	$\frac{1}{12}$	$\frac{1}{12}$	$\frac{1}{12}$	$\frac{1}{12}$	$\frac{1}{12}$

$\frac{1}{3} =$ ______

Problem Solving

Social Studies Connection

Tangram

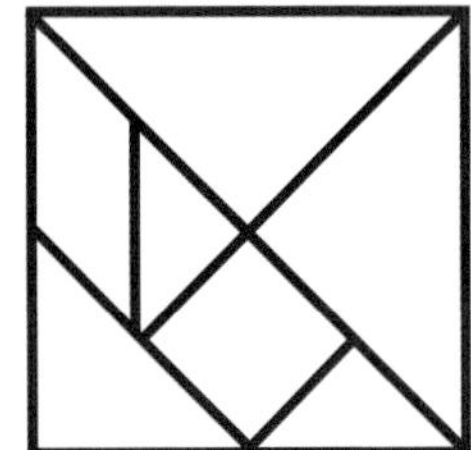

A tangram is an old Chinese puzzle. It is a set of 7 plane shapes that fit together to make a square.

Talk About It Circle the shapes you think cannot be made using tangram pieces. Why?

WEEKLY WR READER eduplace.com/map

Key Topic Review

Pictograph

Use the information in the pictograph to answer the question.

1. How many people voted for yellow?

   ______ people

2. Which 2 colors got the same number of votes?

   __________ and __________

Favorite Color

Red	☺ ☺ ☺ ☺ ☺ ☺
Blue	☺ ☺ ☺ ☺ ☺ ☺ ☺ ☺
Yellow	☺ ☺ ☺ ☺
Purple	☺ ☺ ☺ ☺ ☺ ☺

Key: Each ☺ stands for 2 people.

3. How many more people voted for blue than for red?

   ______ people

4. Which color got the most votes?

   ____

5. How many people voted for a favorite color?

   ______ people

Extra Help at **eduplace.com/map**

Name ______________________  **Chapter Review/Test**

Vocabulary

Complete the sentence.

fraction
greater than
less than

1. A ______________________ names equal parts of a whole.

2. $\frac{1}{10}$ is ______________________ $\frac{1}{2}$.

3. $\frac{1}{4}$ is ______________________ $\frac{1}{8}$.

Concepts and Skills

Write the fraction for the shaded part.

4. 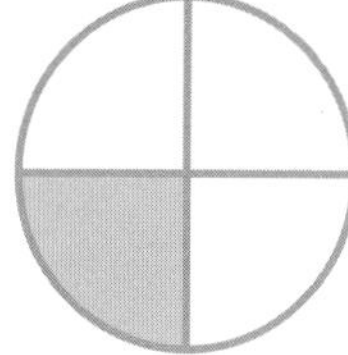
______

5. 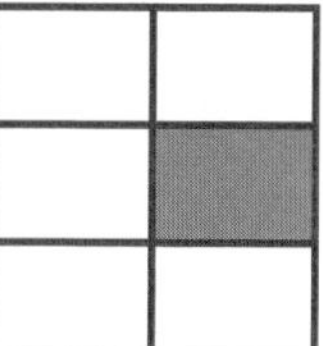
______

6. 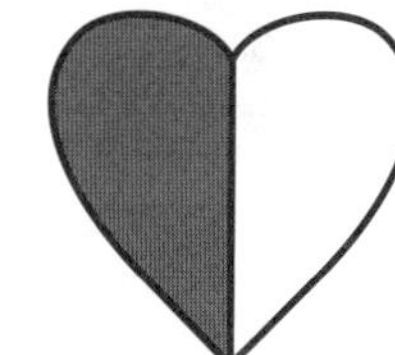
______

Color to show one shaded part. Write the fraction.

7.  ______

8. 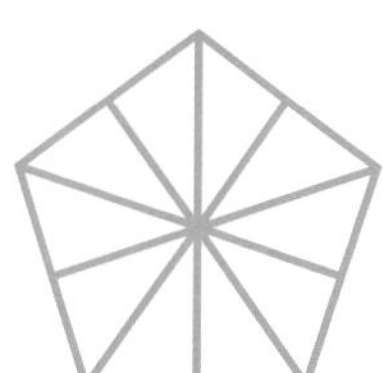 ______

9. 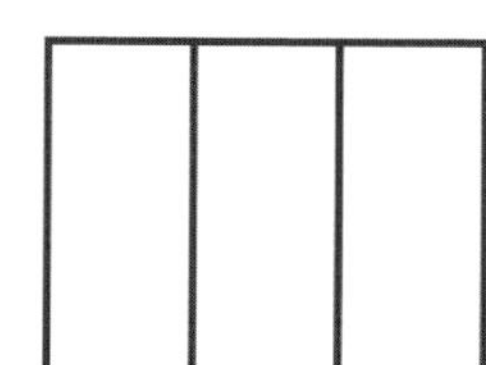 ______

Write the fraction for the shaded part.

10. 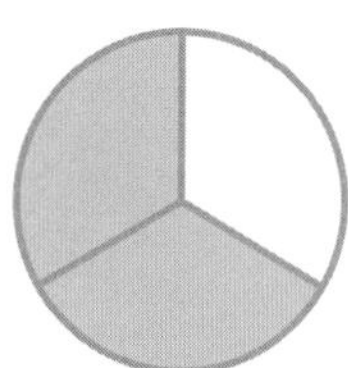
______

11. 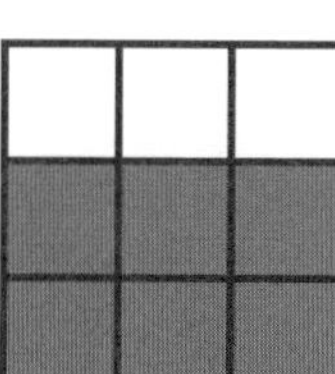
______

12. 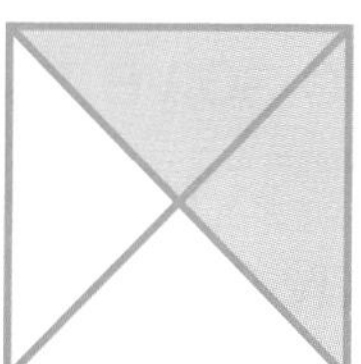
______

Chapter Review/Test

Color to show the number of shaded parts.
Write the fraction for the shaded parts.

13. 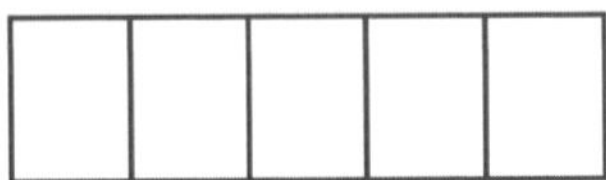

3 shaded parts ______

14. 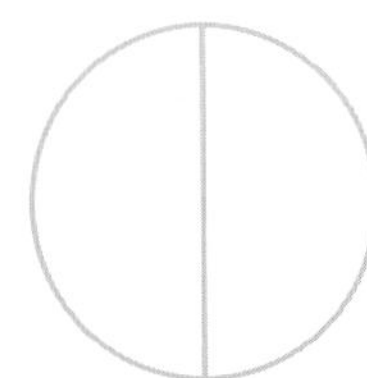

1 shaded part ______

15. 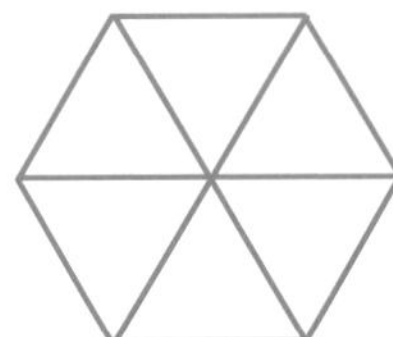

3 shaded parts ______

Circle the fraction that names the shaded parts.

16. 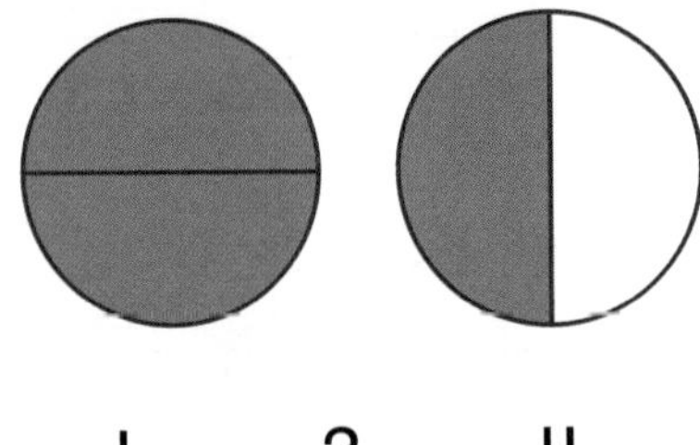

$\frac{1}{2}$ $\frac{3}{2}$ $\frac{4}{2}$

17. 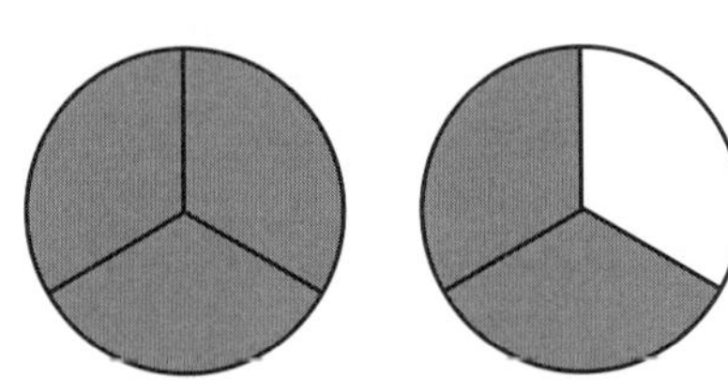

$\frac{1}{3}$ $\frac{4}{3}$ $\frac{5}{3}$

Compare the shaded parts.
Write > or < to compare fractions.

18. 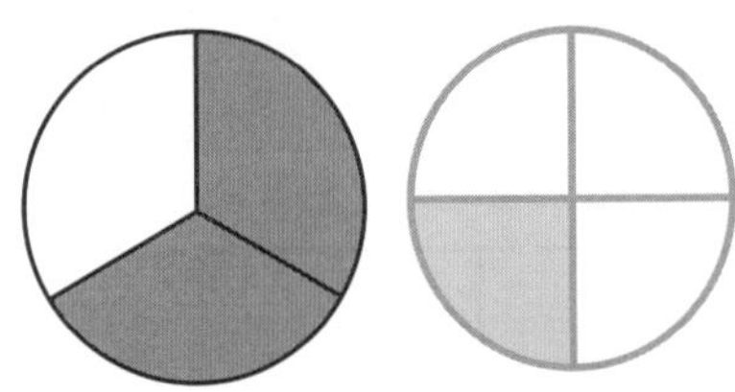

$\frac{2}{3}$ ◯ $\frac{1}{4}$

Write a fraction for each color.

19. 

______ red ______ blue

Problem Solving
Use the picture.
Color to solve the problem.

20. Xavier eats $\frac{5}{8}$ of the pizza.
What fraction of the pizza is left?

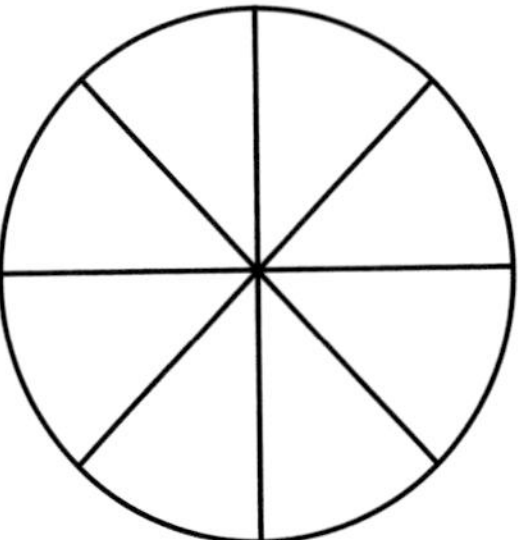

______

Name ______________________________

Sorting by Attributes

You can sort things by finding what is the same or what is different.

Look at this group.
Which shape does not belong? Why?

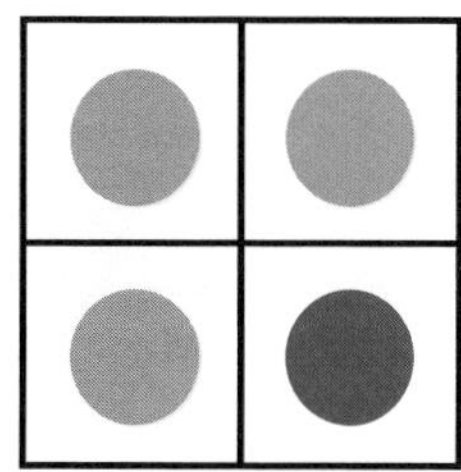

3 of the shapes are orange. 1 is blue. The blue shape is different. It does not belong.

Look at each group. Which shape does not belong?
Cross it out. Tell why.

1. 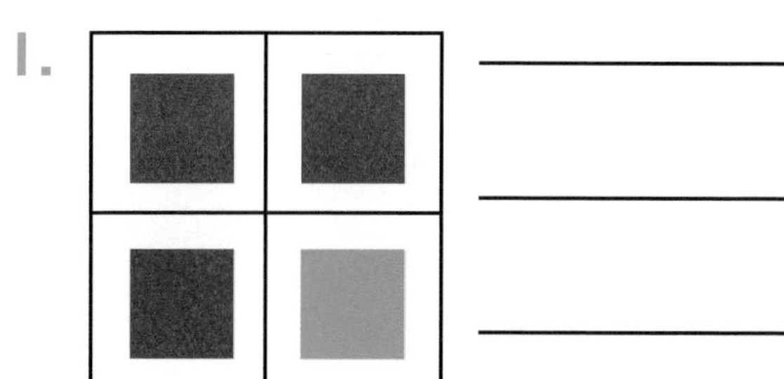

____
____
____

2. 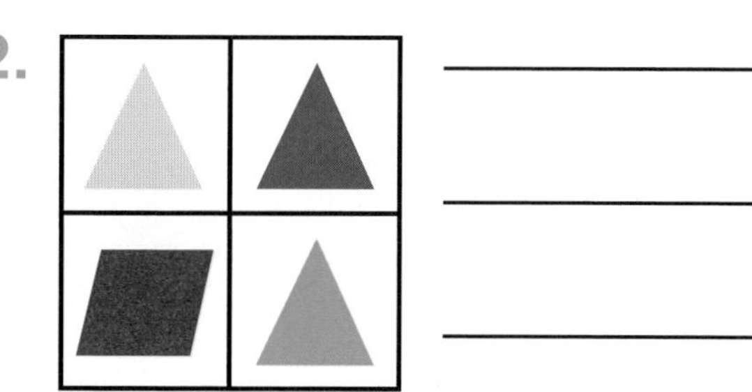

____
____
____

Circle the shapes that can be grouped.
Write a rule that tells why they can be grouped.

3. Circle 4 shapes that can be grouped.

Rule: ______________________________

____

4. Circle 3 shapes that can be grouped.

Rule: ______________________________

____

Write Your Own Use marbles or stickers.
Make a rule to sort by. Ask a friend to guess your rule.

____

Education Place
Visit **eduplace.com/map** for brain teasers.

Computer Pieces of Pie

George the bear likes pie. His mom says he can have $\frac{3}{4}$ of a pie. What does $\frac{3}{4}$ look like?

Use the fraction models found at **eduplace.com/map** to show $\frac{3}{4}$.

1. Put your pointer over the **scissors.** Choose $\frac{1}{4}$.
2. Click on a circle.
3. Click **Fill.** Click 3 sections of the circle.

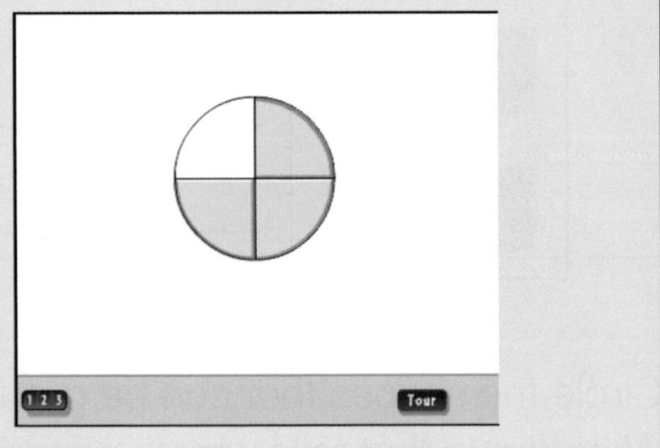

Use fraction models. Draw each fraction.
Then write the fraction for the shaded parts.

1. Split into 4 equal parts.
Fill 2 sections. ____

2. Split into 3 equal parts.
Fill 1 section. ____

3. Split into 2 equal parts.
Fill 2 sections. ____

4. Split into 8 equal parts.
Fill 5 sections. ____

Name ____________________

Vocabulary

Draw a line to match.

congruent
fraction
vertex

1. The point where two sides meet
2. Shapes that are the same size and the same shape
3. Names part of a whole

Concepts and Skills

Write the name of the shape.

cube
cylinder
cone
hexagon

4. 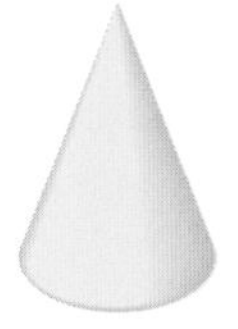

____

5. 

____

Circle the shape if it has a line of symmetry.
Draw a line of symmetry if the shape has symmetry.

6. 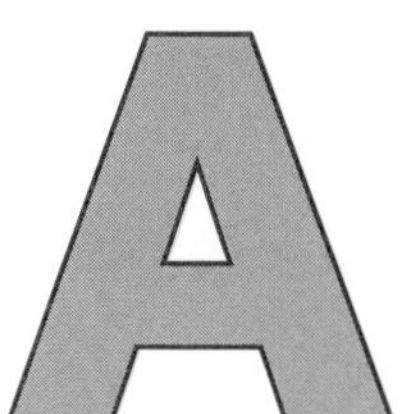

7. 

Circle the shape that is congruent to the first shape.

8. 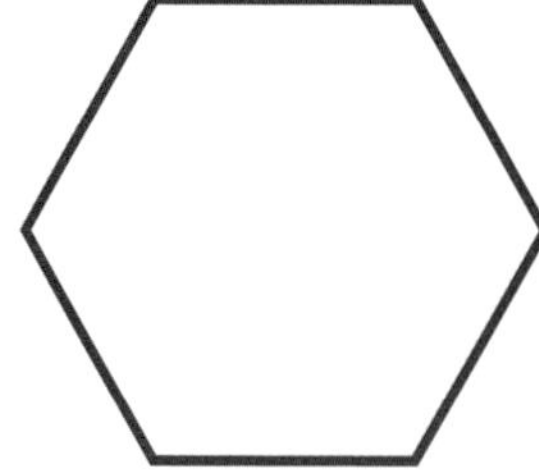

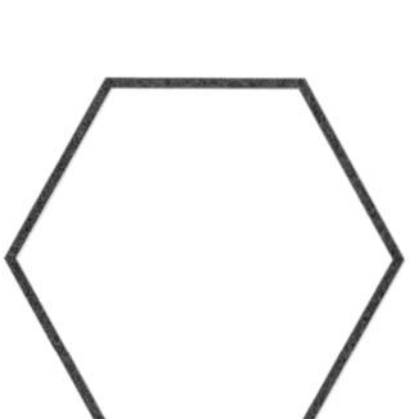

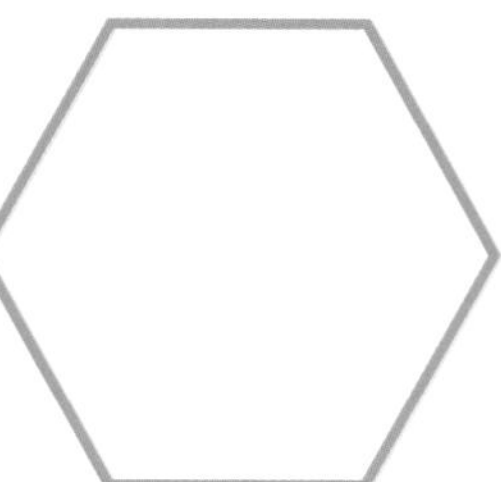

Unit 3 Test

Draw the picture of the plane shape or shapes you would make if you traced the faces on the solid shapes.

9. 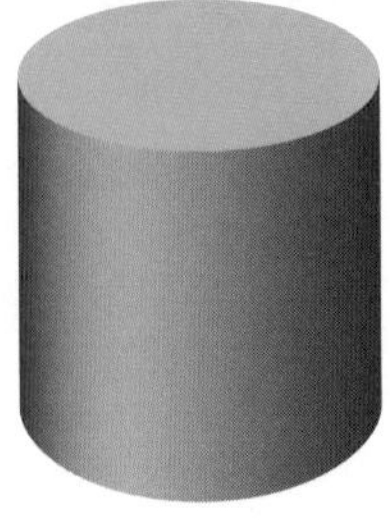

10. 

Write the fraction for the shaded part.

11. 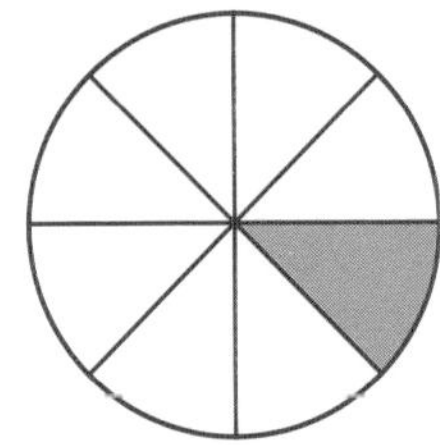

_____

Write a fraction for blue.

12. 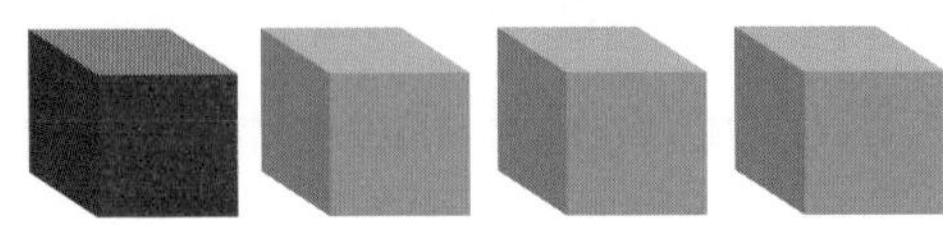

_____ blue

Compare the shaded parts.
Write > or <.

13. 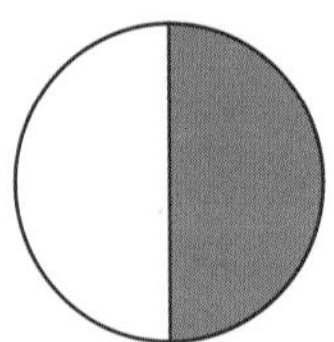 $\frac{1}{2}$ ◯ $\frac{1}{4}$ 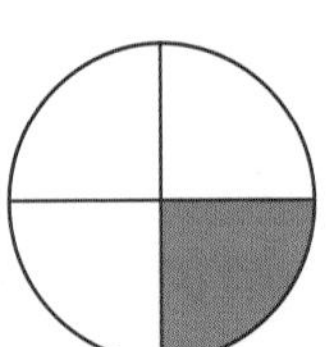

Problem Solving

Draw the three shapes that come next in the pattern.

14. 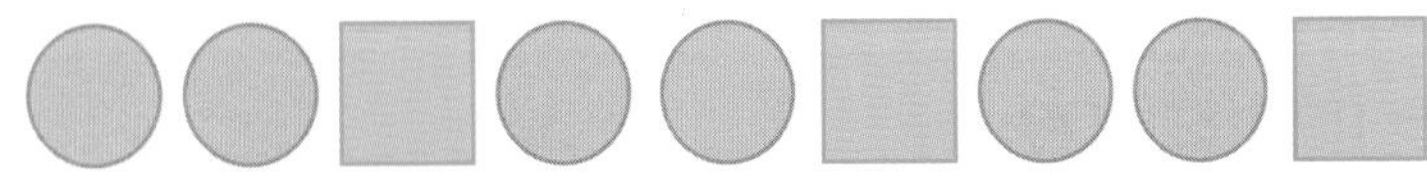

Draw or write to explain.

Use the picture to solve the problem.

15. Jerry eats $\frac{4}{8}$ of the blueberry pie.

What fraction of the pie is left?

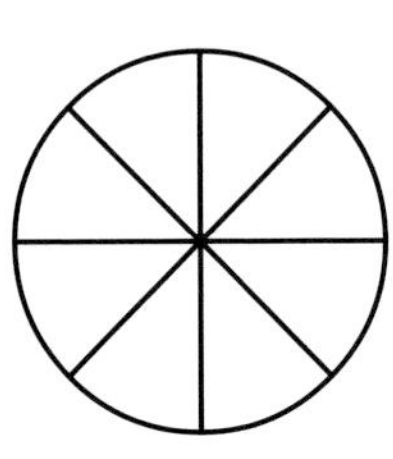

_____ of the pie

Name ____________________________ Cumulative Test Prep

Test-Taking Tips

Look at all the pictures carefully when you read these problems.

If you are not sure of an answer, try to make a good guess.

Multiple Choice

Fill in the ○ for the correct answer.

1. Choose the shape with 4 sides and 4 vertices.

○ ○ ○ ○

2. Mark the fraction of the shape that is shaded.

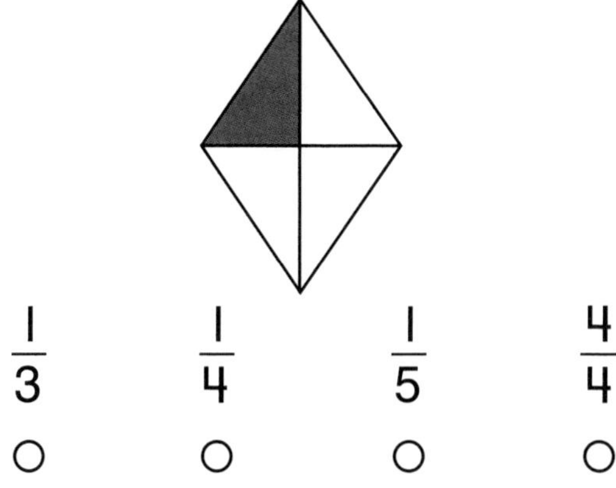

$\frac{1}{3}$ ○ $\frac{1}{4}$ ○ $\frac{1}{5}$ ○ $\frac{4}{4}$ ○

3. Mark the number that comes between.

53 ☐ 71

35 ○ 49 ○ 68 ○ 79 ○

4. Choose the shape that is a cube.

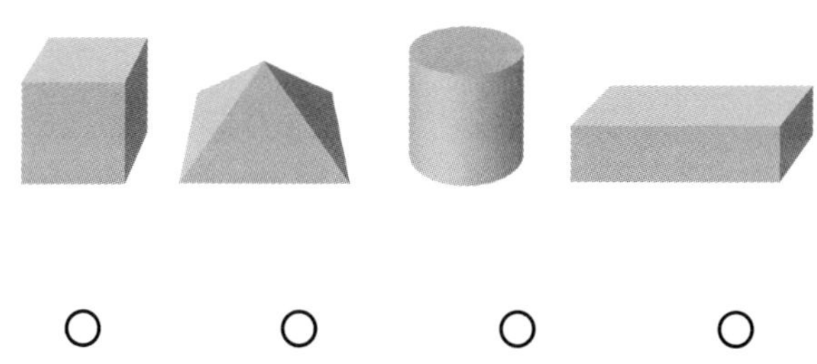

○ ○ ○ ○

Multiple Choice

Fill in the ○ for the correct answer. If the correct answer is not here, choose NH.

5. Mark the number that completes the number sentence.

$16 - \square = 7$

7	8	9	NH
○	○	○	○

6. What fraction of the cubes are shaded?

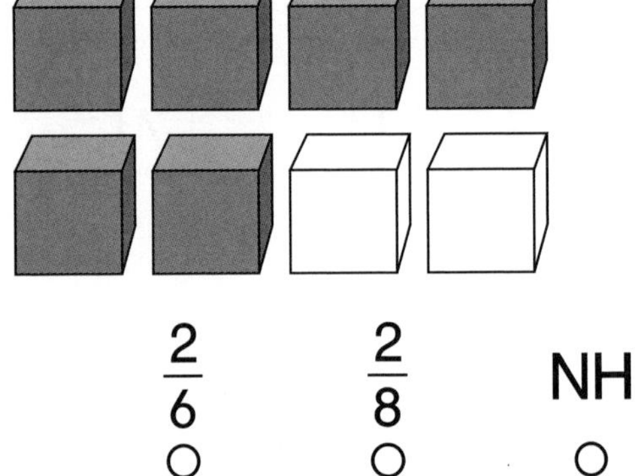

$\frac{6}{8}$	$\frac{2}{6}$	$\frac{2}{8}$	NH
○	○	○	○

7. Choose a sign to make the sentence true.

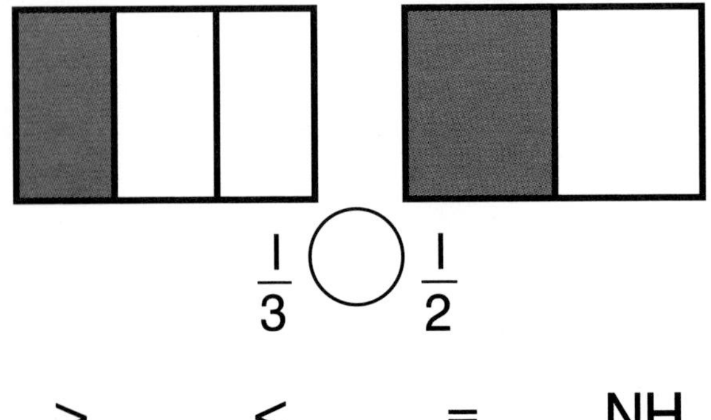

$\frac{1}{3}$ ○ $\frac{1}{2}$

>	<	=	NH
○	○	○	○

Open Response

Solve.

Use the bar graph to answer the question.

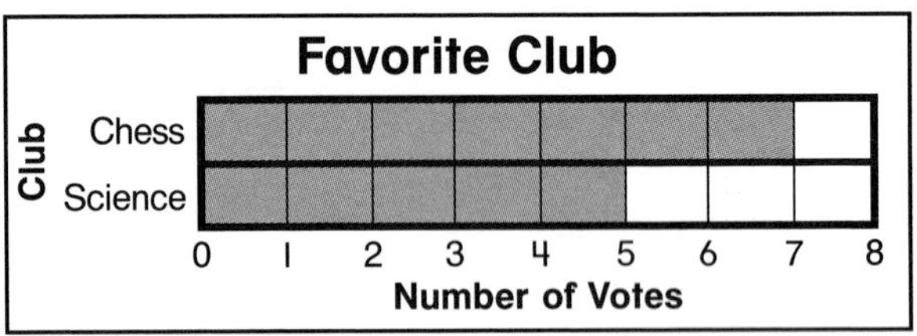

8. Which club was the favorite? Explain.

____

____

9. Patty rakes 4 bags of leaves. Tim rakes 9 bags. How many fewer bags does Patty rake? Write a number sentence to solve.

____

10. Tomás eats 2 parts of the sandwich shown. What fraction of the sandwich does he eat? Explain.

______

____

____

Education Place

Look for Cumulative Test Prep at **eduplace.com/map** for more practice.

Museum Math

Look back at the story to answer these questions.

△ **1.** There are 4 crates of stegosaurs and 5 crates of apatosaurs. How many dinosaurs is that all together?

● **2.** If the dinosaurs came in crates of 5, how would that change the story?

★ **3.** What if the warehouse manager needed 100 dinosaurs, how many crates would he need?

● **4.** What if you order models for the museum store? How many crates of each dinosaur will you order? How many will that be in all?

Answers
1. 9 crates or 90 dinosaurs **2.** All the numbers in the story would be cut in half. **3.** 10 crates **4.** Answers will vary.

Reading Strategies

△ Noting Details ● Cause and Effect
★ Predict ● Draw Conclusions

UNIT 4

Dinosaurs Everywhere!

written by **Sarah Curran**
illustrated by **Gary Johnson**

Ring! Ring! Ring!
HOW MANY stegosaurs will you bring?
10 per crate; 4 crates in all?
Where will I put them? They're really not small.

How many stegosaurs will arrive?

10, 20, ____, ____

Well, now I see that each dinosaur
is a MODEL to sell in the museum store!
There's plenty of room—no problem with space.
And dinosaurs WON'T take over the place!

Wait, wait ... There MUST be a mistake!
There won't be room, for goodness' sake.
The museum director I will call
to find how many crates will be here in all.

How many crates will arrive?

Ring! Ring! Ring!
HOW MANY triceratopses will you bring?
10 per crate; 7 crates in all?
There's not enough space—even in the hall!

How many triceratopses will arrive?

10, 20, 30, ___, ___, ___, ___

Ring! Ring! Ring!
HOW MANY tyrannosaurs will you bring?
10 per crate; 8 crates in all?
Where will they fit? They're big and tall!

How many tyrannosaurs will arrive?

10, 20, 30, 40, ____, ____, ____, ____

Ring! Ring! Not again! Oh, no!
HOW MANY apatosaurs are going to show?
10 per crate; 5 crates in all?
Where will I put them? This isn't a mall!

How many apatosaurs will arrive?

10, 20, ____, ____, ____

UNIT 4

Adding Two-Digit Numbers

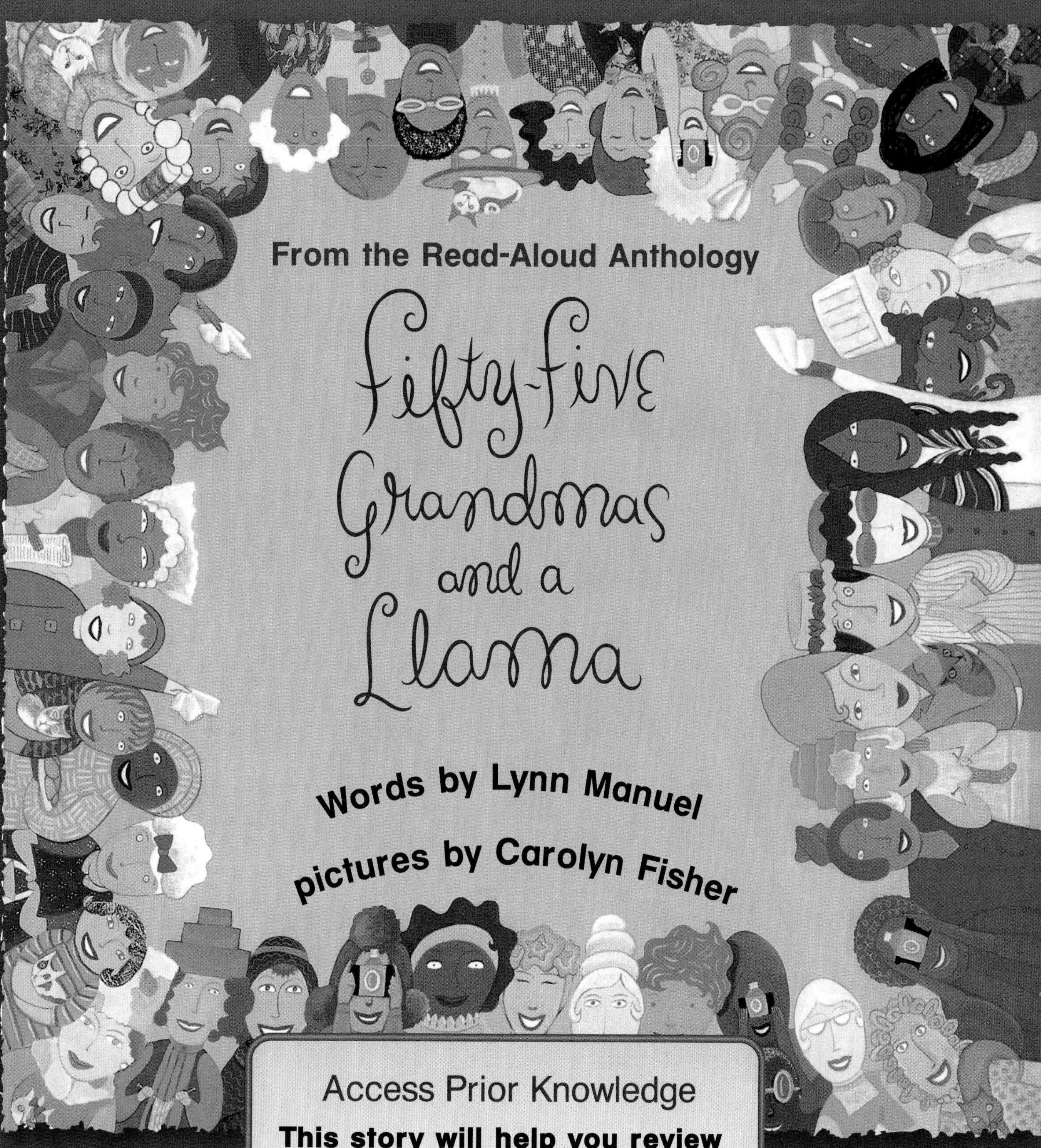

Access Prior Knowledge

This story will help you review

- Basic facts
- Modeling addends and sums

257b from *Fifty-Five Grandmas and a Llama*

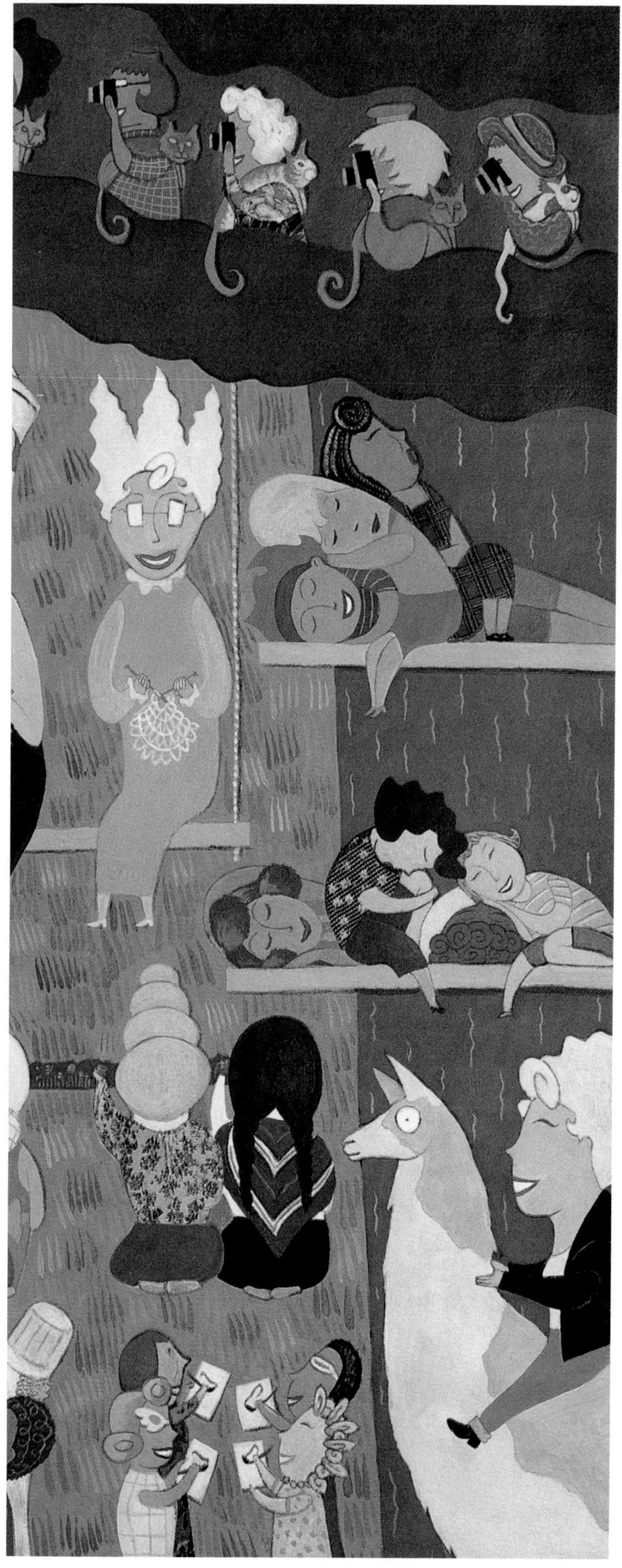

Everywhere he looked, he saw a grandma.

One grandma was sitting on the llama and smiling up at him.

Two grandmas were knitting lace covers for the garbage cans.

Three grandmas were planting lavender plants.

Four grandmas were square dancing on the grass.

Five grandmas were snapping pictures of the cats.

Six grandmas were singing about peanut butter cookies.

Seven grandmas were napping in the tree house.

Eight grandmas were painting pickle pictures.

Nine grandmas were playing bingo.

Ten grandmas were on the way upstairs to hug him.

The grandmas hugged and hugged and hugged!

As soon as they had gone, Sam slipped away. He knew what he had to do.

Name ______________________________

Use the story on page 257b.
Use Workmat 3 and [tens block] and [ones cube].
Solve.

Draw or write to explain.

1. Find and model the number of grandmas in each group. Regroup ones as tens to show the total number of grandmas. How many grandmas are there in all?

_____ grandmas

2. First, 24 grandmas hug Sam. Then, 10 more grandmas hug him. How many hugs does Sam get?

_____ hugs

3. Some grandmas are painting. Others are snapping pictures. 4 grandmas are dancing. How many grandmas are painting, snapping pictures, or dancing in all?

_____ grandmas

4. **Create Your Own** Write a problem about the grandmas. Find the answer.

____

____

____

Dear Family,

My class is starting Unit 4. I will be learning about adding two-digit numbers. These pages show what I will learn and have activities for us to do together.

From, ______________________

Vocabulary

These are some words I will use in this unit.

regroup In addition, to trade 10 ones for 1 ten (This used to be called "carry.")

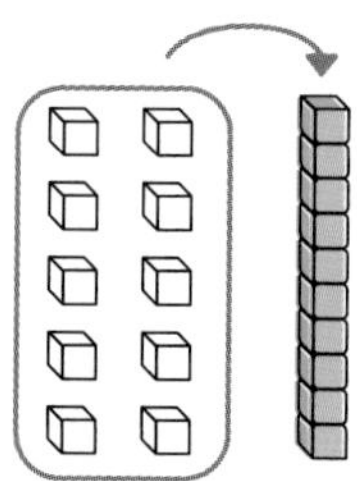

estimate An estimate is an answer that is close to an exact answer.

$$\begin{array}{r} 29 \\ +\ 21 \\ \hline \end{array} \xrightarrow[\text{nearest ten}]{\text{round to}} \begin{array}{r} 30 \\ +\ 20 \\ \hline 50 \end{array} \text{ estimate}$$

sum The result of addition

24 + 53 = 77 (↑ sum)

$$\begin{array}{r} 24 \\ +\ 53 \\ \hline 77 \end{array}$$

sum → 77

round 23 is closer to 20 than 30.
23 rounds to 20.

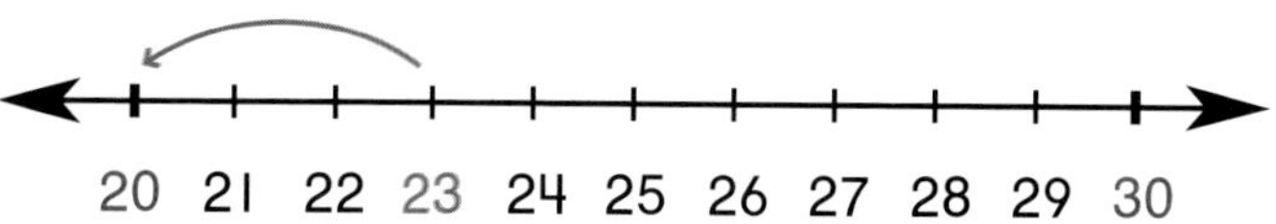

Vocabulary Activity

Let's work together to complete these sentences.

1. In 17 + 48 = 65, the number 65 is the __________.

2. Sometimes when you add, you need to __________ 10 ones as 1 ten.

How To add two-digit numbers

This two-digit addition problem is an example of what I will be learning. Sometimes I will use tens and ones blocks to help me find the answer.

Add 17 and 25.

Show 17 and 25 with blocks. Add 7 ones and 5 ones.

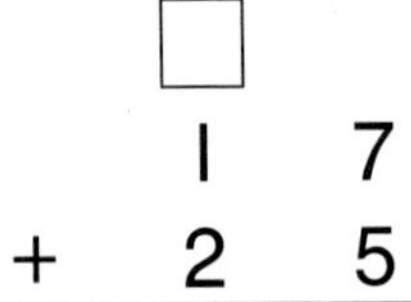

$$\begin{array}{r} 17 \\ +\ 25 \\ \hline \end{array}$$

Regroup 10 ones as 1 ten.

Workmat 3

Tens	Ones

$$\begin{array}{r} 17 \\ +\ 25 \\ \hline 2 \end{array}$$

Add the tens.

Workmat 3

Tens	Ones

$$\begin{array}{r} 17 \\ +\ 25 \\ \hline 42 \end{array}$$

Literature

These books link to the math in this unit. We can look for them at the library.

Arctic Fives Arrive
Elinor J. Pinczes
Illustrated by Holly Berry
(Houghton Mifflin, 1996)

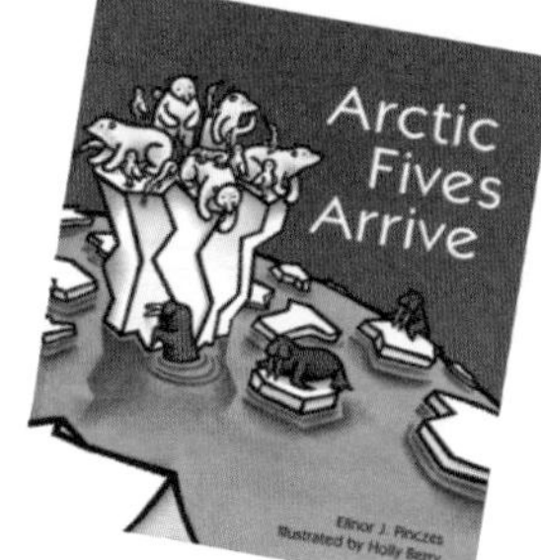

King's Commissioners
Story by Aileen Freidman

Education Place

We can visit *Education Place* at

eduplace.com/maf

for the Math Lingo game, e•Glossary, and more games and activities to do together.

CHAPTER
10
Regrouping With Addition
INVESTIGATION
How many groups of 10 can you find?

Picnic Stories

Listen to the family picnic story.
Use tens and ones to act out the story.

Tens	Ones

Name ____________________

Mental Math: Add Tens

Objective
Use mental math and basic facts to add tens.

Vocabulary
add
sum

When you **add** tens, think of an addition fact.

Find 40 + 20.

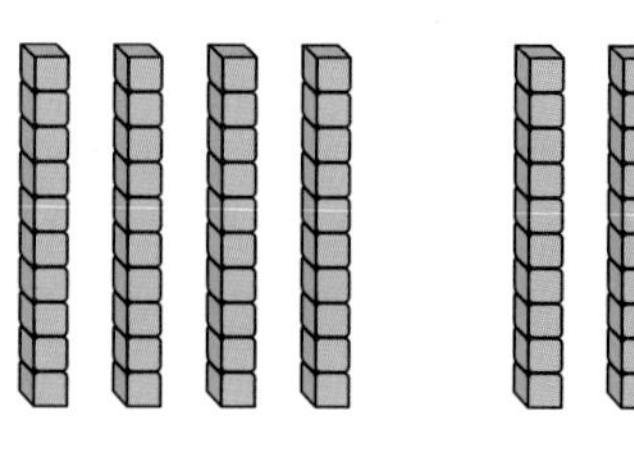

4 tens 2 tens

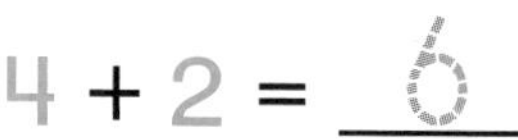

4 + 2 = 6

4 tens + 2 tens = 6 tens

40 + 20 = 60

↑
sum

Guided Practice

Complete the addition sentences. Use a basic fact to help.

Think
6 + 3 = 9 helps me add the tens.

1. 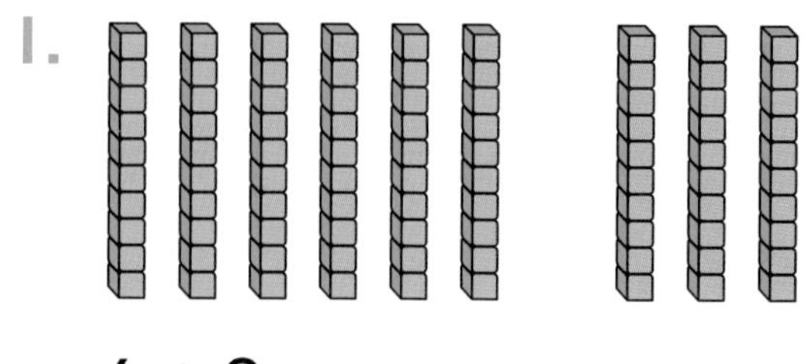

6 + 3 = ____

6 tens + 3 tens = ____ tens

60 + 30 = ____

2. 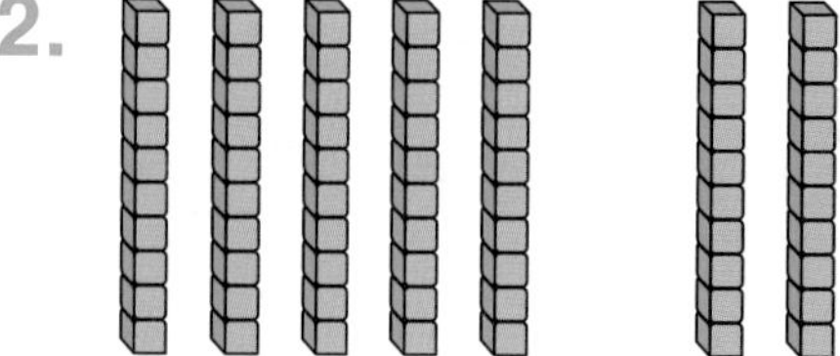

5 + 2 = ____

5 tens + 2 tens = ____ tens

50 + 20 = ____

3. 4 tens + 1 ten = ____ tens

____ + ____ = ____

4. 2 tens + 6 tens = ____ tens

____ + ____ = ____

Explain Your Thinking How does 2 + 6 help you find 20 + 60?

Practice

Remember to think about addition facts.

Complete the addition sentences. Use a basic fact to help.

1. 2 tens + 5 tens = 7 tens

   20 + 50 = 70

2. 4 tens + 3 tens = _____ tens

   _____ + _____ = _____

3. 7 tens + 2 tens = _____ tens

   _____ + _____ = _____

4. 2 tens + 1 ten = _____ tens

   _____ + _____ = _____

5. 5 tens + 3 tens = _____ tens

   _____ + _____ = _____

6. 1 ten + 6 tens = _____ tens

   _____ + _____ = _____

7. 1 ten + 1 ten = _____ tens

   _____ + _____ = _____

8. 3 tens + 2 tens = _____ tens

   _____ + _____ = _____

9. 5 tens + 4 tens = _____ tens

   _____ + _____ = _____

10. 3 tens + 3 tens = _____ tens

    _____ + _____ = _____

Problem Solving ▶ Number Sense

11. Sam tosses two counters on the board. His total score is 50. Show one way the counters may land.

    ____

12. **Talk About It** Does everyone have the same answer? Explain.

At Home Use 7 dimes to show an addition sentence with a sum of 70, such as 30 + 40 = 70. Now ask your child to make another addition sentence with 7 dimes.

Name ______________________

Count On Tens to Add

Objective
Use a hundred chart and count on by tens to add.

Use the hundred chart.
Find 35 + 20.

Step 1

Find 35 on the hundred chart.

Step 2

Count on by tens to add 20.

35, 45, 55

35 + 20 = 55

1	2	3	4	5	6	7	8	9	10
11	12	13	14	15	16	17	18	19	20
21	22	23	24	25	26	27	28	29	30
31	32	33	34	(35)	36	37	38	39	40
41	42	43	44	(45)	46	47	48	49	50
51	52	53	54	(55)	56	57	58	59	60
61	62	63	64	65	66	67	68	69	70
71	72	73	74	75	76	77	78	79	80
81	82	83	84	85	86	87	88	89	90
91	92	93	94	95	96	97	98	99	100

Guided Practice

Use the hundred chart.
Add.

Think
Find 62. Count on by tens to add 30.

1. 30 + 62 = ______
2. 20 + 77 = ______
3. 40 + 54 = ______
4. 45 + 10 = ______
5. 18 + 70 = ______
6. 27 + 70 = ______
7. 50 + 32 = ______
8. 40 + 31 = ______

9. $\begin{array}{r} 68 \\ +10 \\ \hline \end{array}$

10. $\begin{array}{r} 15 \\ +60 \\ \hline \end{array}$

11. $\begin{array}{r} 40 \\ +49 \\ \hline \end{array}$

12. $\begin{array}{r} 13 \\ +20 \\ \hline \end{array}$

13. $\begin{array}{r} 30 \\ +34 \\ \hline \end{array}$

Explain Your Thinking Which number will you start with to find the sum for Exercise 13? Why?

Practice

Remember to move down 1 row for each ten you add.

Use the hundred chart.
Add.

1. 16 + 10 = 26
2. 20 + 34 = ______
3. 69 + 30 = ______
4. 80 + 13 = ______
5. 24 + 60 = ______
6. 40 + 32 = ______

1	2	3	4	5	6	7	8	9	10
11	12	13	14	15	16	17	18	19	20
21	22	23	24	25	26	27	28	29	30
31	32	33	34	35	36	37	38	39	40
41	42	43	44	45	46	47	48	49	50
51	52	53	54	55	56	57	58	59	60
61	62	63	64	65	66	67	68	69	70
71	72	73	74	75	76	77	78	79	80
81	82	83	84	85	86	87	88	89	90
91	92	93	94	95	96	97	98	99	100

7. 28 + 20 = ______
8. 10 + 55 = ______
9. 12 + 30 = ______
10. 60 + 34 = ______
11. 43 + 50 = ______

12. 21 + 10 = ______
13. 20 + 39 = ______
14. 40 + 11 = ______
15. 16 + 70 = ______
16. 60 + 28 = ______

Problem Solving ▶ Missing Addends

Choose a number to complete the addition sentence.

20 30 40 50 60

17. 36 + ______ = 56
18. 47 + ______ = 97
19. ______ + 28 = 58
20. ______ + 53 = 93

At Home Ask your child to explain how to add 45 and 20 on the hundred chart shown above.

Hands-On

Name ______________________________

Regroup Ones as Tens

 **Audio Tutor 1**/29 Listen and Understand

When you have 10 or more ones, you need to **regroup.**

Objective
Regroup 10 ones as 1 ten.

Vocabulary
regroup

Step 1

Here is one way to show 35.

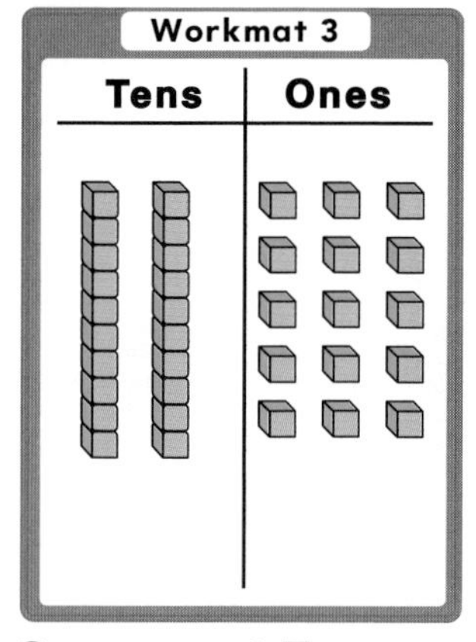

2 tens 15 ones

Step 2

There are 15 ones.
Regroup 10 ones as 1 ten.

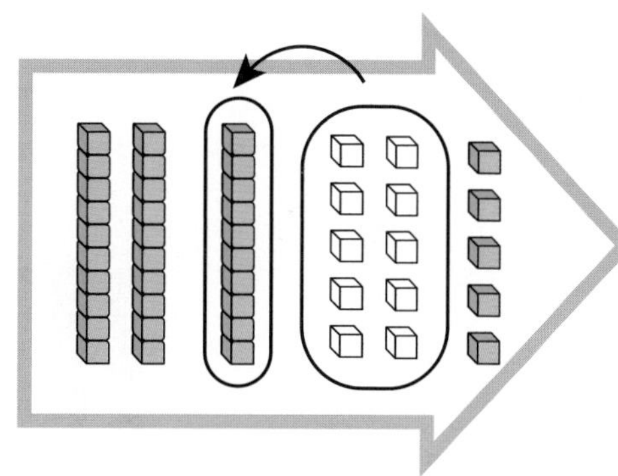

Step 3

Here is another way to show 35.

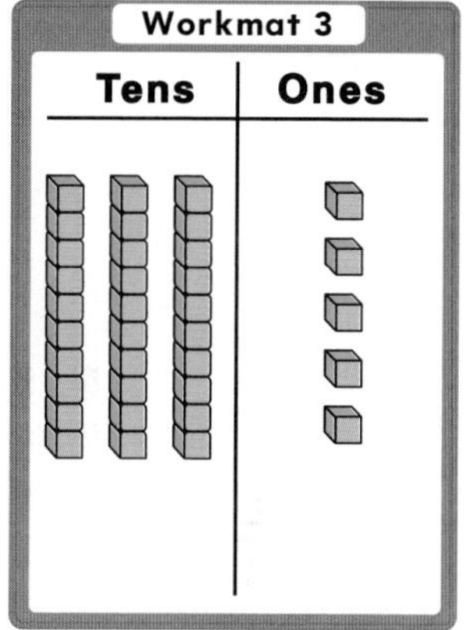

3 tens 5 ones
35

Guided Practice

Use Workmat 3 with [ten rod] and [unit cube].
Show the tens and ones.
Regroup. Write the number.

1. 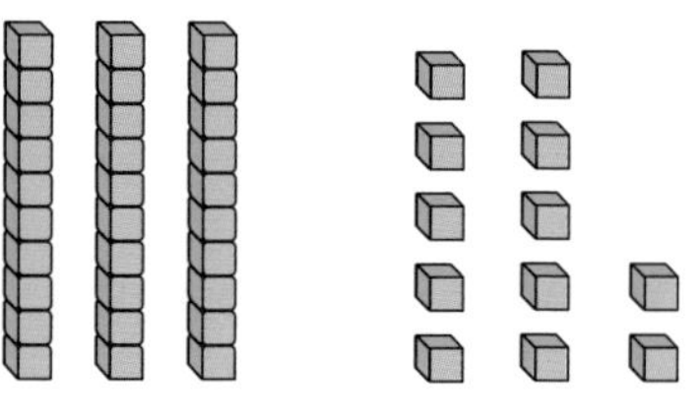

Think
Regroup 12 ones as 1 ten and 2 ones.

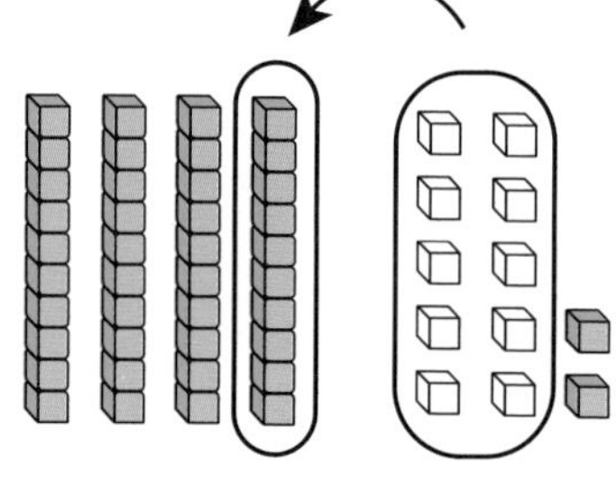

_____ tens _____ ones  _____ tens _____ ones ☐

2. 5 tens 10 ones  _____ tens _____ ones 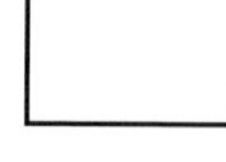

3. 1 ten 19 ones 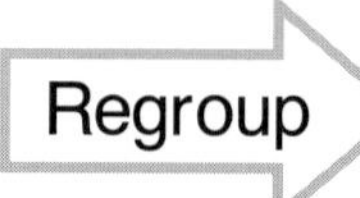 _____ tens _____ ones 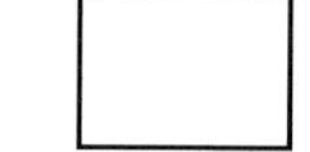

Explain Your Thinking What does it mean to regroup 10 ones?

Practice

Remember to regroup 10 ones as 1 ten.

Use Workmat 3 with [ten rod] and [one cube].
Write the tens and ones.
Regroup. Write the number.

1. 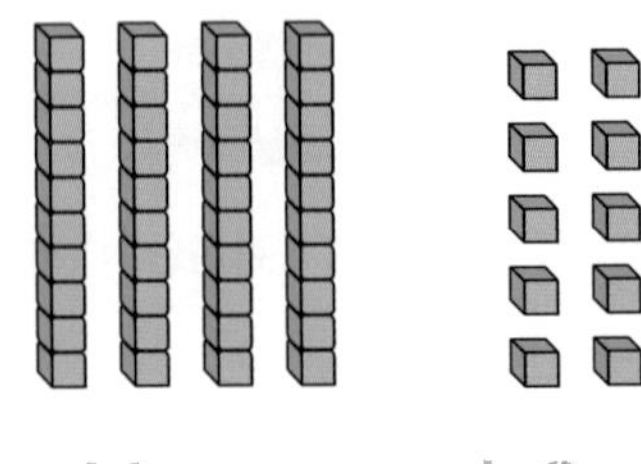

4 tens 10 ones

Regroup →

5 tens 0 ones 

2. 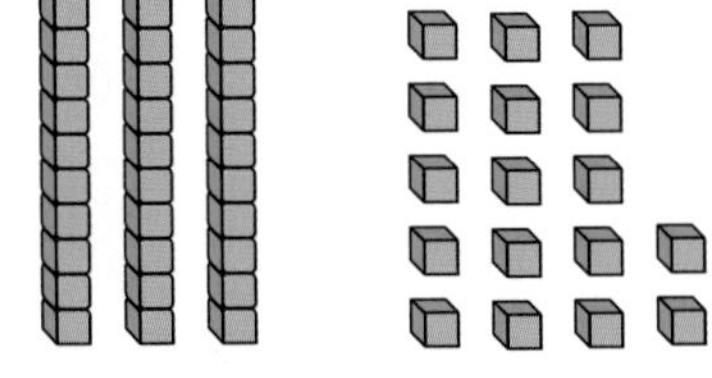

_____ tens _____ ones

Regroup →

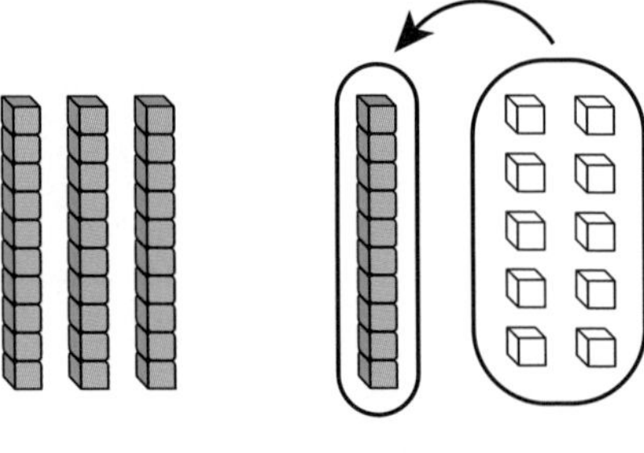

_____ tens _____ ones ☐

Regroup.
Write the number.

3. 6 tens 16 ones Regroup → _____ tens _____ ones ☐

4. 2 tens 14 ones Regroup → _____ tens _____ ones ☐

5. 1 ten 13 ones Regroup → _____ tens _____ ones ☐

6. 7 tens 10 ones Regroup → _____ tens _____ ones ☐

7. 4 tens 15 ones Regroup → _____ tens _____ ones 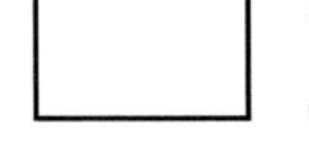

Go on

Name ______________________________

Regroup.
Write the number.

8. 3 tens 11 ones → Regroup → ____ tens ____ ones ☐

9. 6 tens 16 ones → Regroup → ____ tens ____ ones ☐

10. 2 tens 19 ones → Regroup → ____ tens ____ ones ☐

11. 5 tens 14 ones → Regroup → ____ tens ____ ones ☐

12. 3 tens 12 ones → Regroup → ____ tens ____ ones ☐

Problem Solving ▶ Number Sense

13. Circle the pictures that show 40.

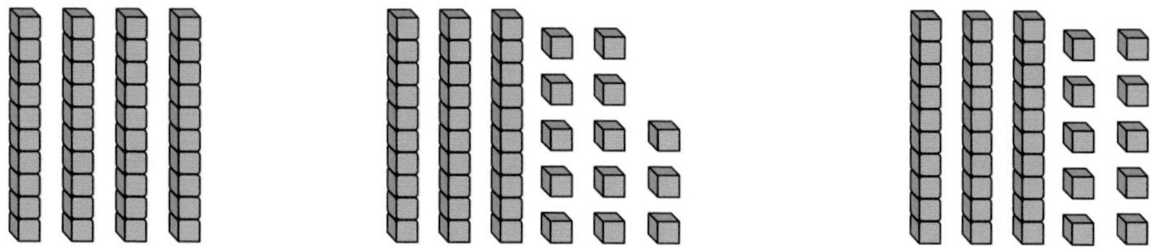

14. Circle the pictures that show 32.

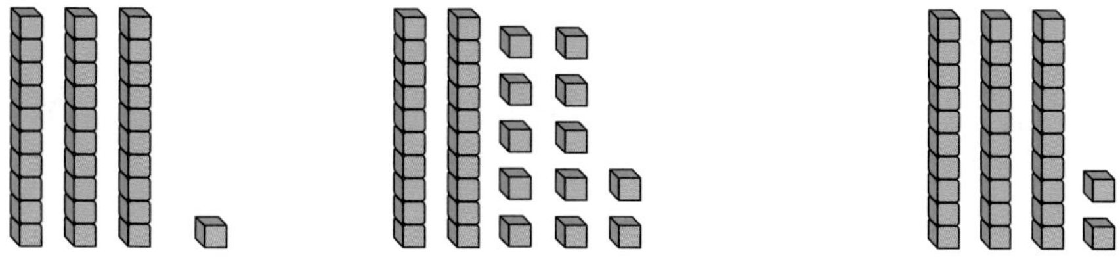

15. **Talk About It** Explain why the pictures you circled in Exercise 14 show 32.

At Home Have your child count a handful of objects, such as cereal or macaroni, by making groups of 10.

Problem Solving

Social Studies Connection
American Flag

Each star on the flag stands for one of the 50 states.

States in the United States	
1890	43
1912	48

How many more states became part of the United States after 1912? _____

Think
How many stars are on the flag?

WEEKLY WR READER eduplace.com/map

Quick Check

Complete the addition sentences.

1. 3 tens + 4 tens = _____ tens

_____ + _____ = _____

2. 6 tens + 2 tens = _____ tens

_____ + _____ = _____

Use a hundred chart.
Add.

3. 19 + 30 = _____
4. 20 + 57 = _____
5. 6 + 40 = _____

Regroup.
Write the number.

6. 4 tens 15 ones → Regroup → _____ tens _____ ones ☐

Facts Practice, see page 671.

Hands-On

Name ______________________________

Decide When to Regroup

Audio Tutor 1/30 Listen and Understand

Objective
Regroup 10 ones as 1 ten when needed.

Add 36 and 7.

Step 1

Show 3 tens and 6 ones.
Show 7 more ones.

Workmat 3

Tens	Ones

Step 2

Add the ones. Regroup 10 ones as 1 ten.

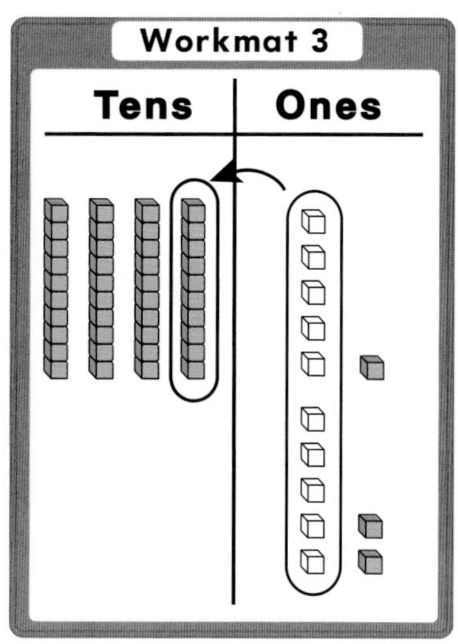

Step 3

Write the sum.

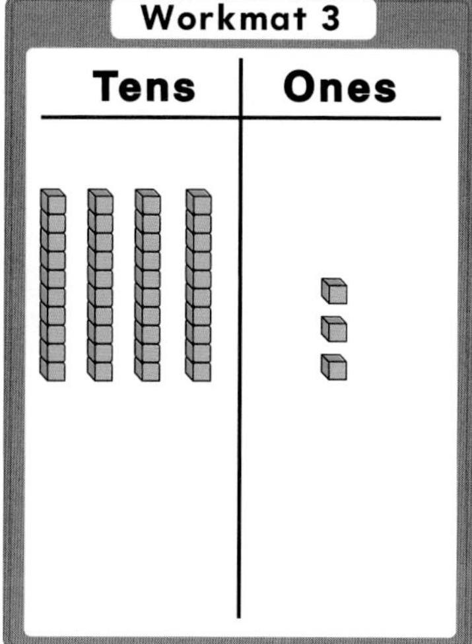

4 tens 3 ones
43

Guided Practice

Use Workmat 3 with [ten rod] and [unit cube].

	Show both numbers.	Add the ones. How many tens and ones are there?	Do you need to regroup?	What is the sum?
1.	23 + 9	2 tens 12 ones	Yes No	
2.	48 + 7	____ tens ____ ones	Yes No	
3.	62 + 5	____ tens ____ ones	Yes No	
4.	52 + 8	____ tens ____ ones	Yes No	

Explain Your Thinking When do you need to regroup?

Practice

Remember to regroup when you have 10 or more ones.

Use Workmat 3 with [ten rod] and [unit cube].

	Show both numbers.	Add the ones. How many tens and ones are there?	Do you need to regroup?	What is the sum?
1.	14 + 7	1 ten 11 ones	(Yes) No	21
2.	28 + 2	______ tens ______ ones	Yes No	
3.	76 + 3	______ tens ______ ones	Yes No	
4.	35 + 6	______ tens ______ ones	Yes No	
5.	61 + 5	______ tens ______ ones	Yes No	
6.	44 + 9	______ tens ______ ones	Yes No	
7.	37 + 8	______ tens ______ ones	Yes No	

Problem Solving ▶ Reasoning

8. Jan has 2 dimes and 5 pennies. She gets 9 more pennies. How many dimes and pennies does she have now?

______ dimes ______ pennies

9. If Jan trades 10 pennies for 1 dime, how many dimes and pennies will she have?

______ dimes ______ pennies

At Home Ask your child to show or explain how 12 pennies can be regrouped using dimes and pennies.

Name ____________________

Add One-Digit Numbers to Two-Digit Numbers

Objective
Add a one-digit number to a two-digit number with and without regrouping.

Audio Tutor 1/31 Listen and Understand

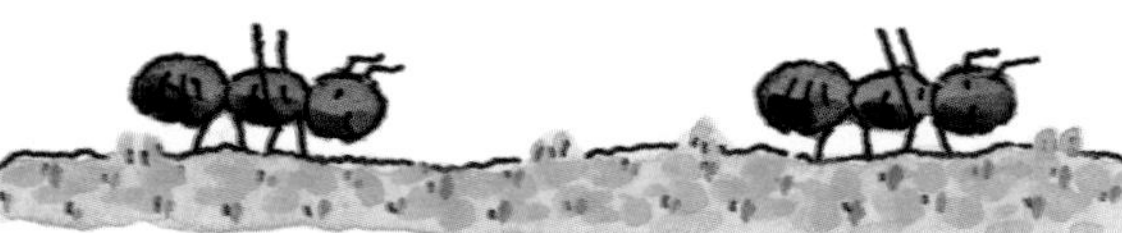

Add 26 and 8.

Show 26 and 8. Add 6 ones and 8 ones.

Workmat 3

Tens	Ones

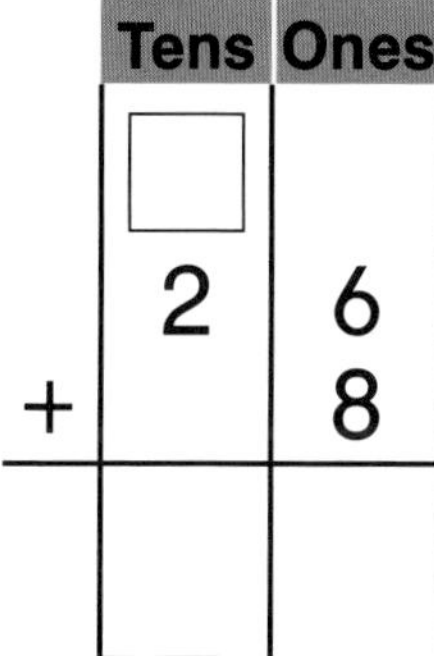

	Tens	Ones
	☐	
	2	6
+		8

Regroup 10 ones as 1 ten.

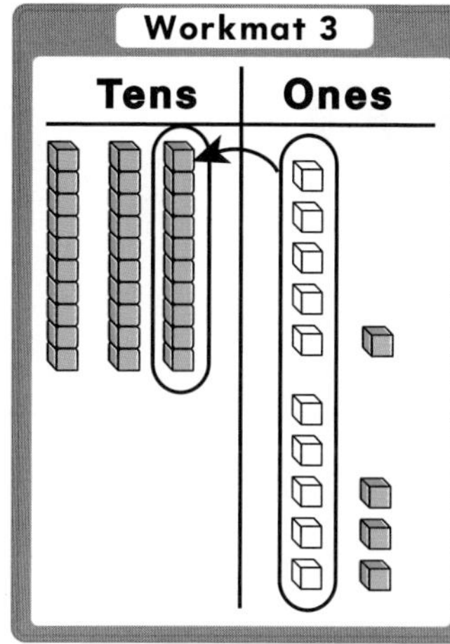

	Tens	Ones
	1	
	2	6
+		8
		4

Add the tens.

Workmat 3

Tens	Ones

	Tens	Ones
	1	
	2	6
+		8
	3	4

Guided Practice

Use Workmat 3 with ▭ and ▫. Add.

1.

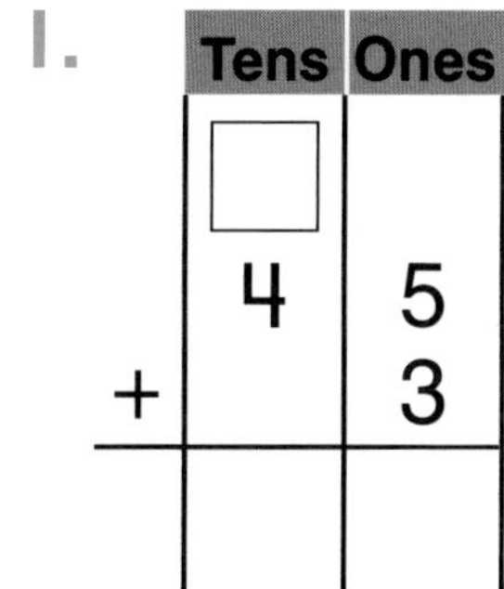

	Tens	Ones
	☐	
	4	5
+		3

Think
Do I have 10 or more ones?
Do I need to regroup?

2.

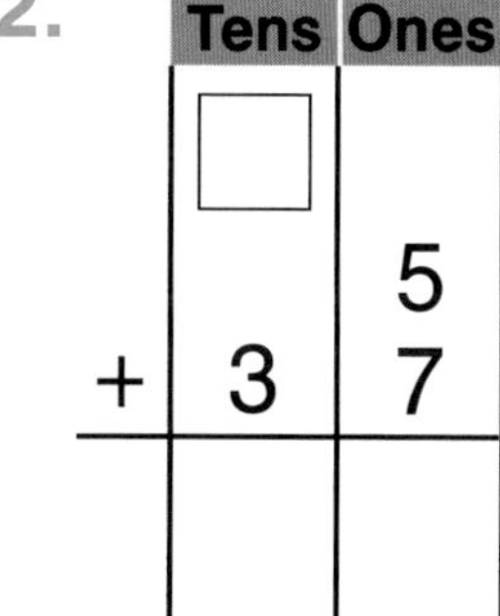

	Tens	Ones
	☐	
		5
+	3	7

3.

	Tens	Ones
	☐	
	5	6
+		7

Explain Your Thinking What does the 1 in the ☐ represent in Exercise 3?

Practice

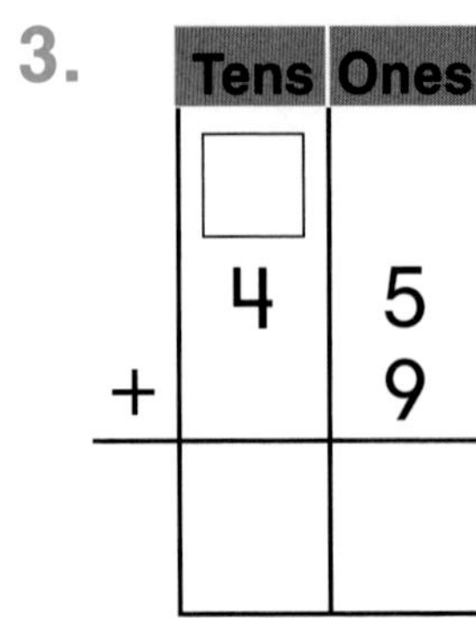

Remember to regroup when you have 10 or more ones.

Use Workmat 3 with [ten rod] and [unit cube].
Add.

1.

	Tens	Ones
	1	
	3	4
+		7
	4	1

2.

	Tens	Ones
	☐	
		8
+	2	9

3.

	Tens	Ones
	☐	
	4	5
+		9

4.

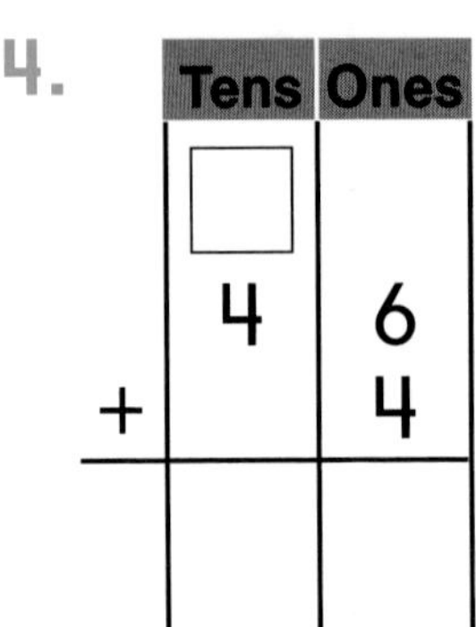

	Tens	Ones
	☐	
	4	6
+		4

5.

	Tens	Ones
	☐	
		3
+	6	3

6.

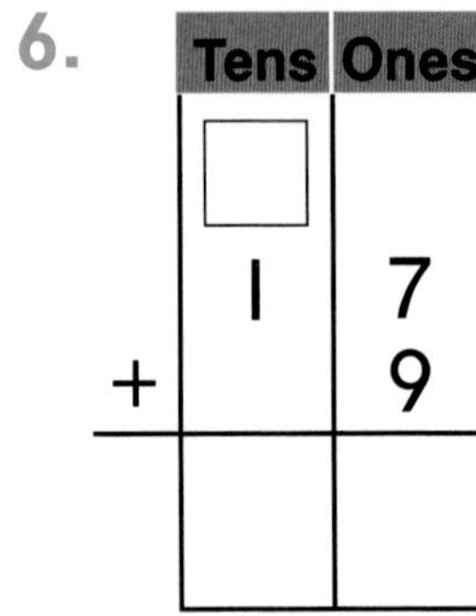

	Tens	Ones
	☐	
	1	7
+		9

7.

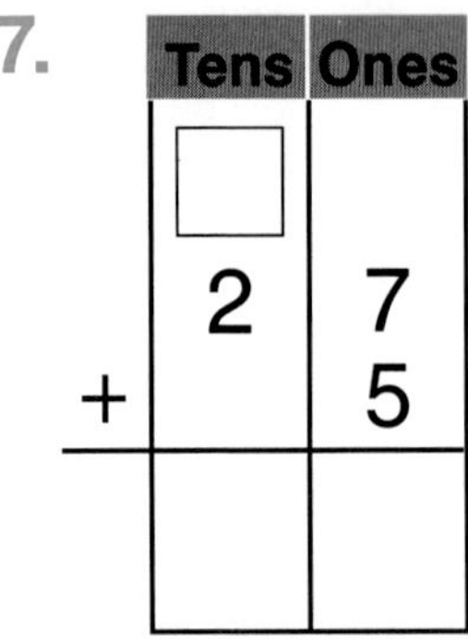

	Tens	Ones
	☐	
	2	7
+		5

8.

	Tens	Ones
	☐	
		8
+	3	5

9.

	Tens	Ones
	☐	
	5	7
+		2

10.

	Tens	Ones
	☐	
		7
+	8	4

11.

	Tens	Ones
	☐	
	9	0
+		6

Problem Solving ▶ Number Sense

12. Don has 24 grapes. Rosa has grapes, too. Don adds to find how many they have together. He has to regroup when he adds. Does Rosa have 6, 3, or 5 grapes?

Draw or write to explain.

_____ grapes

At Home Tell your child your age. Ask your child to add his or her age to yours. Did your child need to regroup?

Name ______________________________

Add Two-Digit Numbers

 **Audio Tutor 1**/32 Listen and Understand

Objective
Add two-digit numbers with and without regrouping.

Add 17 and 25.

Step 1

Show 17 and 25.
Add 7 ones and 5 ones.

Workmat 3

Tens	Ones

	Tens	Ones
	☐	
	1	7
+	2	5

Regroup 10 ones as 1 ten.

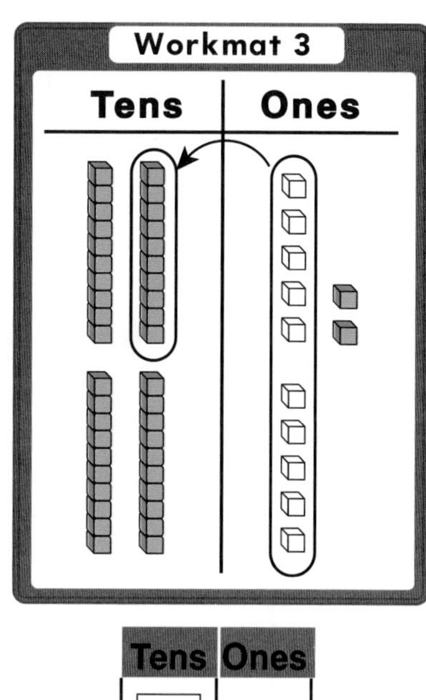

	Tens	Ones
	1	
	1	7
+	2	5
		2

Add the tens.

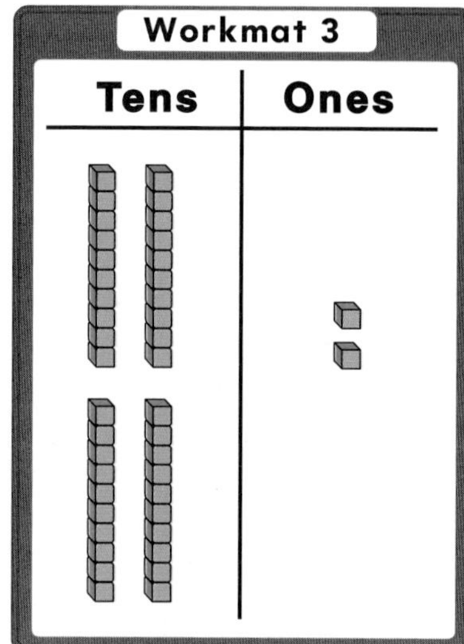

	Tens	Ones
	1	
	1	7
+	2	5
	4	2

Guided Practice

Use Workmat 3 with ten-rods and ones cubes. Add.

1.

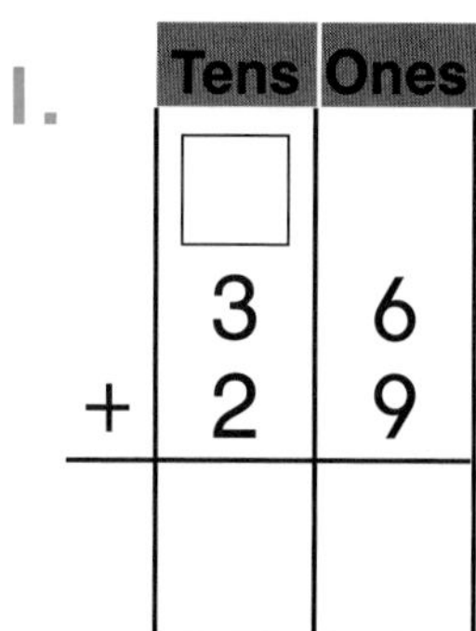

	Tens	Ones
	☐	
	3	6
+	2	9

Think
How many tens can I make from 15 ones?

2.

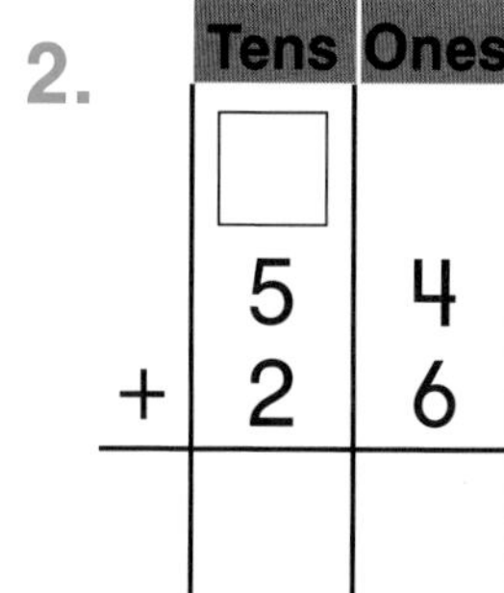

	Tens	Ones
	☐	
	5	4
+	2	6

3.

	Tens	Ones
	☐	
	4	2
+	1	5

Explain Your Thinking How does knowing that 16 ones is the same as 1 ten and 6 ones help you add?

Practice

When you regroup, remember to record the 1 ten you make.

Use Workmat 3 with [ten rod] and [unit cube].
Add.

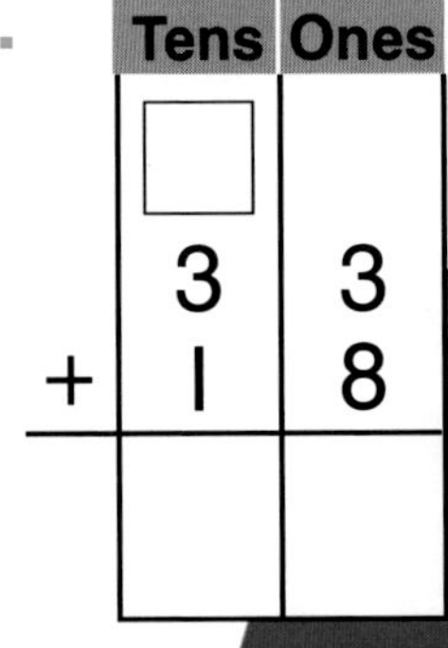

1.

	Tens	Ones
	1	
	2	8
+	3	2
	6	0

2.

	Tens	Ones
	☐	
	4	5
+		8

3.

	Tens	Ones
	☐	
	3	3
+	1	8

4.

	Tens	Ones
	☐	
	2	5
+	4	5

5.

	Tens	Ones
	☐	
	5	4
+	3	7

6.

	Tens	Ones
	☐	
	6	1
+	2	8

7.

	Tens	Ones
	☐	
	2	9
+	2	1

8.

	☐	
	3	2
+		6

9.

	☐	
	2	6
+	5	7

10.

	☐	
	1	9
+	1	4

11.

	☐	
	4	7
+	3	3

12. $\begin{array}{r} 72 \\ +16 \\ \hline \end{array}$

13. $\begin{array}{r} 6 \\ +48 \\ \hline \end{array}$

14. $\begin{array}{r} 36 \\ +26 \\ \hline \end{array}$

15. $\begin{array}{r} 58 \\ +20 \\ \hline \end{array}$

Go on

Name ____________________

Problem Solving ▶ Reasoning

Use Workmat 3 with tens and ones.
Use the picture to solve.

Draw or write to explain.

1. What is the total number of sandwiches and apples?

_____ sandwiches and apples

2. Mrs. Leone made the cookies and the sandwiches. How many things did she make?

_____ things

3. Mr. Lane brings 36 more watermelon slices. How many slices are there now?

_____ slices

4. **Write About It** Use the labels for the plates of food above. Write a story problem that uses addition with regrouping.

____

____

At Home Write a two-digit problem such as 38 + 56. Ask your child to explain how to find the sum.

Activity

Game

Regroup and Score

2 Players

What You Need: Number Cards (as shown)

How to Play

1. Place the Number Cards face up.
2. Choose two Number Cards. Add the numbers to find the sum. If you need to regroup, you score 1 point. Keep the cards.
3. Take turns until all the number cards have been used.
4. The player with the most points wins.

56	24	18	5
12	30	26	7
23	35	27	40
8	14	32	9

Another Way to Play

Place the Number Cards face down. Play the game again.

Name ____________________

Too Much Information

 **Audio Tutor 1**/33 Listen and Understand

Objective
Identify the information you do not need in a problem.

Problem Solving

Sometimes a problem has more information than you need.

On Monday, 30 children visit the zoo. On Tuesday morning 19 children visit. On Tuesday afternoon 20 children visit the zoo. How many children visit the zoo on Tuesday?

Cross out the information you do not need. Complete the number sentence. Solve.

Think
Do I need the information about Monday? If I don't, I will cross it out.

__19__ + __20__ = __39__

__39__ children

Sometimes you need all the information.

At the zoo, 2 bears and 2 tigers are born. 5 chimps are also born. How many animals are born?

Cross out the information you do not need. Complete the number sentence. Solve.

Think
Is there any information that I can cross out?

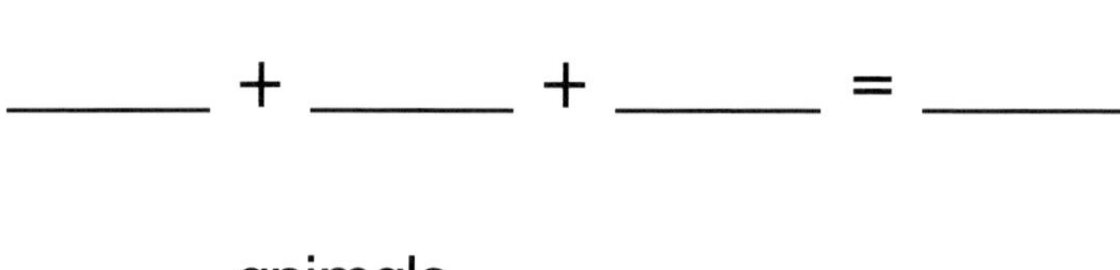

_____ + _____ + _____ = _____

_____ animals

Guided Practice

Cross out any information you do not need.
Then solve.

1. There are 30 first grade children, 40 second grade children, and 4 teachers on the zoo train ride. How many children are on the train?

Draw or write to explain.

Think
Can I cross out any information?

_____ children

2. Larry bought 20 bird cards, 30 fish cards, and 40 stickers. How many cards did Larry buy?

Think
What information do I need?

_____ cards

Practice

3. Tina took 10 pictures of zebras and 10 pictures of the big tigers. She also took 16 pictures of tiger cubs. How many pictures of tigers did Tina take?

_____ tiger pictures

4. Juan has 29 dimes in a box and 59 pennies in a bag. He finds 10 more dimes. How many dimes does Juan have?

_____ dimes

Name ________________________

Strategies
Draw a Picture
Act It Out
Write a Number Sentence

Mixed Problem Solving

Solve.

Draw or write to explain.

1. The zoo has 2 tanks. There are 6 whales in one tank. There are 7 whales in the other tank. How many whales are there?

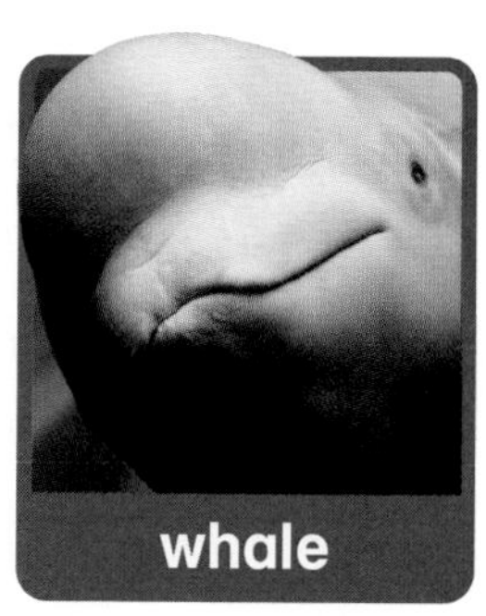
whale

_____ whales

2. There are 20 sea otters in the water. Then 13 more jump in. How many sea otters are in the water now?

sea otter

_____ sea otters

3. The children saw 12 dolphins and 3 whales on the boat ride. On the ride back they saw 3 more dolphins and 1 more whale. How many dolphins did they see in all?

dolphin

_____ dolphins

4. **Multistep** There are 2 seals in the morning show. There are 3 other seals in the evening show. Each seal eats 4 fish at dinner. How many fish do the seals eat at dinner?

seal

_____ fish

At Home Have your child tell which exercises have extra information and identify the extra information.

Problem Solving on Tests • Listening Skills

Open Response

Listen to your teacher read the problem.
Solve.

1. There are 23 eggs in the basket. Byron adds 5 more eggs to the basket. How many eggs are in the basket now?

Show your work using pictures, numbers, or words.

_____ eggs

2. There are 3 fish bowls on a table and 4 fish bowls on a shelf. Each bowl has 2 fish. How many fish in all?

_____ fish

Multiple Choice

Listen to your teacher read the problem.
Choose the correct answer.

3. ○ 20 ○ 27 ○ 17 ○ 72

4. ○ 5 ○ 10 ○ 15 ○ 20

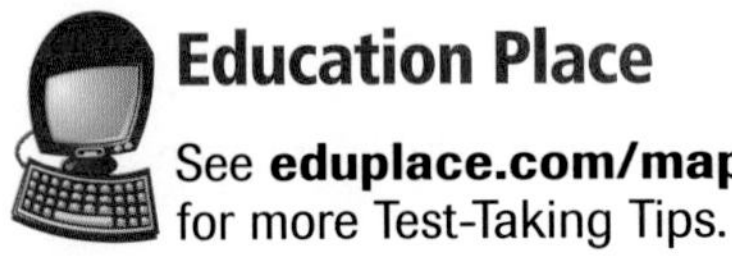

Education Place
See **eduplace.com/map** for more Test-Taking Tips.

Name ______________________________

Now Try This

Use Place Value to Add

Add another way.
Think of place value.

Add the tens.	Add the ones.	Add the tens and ones.
25 + 13	25 + 13	25 + 13
20 + 10 = 30	5 + 3 = 8	30 + 8 = 38

Try it again.

Add the tens.	Add the ones.	Add the tens and ones.
35 + 17	35 + 17	35 + 17
30 + 10 = 40	5 + 7 = 12	40 + 12 = 52

Add. Think of place value.

1. 48 + 31 = 79

40 + 30 = 70   8 + 1 = 9

70 + 9 = 79

Add tens first. Add ones. Then add tens and ones.

2. 19 + 74 = ______
3. 32 + 49 = ______
4. 75 + 12 = ______
5. 82 + 15 = ______
6. 43 + 19 = ______
7. 55 + 25 = ______
8. **Talk About It** What are the other ways to add 43 + 19?

Problem Solving

Math Challenge

Guess My Number

11 37 44 24 55 32

Read the problem.
Find the number.
Write the answer.

1. My number has tens and ones digits that are the same. It is 33 more than the least number. What is my number? ______

2. My number is between 30 and 40. It is 26 more than the least number. What is my number? ______

Key Topic Review

Addition

Add.

1.	2.	3.	4.	5.	6.
6 + 6	10 + 5	9 + 7	12 + 6	7 + 7	11 + 4

7.	8.	9.	10.	11.	12.
8 + 8	5 + 9	14 + 2	4 + 8	5 + 4	9 + 9

13.	14.	15.	16.	17.	18.
11 + 5	14 + 4	12 + 3	9 + 6	10 + 8	13 + 2

Extra Practice at eduplace.com/map

Name ____________________

Chapter Review/Test

Vocabulary

Draw a line to match.

1. **regroup**	To join 2 or more groups
2. **sum**	To trade 10 ones for 1 ten
3. **add**	The result of adding

Concepts and Skills

Complete the addition sentences.

4. 3 tens + 6 tens = ______ tens

   ______ + ______ = ______

5. 2 tens + 3 tens = ______ tens

   ______ + ______ = ______

Add.

6. $\begin{array}{r} 20 \\ +45 \\ \hline \end{array}$

7. $\begin{array}{r} 34 \\ +50 \\ \hline \end{array}$

8. $\begin{array}{r} 71 \\ +10 \\ \hline \end{array}$

9. $\begin{array}{r} 13 \\ +30 \\ \hline \end{array}$

10. $\begin{array}{r} 60 \\ +17 \\ \hline \end{array}$

Regroup.
Write the number.

11. 5 tens 15 ones → Regroup → ______ tens ______ ones ☐

12. 8 tens 10 ones → Regroup → ______ tens ______ ones 

13. 6 tens 11 ones → Regroup → ______ tens ______ ones ☐

Chapter Review/Test

Decide if you need to regroup.
Circle **Yes** or **No**.
Write the sum.

14. 48 + 3 Yes No ______

15. 53 + 6 Yes No ______

Add.

16. $\begin{array}{r} 45 \\ +\ 4 \\ \hline \end{array}$

17. $\begin{array}{r} 6 \\ +39 \\ \hline \end{array}$

18. $\begin{array}{r} 74 \\ +\ 6 \\ \hline \end{array}$

19. $\begin{array}{r} 86 \\ +\ 9 \\ \hline \end{array}$

20. $\begin{array}{r} 53 \\ +17 \\ \hline \end{array}$

21. $\begin{array}{r} 71 \\ +26 \\ \hline \end{array}$

22. $\begin{array}{r} 65 \\ +19 \\ \hline \end{array}$

23. $\begin{array}{r} 48 \\ +29 \\ \hline \end{array}$

Problem Solving

Cross out any information you do not need.
Then solve.

Draw or write to explain.

24. Bridget has 12 gorilla cards. She also has 14 giraffe cards. She finds 3 more gorilla cards. How many gorilla cards does she have in all?

______ gorilla cards

25. The large box of marbles has 45 marbles. The small box has 35 marbles. Ray buys a large and a small box. How many marbles does Ray have?

______ marbles

Using Two-Digit Addition

CHAPTER 11

INVESTIGATION

What strategies could you use to add the 2 groups of fish in this picture?

People Using Math

Sylvia Earle

A building that is 10 stories high is about 100 feet tall. Can you imagine diving 100 feet under the water?

Sylvia Earle loved nature as a girl. When she was older, she learned to scuba dive.

When she dives she studies ocean plants, whales, and the ocean water. She writes books and makes videos about what she sees in the ocean.

Sylvia works very hard to teach others how important the oceans are. She hopes her grandchildren learn from her and help keep the oceans healthy.

Sea urchin named after Sylvia *(Centrostephanus sylviae)* (sent-ro-STEFF-a-nus SIHL-wee-eye)

Sylvia was 17 years old when she first dove under water. 27 years later she set a world record for the deepest solo dive.

How old was Sylvia when she set the record?

Draw or write to explain.

_____ years old

Name ____________________

Rewrite to Add

Objective
Rewrite addition problems in vertical form.

Audio Tutor 1/34 Listen and Understand

Find 46 + 18.

Step 1

Rewrite 46 + 18.
Line up the ones and the tens.

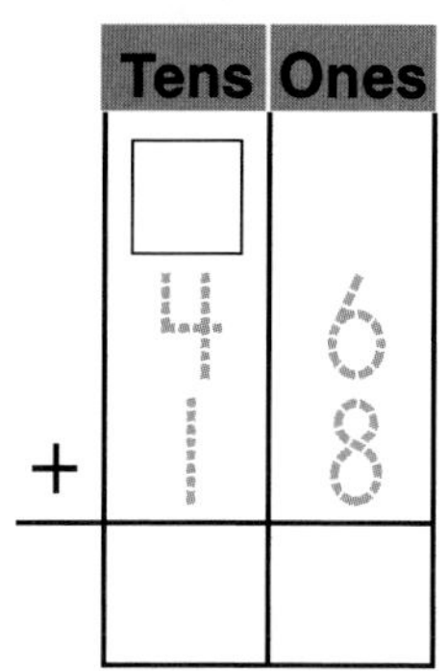

Step 2

Add the ones.
Add the tens.

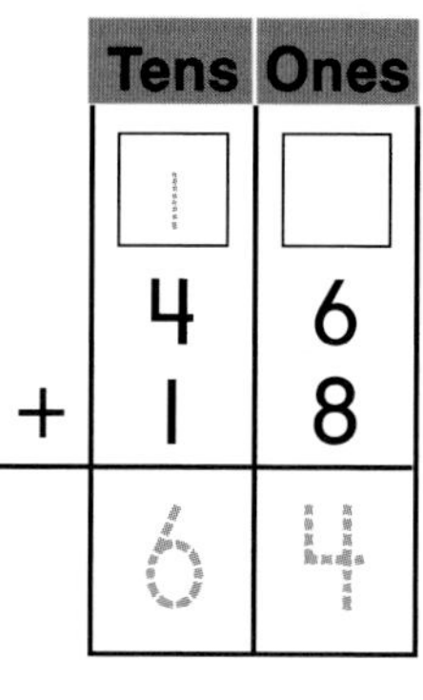

Guided Practice

Rewrite the addends. Add.

1. 37 + 6

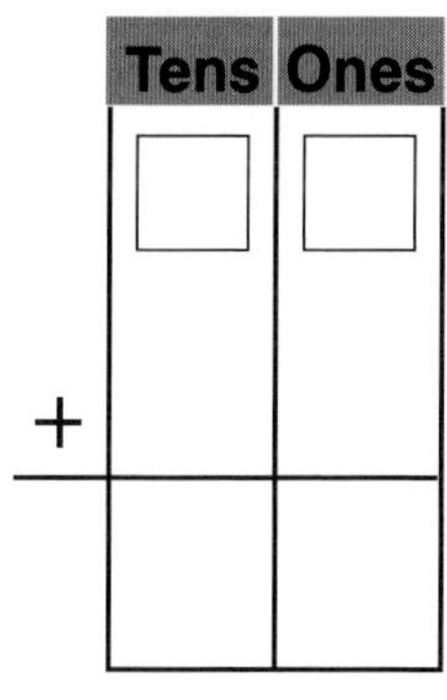

Think
I line up the 7 and the 6 in the ones column.

2. 59 + 16

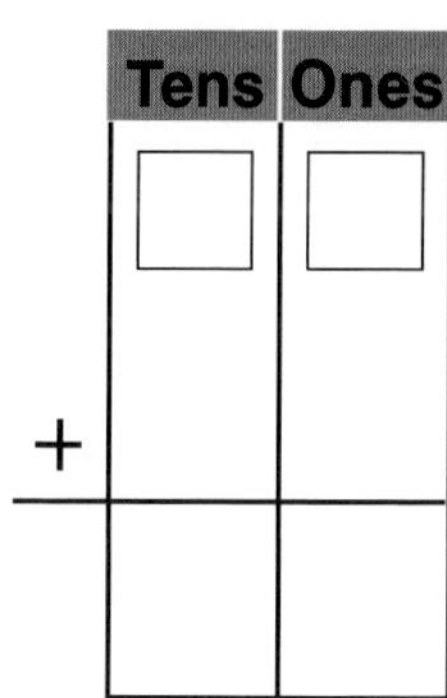

3. 7 + 62

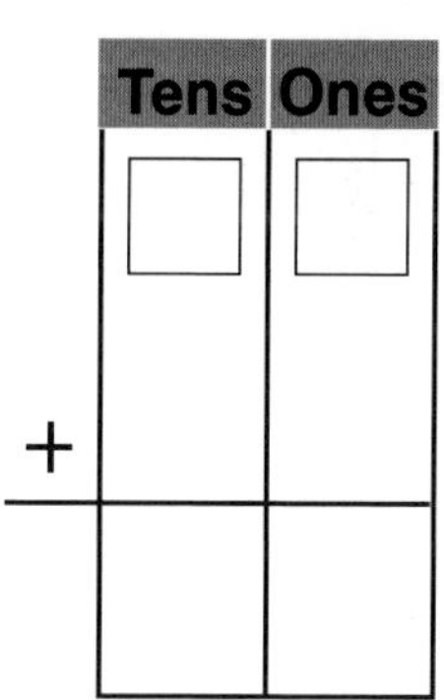

4. 59 + 28

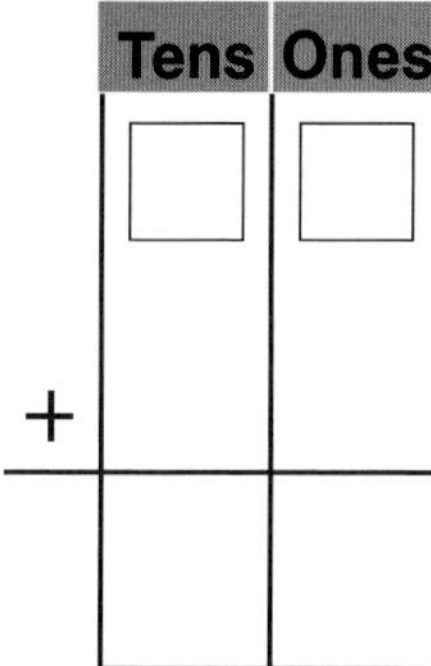

5. 73 + 7

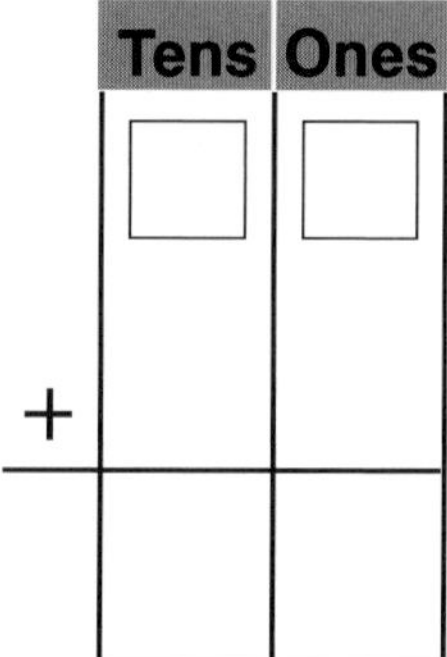

6. 26 + 38

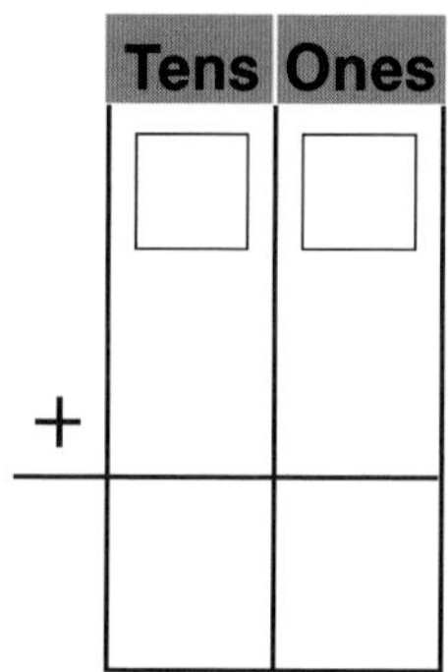

7. 9 + 65

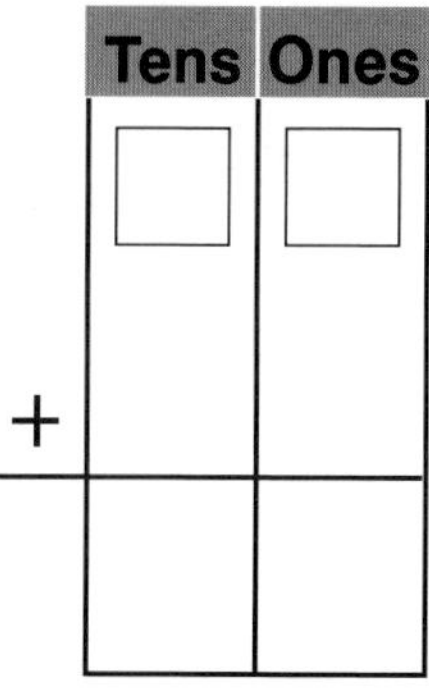

Explain Your Thinking Scott rewrites 49 + 5. Then he adds and gets a sum of 99. What did he do wrong?

Practice

When you rewrite the addends, line up the ones and the tens.

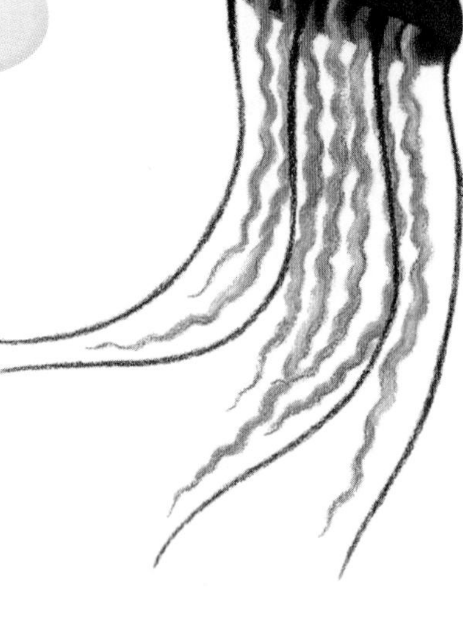

Rewrite the addends. Add.

1. 18 + 72

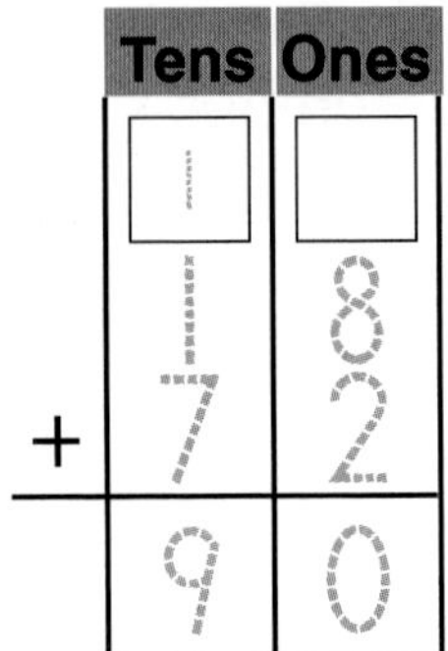

2. 63 + 25

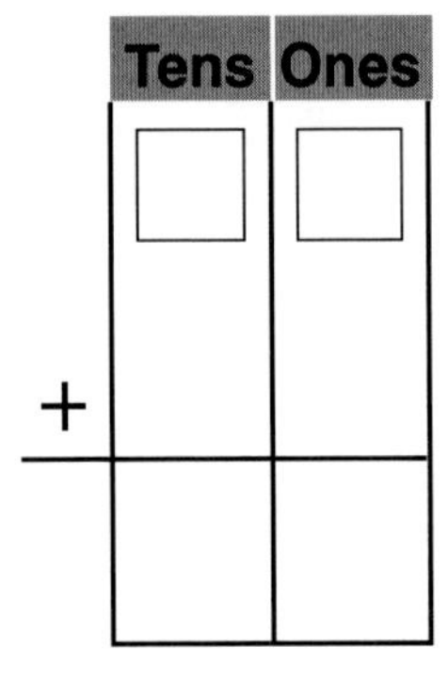

3. 7 + 39

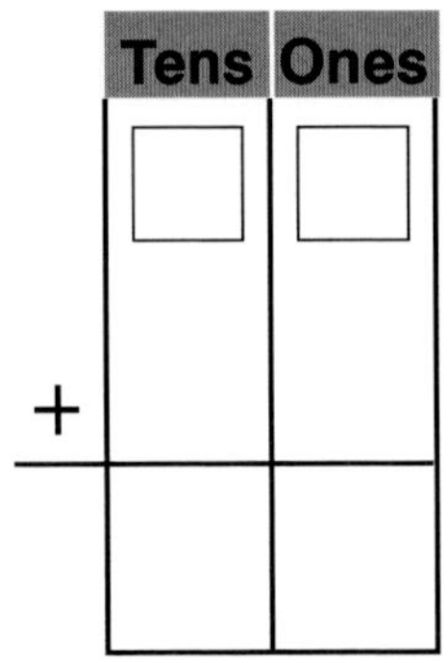

4. 48 + 39

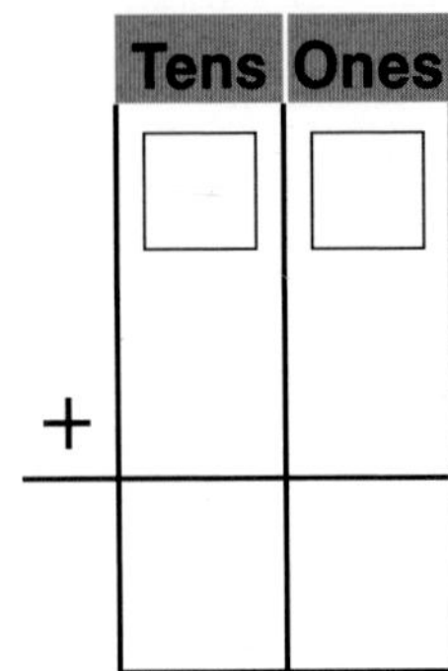

5. 59 + 15

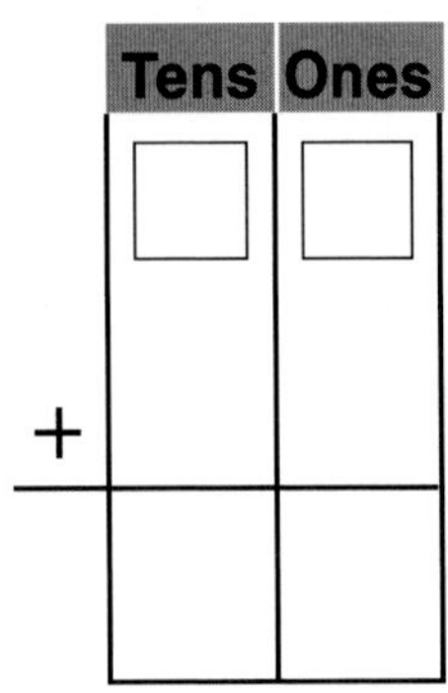

6. 86 + 4

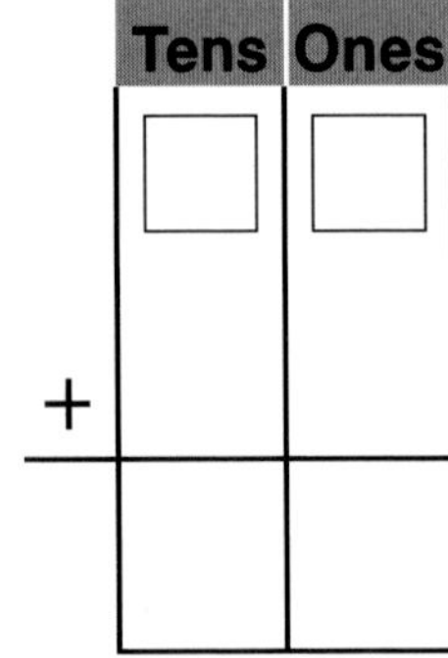

7. 27 + 34

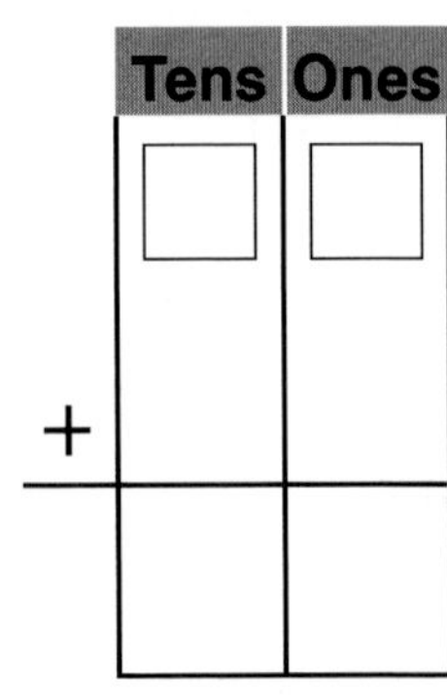

8. 8 + 56

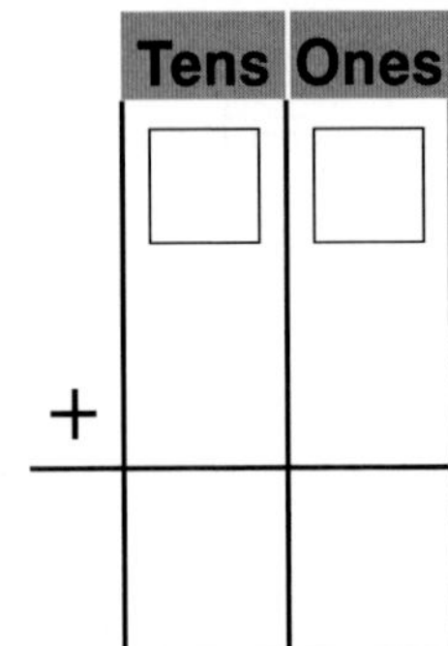

9. 65 + 19

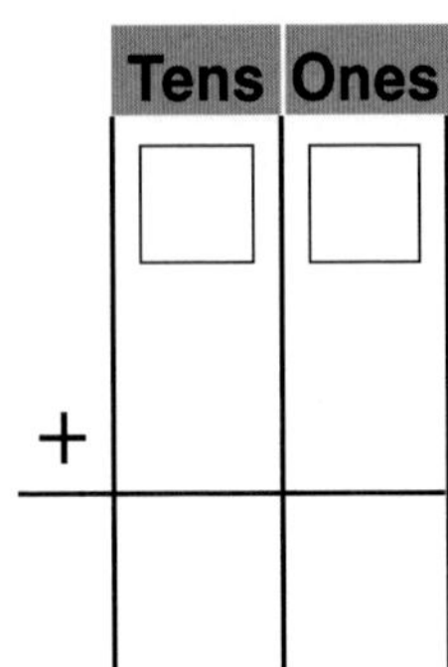

10. 46 + 33

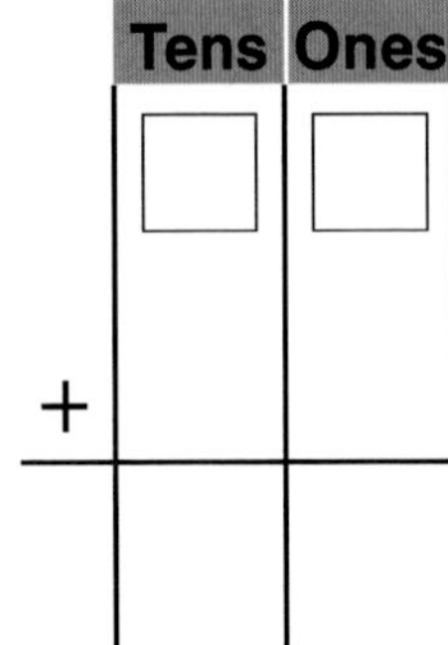

11. 23 + 67

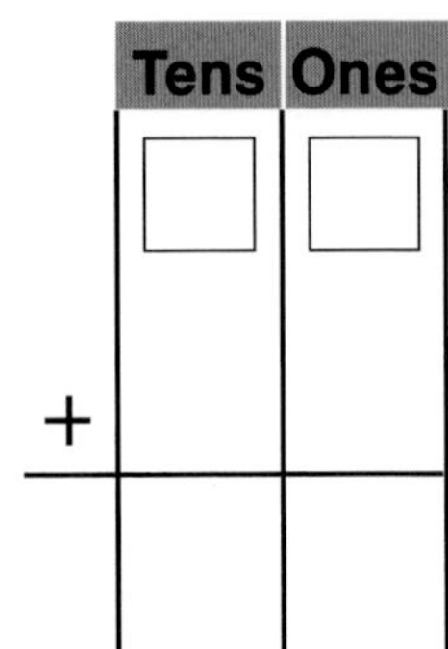

Problem Solving ▶ Number Sense

12. The gift shop needs 75 toys. The shop gets a box of shells and a box of fish. Does the shop have enough toys?

Draw or write to explain.

______

At Home Have your child show you how to rewrite 25 + 46 and 39 + 9 and then find their sums.

Name ____________________

Estimate Sums

Audio Tutor 1/35 Listen and Understand

When you do not need an exact sum, you can **estimate.**

Objective
Estimate the sum of two-digit addends by rounding.

Vocabulary
estimate
round

Estimate the sum of 21 and 35.

Step 1

Round each addend to the nearest ten.

21 is closer to 20. Round down.

35 is exactly in the middle of 30 and 40. Round up.

20 21 22 23 24 25 26 27 28 29 30 31 32 33 34 35 36 37 38 39 40

Step 2

Add the tens to estimate the sum.

20 + 40 = 60

Guided Practice

Round each addend to the nearest ten.
Estimate the sum.

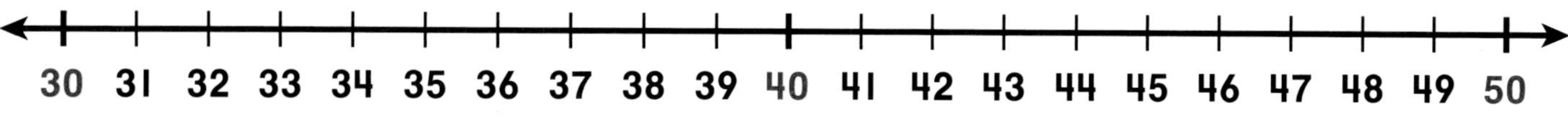

1. 45 + 38

_____ + _____ = _____

Think
I round 38 up to 40.

2. 37 + 49

_____ + _____ = _____

3. 42 + 36

_____ + _____ = _____

Explain Your Thinking Why is 90 a better estimate than 70 for 59 + 28?

Practice

Round each addend to the nearest ten. Estimate the sum.

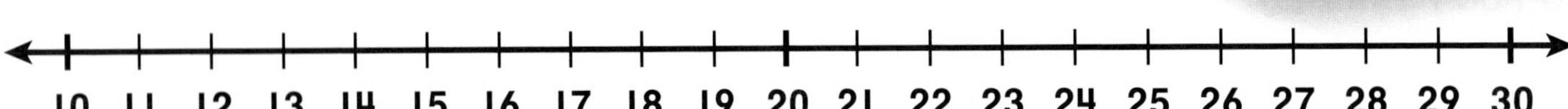

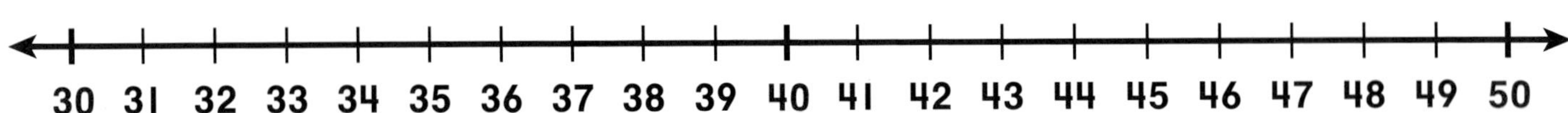

1. 40 + 25

   40 + 30 = 70

2. 27 + 36

   ______ + ______ = ______

3. 22 + 48

   ______ + ______ = ______

4. 15 + 44

   ______ + ______ = ______

5. 19 + 34

   ______ + ______ = ______

6. 31 + 18

   ______ + ______ = ______

Problem Solving ▶ Estimation

Round and estimate to solve.

7. Tony needs 16 starfish stickers and 32 shell stickers to make a design on his notebook. About how many stickers does he need?

Draw or write to explain.

about ______ stickers

Name ______________________

Choose a Way to Add

Objective
Choose an appropriate computation method.

Choose a way to find 64 + 20.

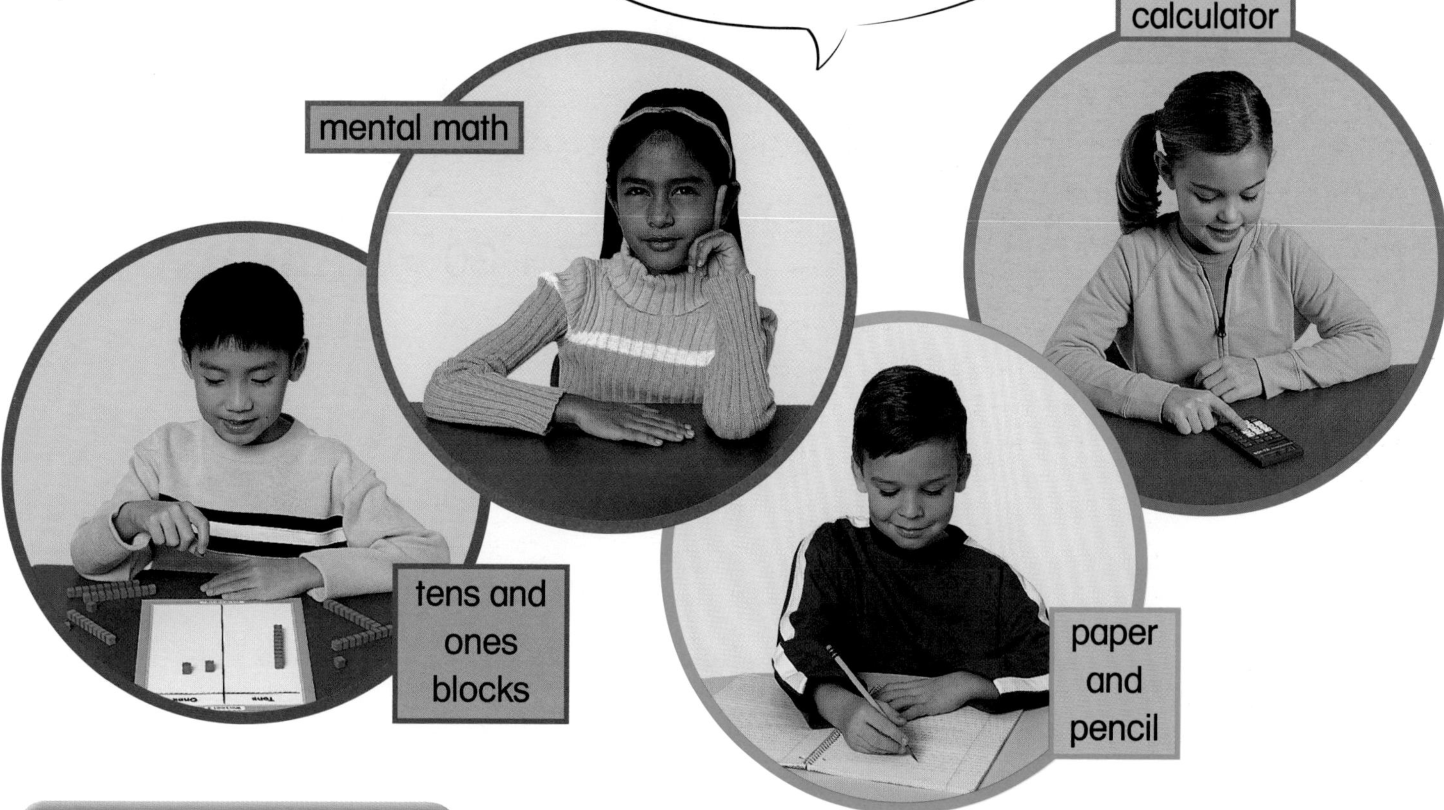

Guided Practice

Circle the way you would choose to add.

Think
Can I do all the steps in my head?

1. 34 + 38
   paper and pencil
   mental math

2. 27 + 56
   tens and ones
   mental math

3. 65 + 26
   mental math
   calculator

4. 45 + 30
   mental math
   paper and pencil

5. 60 + 7
   tens and ones
   mental math

Choose a way to add. Add.
Explain the way you find the sum.

6. 27 + 15 = ______

Explain Your Thinking Is mental math the fastest way to add 60 + 20? Why or why not?

Practice

Remember to choose the way that works for you.

Ways to Add

- **mental math**
- **calculator**
- **tens and ones**
- **paper and pencil**

Choose a way to add. Add.
Explain the way you find the sum.

1. 46 + 28 = _____

2. 57 + 30 = _____

3. 39 + 42 = _____

4. 90 + 6 = _____

Reading Math ▶ Vocabulary

Circle the problem that asks you to find the sum.
Complete the number sentences.

5. 30 = 40 − _____

6. 19 + 36 = _____

7. 5 − _____ = 2

8. 17 + _____ = 22

At Home Have your child show you four different ways to solve 75 + 20 and explain which he or she likes to use.

Name ___________________________

Writing Math: Create and Solve

Write a number story for 25 + 7.
Use the space to draw a picture about your story.
Then solve the problem.

____

____

____

____

Quick Check

Rewrite the addends.
Add.

1. 8 + 56

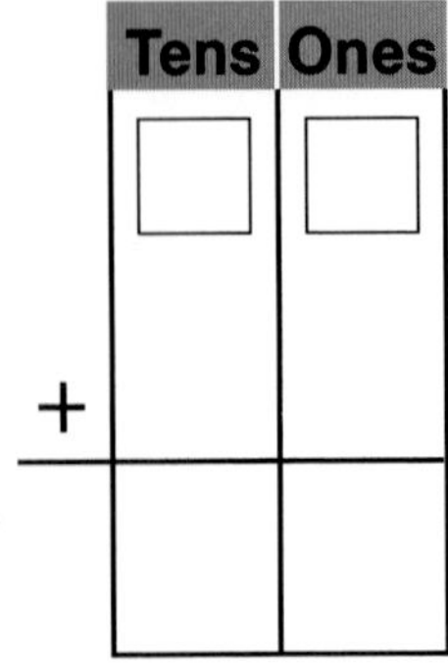

2. 34 + 26

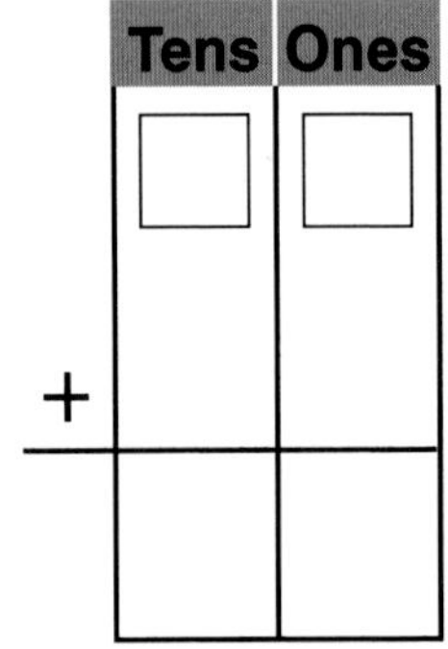

3. 47 + 9

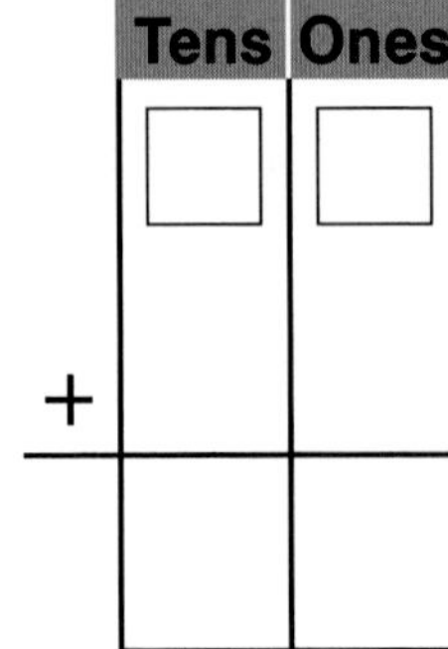

Round each addend to the nearest ten.
Estimate the sum.

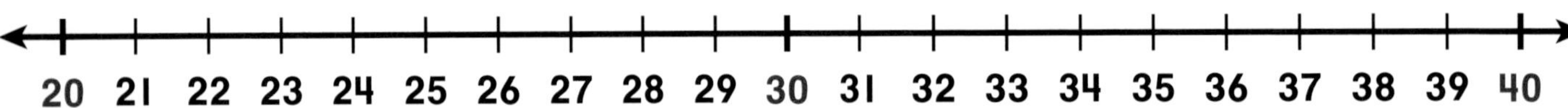

4. 26 + 32

_____ + _____ = _____

5. 38 + 21

_____ + _____ = _____

Choose a way to add.
Add.
Explain the way you find the sum.

Ways to Add
- mental math
- calculator
- tens and ones
- paper and pencil

6. 30 + 56 = _____

7. 27 + 32 = _____

Facts Practice, see page 673.

Name ____________________

Add Three Numbers

Audio Tutor 1/36 Listen and Understand

Objective
Add three two-digit numbers.

There are 17 girls and 23 boys on the whale watch. There are also 13 adults. How many people are on the whale watch?

Add 17, 23, and 13 to find the answer. You can use two ways.

Make a ten.	Use a double.
17 + 23 + 13 = 53; 7 + 3 = 10	17 + 23 + 13 = 53; 3 + 3 = 6

There are 53 people on the whale watch.

Whale Watch ENTRANCE

Guided Practice

Add.

1. $22 + 32 + 10$

Think: I can use a double.

2. $16 + 24 + 2$
3. $45 + 14 + 24$
4. $27 + 15 + 22$
5. $16 + 26 + 11$
6. $25 + 24 + 15$
7. $17 + 12 + 33$
8. $15 + 20 + 34$
9. $42 + 8 + 14$

Explain Your Thinking How did you add the ones in Exercise 9?

Extra Help at eduplace.com/map

Practice

Add.

Remember to look for a ten or a double.

1.	2.	3.	4.	5.
19	66	17	61	27
16	19	30	3	12
+21	+ 4	+52	+13	+57
56				

6.	7.	8.	9.	10.
28	41	2	12	34
11	19	18	13	32
+ 2	+27	+28	+41	+16

11.	12.	13.	14.	15.
14	53	21	18	3
30	17	42	4	34
+14	+ 8	+13	+36	+27

Algebra Readiness  Properties

Complete the number sentences.

Do the work inside the ( ) first.

16. (12 + 4) + 10 = ___?___

 16 + 10 = ______

17. 12 + (4 + 10) = ___?___

 12 + ______ = ______

18. **Write About It** Why does adding the numbers in any order work?

____

____

At Home Tell a story using 3 two-digit numbers. Ask your child to add and explain how to find the sum.

Name ____________________

Guess and Check

Objective
Use Guess and Check to solve problems.

Jack buys 2 different packs of cards. He gets 40 cards in all. Which two packs of cards does Jack buy?

UNDERSTAND

What do you know?

- Jack buys 2 different packs of cards.
- Each pack has a different number of cards.
- Jack gets 40 cards in all.

PLAN

Choose 2 different packs.

Try the medium and jumbo packs.

How can you check your guess? Add.

SOLVE

Add to check.

Medium	16
Jumbo	+ 32
	48

48 > 40
Try again.
Look for ones digits that add to ten.

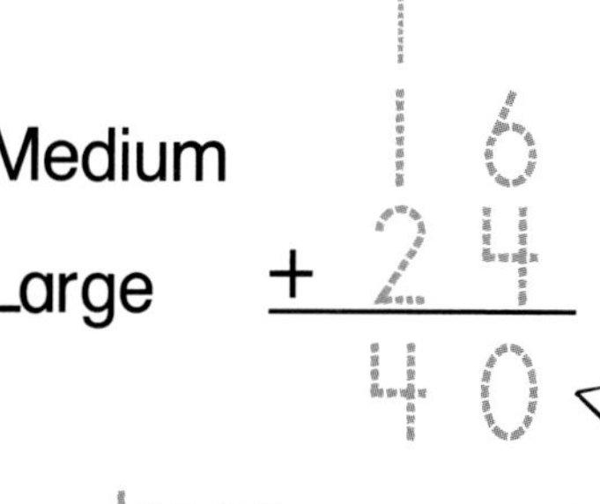

Medium	16
Large	+ 24
	40

The sum is 40, so I am done.

Jack buys a medium and a large pack.

LOOK BACK

Did you answer the question?
Does your answer make sense?

Remember:
- ▶ Understand
- ▶ Plan
- ▶ Solve
- ▶ Look Back

Guided Practice

Use Guess and Check to solve.

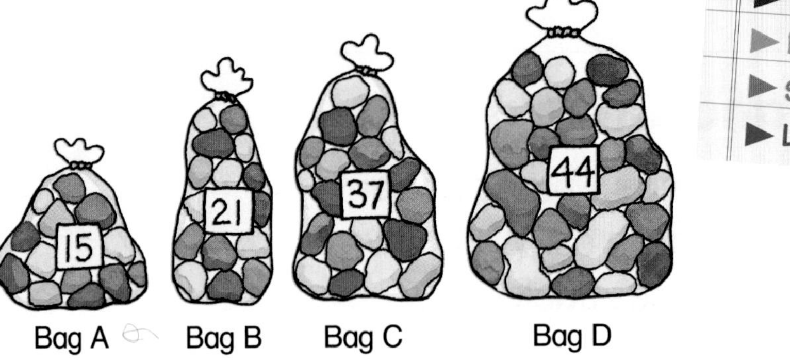

1. Carl buys 52 rocks. Which two bags does he buy?

   Think
   I will pick two that might have a total of 52. Then I add to check.

   Draw or write to explain.

   _____ and _____

2. Maria needs 65 rocks for a project. Which bags should she get?

   Think
   Is my first guess correct? Do I need to try again?

   _____ and _____

Practice

3. Marty drops 58 rocks. Which two bags does he drop?

   _____ and _____

4. The gift shop sells two bags of rocks. 81 rocks are sold in all. Which two bags are sold?

   _____ and _____

Go on

Name ____________________

Mixed Problem Solving

Strategies
Write a Number Sentence
Act It Out
Guess and Check

Solve.

Draw or write to explain.

1. Lobsters come in boxes of 12, 18, and 24. Mrs. Sung wants to buy 30 lobsters. Which two boxes should she buy?

Lobster

box of _____ box of _____

2. The crab shack has 12 crabs. Then 4 are sold. How many crabs are left?

Crab

_____ crabs

3. Sunfish are kept in tanks of 14, 28, and 36. Leon buys 64 sunfish. Which two tanks of sunfish does he buy?

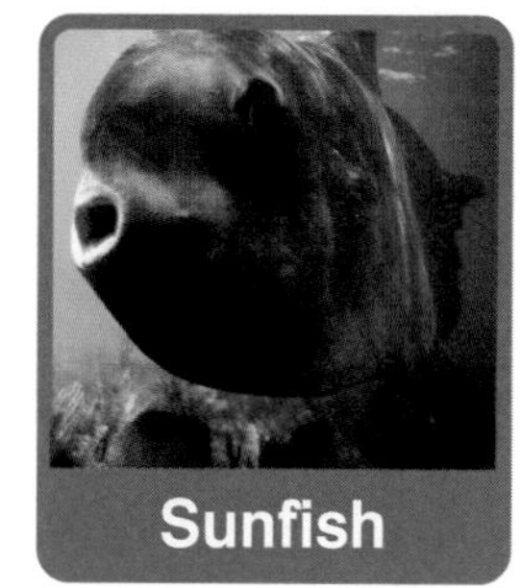
Sunfish

tank of _____ tank of _____

4. **Multistep** Gina has 5 shells in a pail. She finds 8 more shells. Then she gives 4 of them away. How many shells does Gina have now?

Shell

_____ shells

At Home Have your child use objects in your home to write a guess and check problem for you to solve.

Problem Solving on Tests • Listening Skills

Open Response

Listen to your teacher read the problem.
Solve.

1. Mrs. Tucker brings her class of 27 children to the zoo. Mr. Chapel brings his class of 24 children. How many children did Mrs. Tucker and Mr. Chapel bring to the zoo?

Show your work using pictures, numbers, or words.

______ children

2. Jasmine collected 14 rocks. Dan collected 23 rocks. How many rocks did Jasmine and Dan collect in all?

______ rocks

Multiple Choice

Listen to your teacher read the problem.
Choose the correct answer.

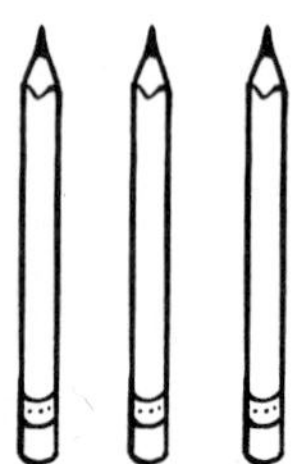

3. 10 ○ 23 ○ 34 ○ 43 ○

4. 31 stickers ○ 41 stickers ○ 53 stickers ○ 72 stickers ○

Education Place
Visit **eduplace.com/map** for more Test-Taking Tips.

Name ______________________________

Now Try This — Front-End Estimation

You can use **estimation** when you do not need an exact answer.

You know how to round to estimate.

Front-end estimation is another way to estimate.

Estimate the sum using front-end estimation. 61 + 32 = ______

Use the tens digit of each addend to estimate.

61 → 6 tens → 60
32 → 3 tens → 30

Add to find the estimate. 60 + 30 = 90

Using **front-end estimation**, you find that 61 + 32 is about 90.

Estimate the number using front-end estimation.

1. 52 50
2. 64 ______
3. 93 ______
4. 82 ______
5. 71 ______
6. 12 ______

Estimate the sum of the numbers.

7. 42 + 32

   40 + 30 = 70

8. 13 + 31

   ______ + ______ = ______

9. 51 + 43

   ______ + ______ = ______

10. 62 + 11

   ______ + ______ = ______

Problem Solving

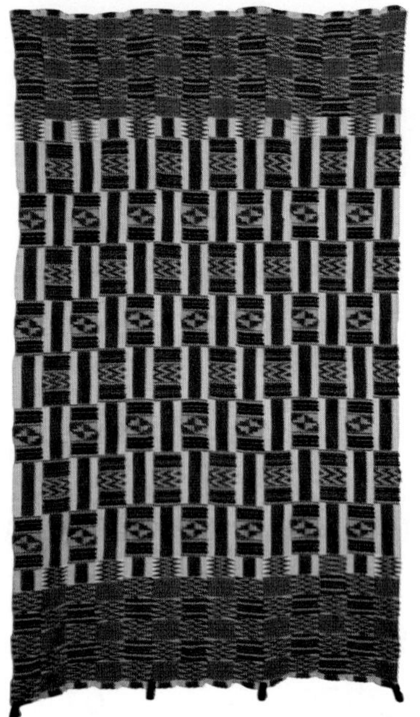

Social Studies Connection

An African Cloth

The Ashanti people of Ghana, Africa weave a cloth called Kente (KEHN tee). Kente cloth has beautiful patterns and bright colors. Clothes made from the cloth are usually worn on special occasions.

Look at the cloth pattern below.
Draw the next two shapes in the pattern.

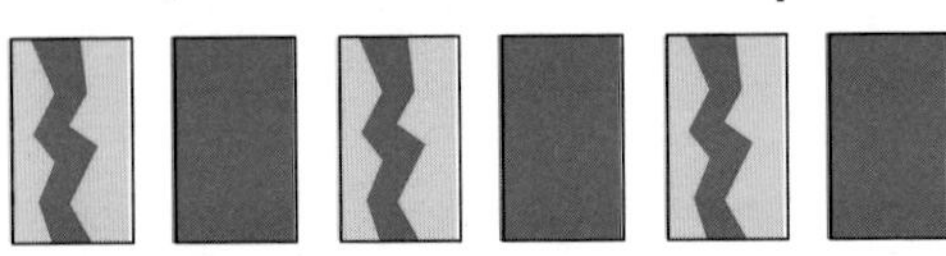

______ ______

Key Topic Review

Pictograph

Use the table to answer the questions.

Tanks of Fish

Tank 1	
Tank 2	
Tank 3	
Tank 4	

Key: Each stands for 10 Fish.

1. How many fish are in Tank 3? ______
2. How many fish are in Tank 2 and Tank 4 in all? ______
3. How many more fish are in Tank 1 than Tank 3? ______
4. How many fish are in Tank 1, Tank 2, and Tank 3? ______

Extra Practice at eduplace.com/map

Name ______________________

Vocabulary

Complete the sentence.

round
estimate
addend

1. I ____________ the sum to find about how many in all.

2. I ____________ the number 18 up to 20.

Concepts and Skills

Rewrite the addends. Add.

3. 39 + 29

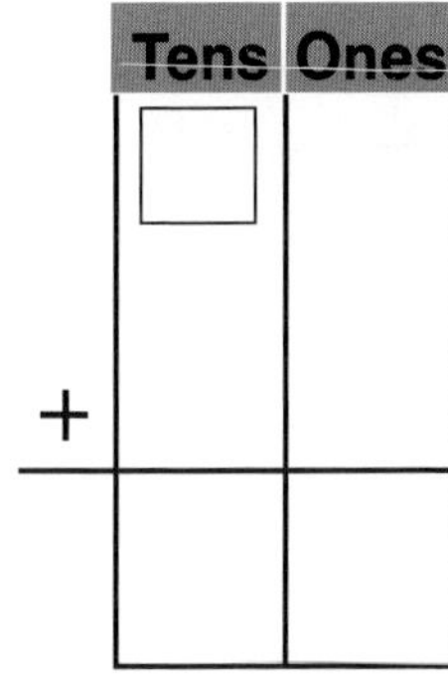

4. 57 + 5

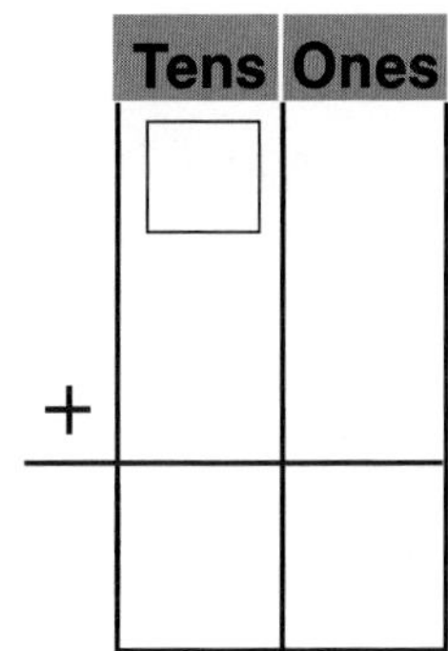

5. 22 + 16

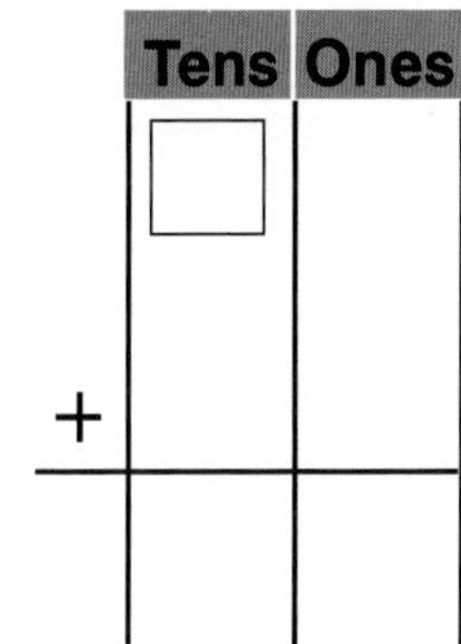

6. 25 + 48

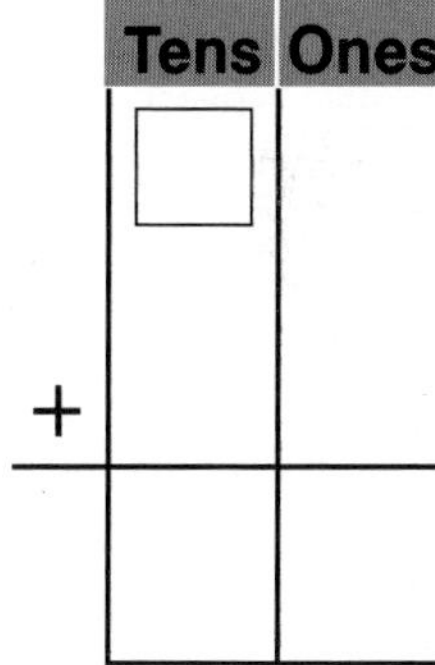

Add.

7. $\begin{array}{r} 23 \\ +38 \\ \hline \end{array}$

8. $\begin{array}{r} 49 \\ +\ \ 6 \\ \hline \end{array}$

9. $\begin{array}{r} 67 \\ +27 \\ \hline \end{array}$

10. $\begin{array}{r} 31 \\ +18 \\ \hline \end{array}$

11. $\begin{array}{r} 34 \\ +35 \\ \hline \end{array}$

12. $\begin{array}{r} 58 \\ +38 \\ \hline \end{array}$

Round each addend to the nearest ten.
Estimate the sum.

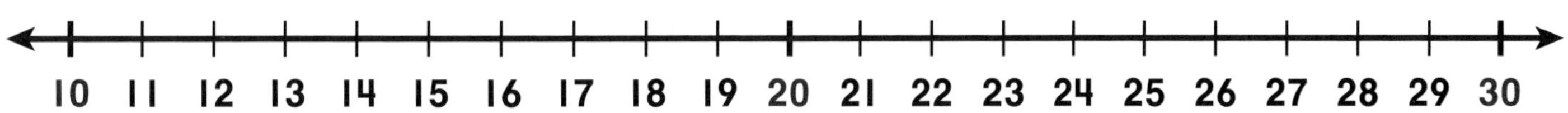

13. 11 + 29

_____ + _____ = _____

14. 24 + 27

_____ + _____ = _____

Chapter Review/Test

Choose a way to add. Add.
Write the way you find the sum.

mental math
calculator
tens and ones
paper and pencil

15. $46 + 40 =$ ______

Add.

16. $\begin{array}{r} 54 \\ 16 \\ +25 \\ \hline \end{array}$

17. $\begin{array}{r} 27 \\ 40 \\ +13 \\ \hline \end{array}$

18. $\begin{array}{r} 35 \\ 5 \\ +11 \\ \hline \end{array}$

Problem Solving

Use Guess and Check to solve.

Draw or write to explain.

19. Bart buys 34 cards. Which two different packs does Bart buy?

______ pack

______ pack

20. Cindy buys 56 cards. Which two different packs does Cindy buy?

______ pack

______ pack

Name ____________________

Comparing Sums

Find the sums.
Use >, <, or = to make the sentence true.

1. 65 + 21 ◯ 21 + 42

   86 (>) 63

2. 50 + 18 ◯ 17 + 62

   ____ ◯ ____

3. 72 + 26 ◯ 26 + 72

   ____ ◯ ____

4. 18 + 36 ◯ 25 + 35

   ____ ◯ ____

Use >, <, or =.
Complete the number sentence without finding the sums.

5. 24 + 42 ◯ 21 + 36

   Explain how you know. ____________________

   ____

Solve without finding the sum.

6. Lia can choose either the red pails of shells or the blue pails of shells. She wants the most shells she can get. Which set of pails should Lia choose?

   red pails   blue pails

   Explain how you know. ____________________

   ____

Education Place
Visit **eduplace.com/map** for brain teasers.

Calculator
Root for a Route

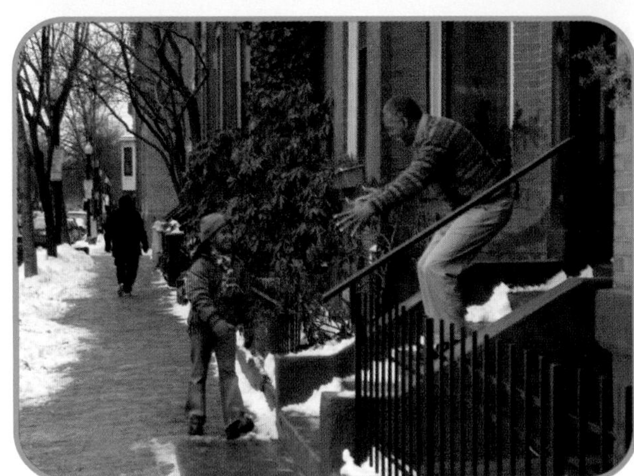

Kelly is going to her grandfather's house. She can travel 4 different routes.

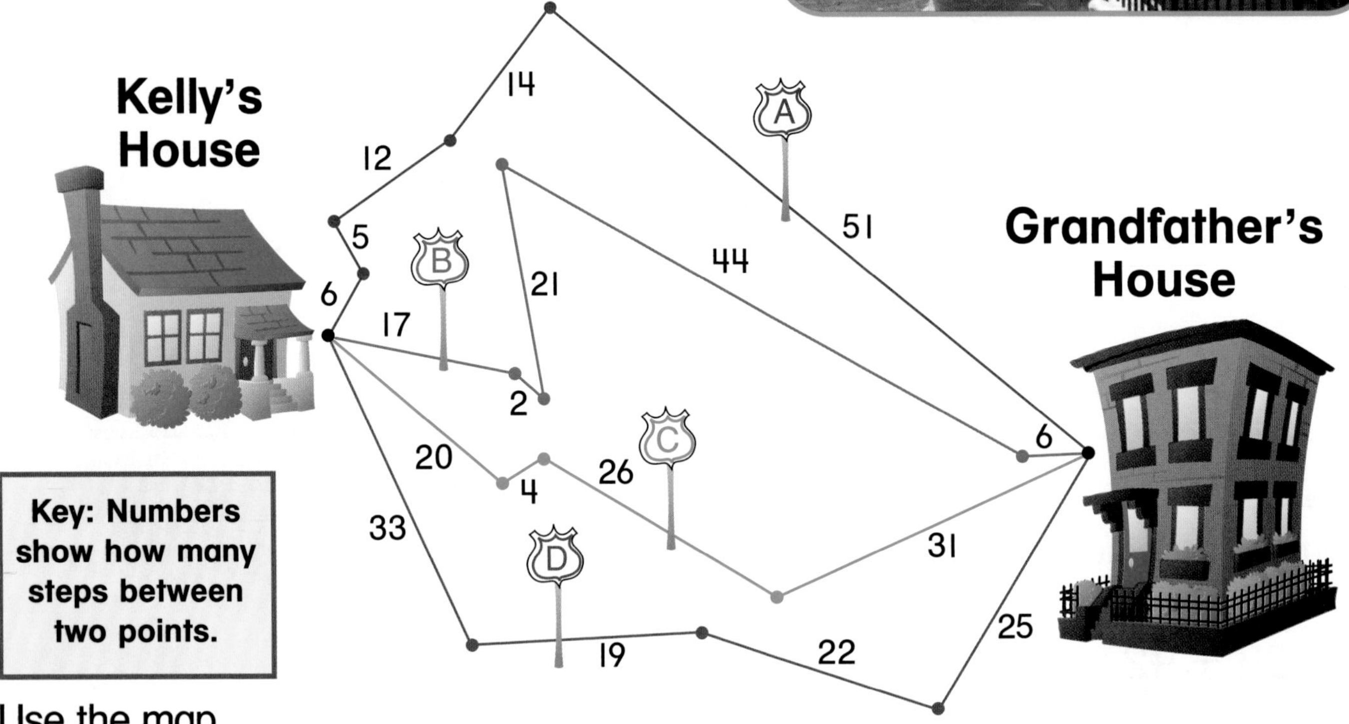

Use the map.

1. Estimate the longest route. Route _____.

2. Write a number sentence to find the length. Use a calculator to solve.

Route A _____ + _____ + _____ + _____ + _____ = _____ steps

Route B _____ + _____ + _____ + _____ + _____ = _____ steps

Route C _____ + _____ + _____ + _____ = _____ steps

Route D _____ + _____ + _____ + _____ = _____ steps

3. Write the routes in order from shortest to longest.

Route _____ Route _____ Route _____ Route _____

4. How much longer is the longest route than the shortest one? _____ steps

Name ______________________________

Vocabulary

Complete the sentence.

addend
estimate
sum

1. I can ____________ if I do not need an exact answer.
2. The answer to an addition problem is called the ____________.
3. In the sentence $15 + 45 = 60$, 15 is an ____________.

Concepts and Skills

Add.

4. $\begin{array}{r} 88 \\ +\ 7 \\ \hline \end{array}$

5. $\begin{array}{r} 28 \\ +\ 28 \\ \hline \end{array}$

6. $\begin{array}{r} 20 \\ +\ 10 \\ \hline \end{array}$

Rewrite the addends. Then add.

7. $46 + 38$

+

8. $9 + 66$

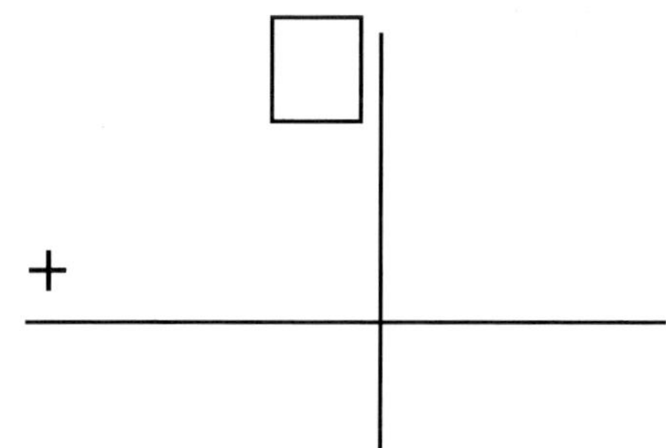

Round each addend to the nearest ten.
Estimate the sum.

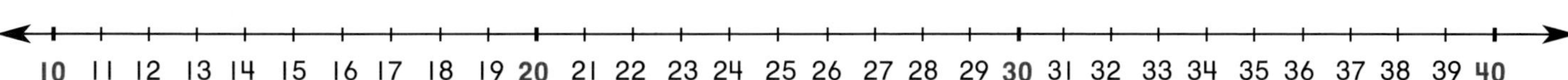

9. $25 + 11$

_____ + _____ = _____

Unit 4 Test

Add.

10.
```
  45
  13
+ 25
```

11.
```
  56
   6
+ 91
```

12.
```
  36
   6
+ 82
```

mental math
calculator
tens and ones
paper and pencil

Choose a way to add. Add.
Explain how you found the sum.

13. 30 + 46 = ______

____

____

Problem Solving

Cross out any information you do not need. Solve.

14. Rebecca has 13 giraffe stickers and 14 turtle stickers. She also has 10 turtle postcards. How many stickers does she have?

Draw or write to explain.

______ stickers

Use Guess and Check to solve.

15. Kaitlin buys 2 of the same size pack of cards. She gets 32 cards in all. Which size pack does she buy?

__________ pack

Name ____________________

Test-Taking Tips

Check your work when you have finished all of the problems.

Reread each problem to make sure you have answered the question.

Multiple Choice

Fill in the ○ for the correct answer.

1. 53 + 37

80 ○ 90 ○ 93 ○ 99 ○

2. 68 + 8

78 ○ 66 ○ 75 ○ 76 ○

3. Celia has 32 beads. Luka finds 17 more. How many beads are there in all?

47 ○ 49 ○ 52 ○ 59 ○

4. Pablo has 78 toy cars. He buys 14 more. How many toy cars are there in all?

82 ○ 84 ○ 93 ○ 92 ○

Multiple Choice

Fill in the ○ for the correct answer. N means Not Here.

5. Choose the number that is greater than 94.

37	49	94	98
○	○	○	○

6. Find the sum.

$$\begin{array}{r} 62 \\ +\ 29 \\ \hline \end{array}$$

71	81	82	N
○	○	○	○

7. Estimate the sum.

26 + 32

about 20	about 66
○	○
about 60	about 80
○	○

Open Response

Solve.

8. Malik thinks of 2 numbers that are named when he skip counts by 5. Their sum is 75. What are the numbers?

____

9. Write a related number sentence for 15 − 9 = 6.

____

10. Are both sums the same? Write Yes or No.

$$\begin{array}{r} 25 \\ +\ 36 \\ \hline \end{array} \qquad \begin{array}{r} 36 \\ +\ 25 \\ \hline \end{array}$$

____

Explain how you know without adding.

____

____

Education Place
Visit **eduplace.com/map** for brain teasers.

READING MATH

Party Packing

Look back at the story to answer these questions.

▲ **1.** Look at page 2. What if Dan had packed 8 boxes of 5 bones? How many dog bones would have been in Dan's van?

● **2.** What if Dog wanted 100 bones? How many boxes of 10 bones would he need?

★ **3.** Look at page 6. How many more bones did Fox have than Frog?

☆ **4.** Look at pages 4 and 6. Estimate how many more bones Cat had than Fox, then find the exact number. Did you make a good estimate? Why?

Answers

1. 40 **2.** 10 **3.** 6 **4.** Answers will vary. 12; Answers will vary.

Reading Strategies

■ Infer ▲ Noting Details ▲ Monitor/Clarify

UNIT 5

A Party at Dog's House

written by **Heather L. Coe**
illustrated by **Jackie Urbanovic**

A friend of Dog's is our neighbor Dan,
with 8 boxes of bones in the back of his van.
In each box there are 10 yummy treats.
That's a lot for just one dog to eat!

How many dog bones are in Dan's van?

10, 20, 30, ___, ___, ___, ___, ___

At Dog's party, poor Dan was quite blue.
He only had 1 box: "Oh, boo hoo!"
Then—surprise!—Cat and Mouse had brought 4.
And Fox and Frog came with 30 bones more.

How many boxes were brought to Dog's house?

How many bones is that?

Frog and Fox saw the bones fly past.
They ran to the boxes and grabbed those bones fast.
Frog got 2 bones plus 1 full box,
and 8 bones plus 1 full box went to Fox.

How many bones does each animal have?
Frog ▭ Fox ▭

Who has more bones?

As Dan was driving to a party for Dog,
his van ran over a very big log.
Bump! Bump! The van gave a jump,
and so 4 boxes fell out with a thump!

How many boxes fell out of the van?

How many bones is that?

Cat and Mouse each gave a shout
when they saw the 4 boxes of bones fall out.
They grabbed every box that they could see.

Mouse carried one box. Cat carried ____.

Down the road, Dan swerved past a tree.
The boxes bounced high—and out fell 3!
Bang! Bam! Boom! They crashed to the ground.
One box burst open, leaving bones all around.

How many boxes fell out of the van?

How many bones is that?